D0722283

NARCOTIC CULTURE

FRANK DIKÖTTER
LARS LAAMANN
ZHOU XUN

Narcotic Culture

A History of Drugs in China

THE UNIVERSITY OF CHICAGO PRESS

The University of Chicago Press, Chicago 60637
C. Hurst & Co., London, England
© Frank Dikötter 2004
All rights reserved. Published 2004
Printed in Hong Kong

12 11 10 09 08 07 06 05 04   1 2 3 4 5
ISBN: 0-226-14905-6 (cloth)

Cataloging-in-publication data have been
requested from the Library of Congress.

ACKNOWLEDGEMENTS

The authors acknowledge with gratitude grant R000239272 from the Economic and Social Research Council (ESRC) which allowed them to carry out the research for this book from start to finish. The ESRC is not responsible for any of the views expressed in this book. Zhou Xun and Lars Laamann worked full time on all aspects of the project as research fellows, although I, as the principal applicant, bear final responsibility for all errors and omissions.

A number of people have generously shared their ideas and suggestions with us and read and commented on draft versions, in particular Stephen Averill, Michigan State University; Inga-Britt Bengtsson, Sahlgrenska University Hospital; Gregor Benton, University of Wales, Cardiff; Virginia Berridge, London School of Tropical Hygiene; Jerome Ch'en, York University, Toronto; Gervase Clarence-Smith, School of Oriental and African Studies, University of London; Mark Elvin, Australian National University; David Faure, Oxford University; Sander Gilman, University of Illinois; David Hodson, Centre for Criminology, University of Hong Kong; Virgil Ho, Hong Kong University of Science and Technology; Mike Jay, London; Bill Jenner, Australian National University; Alfred Lin, University of Hong Kong; Richard Newman, School of Oriental and African Studies, University of London; Geoffrey Pearson, London School of Hygiene and Tropical Medicine; John Richards, Duke University; Edward Slack, Eastern Washington University; Harold Traver, University of Hong Kong; Frances Wood, The British Library; Zhou Zhaoxi, Chengdu.

London, April 2003   F. D.

v

CONTENTS

ILLUSTRATIONS

between pages 146 and 147

CONVENTIONS

The symbol '$' and the term 'dollar' refer to Chinese dollars before 1933 or Chinese yuan after 1933; the two were approximately equivalent. The value of copper varied in relationship to silver, and in the 1930s one silver dollar could generally be exchanged for 300 to 330 coppers. One fen is a hundredth of a dollar. China suffered huge inflation in the 1940s, and prices bore little relation to actual value.

The terms 'grams', 'feet' or 'metres' refer to European units unless indicated otherwise. Much confusion was caused in China by the lack of uniformity in standards of measurement. The unification of weights and measures was only undertaken by the government in 1930, although it was carried out in different periods by different provinces and municipalities, and a variety of standards remained in use for many years. One *mu* corresponds to 648 square metres (0.0648 hectares or 0.16 acres). Chinese 'ounces' (*liang*) measure 37.7 grams (1.33 avoirdupois ounces). English weights quoted refer to the avoirdupois and apothecaries' systems. One picul, or a chest, is equivalent to 133.3 pounds or 60.5 metric kilos; one drachm to 60 grains, corresponding to 3.9 grams; one mace weighs 3.78 grams; one dram represents 1.772 g.; one grain equals 0.065 g.; one ounce is 28.35 g.; one pound contains 453.6 g.

Pinyin romanisation is used throughout, except for names and terms better known in a different spelling (Canton rather than Guangzhou, Taipei rather than Taibei) or where they appear in published works using alternative conventions. Beijing was renamed Beiping after the capital moved south to Nanjing in 1927. Contrary to general usage, and in the interest of clarity for readers who are not specialists of modern China, we have used the spelling Beijing for the entire republican period.

1

INTRODUCTION

In the *Cambridge History of China* John King Fairbank, doyen of modern Chinese studies, characterised the opium trade as 'the most long-continued and systematic international crime of modern times'.[1] Britain, in its merciless pursuit of financial gain, trampled on the sovereign rights of China to enforce a shameful trade which reduced the country to a state of opium slavery. As the silver which Britain had to spend on buying tea from China began to drain the treasury, British merchants discovered that opium found an eager market in that country, starting a huge addiction problem among the local population. The emperor of China was alarmed by opium's devasting impact on his people, and tried to ban the substance and bar foreign smugglers from the country. The British government decided to send an army to fight for the opening of China to foreign trade: it crushed the imperial army with overwhelming military superiority, enforced the opium traffic with gunboats, burnt down the Summer Palace in Beijing, and imposed several unequal treaties during the 'Opium Wars' in the 1840s and '50s.[2] In these first Wars on Drugs, a highly sophisticated civilisation was powerless against the pernicious forces of imperialist aggression, as Britain gradually extended its control over the ports of the country the better to further the opium trade. The evil of opium turned China into a nation of hopeless addicts, smoking themselves to death while their civilisation descended into chaos.

As Mike Jay observes, the image at the core of this belief has rarely been examined, either at the time by contemporaries or more recently by historians, as a variety of interests intersect to replicate it in different contexts: nationalists in China were eager to find a scapegoat in imperialism by emphasising the catastrophic results of the opium trade, at the same time as foreign missionaries and campaigning journalists published sensational reports portraying China as a victim of gunboat policy.[3] During the first decades of the twentieth century, as a narcophobic discourse gradually established itself in other parts of the world, the image of China as an opium slave became the *locus classicus* of the modern drug debate, the cornerstone of the anti-opium movement, the founding case of concerted international efforts to enforce increasingly draconian measures not only against opium but against all illicit drug use in America, Europe and Asia. China is 'Patient Zero' in what is represented as a drug plague that has contaminated the rest of the globe; it is the single most important example in history of a culture commonly claimed to have been 'destroyed' by an intoxicant other than alcohol. This book systematically questions this image on the basis of extensive primary sources in several languages, including archival evidence from China, Europe and the United States.

'An essential first step in demythologising the Chinese opium problem is to understand the [lack of] scientific evidence about the drug's impact... upon the health of the individual consumer.' Referring to historians of modern China as 'victims of the [opium] myth', the historian of India Richard Newman has criticised the China field for uncritically reproducing the anti-opium stance adopted by prohibitionist missionaries in the late nineteenth century.[4] Newman shows that opium rarely undermined the health or shortened the lives of the majority of smokers in nineteenth-century China. Others have underlined that in England, where opium was widely available from local shops during the nineteenth century, frequent and chronic users did not suffer detrimental effects from opium: many enjoyed good health well into their eighties.[5] In South Asia a diversity of evidence offered by both Indian and British physicians in the nineteenth century showed that opium pills were commonly taken throughout the subcontinent without creating serious social or physical damage, in contrast to the strong spirits imported from abroad in the face of opposition from both the Hindu and Muslim communities.[6]

This book challenges the image of China as a victim of the opium plague by documenting that in most cases habitual opium use did not have significant harmful effects on either health or longevity: moderate smoking could even be beneficial, since it was a remarkable panacea in the fight against a wide range of ailments before the advent of modern medications. In Southeast Asia, South Asia, the Middle East and Europe, it was primarily used as a painkiller before the discovery of aspirin or penicillin in the twentieth century. Opium was extremely effective in fighting fever, blocking dysentery, relieving pain, suppressing coughs and abating hunger. Negative representations often confused the medical symptoms of the diseases, against which opium was taken as a palliative, with the imagined physiological effects of 'addiction'. For instance, its consumption in the countryside tended to increase in times of malnutrition: foreign visitors passing through such 'opium villages' would often attribute the physical effects of famine to those of opium smoking.[7] The Wesleyan missionary and opium opponent John Turner noted at the end of the nineteenth century that the very few emaciated cases which could be found in Canton were rarely due to the 'opium habit': 'He may be a victim of some incurable disease, and smoking merely to dull his pains.'[8]

A second aspect of the opium myth is the conflation of 'opium' with 'China'. Historians of China rarely mention that any respectable person in Europe or America could walk into a pharmacy in 1900 and routinely buy a range of hashish pastes, exotic psychedelics or morphine (complemented by a handy injection kit), and that opium products were widely on sale in Britain. As Virginia Berridge outlines, opium fulfilled a crucial role before the availability of modern synthetic drugs: it was a medical panacea for the many in nineteenth-century England and in other parts of the world.[9] In his book on the widespread culture of opium in Laos, Westermeyer astutely observed that the popular link made between China and opium allowed every government in Asia to define opium use as a 'Chinese problem' and hence ignore or downplay indigenous narcotic cultures.[10] Opium was widely cultivated and consumed in India, Persia and Turkey, although historians of China still have to explain why they consider it to have been a 'problem' in China but not in other parts of the world.

As a global commodity, opium can only be studied within its proper global context, as the first chapter shows. It could be taken in a diversity of ways around the world that need to be accounted for by placing greater emphasis on social context and cultural meaning. Through the rectum as an enema or a suppository; as a liquid when mixed with alcohol; and eaten directly or patched onto wounds as a plaster: how and why these different modes of delivery, including the very choice to smoke opium, were used by different social groups in changing historical circumstances is one of the many questions which we seek to address.

A third element of the opium myth is the refusal to accept that most opium use in Europe, the Middle East and Asia was light and moderate. As Virginia Berridge argues, the existence of a class of moderate users was one of the most controversial issues in the opium debate in the late nineteenth century: recognising that the majority of consumers used the substance in moderation and without any fatal 'loss of control' would have undermined the case against cultivation of the poppy.[11] The denial of moderation would also have damaged the medical argument that dosage increases could not be reversed and addiction was unavoidable, making all regular users of the drug hopeless 'addicts' and hostages to the medical authorities who alone could prevent their physical descent to certain death. This book shows that opium was used by many people in moderate quantities: the relative absence of problematic users—rather than a proliferation of 'drug fiends'—is the most striking feature of narcotic culture in late imperial China. Even heroin, which circulated as a substitute for opium in a climate of prohibition during the first decades of the twentieth century, was not used in life-threatening doses by a small circle of social outcasts, as conventional imagery might have it; rather it was taken by many social categories in relatively small and innocuous quantities: in some cases 'heroin pills' contained no heroin at all but consisted of lactose laced with quinine or caffeine.

Users of opium did not become irremediably enslaved or necessarily caught in a destructive downward spiral. Opium is portrayed in narcophobic discourse as a drug which produced an irresistible compulsion to increase both the amount and frequency of dosage, although the historical evidence shows that very few users were 'compulsive addicts' who 'lost control' or suffered from a 'failure of will'. Richard Miller and others have pointed out that most reach a plateau beyond which they will not increase their consumption levels: users want reliable, not infinite supplies.[12] Tolerance to opium does not increase illimitably, and the idea that smokers become physically dependent on their drugs needs to be examined, since there is relatively little evidence of an 'organic' need for the substance. Like nicotine, opium is a psychotropic which is generally taken in determined amounts rather than ever-increasing ones: even the habitual smoker reaches a plateau, often between seven and fifteen pipes a day, a number rarely exceeded. The same daily dosage could easily be maintained year after year without developing a tolerance that required the user to smoke more and more.[13] The riddle of opium, as Jean Cocteau observed, is that the smoker never has to increase his dose.[14]

Another important aspect of the opium myth which needs to be questioned is the narrow concern with the presumed pharmacological properties of the drug, stripping opium use of its cultural meanings and social dimensions. Anti-opium propaganda, Virginia Berridge rightly observes, considered opium smoking in China and opium eating in India in isolation from the cultural and social factors sustaining these practices.[15] The exclusive focus on the pharmacological effects of psychoactive substances, at the expense of an analysis of the social practices and cultural connotations structuring consumer choices, is reflected in the idea that 'drugs' have predetermined effects on all users alike. Michael Gossop believes that 'the idea that specific drugs have fixed and predictable effects which are the same from person to person is extremely widespread but remains a fallacy', since the faith users place in a drug and their expectations largely condition their responses.[16] Opium, like other psychoactive substances, could be used in a variety of social contexts and endowed with different cultural meanings which defy simple stereotypical explanations. We thus shift our analysis away from an emphasis on 'abuse' and 'addiction', which has long dominated the China field, towards use and context.

By reconstructing the narcotic culture which endowed opium smoking with social significance, we seek to understand why and how this substance assumed such historical importance in parts of China. The use of opium, as of other psychoactive substances, was a social ritual in which users learnt what to feel and what to expect. Those who smoked opium for the first time may have felt nothing in particular. Oden Meeker tried it in Laos in the 1950s and was surprised that 'nothing happened'.[17] In other cases the first experiences of smoking opium may be nausea or constipation.[18] As two experts on opium detoxification in Java commented in 1930, 'practically all opium users report that they became indisposed after the first pipe and that they became accustomed to it and began to like it only very gradually.'[19] These initial reactions had to be overcome by the user, who would learn to appreciate and experience opium as part of an elaborate smoking ritual. Richard Hughes, who tried it in the world's biggest opium house in Bangkok in 1959, thought that he would have derived far more enjoyment from six whiskies than from his six pipes. He noted that many who tried opium would consider it to be overrated: 'Opium is a cultivated taste. And, Western notions to the contrary, talk about opium-smoker's dreams—exotic or terrifying—is mostly nonsense. Whatever the poet says, the poppy opens no "scarlet purse of dreams". De Quincey suffered his monstrous dreams because he drank laudanum and ate opium; that is just as barbarous as smoking opium by yourself; if you smoke, you always smoke in agreeable company.'[20] Peter Lee, a careful and nuanced observer of opium culture, notes: 'Nothing forces the smoker to smoke. The only force at work is the volitional force of the smoker's own free will. For all the various reasons and rationalisations that opium smokers might cite to justify their decision to adopt an addictive and toxic substance as a mainstay of their daily lives, the bottom line still remains their own volition and will.'[21] As the famous 'opium addict' Jean Cocteau found, opium was a choice to be made.[22]

Opium was prepared and appreciated in highly intricate and complex rituals with inbuilt constraints on excessive use, very much like the tea ceremony which signified social distinction among the ruling elites. It also fulfilled a variety of social roles which endowed its consumption with positive meanings: opium could be alternatively or simultaneously a medical product, a sign of hospitality, a recreational item, a badge of social distinction and a symbol of elite culture. Opium houses, contrary to the myth of the opium den as a dark and depraved trap in which the opium lamp threw a feeble light on the gaping mouths of dazed addicts, were respectable sites of male sociability in which small amounts of opium were shared together with tea, fruit, sweets, snacks and food. In a culture of restraint, opium was an ideal social lubricant which could be helpful in maintaining decorum and composure, in contrast to alcohol which was believed to lead to socially disruptive modes of behaviour. In Java too, as James Rush has observed, opium relaxed the smoker without upsetting social etiquette.[23] Among the hill tribes of northern Thailand, where opium smoking was widespread until it was banned in 1959, alcohol and marijuana were also considered socially undesirable, as these substances tended to excite the user, and thus represented a potential cause of conflict or embarrassment in tight-knit village communities.[24]

Equally erroneous is the convention that supply determines demand: inanimate substances are granted agency, while human beings become passive objects. Researchers working on the history of opium in China have thus trained their gaze exclusively on issues of supply and policy.[25] However, opium pipes and morphine needles do not have lives of their own: they are granted social lives by their users, the sentient beings who have disappeared behind the smoke-screen of the opium myth which continues to cloud the China field to this day. Outside sinological circles, a consumer-centred approach has been at the heart of the revival in drugs studies since the 1960s: historians and sociologists no longer seriously consider all users to be 'addicts' governed by physical dependence but see them rather as complex human beings whose social experiences should be the main focus of attention if we are to understand substance-influenced behaviour. As David Lenson has observed, the intricate and diverse ways in which drugs interact, collude and even collaborate with human beings in a range of diverse social contexts give psychoactive substances their particular epistemological interest.[26] Opium was not merely 'imposed' by 'imperialism'—although it cannot be denied that better modes of production and transportation significantly lowered its price and that Qing government objections to free trade were met with a military response. Opium was appropriated and used for different reasons by a variety of consumers. The present study attempts to approach the history of opiates 'from below' rather than from a 'trickle-down' perspective. Historians have tried to reconstruct the colonial view from the deck of the gunboat or from the international negotiating table, failing to ask why and how opiates, rather than coffee or cannabis, were so eagerly consumed in the first place.

Another problem which needs to be addressed is the demonisation of 'opium' into a single and uniform substance. As the first chapters show, the paste varied immensely in strength and quality, while many consumers were keen connoisseurs who could distinguish between a large variety of products, ranging from expensive red Persian opium to qualitatively poor local produce.[27] Opium is an extremely complex compound containing sugars, gums, acids and proteins as well as dozens of alkaloids which vary in proportion and content. General statements about the purported effects of 'opium' are thus as vague as blanket condemnations of 'alcohol': a world of difference exists between beer, wine and whisky, which are used in radically different social contexts. Most of the imported paste from India and the locally cultivated opium in China had a relatively low morphine content (on average 3–4 per cent), much of which never reached the users' lungs, since smoking was a very wasteful mode of delivery. On the other hand, the opium imported every year into England from Turkey in tens of thousands of tonnes was very rich in morphine (10–15 per cent). Products from India also varied substantially, and these differences are vital in understanding the historical shifts in opiate consumption in China: only when colonial authorities took drastic action to improve the quality of Patna opium in the 1790s would exports significantly increase, overtaking the demand for poor-quality Malwa cultivated and traded by Portugal.

Finally, if opium was a relatively benign substance when used in moderate amounts, as it was by a majority of smokers in late imperial China, this book provides abundant evidence that the transition from a tolerated opium culture to a system of prohibition produced a cure far worse than the disease. Opium was medicine as much as recreation, and its demonisation was a public health disaster: heroin, morphine and cocaine flooded the market in the wake of the anti-opium movement, and countless other new psychoactive substances were snorted, smoked, chewed or injected. The existence of these substances—many used in conditions far more harmful to health than opium smoking—escapes the confines set by the 'opium myth' and hence the gaze of many historians of China, who seem hardly even to be aware of their existence.[28] However, even cursory examination of the primary sources reveals that the crusade against opium encouraged, however inadvertently, the development of new substances, as well as the existence of criminal gangs who relied on prohibition for their prosperity. Official campaigns facilitated a shift towards morphine injection which proved disastrous for many poor consumers: prohibition priced opium out of their reach, and contributed to the spread of cheaper semi-synthetics like morphine and heroin, encouraged the spread of adulterated products, engendered social exclusions, spawned corruption, and created a criminal underclass. It is not opium that was an imperialist imposition, but the morphine and heroin contained in the 'opium cures' distributed by medical missionaries at the end of the nineteenth century. Supported by moral crusaders abroad and nationalist elites at home, prohibition in China exacerbated rather than contained a 'drug problem'.

2

THE GLOBAL SPREAD OF PSYCHOACTIVE
SUBSTANCES *c.* 1600–1900

This chapter places the spread of opium in a global context marked by the dissemination of psychoactive substances from the fifteenth century onwards. David Courtwright has called the discovery and spread of the world's psychoactive resources—tea, coffee, coca, spirits, opium, tobacco—after the fifteenth century a 'psychoactive revolution'.[1] At first confined geographically and limited in their social uses, an array of different substances gradually entered the stream of global commerce, reaching new parts of the world and percolating down to less privileged users. This chapter assesses the importance of opium in relationship to other psychoactive substances and highlights the global nature of its use. 'Opium' and 'China' have become all but indistinguishable in the popular imagination since the end of the nineteenth century, although opium consumption was common in many other parts of the world. It was widely used for recreational and medical reasons in Turkey, Persia and India: the psychoactive revolution would bring the opium cultivated in these regions to China in the seventeenth century. Britain was also awash with opium at all social levels until the beginning of the twentieth century: in a drinking culture dominated by caffeine and alcohol, it was generally taken in liquid form.

THE PSYCHOACTIVE REVOLUTION

Much has been written about the global movement of people, germs and plants, as smallpox and measles eradicated millions in the Americas while the potato and maize sustained massive population growth in Europe and Asia.[2] Psychoactive substances hitherto confined to particular geographical locations and reserved for specific social groups also spread thanks to their inclusion in the global stream of commerce from the fifteenth century onwards. Tea, coffee and chocolate, for instance, were imported to Europe from great distances as luxury products before reaching a much larger market in the eighteenth century, while opium spread in the nineteenth century thanks to lower production prices: all were consumed as beverages in a rapidly expanding drinking culture.

Tea was first reported in Europe by travellers and missionaries in China in the sixteenth century before it reached a privileged clientele as an exotic commodity less than a century later. Extravagant claims for its medicinal virtues were made by medical writers, the Dutch physician Cornelis Bontekoe even recommending consumption of up to fifty cups of tea per day. The penetration of tea into elite consumption accorded well with the social values heralded by burgeoning commercial and professional groups in Britain, for whom tea represented sobriety and respectability. However, by the end of the seventeenth century, tea was no longer restricted to the fashionable few but had spread to all social classes, transforming the dietary habits of the poor by gradually displacing home-brewed beer and infusions of indigenous plants.[3] Tea became more affordable after the British East India Company started direct trade with Canton in 1713: responding to growing demand, the trade steadily expanded until European powers introduced tea cultivation to their colonies in the mid-nineteenth century. The Dutch brought the plant to Java, while tea plantations were also promoted by the colonial authorities in India and Ceylon. By the 1880s tea was produced more effectively and economically in India, and imports from China rapidly declined. Tea from India was popular in Britain because it was stronger and needed to be consumed in combination with sugar, a nutritious complement which allowed the beverage to replace beer for breakfast in the working-class diet. Thomas Lipton, an aggressive retailer, used a massive turn-over to offset narrow profit margins, making tea an affordable excitant even for the poor in Europe.[4] From being a fashionable item associated with the Orient, tea had crossed regional, class and gender boundaries to become an integral part of everyday life in less than two centuries.

If tea was particularly popular in Britain, coffee acquired a position of general acceptance in most other European countries after the fifteenth century. An excitant like tea, coca and tobacco, it was also an expensive luxury associated at first with royal courts before spreading to aspiring members of the urban bourgeoisie in the seventeenth century. It was imported into Europe from Constantinople by Venetian merchants after 1600, appearing in the coffee houses which emerged in parts of Europe during the second half of the seventeenth century. Like so many other psychoactive substances, it was attributed both extraordinary therapeutic powers and menacing medical properties, and was classified with medicines and spices. Coffee houses were viewed with suspicion in England by Charles II (reigned 1660–85), who attempted to close them down on moral and political grounds, although they continued to thrive as the literary, political and commercial centres of London. By the end of the century coffee had started to move into wealthy households and later it would enter the middling ranks of society, where it was offered to guests as an alternative to tea and chocolate.[5] In other European countries coffee also started to spread as a temperate alternative to beer, as coffee and coffee houses came into general use across the breadth of the Hapsburg empire in the eighteenth century, although in Prussia, Frederick the Great (1712–86) endorsed the medical verdict that coffee was a threat to health, causing effeminacy in men and sterility in women. In a mercantilist age he waged war on the substance for several decades, although its progress proved unstoppable: not only did the pursuit of real coffee create a thriving black market, but numerous substitutes brewed from wheat, barley and chicory were developed. Bans on coffee were also passed in Sweden during the second half of the seventeenth century, although the *per capita* consumption of the stimulant soared to become one of the highest in the world in the following centuries.[6] The ambiguous relationship between prohibition and consumption is also an important theme in the history of other psychoactive substances, as we see in the case of opium.

The Spanish *conquistadores* encountered the cocoa beverage in the Maya and Aztec empires, consisting of cocoa powder and a variety of spices. Chocolate was drunk cold and without sugar in Europe and was confined to members of the social elite, who would offer the beverage to guests at banquets with tobacco. The elite associations of chocolate were replicated by the aristocratic households of Europe, in particular Spain, although some added sugar.[7] The French Revolution resulted in a relative decline in the consumption of chocolate, as the urban bourgeoisie embraced the less negatively marked beverages of tea and coffee instead.[8] In the longer run, however, the middle classes' desire for luxury consumables ensured that sweetened chocolate would be drunk or eaten by a rising number of people, including women and children. The addition of milk to liquid and solid chocolate popularised cocoa even further, so that consumption in Europe somersaulted to some 50,000 tonnes by 1899, with the cultivation centre shifting from the Americas to Africa.[9]

The addition of sugar and milk to chocolate, tea and coffee helped transform dietary habits in Europe during the nineteenth century. Once the prized luxury of a small elite, tea and bread had become the standard fare of the working classes in several regions of northern Europe, notably England and northern Germany, while coffee taken with bread was prevalent in others (Austria, Scandinavia). When tea and coffee became substitutes for beer as standard working-class fare, the addition of sugar could only partly compensate for the shortfall in calories. However, with the addition of milk, the days of the 'ploughman's breakfast' based on beer were numbered.[10]

Caffeinated beverages sustained rather than eliminated the spread of alcoholic drinks: caffeine and alcohol worked together to create a thriving drinking culture in Europe. As Fernand Braudel has noted, the revolution in Europe was the appearance of alcohol, created in the sixteenth century, consolidated in the seventeenth and popularised in the eighteenth.[11] During the Middle Ages the populations of Mediterranean Europe accompanied their meals with a mixture of weak wine and water, the everyday liquid food in the north being 'small beer' of around 2 per cent alcohol. 'Strong beers' needed to undergo a process of 'mashing', and depended in their alcohol content on the type of fermentable ingredients used: before the advent of hops, beer had to be brewed daily, a task usually performed at home.[12] However, the real breakthrough came with distillation, invented in the sixteenth century. Fermented liquids were weak and spoiled quickly, while distilled drinks were strong and kept well. As distillation spread, brandy broke away from apothecaries, wines were given new body by the addition of spirits, and alcohol gradually appeared wherever the raw material was available, from Cognac to Jerez. Technological changes in the eighteenth century lowered the manufacturing costs and contributed to the huge availability of alcohol in the nineteenth century. Alcohols made from grain started to compete with brandy and spirits during this period, as vodka, whisky and gin were modest in price and found a large market to the north of the area reached by the vine.[13] To the huddled masses who had flocked to the factories of industrial Britain, gin often provided an important solace for those suffering from mental exhaustion and physical hardship.[14] The proliferation of gin consumption in England between 1720 and 1750 generated social anxieties among the ruling elites which lasted well into the twentieth century.[15]

Europeans also exported distilled drinks and the stills which allowed the production of spirits. People in Asia, Africa and the Americas took to imported alcohol and from the seventeenth century onwards produced liquor locally. Rum, arrack, gin and brandy became global commodities, although distilled beverages did not take hold everywhere. For instance, grain spirits created more havoc in the north of Europe than in the vine-growing regions of the south. Cultural norms, social structures and historical circumstances varied enormously from place to place, shaping the spread of drinking cultures and the prevalence of drink problems. In Islamic countries alcohol generally failed to become part of local patterns of intoxication, and tea and coffee, as well as opium and cannabis, were the main psychoactive substances. No alcohol revolution occurred either in China, where distillation had been known since the twelfth century at the latest. A smoking culture appeared instead during roughly the same period: introduced in the seventeenth century and consolidated in the eighteenth, smoked tobacco and smoked opium spread to all social categories during the nineteenth century. Foreigners visiting China observed with interest that alcohol was not the 'great evil' they considered it to be at home. Millet beers (*huangjiu*) and rice wines (*mijiu*) were weak compared to the stronger spirits consumed in Europe. Other distillations such as burnt wine (*shaojiu*) were at least of equal strength, although they were more often used in cooking and in medicinal recipes.[16] In a period of rapid population growth and concern over grain shortages, moreover, distillation was prohibited several times during the eighteenth century, contributing to the low visibility of alcohol consumption.[17] As John Barrow, high-ranking member of the Macartney mission to the Qianlong court, observed,

[Public inns] are no incitement, as those are of a similar kind in Europe, to jovial pleasures or to vulgar ebriety. From this odious vice the bulk of the people are entirely free… Whenever a few Chinese happen to meet together it is generally for the purpose of gaming, or to eat a kettle of boiled rice, or drink a pot of tea, or smoke a pipe of tobacco. The upper classes indulge at home in the use of opium.[18]

The explanation for the relatively low occurrence of alcoholism is probably to be found in established cultures of consumption, although reliable evidence is so far lacking: alcohol, at the close of the nineteenth century, was drunk in conjunction with meals in egg-cup quantities. It was rarely taken as a social lubricant, a use reserved for tea, tobacco and opium. The relatively high price even for weaker liquors made alcoholic beverages a luxury item, compared to the base-grade opium smoked by the poor during the late Qing.[19] Even after China was opened for trade by the Treaty of Nanjing (1842), foreign traders quickly discovered that there was almost no demand for wines and spirits: as one merchant of Fenchurch Street, London, was advised, 'We have for years past urged on our friends the impolicy of sending out large quantities of Wines and such articles to a country like this, where no demand exists for them beyond the few hundred individuals composing the foreign community'.[20] Gin, rum, brandy, whisky and other distilled drinks never became popular in China, with the exception of beer and sweet wines at the end of the Qing. Another factor in the failure of foreign traders to export liquors and spirits to China may have been taste, although more research would be necessary to confirm this hypothesis. Zhang Deyi, diplomat to Europe in the 1860s, described the taste of red wine as acid (*suan*) and bitter (*se*), and could only swallow it with water added.[21] Some evidence has also been offered to suggest that a significant proportion of the population were deterred by a response referred to as an 'alcohol flush reaction', characterised by a rush of blood to the face, neck and chest, accompanied by rapid heartbeat, headache, nausea and extreme drowsiness.[22] A higher vulnerability to alcohol poisoning may also have prevented the spread of a wider drinking culture in China. Moreover, in Europe wine, beer and spirits were safer alternatives to potentially contaminated water,[23] a problem circumvented by the use of boiled water in a tea culture established well before the advent of the psychoactive revolution: the poor who could not afford tea would sip hot water instead.[24] More important, opium smoking fulfilled so many medical, social and recreational roles that it successfully prevented distilled alcohol from devastating the local population, as happened in other parts of the world.

OPIUM IN EUROPE AND ASIA

As a drinking culture spread to all social levels in Europe after the sixteenth century, alcohol was increasingly perceived by the ruling elites as a threat to social order and public health.[25] Coffee from the Middle East, cocoa from the New World and tea from China were seen as suitable alternatives to brandy and gin. Opium was also considered an appropriate replacement for alcohol: in nineteenth-century England children were given a cordial with laudanum in the pub rather than an alcoholic beverage. Generally chewed and eaten in tiny portions or dissolved in tinctures, opium became a drug of convenience for consumers of all social categories, although it carried different connotations from literary circles (Thomas de Quincey and Samuel Taylor Coleridge) to working-class homes. It was regarded as a beneficial medicine which could lead to physical dependence if used excessively, just as an uncontrolled passion for the bottle could lead to alcoholism.[26] Belief in the wholesome properties of opium as a panacea for all human ailments was only shaken with the emergence of medical science around the end of the nineteenth century.

Most of the opium in Europe was imported from Turkey rather than from India: it had at least twice the morphine content (10–15 per cent rather than 3–4 per cent)[27] and was considered of higher quality. Smyrna opium was traded by a handful of intermediaries via Italian ports in conjunction with spices imported from the Middle East. Britain was also supplied directly from Turkey in consignments commissioned by the Levant Company. By the middle of the nineteenth century opium was increasingly shipped directly to London, where it would be inspected and purchased by private arrangement rather than at public auctions. It was also imported from India, Persia and France, China exporting up to 16,000 kilos a year to Britain in the 1880s. Although the amount consumed is difficult to assess in the absence of reliable statistics, estimates vary from 600 to 1,600 grams per 1,000 population in 1827–60.[28] Attempts were also made to cultivate the poppy in England during the early nineteenth century, mostly in the fenlands of Norfolk and Cambridgeshire, but the quality and the relative yield were disappointing. Detailed plans were drawn up to finance the harvesting of the poppies, an arduous task for which the use of Irish labourers was suggested. Similar schemes to produce opium on a commercial scale were also devised in Germany and France, although the only successful commercial venture was in poppy heads rather than in opium.[29]

Wholesale pharmacists in England manufactured their own opium preparations, and many of their standard concoctions—Dover's Powder, Battley's Sedative Solution, Black Drop and countless others—were available at chemists' shops throughout the country. Opium was marketed in a wide variety of pills held together by soap or lead, lozenges, powders, confections, plasters, enemas or liniments. Before the advent of the Pharmacy Act in 1868, opium preparations could be bought freely in pharmacies, street markets, pubs and local shops crowded with food, clothing and fabrics: in the 1850s between 16,000 and 26,000 people were engaged in selling them. Opium was dissolved in beer, wine or vinegar, as potent laudanum or simply as an infusion prepared out of boiled poppy heads; powdered opium was used in suppositories and raw opium was rolled into pills. Opium remedies were bought by working men in many manufacturing towns. Laudanum could be found in every home, often made to order by shopkeepers, while going to the grocer's for opium was a child's errand.[30] Laudanum was so popular that *The Lancet*, reporting in 1844 that restrictive legislation had been introduced in St Petersburg that required clear labelling and shaping of laudanum bottles, doubted 'whether such despotic measures would be tolerated in England'.[31]

Opium use was the cornerstone of self-medication, and a good housewife was expected to be able to blend cough syrups and other opiate remedies at home. In the opinion of Dr Francis Anstie, editor of *The Practitioner*, the poor 'would never think of narcotising themselves, any more than they would be getting drunk; but who simply desire a relief from the pains of fatigue endured by an ill-fed, ill-housed body, and harassed mind'.[32] Opium pills and laudanum were a remedy for 'fatigue and depression' as well as a whole range of minor complaints of working people. It was a standby for coughs and colds, used to combat cholera and deployed against diarrhoea. The populations of the cold and humid marshlands (e.g. the Fens between Cambridge and the Wash), where fevers, rheumatism and neuralgia were common, readily spent a considerable portion of their earnings on opium. Chewed, eaten in bread and biscuits, brewed in tea or dissolved into beer, administered as drops, but never smoked, opium became the Fenman's best friend. Working women, kept awake at night by their children, embraced the soothing qualities of the drug, as the instant effect of laudanum or paregoric on crying infants was common knowledge. Older children could be pacified by sucking on opium lollies and lozenges.[33] Only at the very end of the nineteenth century did it become normal to look askance on the use of opiates on infants, in particular among the lower classes ('A nurse who boasts much of her ability to keep an infant quiet… should be an object of suspicion').[34]

In France, too, opium had been appreciated for many centuries as an essential ingredient of self-medication. The Capucin Rousseau, operating under the tutelage of Louis XIV, was the inventor of a potent laudanum concoction known as the *goutte noire* (black drop), which proliferated in Europe up till the end of the nineteenth century. As in most other European countries, the opium was supplied by sea from the opium-rich provinces of central Anatolia and Isfahan, reaching central Europe via Venice, Leghorn (Livorno) or Marseille.[35] However, one important difference was that smoking opium became popular towards the end of the nineteenth century, first among colonial administrators returned from Asia and later mainly among naval officers. The sudden appearance of hundreds of opium houses in ports such as Toulon, Marseille, Brest, Cherbourg and Bordeaux aroused widespread public interest. They also became a feature of the Belle Époque in Paris and other large cities, catering to various social classes. When the existing legislation was tightened in 1908 at the specific request of the Navy, many opium smokers such as the poet Antonin Artaud and the popular writer Claude Farrère (alias Charles Bargone) defended the eating and smoking of opium, which they considered far less destructive than alcohol. However, in the aftermath of the Hague Convention opium and other narcotics were outlawed in 1916.[36]

If opium use was popular at all social levels in nineteenth-century Europe, it was even more prevalent in regions where the poppy had been cultivated over many centuries. Originally cultivated in Egypt, the poppy spread to Asia Minor and Greece in the ancient world while Arab traders brought it to Persia, India and China. While vineyards were torn up and the vines burnt by the followers of the Prophet Muhammad after the seventh century, cannabis and opium were all the more freely indulged in without alcohol to rival them.[37] Between the eighth and sixteenth centuries, traders from the Middle East—Jews, Christians and Muslims—regularly included opium in their merchandise, alongside jasmine and henna. The opium pills were at times sealed with labels inscribed with the dedication *mash allah* ('gift of god') so often encountered in Muslim countries.[38]

In the case of Turkey, which provided Europe with most of its opium, an astonishing lack of research makes even a cursory overview of the history of opiate use rather difficult. While Turkey was one of the largest opium producers in the nineteenth century, at least one historian has claimed that a strong taboo against the consumption, as opposed to the exportation, of opium helped the local population avoid a 'major addiction problem': if true, that would at least invalidate the common assumption that the mere availability of a substance inevitably leads to its use.[39] However, the idea that the crop was reserved for exportation seems dubious, if only because individual farmers rather than large landowners were the main cultivators, while the state would have had insufficient power to prevent its consumption.[40] The recreational use of opium was widely observed in the Ottoman empire by foreign visitors from the sixteenth century onwards. William Biddulph noted after 1600 that Turkish men congregated in coffee houses and used opium,[41] which, according to Engelbert Kaempfer (about 1687), was flavoured with nutmeg, cardamom, cinnamon or mace and eaten for pleasure.[42] Opium was also popular in Egypt, where local produce was of a relatively poor quality and was sold in round cakes flattened and enveloped in leaves. It was used over the centuries for ritual, medicinal and recreational purposes although, as in most opium-producing countries, it was eaten rather than smoked.[43]

Opium appeared in India in the seventeenth and eighteenth centuries as one of several ingredients in prescriptions for diarrhoea and later still as a painkiller.[44] In the nineteenth century its consumption was already common throughout the subcontinent, although more prevalent in the northern and western regions than in the extreme south. Habitual users often took opium pills twice a day in increasing dosages until a level of tolerance had been reached: the same dosage would then be kept for life. A diversity of evidence offered by both Indian and British physicians showed that the habitual use of opium did not have harmful effects on either health or longevity. Opium was an important household remedy in India, as local populations reached for the pills to treat diarrhoea, dysentery, chills, malarial attacks, asthma, chronic coughs and rheumatic pains. Small doses could be given to infants soon after birth until the ages of two or three, keeping them quiet and in good health. It helped their digestion and relieved a variety of infant ailments, including teething pains and fevers. In Gujarat, Rajasthan and central India its use in ceremonies was common, as a solution of opium was offered in water during formal receptions at court and at home. Religious festivals, births and funerals were also marked by the offering of opium water, which was accepted even by participants who might not ordinarily take opium. While some of these practices were dying out as a result of the increasing consumption of alcohol and the rising price of opium from the late nineteenth century onwards, opium continued to be taken without challenge until independence in 1947. Its use in India was widespread and generally moderate, rarely leading to excessive consumption, contrary to the social and physical damage caused by strong spirits, imported into India despite the opposition of both Hindu and Muslim communities.[45] With the unfolding of the psychoactive revolution, India was to become the world's largest exporter of opium.

THE OPIUM TRADE IN EAST ASIA

Already in the sixteenth century, visitors to India such as the Venetian Caesar Fredericke (1581) and the Englishmen Ralph Fitch (1591) and William Finch (1608) exalted the wealth which the opium trade could generate.[46] Portuguese and Spanish fleets were the first ones to compete directly with the established sea merchants of Asia, the discovery of the alternative route around the Cape of Good Hope dealing a blow to the virtual monopoly of the Arab maritime trade. The arrival of Dutch, English, Danish and French ships in the sixteenth and seventeenth centuries heralded a new global order:[47] their trade concessions and East India Companies were a deliberate attempt to destroy the indigenous sea trade and form monopolies over the highly coveted goods of the East, including pepper, spices, tea and silks, as well as opium, which was portable and durable and soon became a substitute for silver coins or gold.[48]

The first opium imported on behalf of the London East India Company (founded 1600) reached England at the very beginning of the seventeenth century, on Dutch and Portuguese vessels. The Dutch were also the first to establish a monopoly over the East Asian opium trade by controlling the opium grown in the Hugli region of Bengal. Bengali opium was destined for shipment to the Dutch possessions in Ceylon, the Malacca Straits and in the Malay archipelago. Opium began to figure prominently in the Dutch Batavia trade from 1640 onwards. Once established as a trade item and as a form of payment, it followed Dutch seafarers in their search for spices: from Bengal to Borneo and from Malacca to Cochin, Dutch trade popularised its use.[49]

In the same period the Portuguese established a monopoly for opium produced in Malwa, which was shipped from the Gulf of Cambay to East Asia via Macau.[50] Opium had already played a role in the Portuguese trade between India, Malacca and Singapore in the second half of the sixteenth century, and other European powers followed in their wake, Britain gradually eclipsing them in influence over India. The British conquest of Bengal and Bihar in 1758 in particular provided a unique opportunity for the colonial authorities to collaborate with wealthy opium cultivators.[51] Competing interests between the different opium-growing and opium-exporting states in India, as well as rivalry between British India and Portuguese Goa, which relied heavily on opium exports from its ports of Diu and Daman, meant that the origin of the opium reaching the East Asian markets was as much determined by political as by commercial considerations. It required decades before such fiscal and political difficulties could be overcome and opium from Malwa and Bengal could become more profitable for export.[52]

The British East India Company traded opium throughout the eighteenth century, but towards the end of the century the profit margins of the earlier period were reduced to net deficits, a fate shared by most European East India Companies. The problem reached a climax when the British government decided drastically to reduce tea duties in 1785. The ensuing financial pressure on the East India Company led to complex negotiations on the future of the opium monopoly.[53] It lost its trade monopoly under the Charter Act in 1813, although the company kept control of opium production and manufacturing in Bengal. The new arrangements led to an influx of Turkish opium into the Bengal and Bombay Presidencies:[54] in the new global trading system, competition between different opium providers created vast private business empires.

Competition was particularly intense between the controlled trade in Patna opium and the freely traded Malwa variety, which had escaped government prohibitions and export bans by locating new ports, carriers and markets for export. The right of Indian states to levy a transit tax on the officially traded commodity was one of the main factors which made Patna too expensive to be commercially attractive. When prices collapsed in the 1820s, after a price war between cultivators in Bengal and in Malwa, new exports to Southeast and East Asia presented the only option for survival. Following the submission of the state of Sind in 1843, the colonial government controlled most of the coastline, except for Portuguese Goa, and was therefore free to fix export duties for all opium leaving India. This made it easier for the British Indian administration to control and tax Malwa opium, which had formerly gained fame as the contraband commodity *par excellence*, all but escaping from the clutches of the tax collectors. The ever-increasing availability of Indian opium led to a dramatic increase in the quantity of opium auctioned publicly, as well as a general reduction in its price.[55]

Opium in India, including that produced under government monopoly and put up for auction at the Calcutta sales, was bought by private merchants, often British or Parsi, who shipped it to other countries on their own account. As most of the opium imported into Europe came from Turkey, the single most important destination for opium from India was China, where demand had grown steadily from the end of the eighteenth century, as the next chapter explains.

3

OPIUM BEFORE THE 'OPIUM WAR'
(*c.* 1600–1840)

The last chapter examined the global spread of psychoactive substances, showing how after the fifteenth century opium was used widely in many parts of the world, including Europe and India. The ways in which it was administered could vary greatly and often depended on patterns of consumption already in place before its advent. In Britain opium was swallowed in liquid form: opium tinctures consisted of a solution in alcohol and water and were very popular in a culture of self-medication. Where hashish was eaten in India for complex social reasons, opium was administered orally to combat numerous medical problems. However, its spread in China depended on the discovery of an entirely novel mode of delivery: smoking. The history of opium in China thus starts in America, where European settlers enthusiastically adopted the local habit of inhaling tobacco before spreading it to the rest of the world.

TOBACCO AND THE CULTURE OF SMOKE

While a wide range of plants had been used for centuries by the indigenous populations of Central and North America for both ceremonial and recreational purposes, the origins of tobacco smoking remain relatively obscure. By the time European settlers arrived along the east coast of North America, tobacco cultivation was widespread. The Montagnais of Quebec were apparently so committed to their smoking habit that they even inhaled the incinerated wooden stems of their pipes once the tobacco

itself had been used up. As a powerful hunger-suppressant, nicotine enabled warriors, traders, hunters and farmers to remain alert
over long periods of time.[1] Europeans eagerly adopted the habit
of smoking tobacco themselves, and by the 1570s pipe smoking
was spreading rapidly through their settlements of the Americas,
while it became a popular pastime in Europe in the early seventeenth century.[2] It was also quickly disseminated throughout
Africa, facilitated by Portuguese and French traders. Within barely
two generations the use of tobacco had become entirely incultura-
ted, producing a rich African smoking culture which extended
into social ritual and religious rites.[3]

Tobacco was first introduced in parts of Asia at the end of the
sixteenth century, though not always smoked: in Java it became an
important additive to the betel chew, along with areca, betel and
lime; smoking would also become widespread in the seventeenth
and eighteenth centuries.[4] In Japan smoking through long-stemmed
clay pipes (*kiseru*) became popular among members of the imperial elite during the first decades of the seventeenth century.[5]

Snuff was introduced to China by the Jesuit Matteo Ricci in
1581 and rapidly became a luxury item among the ruling elites.[6]
Wang Shizhen (1641–1711) noted how it had become a prized
commodity in the capital by the end of the seventeenth century:

Recently, somebody made snuff (*biyan*) from tobacco in the imperial
capital. It is claimed that snuff can be used to sharpen one's eyes; it is especially useful in remedying various illnesses. Snuff bottles are made of
glass, and they come in all shapes, sizes and colours, including red, purple, yellow, white, black and green. The white ones are like crystal and
the red ones look like fire…[7]

Finely crafted snuff bottles were prized by tobacco connoisseurs,
not unlike the expensive opium pipes which would appear on
the market in the following two centuries. Snuff often contained
rare fragrances such as musk and was thought to alleviate the
symptoms of colds,[8] although its use remained confined to social
elites and foreign missionaries.

Smoked tobacco (*danrouguo, danbagu* or *yancao*) was also introduced to China by European traders in the Wanli period (1573–

1620), probably on Spanish or Portuguese vessels from Manila and through the ports in Fujian.[9] Dutch traders may have been involved too, since copious amounts of tobacco were kept in loading bays for their personal consumption.[10] The smoking of tobacco rapidly spread to the court, despite numerous bans passed by the Manchus already before their conquest of China in 1644, as it was considered 'a more heinous crime than even that of neglecting archery'.[11] Despite these legal constraints, smoking soon became popular at the highest level: all the women put in charge of Kangxi's upbringing, including his wet-nurse, took to the habit. A series of prohibitions were loosely enforced and then quickly abandoned, as Kangxi himself tolerated the habit.[12] Within two generations the Manchus had acquired a thriving smoking culture.

The tobacco plant became a popular crop in the seventeenth century, particularly in the tropical south.[13] Yao Lü (d. 1622) was an early observer of the smoking habit: 'You light one end and put the other in your mouth. The smoke goes down the throat through the pipe. It can make one tipsy, but it also protects against malaria.'[14] An important passage in the *Siku quanshu* also traced the origins of tobacco smoking in 1701:

From officials to servants and women, everyone smokes tobacco today. Many farmers have planted the crop and make enormous profits. I looked it up in various pharmacopoeias and in the *Er Ya* [encyclopaedia of the third century], but did not find any reference to it. In the work of Yao Lü it is suggested that the plant is known as *danbagu* [tobacco, transliteration] in Luzon, as well as *jinsixun* [gold threaded intoxicant]. The smoke enters the lungs via a tube and can be intoxicating. It can also be used as a prophylactic against malaria (*zhangqi*). Its juice can be used to poison snakes. It was originally imported from overseas by someone from Zhangzhou. It has also been planted in Putian. Today more tobacco is being grown [in Putian] than in Luzon. It can be seen almost everywhere.[15]

Ye Mengzhu also noted the rapid spread of tobacco despite imperial prohibitions:

Tobacco originally came from Fujian. When I was a child, I heard my grandfather say that it was cultivated in Fujian, and that one could become intoxicated when smoking it. He claimed that it was also called 'dried liquor', but that it did not grow in our region... Later it was prohibited by imperial edict. It was claimed that wandering bandits used it against the symptoms of cold and rheumatism. Common people were not allowed to plant it or the merchants to sell it... It did not take long for tobacco cultivation to die out as a result. In the beginning of the Shunzhi period [of the early Qing], however, everyone in the army used tobacco. Tobacco merchants suddenly reappeared and farmers cultivated it as profits shot up.[16]

The medical qualities of tobacco, despite early imperial edicts against its use, were praised by a number of scholars. Zhang Jiebin (1563–1640), one of the first medical writers to comment on tobacco, concluded that soldiers who smoked in Yunnan were protected from malaria, while its juice was a potent antidote against lice on the scalp: its fine quality earned it the name 'golden silk smoke' (jinsiyan). He recommended occasional smoking, but cautioned that excessive use could cause the smoker to faint.[17] Fang Yizhi (died 1667), another medical authority, prescribed it against rheumatism and the common cold, but warned that too much smoke could lead to 'dried-up lungs' and premature death.[18] In a similar vein Wang Pu mentioned in 1679 that 'the people beyond the [northern] border are subject to diseases caused by extreme cold, and cannot be cured without tobacco'.[19] Qing author Wang Ang (born 1615) remarked that smoke 'circulates throughout the whole body' (zhou yishen), invigorating the smoker and suppressing hunger. Its medical properties could be enhanced by boiling the tobacco and applying the hot paste to the affected body parts.[20] In the beginning of the eighteenth century, the celebrated writer Quan Zuwang (1705–55) even lauded tobacco as a medical panacea in his Danbagu fu (An essay on tobacco):

Alcohol is good at dispersing depression. Tea is good for quenching thirst. Yet neither can be compared to tobacco... When depressed, tobacco can cheer the spirit, guide the qi and open up spiritual passages—a plant of immortality. Betel can be used to eradicate malaria ['to chase away bad air'], while olives can help extract poison, yet none can compare to the usefulness of tobacco... It can sober up the drunk, yet may also be intoxicating... As a good gastric remedy, it can relieve hunger and boost the appetite. It can dispel boredom and preoccupation—a necessity for daily life.[21]

Popular opinion in the eighteenth century likened it to the betel nut, although its taste was considered more refreshing.[22] Betel nut chewing was widespread as a prophylactic against malaria,[23] but tobacco, and later opium, would become much more effective and popular remedies against fever, as will be shown in another chapter.

The perceived medical benefits of tobacco and the positive reception of smoking as a new mode of delivery may well have thrived on the positive meanings traditionally associated with smoke. Incense sacrifice originated in Buddhist India and was incorporated into the ancestral rites during the Song, aided by Buddhist scholars such as Channing (919–1001). Incense was burnt not only for ritual purposes but also for the soothing effect it had on participants: 'Incense clears foul odours by exuding a fragrant scent.'[24] Healers used the fumes of burning herbal drugs to exorcise demons and release evil *qi* ('vapours' or 'energy').[25] Moxibustion, in which a herbal substance was burnt on the skin as a counterirritant, also drew on the healing powers attributed to smoke. The famous physician Li Shizhen (1518–93) praised moxa fumes as an effective cure against illness, especially rheumatism, while burning moxa was used in sacrificial ceremonies to obtain protection from evil. Moxa was even hung outside the house to repel evil spirits with its protective veil of smoke.[26] While relatively little is known about folk remedies in late imperial China, ordinary people may of course have been less impressed with the ability of smoke to offer spiritual protection than with its effectiveness in repelling insects, which were a constant and ubiquitous irritant if not a direct threat to personal health.

By the 1780s tobacco was cultivated widely in China. The rage for tobacco smoking was noted by Macartney in 1793: 'They almost all smoke tobacco', the British ambassador elaborated, 'and consider it as a compliment to offer each other a whiff of their pipes. They also take snuff, mostly Brazil, but in small quantities, not in that beastly profusion which is often practised in England, even by some of our fine ladies.'[27] Tobacco pipes could be elaborate and made of valuable materials, whereas ordinary pipes were small compared to contemporary European pipes, often consisting of a brass bowl and a brass or stone mouthpiece, connected by a reed stem. Such implements, mainly used in eastern China, merely yielded a handful of inhalations per pipe-load. The ash would then be knocked out on to the floor.[28] Tobacco smoking also accorded well with a thriving tea culture, as the next section shows.

MINERALS, ALCOHOL AND TEA CULTURE

A tea revolution marked the Tang dynasty (618–906), permanently relegating alcohol to a lesser position among the culturally privileged intoxicants. New processing techniques and advances in cultivation methods combined with the widespread promotion of tea as a suitable substitute for alcohol by monastic Buddhism.[29] Tea was important for the long periods of sleepless meditation practised in Chan (i.e. Zen) monasteries, while itinerant monks further disseminated tea drinking all over the country in the second half of the eighth century, encouraging temperance by highlighting the social problems associated with alcohol.[30] Pious tracts extolled the virtues of tea while rebuking the objections made by proponents of alcohol.[31] Medical writers also acknowledged its medicinal and therapeutic qualities, recommending tea to nurture the stomach, clear inflammations in the throat and aid digestion. Liu Yuanliang attributed ten virtues to tea, including its taste, nutritional and stimulating virtues, and its value against depression and tiredness. He regarded it as instrumental in the promotion of rites and general civility, which was indispensable for 'reaching enlightenment' (mingde).[32]

The rise of a tea culture during the Tang was a significant shift away from heavier patterns of intoxication, all the more so since the previous period had been a 'golden age' for alcohol.[33] During much of this early period, mineral powders were taken in conjunction with alcohol to act as powerful 'immortality drugs', and usually had the opposite effect. The most popular of these substances was called 'cold eating powder' (hanshisan), used in alchemy with cinnabar (dan) and consumed with copious amounts of alcohol between the Latter Han (25 bc–220 ad) and the Tang (618–907).[34] Alchemist Zheng Xuan (127–200) specified that the medically active minerals chalcanthite (*shidan*), cinnabar (*dansha*, red arsenic sulphide), realgar (the arsenic sulphide *xionghuang* or *xiongshi*) and magnetite (*cishi*) should be enclosed in an earthen receptacle, continuously heated over three days.[35] The drug obtained from the concoction could then be applied to the affected areas of the sick body. Resembling fresh blood, the realgar was probably an early ingredient in alchemical attempts at creating an elixir of immortality. Iron, saltpetre and mercury were also standard ingredients, while other pharmacopoeias mentioned over forty different minerals.[36] Alcohol was seen as an indispensable ingredient of the 'cold eating powder', to be taken either cold or heated to prolong life and avert death.[37] The effects of the powder-alcohol concoction could be overpowering. The medical expert Huangfu Mi (214–82) recalled that it could give rise to sensations of sudden heat and cold, sleeplessness, amnesia, anxiety and suicidal impulses. From the Song onwards, mineral powders became more varied, including increasing quantities of medical herbs, ginger, ginseng and oyster extract, thus changing in character from alchemical substances to formal medicines (*yao*).[38]

While the use of immortality drugs remained confined to a small number of literary figures in search of longevity, tea culture gradually percolated in late imperial China to lower social levels. The beverage became particularly popular during the Ming, largely because monks and scholars actively promoted it as an alternative to alcohol.[39] The medicinal properties of tea were widely appreciated and undoubtedly contributed to its spread. For instance, a southern variety known as *kudeng* was thought to have a cooling effect and was often used with local herbs to treat malarial fever.[40] While high-grade tea required pure water, the scent of flowers could disguise the poor quality of ordinary water as well as the bitter aroma produced by cheaper tea leaves. In late imperial China the addition of flowers such as jasmine (*molihua*) as well as herbs and petals thus allowed tea consumption to permeate throughout the population.[41]

Well into the twentieth century, high quality tea nonetheless remained a relatively expensive beverage, since clean water was beyond the means of many people. Tea houses put a premium on pure water, not for reasons of hygiene but because it enhanced the taste of the tea they served. In Suzhou tea houses collected rain water or obtained it from selected wells or unpolluted canals outside the city, where boats operated specifically for this purpose.[42] Frequent water shortages in large areas of Shaanxi and parts of Shanxi may have been one reason for the spread of smoking, first of tobacco and later of opium. Since pure water was an important ingredient for tea and alcohol, the quality of both suffered when water supplies were inadequate: tobacco and opium provided convenient alternatives.[43]

Tea also fulfilled a variety of social roles which account for its success in late imperial China. As tea varied widely in price and quality, from rare leaves brewed with imported water down to cheap jasmine tea made with ordinary rainwater, it was ideal as an indicator of elite status—a role that opium would replicate in the nineteenth century. Discerning customers distinguished between different regions, types and even parts of the leaf, while certain varieties such as Pu'er tea attained the status of luxury items. An elaborate tea ritual remained the exclusive occasion for the conspicuous display of good taste and social status, while tea utensils and porcelain ware were cherished by connoisseurs as *objets d'art*.[44] While less complex than the tea ritual in Japan, the quality of the tea, the heat of the water and the type of teapot used were important in the preparation of the beverage. On the other hand, tea culture was also a vector of social inclusion, as teahouses (*chaguan*) developed during the Ming into meeting places comparable to coffee houses in Europe. Popular venues included luxurious tea salons (*chasi*), tea rooms (*chawu*), simple tea stalls (*chatan*), tea huts (*chapu*) and the teahouse (*chaguan*), each catering to a different category of people. Teahouses provided entertainment in the guise of popular plays, story-telling and games, while fruit, snacks and deserts were also served.[45]

Tobacco was the ideal companion of tea before the spread of opium: the teahouse acted as a venue for a combined activity which became known as *yancha*, namely 'smoke and tea'.[46] Guests would first smoke and then drink tea, which was supposed to cleanse the palate of the lingering taste of tobacco. Water also took time to boil: customers were offered a smoke while waiting for tea to be prepared.[47] Tobacco was also used in conjunction with alcohol, a combination celebrated by the poet Han Tan (1637–1704), but its association with tea enabled its exceptionally swift reception outside scholarly circles.[48] With the spread of opium during the nineteenth and early twentieth centuries, the distinction between social spaces for the consumption of opium and tea would become blurred, with most opium houses serving tea and most teahouses offering smoking: opium replicated the role of tobacco in a culture of *yancha*. Before opium was smoked pure, however, it was laced with tobacco: madak is the topic of the next section.

THE SPREAD OF MADAK *c.* 1660–1780

Opium was available in China via Arab merchants from the eighth century onwards. Taken orally as a medicine, however, opium left a bitter taste. When smoked it released a sweet, pleasurable aroma, which rapidly became known for relieving boredom (*jiemen*) and anxiety (*xinjiao*). To be smoked more easily, raw opium was mixed with other substances. Engelbert Kaempfer, a Westphalian physician working for the Dutch East India Company, recorded that the Javanese soaked their tobacco in water that made the head 'spin violently'. The opium required for this preparation quickly became the most precious traded commodity in Batavia.[49] The first traders to introduce opium for smoking to China were probably the Dutch between 1624 and 1660, first to their trade posts in Taiwan, and from there to Fujian. During the tumultuous decades of the Ming-Qing transition, opium (madak) smoking was confined to the Taiwan Strait, and not noted by the Qing authorities until Xiamen was captured in 1683.[50]

Javanese opium was blended with roots of local plants and hemp, minced, boiled with water in copper pans and finally mixed with tobacco: this blend is called madak.[51] The mixture was prepared by the owners of smoking houses and fetched prices significantly higher than for pure tobacco. Opium house owners in Taiwan also provided the smoking implement: a bamboo tube with a filter made of coir fibres produced from local coconut palms.[52] Early reports from Taiwan indicate that they often offered the first smoke of madak free, serving copious amounts of appetisers, food, and desserts.[53] Travellers to Fujian and Taiwan observed that honey, candy and fruits were eaten as the opium was budding and crackling above the lamp.[54] Contemporary observers such as Zhu Jingying also mentioned that opium (*yapian*) originated from parts of Southeast Asia which correspond to Indonesia and the Philippines today. The same author described the first opium pipes: made of bamboo, round, slender and with a fine opening, with a mouthpiece made of china clay. The substance was smoked with a hollow pot made of yellow clay, which was used to cook the opium. While the cleaning tool and the opium box were made of bamboo, opium paste scrapers were based on either iron or bamboo, flat or curved.[55]

Although these early reports were condemnatory, the habit of smoking madak spread throughout the coastal provinces of south China, even though never exceeding the popularity of tobacco. A precise chronology is not possible in the absence of reliable source material. The first references to opium smoking date from the early eighteenth century and come from Fujian and Guangdong, the same ports of entry as for tobacco: 'The opium is heated in a small copper pan until it turns into a very thick paste, which is then mixed with tobacco. When the mixture is dried, it can be used for smoking by means of a bamboo pipe, while palm fibres are added for easier inhalation. There are private opium houses where people gather to lie on couches and smoke in turns by passing the pipe around. This carries on till late at night and goes on night after night without a break.'[56] Another description is provided in a memorial sent to the Yongzheng emperor in the 1720s:

Opium (*yapian*) is produced overseas, and the foreign merchants who import it as medicine (*yaocai*) derive a lucrative business from this trade, in particular in the Fujianese districts of Xiamen and Taiwan. Shameless rascals (*wulai guntu*) lure the sons of good families into [the habit] for their own profit. The opium is boiled down to a paste and is blended into tobacco (*yan*) in order to produce smoking opium (*yapianyan*, i.e. *madak*). Privately run inns are established, where [smokers] congregate at night, only to disperse at dawn (*ye ju xiao san*), leading to licentious behaviour. The truth is that youngsters become corrupted (*xie*) by smoking (*xi*) it until their lives collapse, their families' livelihood vanishes, and nothing is left but trouble. If one is intent on extirpating this evil (*hai*), one must tackle it at the root by ordering the imperial officials of Fujian and Guangdong to be strict in prohibiting the trade. Strict legal measures... will prevent any resurgence of the opium trade and lead to the closure of private opium houses.[57]

The memorial is significant for several reasons. It emphasises that opium smoking was an 'evil' afflicting only the south-eastern coastline; it shows that the 'opium' smoked was in reality madak; and it indicates that opium smoking advanced from the bottom of the social order—opium houses run by disreputable locals—threatening to ensnare the sons of 'good families'. The moralising language is reminiscent of the concurrent anti-'heresy' (*xiejiao*) edicts, in particular the allegation that people congregate throughout the night, thus reversing the 'natural order' promoted by the Confucian state. Such heterodox gatherings, as in the case of religious heresy, would inevitably lead to lewd behaviour, economic ruin and eventually social decay.[58]

The Yongzheng edict of 1729, which banned the importation of opium for madak, still referred to smoking as a practice confined to Fujian, Taiwan and Guangdong. The consumer base must have been very narrow indeed, if the official trade statistics of the Oost-Indische Compagnie can be trusted. The Dutch trade in Bengali opium to Batavia outstripped the Chinese trade by a ratio of nearly seven to one; some 80 tonnes exported to the archipelago between 1738 and 1745, as opposed to a peak of 12 tonnes reaching China during the Yongzheng period.[59] Even if allowance is made for illegally traded opium, few eighteenth-century sources comment in any detail on the use of madak, let alone pure opium. Consequently the Yongzheng edict, mentioned in most standard histories of opium as a landmark in the struggle against the foreign drug, cannot be understood by reference to opium only and must be placed in a wider political context.

The Yongzheng emperor (1723–36) took over the imperial throne in 1723 in a military coup after a brutal internecine power struggle. The young emperor enacted a welter of measures designed to consolidate his grip on power, including the strengthening of the old *baojia* system of mutual surveillance.[60] He also promoted a policy of integrating outcast groups into one homogeneous body of commoners (*gejian weiliang*). Whereas duties and privileges traditionally depended on a stratification which divided officials from merchants, workers from peasants and commoners from outcasts, the new regime mandated a uniform standard of criminal liability across all social boundaries. Status performance, as Matthew Sommer has argued, was replaced by gender performance, in which all people were expected to conform to gender roles defined in terms of marriage. In a new age of prosperity and anxiety, increasing alarm at the presumed breakdown of moral and social order in a context of rapidly changing socio-economic realities led to heightened concern over proper behaviour. With this paradigmatic shift emphasising rigid norms of behaviour for all commoners, the Yongzheng emperor sought to reform their moral character and to wipe out social activities deemed reprehensible: adultery, prostitution, sodomy and the forced remarriage of widows, for instance, were all severely punished.[61]

Smoking, increasingly at the centre of male sociability, was also seen to constitute a heterodox activity. The use of madak by ruling elites may have seemed tolerable, but popular consumption raised fears of social disorder. James I, who attempted to rule in 1603–25 as absolute monarch in England, called tobacco smoking 'loathsome', 'hateful', 'harmful' and 'dangerous' to the body in his treatise *A counterblaste to tobacco*, while contemporary pamphlets predicted a society of 'idle' and 'bewitched' smokers. His edict against tobacco portrayed smoking as an heinous activity which needed to be strictly controlled.[62] In a similar vein, the 1729 edict in China should be seen as a continuation of the earlier prohibitions against tobacco and as part of a more general attempt to cope with broader social changes rather than as an attack on opium only.

The smoking of madak first became popular along the coasts of Fujian and in Taiwan, frontier regions which were considered of strategic importance to imperial control and political stability. People in the south were farther away from the centre of the empire and were traditionally regarded as less well educated and more prone to rebel. For potential rebels to 'gather in groups' (*juzhong*) in order to pursue a 'corrupt' (*xie*) and 'lustful' (*yin*) habit seemed to pose an even greater danger to dynastic rule in this part of the empire. These official restrictions did not extend to the medical uses of opium: 'Opium is used for making medicinal paste or pills, for the treatment of diarrhoea… It is a medicine required by physicians and doctors. It becomes immoral and harmful only when it is made into opium for smoking.'[63]

FROM MADAK TO OPIUM c. 1780–1820

The British trade colonies in Southeast Asia encouraged a policy of free competition in the distribution of opium, but trade with China was under the strict auspices of India House. The reason for the Company's circumspection was the prohibition of 1729, which forbade the importation of opium for smoking while deeming trade in medicinal opium legal. Foreign firms residing at Canton risked having their licences revoked or faced heavy fines. These restrictions ensured that the ships of the East India Company, with few exceptions, steered clear of opium cargoes during most of the eighteenth century.[64]

Until the last decades of the eighteenth century, opium exports from India and the Ottoman empire to China were exclusively shipped on Portuguese vessels to Macau, all intended for medical use. During the Qianlong period, a maximum of 200 chests of Malwa per year (circa 12 tonnes) thus found their way on to the market.[65] The demands of the market must have remained limited until the end of the eighteenth century, since attempts to trade opium illegally were largely unsuccessful. When the Indian possessions of the East India Company faced bankruptcy in 1780 (the result of several factors, including the cessation of transfers from Britain following American independence, increased piracy, the falling price of opium, and wars with the French and Indian powers), two of its ships were authorised to sail to Guangdong, disguised as warships free of any cargo, in order to seek private outlets for smuggled opium. The operation resulted in an expensive embarrassment, although the cargo was eventually sold at a substantial loss to Sinqua, an influential *hang* merchant at Canton, already in the habit of acquiring opium directly from the independent 'country ships'. However, the *hang* merchant merely managed to sell some 15 per cent of his purchase within China, the remainder being distributed via the junk trade in and beyond the South China Sea.[66] Sinqua's difficulties indicate that the demand for smoking opium was still relatively low in 1780.

The smoking of pure opium had been observed in China only a decade or two earlier, leaving the smoking of madak to the Malay populations of Southeast Asia.[67] The earliest description comes from medical writer Zhao Xuemin, who quotes a source from Taiwan and wrote in 1765:

Opium smokers invite many people to congregate and smoke in turn. They roll out a bamboo sheet on the bed and sit on it. In the middle an opium lamp is placed for communal smoking, yielding anything from one hundred to several hundred puffs. The pipes are often made of bamboo, about 8–9 inches wide and filled with coir fibres or hair, silver decorating both ends. The top end has a tiny hole about the diameter of a small finger. A bowl made of clay is fixed on top of this hole, into which opium is placed: the substance is consumed in one inhalation.[68]

More concrete evidence for the transition to pure opium smoking only appeared at the end of the eighteenth century, the scholar Yu Jiao, for instance, noting that imported opium resembled slightly green horse manure. When boiled in water, it reduced to a treacly substance similar to the paste used by practitioners for treating the sick. Pellets the size of millet, Yu Jiao observed, were placed into a lamp adorning flute-like bamboo pipes. Smokers in reclining position would pass the pipe around in alternating mode, deeply inhaling the smoke.[69]

The reasons for this important change in the mode of delivery are not easily gauged, all the more as reliable sources for the eighteenth century are relatively rare. One hypothesis is that opium was used to enhance the sex performance. Well before opium was ever smoked, medical writers already pointed to the use of ingested opium in the bedchamber, as the chapter on the medical uses of opium will show in much greater detail. This hypothesis is reinforced by Zhao Xuemin's observations that in Taiwan 'the local people use opium as an aid to indulge in excessive sexual intercourse (*daoyinju*).'[70] Zhu Shijie's travel account of Taiwan, published in 1765, also noted that opium was smoked pure as a sex aid (*fangyao*).[71] Another explanation, ventured by the historian Xiao Yishan, is that the edicts against smoking which were enforced in Fujian and Guangdong prompted local users to resort to pure opium instead, the use of which could be justified for medical reasons.[72] Soon after the passing of the Yongzheng edict, this argument was already invoked by smokers of madak: in 1729, the commoner Chen Yuan, accused of breaching the edict, retorted that he had purchased the opium at a pharmacy and that it could therefore not be smoking opium (*yapianyan*). The official verdict was that 'opium is a pharmaceutical substance required by medical practitioners. Only when it is blended with tobacco can it become harmful and lead to lustful acts: it can then be referred to as an illegal item.'[73] It is conceivable that the tobacco content was gradually dropped in order to avoid being convicted of smoking madak. As we shall see, restrictive policies on psychoactive substances more often than not result in a shift in consumption patterns. A third possibility is that the smoking of pure opium allowed it to become a marker of social status: in a period marked by increased social mobility and conspicuous consumption, large amounts of money could be spent in one evening on pure opium. Wealth and status could be displayed far more effectively by smoking many pipes of pure opium than by drinking expensive tea or alcohol. This last interpretation is partly supported by available evidence, in particular the fact that a shift away from relatively cheap Malwa shipped by Portuguese traders towards more expensive Bengali opium in the 1790s marked the beginning of

considerable expansion in the opium trade. Malwa not only varied in quality, but was also fiery and irritating when smoked
pure, while high-quality Patna was mild and pleasant to the palate.[74] Where Patna opium circulated in Southeast Asia, it was a
relatively low-grade paste bulked up with anything from horse
dung to sand. The quality improved considerably after poppy
cultivation in Bengal was more carefully controlled by the East
India Company in the 1790s and the output reduced against
the wishes of the Indian opium farmers. A supply of cheap and
impure Patna during the 1760s and '70s may have led to excess
quantities which some madak smokers attempted to smoke on its
own. Affluent smokers may have appreciated the sudden im-
provement in the quality of the opium paste in the 1790s, fuelling
an ever-increasing demand for top quality Patna.

In 1793 the East India Company started its monopoly over
opium production in Patna. Four years later the Company declared a temporary cultivation ban in Bengal, with the aim of
draining the market of cheap, low-grade opium.[75] The Qing rigorously outlawed the trade in opium in all its forms between
1796 and 1800, contributing to the emergence of a lucrative black
market. We may provisionally conclude that the decades of cheap
but unmarketable opium up till 1793 created a market for madak
smoking and for experimenting with the smoking of pure opium.
Once opium had become an expensive, high-quality black market commodity, it became more suitable for conspicuous consumption. Consumer response to Patna, as the following section
shows, was extremely positive, leading to rapidly growing exports
to China during the decades before the 'Opium War'.

TRADERS, PIRATES AND OPIUM 1793–1820

Opium, whether laced with tobacco as madak or smoked pure,
remained a relatively rare product consumed mainly by local people in a few coastal provinces until the very end of the eighteenth
century. Descriptions of the reception extended to the McCartney
embassy by local officials in 1792–4, for instance, never even mentioned opium, although there were references to the smoking and

chewing of the areca nut at official banquets.[76] On the other hand, George Staunton observed that tobacco smoking was widespread, including women and children as young as eight: 'The smoke of the tobacco is inhaled through bamboo tubes. Its powder, too, is taken as snuff as is likewise pulverised cinnabar; and opium and odoriferous gums are sometimes made use of for smoking'.[77] Moreover, madak was still smoked for several decades in the nineteenth century, as the British traveller Clarke Abel noted during the Amherst mission of 1816:

No opium is exposed for sale in the shops, probably because it is a contraband article, but it is used with tobacco in all parts of the empire. The Chinese indeed consider the smoking of opium as one of the greatest luxuries; and if they are temperate in drinking, they are often excessive in the use of this drug. They have more than one method of smoking it: sometimes they envelope a piece of the solid gum in tobacco, and smoke it from a pipe with a very small bowl; and sometimes they steep fine tobacco in a strong solution of it.[78]

According to H. B. Morse, who researched the opium trade extensively on the basis of sources in Chinese now lost, 'There is no evidence to show when opium ceased to be mixed with tobacco; ... it is probable that opium was not much, if at all, smoked by itself before the year 1800.'[79] The use of pure opium only became socially significant during the first decades of the nineteenth century. Its spread up the social scale and out of the coastal provinces may have been the combined result of a shift in the quality of opium and of a stricter ban on trade during the 1790s: high-quality Patna successfully replaced poor-quality Malwa. However, even during the first decades of increasing opium imports the supply was at best haphazard, depending on price fluctuations and piracy as much as on local insurrections and administrative whims. In 1802 the foreign Council of Canton concluded that the annual consumption had risen to a mere 3,000 chests (i.e. some 180 tonnes):[80] England, by comparison, imported up to 100 tonnes of opium every year from Turkey during the decades before the Sino-British War (1839–42), although its population was much smaller.[81] The unpredictable nature of the trade meant that the *hang* merchants often refused to engage in illegal transactions, increasing the risk for foreign traders involved in contraband activities. On the other hand, the illegal trade had become so lucrative that it was indispensable to British commerce:[82] the ranks of independent English and Scottish traders ('agency houses'), such as Fairly Fergusson & Co., were soon joined by Parsis and Armenians eager to exploit a market niche.[83]

In addition to the increased activity of country traders, pirate fleets ruled the waves of the South China Sea between the 1780s and the 1810s. The pirates would seize the cargo of entire convoys, both of local junks and of foreign vessels, which was then traded with coastal merchants for silver and provisions. The uncompromising attitude of the pirates ensured that the coastal sea routes fell under their influence, as the burning of two commercial fleets in 1805, resulting in the loss of 180 government junks, demonstrated.[84] Once fleet owners had been forced into paying bribes, mutual arrangements with powerful protectors such as the salt merchants offered substantial advantages for the pirates, including the provision of arms and food. The collaboration of local officials was frequently guaranteed by similar means. Damage inflicted on the mainly British-owned opium vessels was described as 'frequent' in contemporary accounts.[85]

Despite the lack of precise figures, it can be safely assumed that considerable quantities of opium found their way onshore with the pirates as intermediaries, possibly outperforming the equally illegal activities of country traders. Moreover, in 1820 the Qing government declared tough new anti-opium legislation which forced the foreign Canton trade to Lingding (Lintin) Island, some 125 kilometres south of the city, at a great distance from any supervision that Qing officials could effectively have imposed. The new-found isolation suited the country traders, who turned the island into a harbour for a new breed of fast, armed opium clippers. The new harbour thus formed an ideal starting-point for the contraband traffic which culminated in the 1830s.[86]

Between 1797 and 1820 high-quality opium percolated the coastline in south China through well-established contacts between local merchants, official intermediaries and contraband traders. Such smuggling could either be undertaken by British, Parsi, Jewish, Dutch, Portuguese, Danish and American traders or by local pirates. After 1820, when supplies were built up systematically in Lingding harbour, market conditions were ready for a dramatic expansion of Chinese opium imports.

WAR ON DRUGS: THE 'OPIUM WAR'

Far from eliminating the illegal trade in opium, the expulsion of the foreign merchants from Canton to Lingding island in 1820 on the contrary increased contraband considerably: up to 7,000 chests, or 420 tonnes, were traded in 1821. Opium trade continued to flourish during the next two decades. In the years immediately preceding the war, 307 foreign residents, belonging to fifty-five firms with 200 ships, produced profits through commerce and financial services which employed thousands of labourers, runners and petty officials.[87] The value of contraband opium rose to £ 3 million per annum paid for in silver bullion.[88] Moreover, in 1819 the East India Company started to buy all Malwa opium which was competing against its own Bengal produce and sold it in China: the result was a huge supply capable of responding to the growing demand for opium in parts of China beyond the southern coast where smoking was becoming popular. Control over Malwa opium was ensured by allowing it through British territory on payment of a fee, while new districts were developed for poppy cultivation between 1831 and 1839.[89] In 1833 the East India Company's monopoly of trade in China was abolished, opening up the market to ambitious entrepreneurs like William Jardine and James Matheson who had little patience with the trading restrictions imposed by the Qing. These were not confined to opium: large quantities of saltpetre and salt were also illegally imported (the import of both products continued to be strictly forbidden even during the republican period),[90] while official prohibitions on the export of silk were not respected either: attempts by the court in Beijing to restrict commercial transactions between their subjects and foreign merchants had all but failed by the 1830s.[91] This observation holds good equally for other parts of the empire; opium, for instance, was also being carried to China in considerable quantities by Kokandi traders via Inner Asia,[92] but camels were less efficient than clippers. It is interesting to note that Joseph Fletcher has referred to the military victory of the Kokand over the Qing army in Xinjiang in the 1830s as the 'First Opium War': the concessions granted to the coastal trading powers in the Nanjing treaty several years later (mainly extraterritoriality, an indemnity, taxation rights, and most-favoured-nation treatment) were directly based on the trade advantages wrung from imperial negotiators under the threat of military power by the Khan of Kokand between 1831 and 1835.[93]

The sheer amount of illegally imported opium was blamed by some officials for reducing the empire's silver holdings. Historians have also underlined that massive opium imports produced a substantial trade deficit and severe economic dislocation, leading to the 'Opium War' and the forced integration of China into a world order dominated by imperialist powers. While there is little doubt that a world economic recession in the second quarter of the nineteenth century significantly affected China, economic difficulties may not have been caused only by the outflow of silver or the importation of opium. As Dermigny already underlined in his study of Canton, the scale of opium imports could not account for more than half of the outflow of silver.[94] The 'balance-of-trade' theory of bullion flows is inadequate in accounting for the changing fortunes of silver in late imperial China, as it fails to consider precious metals as commodities. As one observer commenting on the relatively low value of silver noted in the 1850s, 'silver is, in China, not money, but merely merchandise.'[95] As Richard von Glahn underlines, China was not a passive participant in the international market: merchants in China traded the commodities they possessed in abundance (porcelain, silk) for a commodity they lacked (silver) in the sixteenth century, while merchants in Europe brought silver to China because they too benefited tremendously from this trade. The flow was reversed from the late eighteenth century onwards as a consequence of a global shortage of silver. The silver had a higher value in Europe and the United States, relative to that of gold on world markets, than in China, a trend which eliminated the incentive to export the metal to that country. Commercial growth in eighteenth-century China also fuelled local demand for copper coin as an instrument of exchange: copper reclaimed the functions assumed by silver, which had been adopted by the Ming as a basis for state finance. In short, merchants in China traded silver during the first half of the nineteenth century because they could make a profit and bought a commodity they lacked (opium) in response to local demand.[96] Even without any opium imports at all, China would have been adversely affected by a global recession after 1820.

Imperial elites may not have been in a position to question the economic significance of the drain of silver out of China, yet recent scholarship has indicated that in the decade preceding the 'Opium War' official opinion was divided about the amount of silver outflow that could be attributed to payments for opium. A majority of court administrators, including the Daoguang emperor, did not even regard a trade embargo on opium as an effective solution to domestic monetary problems. Some officials pointed to the existing deficiencies in currency management and proposed to solve the financial crisis by monetary reforms; others advocated legalisation of the opium trade to reduce the price and bring down the volume of imports. Few favoured a frontal attack on the opium trade, because of the enormous practical problems posed by tough action against foreign and local traders, efficient prosecution of smugglers and effective enforcement of legal controls by the military in a province far away from the capital. Had these views prevailed, James Polachek hypothesises, 'there probably never would have been an opium war.'[97]

The reasons for the abrupt change in favour of a policy of opium prohibition had more to do with internal court politics, in particular tensions between Han officials and Manchu aristocrats, than with the actions pursued in the 1830s by the British government in favour of free trade. James Polachek has demonstrated that Han scholars turned opium prohibition into a political agenda, enabling them for the first time since the Manchu conquest in 1644 to challenge the dominant position of the court aristocracy. These scholars not only believed that it was their mission to sound the alarm over moral decay and an alleged breakdown in social order, but also wished to restore the scholar-official class to the position of collective power and moral authority which it had enjoyed under the Ming. The central political system under Daoguang was particularly responsive to local interests, including reckless regional administrators from Guangdong with strong links to sympathetic officials who wielded considerable influence at court level. Han scholars effectively used their networks of patronage to undermine the Manchu-Mongol strategists who dominated military thinking. Influential officials, in particular Lin Zexu and Huang Juezi, believed that they could profit from an opium embargo as they used the fiscal woes of the 1830s as an opportunity to challenge Manchu-imposed administrative priorities.[98] When the Daoguang emperor finally sided with the prohibitionists, conflict with foreign opium traders was inevitable. Prohibition, in other words, was a political tool exploited in court politics by Han scholars against Manchu diplomats.

As part of its new prohibition policy, the imperial administration despatched Lin Zexu (1785–1850) in 1839 as commissioner to Guangdong in order to bring all opium imports to a halt. Opium stocks were confiscated, the movement of foreigners was further restricted, and in a highly symbolic act of purification, 20,000 chests of imported opium were burnt in public. The retaliatory action by British forces provided the spark for the first Sino-British War (1839–42), later remembered as the 'Opium War'.[99] As John Quincy Adams commented in a lecture before the Massachusetts Historical Society in December 1841, opium was a 'mere incident to the dispute but no more the cause of the war than the throwing overboard of the tea in Boston harbour was the cause of the North American revolution.'[100] Free trade and the 'opening' of China prompted the first Sino-British War in 1839, just as the United States would force Japan to 'open' in 1868.

4

OPIUM FOR THE PEOPLE: STATUS, SPACE AND CONSUMPTION (*c.* 1840–1940)

This chapter explores the many different and shifting functions which opium fulfilled within specific social circles: opium could be alternatively or simultaneously a medical product, a recreational item, a badge of social distinction and a symbol of elite culture. Moreover, it was prepared in highly intricate and complex rituals, much like the tea ceremony which conferred social distinction to the ruling elites. The elaborate ritual of opium smoking was in marked contrast to the simplicity of opium ingestion in contemporary Europe, and contributed to the relatively low incidence of problematic consumption. While important differences in social status existed between a variety of consumer groups, ranging from the wealthy merchant who indulged in imported Patna to the poor coolie who resorted to dross, the smoking of opium had nonetheless become one of the chief factors of social inclusion rather than exclusion by the end of the nineteenth century.

THE EXPANSION OF OPIUM CULTURE

'So far back as the year 1793, Mr Barrow found this fascinating drug very generally indulged in by the opulent, though its price placed it beyond the reach of the poorer classes.'[1] We saw in the last chapter how tobacco laced with opium became popular in a few coastal regions of south China during the late seventeenth century. The habit of smoking opium pure appeared in the 1760s but remained relatively rare till the 1790s, as cheap and impure

Malwa was competing with high-quality Patna. Pure opium was expensive and exclusively used by wealthy elites. From the 1820s larger imports and lower prices led to broader social participation in narcotic culture. In the second half of the nineteenth century the advent of steam navigation improved the transportation of opium, innovations in banking facilitated monetary transactions, and modern chemistry made possible a qualitative expansion of the range of opiates on offer. By the end of the century, as local production surpassed imported varieties in quantity, opium was used across the social scale, from the imperial household down to the poor rickshaw puller.

By the middle of the nineteenth century an effective system of cultivating and processing opium had already developed in parts of the country.[2] The cultivation of the poppy required intensive fertilisation, usually achieved with soybean cakes, night-soil and ammonium sulphate, applied at least three times per year. Opium fields were also labour-intensive, which suited regions which had an abundant and cheap source of labour. Wet-rice cultivation, widespread in China, also demanded intensive labour, producing work habits which were easily replicated in the poppy field. Since harvesting the poppy sap required more dexterity than physical strength, the task was often taken over by women and children, leaving the male farmers time to devote themselves to other agricultural work.[3] The poppy thrived best on fertile but dry soils, often even on top of sandstone.[4] Ordinary crops required less investment, in terms of both fertilisation and labour, but yielded smaller returns. As a winter crop, opium poppies were succeeded by cotton, beans, maize and rice, although some farmers were driven by profit to replace their ordinary food crops by opium during the late nineteenth century.[5] In the arid central-western provinces, principally Shaanxi, Shanxi and Gansu, farmers could make an actual decision whether to plan for a food or opium cultivation. In the fertile south, including Sichuan and Yunnan, they faced no such choice, since a second or even third harvest often sufficed for purposes of subsistence. During the last decades of the nineteenth century the poppy was the most prominent winter crop in Sichuan.[6]

Opium had the added advantage of not depleting the soil of its nutrients as rapidly as rice, wheat or vegetables. Late nineteenth-century comparisons between the relative yields of wheat and poppy produced a profitability ratio of two to one in favour of the latter, further increased by the fact that opium was cheaper to transport to the marketplace than wheat.[7] After extraction of the flower's precious sap, the poppy plant also provided fodder and seeds. The oil was particularly popular with farmers, who used it for food and lighting.[8] The lower leaves could be prepared as food, resembling spinach in taste, while the remainder would be used as fodder.[9] Finally, after incineration, the stalk produced a sought-after dye.[10]

The extraction of juice contained in the poppy heads required skill and patience. A series of incisions had to be cut into the seed capsule at sunset with a little stylus or a hook, and the white fluid would ooze through it.[11] Around Chongqing in the 1880s farmers were 'armed with a short wooden handle, from one of the ends of which protrude three or sometimes four points of brass or copper blades, firmly inserted in the wood'.[12] Each capsule was incised three or four times, at intervals of two to three days, although some were exhausted by only one incision. The exuded juice would coagulate overnight on the capsules, turning brown on contact with the air. The following day, the brown 'latex' would be scraped off with a pruning knife and collected in vessels, where it separated into two parts. However, in Wenzhou (Zhejiang) poppies were not incised but the outer skin was shaved off with a little plane, leaving the sap to seep out along the exposed surface. When employing the shaving method, it was imperative to collect the juice almost immediately with a hollow bamboo. Once harvested, the drained residue was exposed to the air for several weeks, during which time it set into a soft brown mass, which would deepen in colour with age and with exposure to air and light, constituting what was known as 'raw opium'.[13]

Opium was compact and light, and could be carried over great distances and difficult terrain—steep mountains, deep valleys and wild rivers. As the Prussian traveller Ferdinand von Richthofen testified regarding central Shanxi, opium was unlike rice or wheat

in that it repaid rugged travel along winding trails in the hinterland.[14] As one observer noted, 'No other product is so easy to
transport as opium. A man can carry several hundred dollars'
worth on his person; a man with a mule can carry several thousand
dollars' worth. That is one of the reasons why opium is a more
profitable crop than potatoes or wheat.'[15] It also remained relatively impervious to changes of climate and could keep its quality
over a long period, unlike more delicate crops such as rice and
wheat, which presented storage problems as soon as they were
harvested.[16] But even in less harsh conditions as in the plains of
Manchuria or the maritime provinces, opium production boomed
during the late nineteenth century. In some cases, opium complemented or replaced other cash crops such as tobacco, sweet
potatoes, rhubarb or sugar cane.[17] For many farmers in Yunnan,
it formed an additional cash crop, intended to supplement the
meagre income derived from other winter crops such as cereals,
potatoes and beans.[18] To the farming communities and commercial districts of Sichuan it was a valuable export commodity.[19]

After 1870 domestic production exceeded imported opium in
quantity, as the poppy provided an important impetus for the re-
building of the local economy after the devastation of the Taiping
and other rebellions.[20] By 1879, when Indian imports were at
their peak of nearly 5,800 tonnes, the production of opium in
Sichuan alone (c. 8,500 tonnes) easily outstripped the total of
all foreign produce reaching China. Opium from Yunnan came
second (1,600 tonnes), while Guizhou, Zhejiang, Henan, Gansu,
Shanxi and Shaanxi also played a certain role (in this order). By
1906 the output of Yunnan opium (*yuntu*) had risen to 4,700
tonnes, but it was still dwarfed by the production of Sichuanese
opium (*chuantu*), at 14,400 tonnes.[21] While local production far
exceeded imported opium in quantity in the late nineteenth century, it varied significantly in quality, as the next section explains.

VARIETIES OF OPIUM

The cultivation of the poppy in various parts of China added to
the variety of opium products available. Opium came in different

shapes, colours, textures, fractures or 'touches', gravities, consistencies, strengths and aromas, as well as degrees of purity: in the narcotic culture of the nineteenth and early twentieth centuries, producers and consumers were acutely aware of the many differences between opium types, some subtle enough to require connoisseurship, others obvious even to an outsider.

By the early 1880s the vast majority of the imported opium came from India, the high-quality Patna variety from Bengal accounting for more than 37 per cent of the total, just under 20 per cent coming from Benares (Bengal) and the remaining 42 per cent from Malwa. Other imports consisted of Persian and Turkish produce, and smuggled Bengali opium.[22] Patna and Benares opium (both known in China as *datu*, Patna also being called *yangyao* or *bantu*, Benares as *guyangyao* or *lazhuangtu*) were carefully examined by experts for quality before being placed on the market, where it was usually presented in the form of balls which had an outer shell or covering. Malwa opium (called *xiaotu, baipitu, baiyangyao* or *gongsibai*) was worked by hand into balls which were rolled in poppy leaves or chaff, to be packed in chests as soon as they were sufficiently hard. Malwa opium varied in quality and was usually considered inferior to Patna and Benares. When smoked, it was strong and fiery and caused irritation, while Patna and Benares opium were mild and preferred by most smokers, particularly in hot climates. Persian opium (*bositu* or *jinhuatu*) was prepared with oil and was often highly adulterated. It was usually made into cakes rolled in red paper, and tied with red string.[23] Even some African opium was traded in China in 1884, 'the first African imports ever' according to a commercial report.[24]

Bengal opium originated from poppy fields in the Ganges plain, was processed and packed at government factories in Ghazipur and Patna, and reached China by way of auction houses in Calcutta. Once sold on to the free market, the successful bidder would transport the opium to markets spanning the globe, from London to Manila. The same went for Malwa opium, which was grown and produced in the central Indian states, and privately exported from Bombay—against payment of a fee to the British authorities. An important difference was that Malwa opium contained less evaporable matter than its Bengali rival, reducing to about 72 per cent after processing by repeated boiling and filtering of the opium-water solution. Patna reduced to nearly half its original weight, at 52 per cent.[25]

Consumers in China were well aware of the differences in taste and quality between the two Bengali types, which was reflected in price levels. In order to influence the price, but also in reaction to consumer demand for specific flavours, opium from plantations in China was blended with Malwa and Patna produce, not unlike tea, coffee or tobacco.[26] Locally produced opium, on the other hand, had little success outside China. In British Malaya it was considered inferior: as one observer noted as late as the early 1930s, 'Because of the large quantity of the highly flavoured Indian and Persian opium consumed in British Malaya, it is not likely that Chinese opium—which every smoker knows to be the least desirable—has a good market there. Unmixed with Indian or Persian opium, Chinese opium would not be smoked by the discriminating smoker.'[27]

Indian opium, in particular from Bengal, thus dominated the market in the nineteenth century, establishing a reputation which was to last well into the twentieth century. Its price depended largely on its quality and place of origin, but also on the prevailing market conditions.[28] If market prices happened to be too low, traders had an additional means of effecting higher returns; following the Treaty of Tianjin (1858), they could delay the unloading of their opium cargoes by leaving them on board the vessels without payment of any excise duties or taxes for an indefinite period.[29] Indian imports peaked in 1879–80, declining by half to an average of some 50,000 chests in the later 1890s and most of the 1910s. Imports ceased in 1913, when the Sino-British treaty of 1908 on the suppression of the opium trade came into full effect.[30]

ESTIMATES OF OPIUM CONSUMPTION

While it is beyond doubt that opium culture expanded enormously throughout the nineteenth century, estimates on the number of opium users differ wildly in the absence of reliable and meaningful statistics. Estimates ranged from 0.66 per cent of the adult population to 60 per cent or more, while consumption patterns could be finely differentiated or on the contrary lumped together into a single category.[31] The difficulty of compiling reliable statistics lies in the nature of the object: rather than merely gauging the number of smokers, smoking patterns have to be established and an average consumption quantified. Moreover, estimates can vary greatly, often depending on the extent to which opium was defined as a 'problem'.[32] A common method used by a number of organisations in the first decades of the twentieth century was to use the official import figures, with estimated domestic production output, to be divided by an estimated number of smokers, based on counts in 'representative districts'. A survey carried out at a national level by the National Anti-Opium Association in 1929 produced an average total of 3.85 per cent, with results for the individual provinces differing substantially (e.g. Shandong 0.6 per cent, Hubei 29.14 per cent).[33] Accordingly, China would have had some 18 million smokers, although the authors of these statistics failed even to allude to the important differences existing between occasional, intermittent, light and problematic smokers.[34]

Medical uses aside, the amount of opium smoked for recreational purposes could vary from a single puff on the arrival of friends, over light social smoking, to the ceaseless heavy smoking of a minority who were physically dependent.[35] Robert Hart, Inspector General of the Imperial Maritime Customs, commissioned a survey that his department carried out in 1879, revealing that 3.5 per mille (0.35 per cent) of all inhabitants were smokers of foreign opium.[36] Taking into account a number of demographic considerations, including the facts that about half of the population were children and that women smoked much less than men, the historian Richard Newman recently reached the following estimates for 1879. Including not only imported and local raw opium, but also the recycled ash from pipes and the extracts from boiling, as was usual in the calculations of consuls and customs officers at the time (a method curiously overlooked by historians of China), he arrives at a total of smokable material of over 423,000 piculs, or roughly 25,000 tonnes. Of the estimated population of 400 million, around 30 per cent were adult males, 30 per cent adult females and the rest children. Any smoker who used more than a mace (3.78 grams) per day could be seen as 'dependent'. Around one gram would have been sufficient for one daily pipe, or one long smoke every ten days.[37] While the vast majority of smokers used opium intermittently for medical purposes (estimated at four mace a year) and occasionally at festivals (one mace per year), about 20 per cent of men could be characterised as light or moderate smokers, with individual amounts varying from two-fifths of a mace every three days to one or two mace a day. Heavy and regular smokers, using more than five mace a day, constituted no more than 1 per cent of the total population, or 5 per cent of all recreational smokers. Taking detailed figures supplied by the Qing government to the International Opium Commission, the total of smokable opium, including ash, increased to approximately 813,000 piculs in 1906, or roughly 50,000 tonnes. While Newman would never claim complete accuracy for these estimates, he believes that official observers may have overestimated the amount of raw opium, leading to slightly inflated figures. He uses these numbers to show that the number of heavy and regular smokers probably increased to 2.5 per cent of the total population in 1906. However, the most important qualifying statement is that the health and longevity of these 'addicts' would hardly have differed from those of light or moderate smokers, and a considerable number would have led normal lives.[38]

The emphasis in Sir Robert Hart's survey, on the other hand, was less on the quantity consumed (on average given as 11.34 grams, sufficient for thirty to forty inhalations),[39] but on the period of the habit's enjoyment: answers differed wildly, with some defining a mere two months of opium smoking as leading to addiction, and others stating a period in excess of ten years. The average duration was placed between one and three years.[40] In interviews with 2,000 opium smokers conducted in the middle of the nineteenth century by the French physician Libermann in Shanghai and Tianjin, 646 confessed to consuming one to 8 grams per day, 1,250 consumed between 10 and 20, and only 104 between 30 and 100 grams, an amount the author considered '*une grande habitude du narcotisme*'. Libermann's figures differ also in the amount of opium estimated to suffice per smoke (0.1–0.15 g per one minute session), but not in the conclusion that only a tiny minority (circa 5 per cent) of all smokers were dependent.[41] The German traveller Eugen Wolf observed in 1896 that rickshaw pullers commonly made use of their spare time by smoking small amounts of opium very slowly: three pipes an hour, with each pipe lasting no longer than for three deep inhalations.[42] The American surgeon Robert Coltman, on the other hand, dutifully noted in the 1880s that entire villages in Shanxi were 'debauched', though he added that his own acquaintances mostly smoked opium in modest quantities, and usually in the course of hospitality. The consumption of opium for recreational purposes, according to his observations, averaged between 4 to 8 grams, rarely exceeding 12.[43] Higher *per capita* figures could also be found, though heavy smokers were capable of managing their lives despite the large amounts of opium they consumed.[44] As one close observer exclaimed while on a mission to Sichuan in 1882, 'Nowhere in China are the people so well off, or so hardy, and nowhere do they smoke so much opium.'[45] Even the League of Nations had to concede in the 1930s that people in China had 'better control over themselves, avoiding excessive use and keeping the daily consumption within the limits', and that individuals would find by experience a quantity 'which will not endanger his earning capacity or bring other undesirable results.'[46]

Many smokers only took up the pipe on special occasions: the official He Yongqing exclusively smoked opium to treat diarrhoea,[47] while countless others smoked no more than three or four mace a year strictly for medical purposes. Many were intermittent smokers, drifting in and out of narcotic culture according to their personal and social requirements. Men and women would smoke a pipe or two at festivals and ceremonies several times a year without ever becoming regular users. R. A. Jamieson, a doctor in Shanghai, noted at the end of the nineteenth century that if those who smoked a few pipes on the occasion of a festival such as a marriage were to be counted, few adult males could be excluded, although habitual consumers were very rare.[48] A British consul based in Hainan, an island notorious for malaria, also reported that 'although nearly everyone uses it... one never meets the opium-skeleton so vividly depicted in philanthropic works, rather the reverse—a hardy peasantry, healthy and energetic.'[49] In Taiwan, opium could be smoked after local ceremonies taking place during the festive season.[50] As late as in 1932 missionaries based in the Hubei and Hunan region reported that 'at funerals, weddings, or feasts, on any occasion when many guests are invited, a number of rooms is prepared for smoking with beds, pipes, lamps and opium provided for all smokers... Opium is provided as a matter of course, just as is wine.'[51]

As the journalist Richard Hughes noted, even foreign bankers and merchants in cities like Shanghai and Hong Kong occasionally enjoyed a few pipes without ever developing a craving for the substance: 'Those few who became addicts would have become alcoholics had they stuck to liquor.'[52] Even ardent opponents of opium in the early twentieth century had to concede that only a minority of smokers were physically dependent. In *Drugging a Nation* (1908), Samuel Merwin observed that 'probably the majority of the victims take it up as a temporary relief... it is a social vice only among the upper classes.'[53] Similar observations came from local anti-opium associations: 'In Yunnan and Guizhou, few have not smoked a couple of puffs of opium. However, not everybody has become addicted. Even among habitual smokers, degrees of craving can vary enormously.'[54] J. F. Molyneaux, working as a surgeon in Ningbo at the end of the nineteenth century, confirmed that many men 'habitually smoke a limited amount with so little effect that they are easily able to conceal the fact.'[55]

There is no doubt that opium could also be smoked in excessive quantities among wealthy circles, some scholars retiring to their mansions, rich merchants leaving business to their partners, or government administrators handing over their districts to clerks in order to smoke away their assets: they could develop a complete dependence and spend their lives in compulsive reliance on opium.[56] On the other hand, many individuals did not take to opium at all because they could not inhale the smoke or were repelled by the taste.[57] Zhou Zhaoxi recalls that as a child he was once offered an opium pipe by his aunt when suffering from a stomach pain but disliked the taste.[58] Shushan, a keen reader of Cocteau, had tried opium several times but found the smell too foul (*chou*).[59] Countless others smoked opium once or twice only to reject it.

Not unlike tobacco, opium was a substance generally taken in determined amounts rather than in ever-increasing ones: even habitual smokers reached a plateau, often between seven and fifteen pipes a day, a number rarely exceeded. The same daily dosage could easily be maintained year after year without developing a tolerance that required the user to increase the dose over time.[60] The riddle of opium, as Jean Cocteau observed, is that the smoker never had to increase his dose.[61] Opium smokers, in short, were perfectly able to determine the desired level of consumption. They could moderate their use for personal and social reasons and even cease taking it altogether without help. The idea that smokers felt an irresistible compulsion to use increasing doses of opium has little foundation, and none can be found for the supposition that consumers suffered from 'loss of control' in their use of opium. The idea that opium smoking had devastating economic consequences, inevitably leading to financial ruin, is equally simplistic: smokers could determine the quantity and quality of opium they wanted to consume, while abundant supplies of cheap local produce, including recycled dross, made the practice affordable even for regular smokers among the poor. In the late 1930s, when opium prices soared in Canton, most smokers halved the amount they consumed in order to make ends meet: few would rigidly hold on to their usual dose.[62]

Many occasional, intermittent or moderate smokers may even have been unaware of any undesirable effects. Even the medical missionaries Lockhart and Medhurst considered the use of 3.5 to 4 grams, as smoked daily by many consumers, to be entirely 'harmless', since the effects of opium were reduced by 90 per cent through burning.[63] However, the authors stated that the same quantity ingested orally in a solution with alcohol, as was common

in England, could lead to poisoning.[64] According to another medical author opposed to opium, the substance was six to seven
times more powerful when swallowed than when smoked. He
also underlined that domestic opium had a morphine content
of merely 3–7 per cent, thus being considerably weaker than
produce imported from India.[65] Smoking was generally acknowledged to be more wasteful than ingestion, although the morphine content reached the bloodstream more quickly and caused
a rush: 80–90 per cent of the active compound was lost from
fumes which either escaped from the pipe or were exhaled unab-
sorbed by the smoker.[66] An expert of the League of Nations confirmed in the 1930s that eating opium or dross was more harmful
than smoking prepared opium, since much larger quantities of
morphine entered the system via ingestion than by smoking.[67]
Dr P. L. McAll, on the other hand, had already concluded from
his experience with opium patients in 1903 that 'one part of
opium swallowed by the mouth has the same effect as smoking
six or seven parts' through a pipe.[68]

A variety of figures indicate that opium was smoked widely
but in relatively small quantities in the nineteenth century. While
the available statistical evidence is often contradictory, it does not
support the prevalent view that a majority of smokers lived in the
grip of addiction and were compelled to take ever-increasing
amounts of opium. However, mere numbers fail to convey the
cultural meanings and social uses of opium in late imperial China,
which are analysed below.

OPIUM AS SOCIAL STATUS

Opium is often understood to have been widespread in China
because of its addictive properties, foreign traders using the drug
to create a physically dependent market. This popular explanation defies common sense, since opium was also used in many
other parts of the world, not least in India, Turkey and Persia
where it was traditionally produced. Rather than focusing exclusively on the pharmacological properties of opium, it would be
more fruitful for us to examine the cultural norms and social

factors which sustained its consumption in the specific historical context of the late imperial period. At the core of such research is the analysis of opium as a marker of social status in a culture of conspicuous consumption.

Patna opium was an exotic commodity which became an object of connoisseurship for wealthy scholars and rich merchants during the early nineteenth century. Within these privileged circles, opium was appreciated in intricate rituals, very much as the careful boiling of high-quality tea could confer social distinction. Terms such as 'yellow' (*huang*), 'long' (*chang*) or 'loose' (*song*) were used to describe the proper preparation of opium (*zhuangyan*). A rich family normally had at least one 'opium sous-chef' (*xianzi shou*) to prepare its pipe.[69] The cooking would be done by using two needles (*yanzhen*), one in each hand, kneading and rolling a wad of opium between the two points in the heat above the lamp. A properly trimmed wick in the lamp would generate a flame with just the right temperature, over which the carefully cooked opium would gradually acquire a dense rubbery texture and a deep tan, the appearance and colour of the substance signalling that it was ready for smoking. Once cooked, the wad was removed and hardened like caramelised sugar. Most of the opium would set on one needle, while a small pellet was left on the other for smoking. After being pulled out of the heat, the pellet was rolled into a cone and inserted into the hole of the bowl for smoking.[70]

Inserting the pellet into the hole was a delicate operation: the bowl was first held inverted over the flame to heat the hole, then the tip of the needle would be spun back and forth over the heat, allowing the pellet to soften slowly without melting or charring. When sufficiently soft, it was plunged into the hole and pressed down, forming a small compact ring on the hole like a miniature doughnut. After withdrawing the needle, a round hard clump of opium with a hole in the middle was ready to be smoked. The pipe would be held with the pellet exposed towards the lamp at a 45 degree angle. Lips had to be pressed against rather than around the mouthpiece to create an airtight seal. A slow and steady draw on the pipe with the bowl securely in place over the lamp would cause the pellet to sizzle and vaporise as the fumes were sucked into the bowl, which cooled and distilled the smoke before it moved through the pipe into the smoker's lungs. The opium vapours, by abruptly expanding and condensing in the pipe, separated from any impurities which gathered as a crust, also known as 'dross', on the chamber walls. A smoker would therefore only inhale the chemically purest form of alkaloidised vapour, unencumbered by any unpleasant by-products.[71]

Before the smoke reached the lungs, a smoker would feel a bittersweet sensation on the palate, followed by a pleasant tightening of the capillaries.[72] A single breath sufficed to absorb each serving, as larger pellets tended to sputter and evaporate unevenly and to overheat the bowl. When the pipe was finished, the hole was cleared with the needle and a cloth was used to wipe the surface of the bowl.[73] Here is a description from Emily Hahn, who happily acquired a smoking habit during her days in Shanghai:

Heh-ven never stopped conversing, but his hands were busy and his eyes were fixed on what he was doing—knitting, I thought at first, wondering why nobody had ever mentioned that this craft was practiced by Chinese men. Then I saw that what I had taken for yarn between the two needles he manipulated was actually a kind of gummy stuff, dark and thick. As he rotated the needle ends about each other, the stuff behaved like taffy in the act of setting; it changed color, too, slowly evolving from its earlier dark brown to tan. At a certain moment, just as it seemed about to stiffen, he wrapped the whole wad around one needle end and picked up a pottery object about as big around as a teacup. [The bowl] looked rather like a cup, except that it was closed across the top, with a rimmed hole in the middle of this fixed lid. Heh-ven plunged the wadded needle into this hole, withdrew it, leaving the wad sticking up from the hole, and modelled the rapidly hardening stuff so that it sat on the cup like a tiny volcano. He then picked up a piece of polished bamboo that had a large hole near one end, edged with a band of chased silver. Into this he fixed the cup, put the opposite end of the bamboo into his mouth, held the cup with the tiny cone suspended above the lamp flame, and inhaled deeply. The stuff bubbled and evaporated as he did so, until nothing of it was left.[74]

Smoking utensils could become sought-after collectables. Expensive pipes were made of precious black wood, ivory, jade or tortoiseshell, with ornate silver decorations.[75] The stem could be long or short, the knot carved out of silver or precious wood and the bowl carefully polished. Flowers or leaves would climb along slender silver pipes, with blooming hibiscus surrounded by leaves of wild mint, while some ivory or jade pipes resembled an elephant's tusk.[76] Some connoisseurs cherished the accessories to such an extent that they became more important than the substance itself, and affluent households saw expensive pipes as a symbol of wealth and social status.[77] The lamp even came to signify for many the most atmospheric aspect of the smoking experience. The invitation to 'light the lamp' (*diandeng*) meant to share the comfort and peace of the smoking chamber.[78]

The close interrelation between status, consumption and connoisseurship was not confined to China, as the *chinoiserie* craze of eighteenth-century Europe shows. As tea became a sign of gentility and respectability in the higher echelons of British society, serving the beverage became associated with other novel objects of conspicuous display—fine china porcelain tea ware, gilded mahogany tea furniture, silver tea *equipages* including tea caddy, teapot, tea-kettle, milk or cream jug, sugar bowl and spoon-tray.[79] China's opium utensils, likewise, were an integral part of the smoking ritual. The wealthier the smoker, the more expensive the material chosen, with exquisite jewels embellishing the pipe. Seduced by beautifully carved woodwork, illuminated by soft light intermingling with the smoke and the scent of opium, smokers experienced—according to enthusiasts—an intoxicating 'journey of immortality' (*si shenxian*), a veritable 'ascent to the moon' (*dao yuezhong*).[80] The following observation in 1801 by Yu Jiao (1751–1820) is one of the earliest on record:

My friend Yao Chunpu has praised opium in front of me. He said that it is fragrant and sweet in taste: 'On a miserable rainy day, or when you feel down, light up an opium lamp on a low table, recline face to face, pass the pipe around and inhale. At first there is a sudden feeling of refreshment, one's head and eyes becoming very clear. Soon afterwards, there is quietude and profound well-being. After a while, one's bones and joints become extremely relaxed and the eyes heavy. This is followed by a gradual descent into slumber, and detached from all worries, one enters a world of dreams and fantasies, completely free like a spirit: what a paradise!'[81]

In a period marked by social mobility and anxiety over class distinctions, the traditional attributes of the scholar—calligraphy, art, literature—were perceived as being less desirable than clear markers of social status: opium clearly contributed to this role.[82] The ability to spend money on opium became a direct manifestation of wealth and status, while opium houses became known as 'money-spending holes' (*xiaojinku*) where customers vied to outdo each other in the conspicuous consumption of the prized narcotic.[83] As the following account demonstrates, great amounts of money filled the pockets of enterprising opium house owners in the prosperous Jiangnan region:

Frequenting opium houses was as common as going to inns and tea-houses. These places of entertainment possessed exceptional charm, and customers visited them as often as they could… In the most prestigious places, couches were made of red sandalwood, mattresses beautifully embroidered with soft cushions and spittoons made of white copper. The servants were usually very attentive and took pride in making customers feel at home. There were also many peddlers who sold food all day long. Besides smoking, customers indulged in desserts and fruits, such as toffee apples, Huzhou lotus rice and other fancy snacks… Some big spenders could smoke up to thirty or forty holders a day… an attraction exclusively for the rich, for whom the couches had to be exquisite. The same was true for the [smoking utensils]: rainbow-coloured bowls from the Yongzheng period, equipped with silver lamps, ivory pipes with translucent jade heads. How could anyone not be seduced by this experience?[84]

A committed opium user would, in competitive conspicuousness, strive to become an 'opium connoisseur', connoisseurship being a carefully cultivated gentleman's art. Connoisseurs were defined not only by their expertise, but also by their ability to spend considerable amounts of money in expensive opium houses on the highest quality of opium. However, the availability of cheaper opium also meant that narcotic culture was shared by less wealthy social groups, who had little more than an oblique relationship to the cultural attributes of elite connoisseurship. One disapproving observer already noted in the 1840s that 'everyone becomes fond of [opium smoking] and eventually succumbs to it. Together they have turned our Divine Land into a world of smoke. All good fields have now been cultivated with poppies; all good homes display smoking utensils; all famous red light districts are lined with smoking houses.'[85]

As opium smoking progressed down the social scale during the second half of the nineteenth century, it gradually became a popular marker of male sociability. It emerged as a vector of hospitality: the 'welcome smoke' (yingchou) offered to guests became an indispensable aspect of social etiquette, and failure to offer opium was considered a serious faux pas. Refreshments and tea would also be served, while the honoured guest reclined on a cushioned platform (mukang), at times covered in auspicious red, in order to receive his pipe.[86] Discussions would be animated, while the elderly were allowed to drift into a light slumber, as one foreign observer noted in 1891.[87] Even among the less privileged, the example of the 'lonely smoker' was generally eschewed: smoking was a collective experience, an occasion for social intercourse, a highly ritualised event which set strict parameters for the consumption of opium. Either in public opium houses or in the privacy of one's home, opium would be smoked by friends while enjoying leisurely conversations or in groups where the pipe was passed around. During the socio-economic changes experienced in the second half of the nineteenth century, opium and teahouses as well as alcohol-serving inns provided spaces of social comfort where even less privileged groups could meet and socialise.[88]

OPIUM CONSUMPTION AND CONSUMER TASTE

As we have seen, opium, just like tea, came in different grades which were marketed for carefully targeted social groups.[89] In order to suit the different tastes of consumer groups, raw opium was often refined. Opium from Yunnan, for instance, was turned into four varieties before being transported to the markets. 'Horseshit' (mafen) was made of raw opium from the southeast of Yunnan; blackish-red and wrapped in bamboo leaves, it had the distinct appearance of horse manure. However, it was considered the best of all domestic opium and was custom-made for the Guangdong market. 'Buns' (*baozi*) came second, consisting of raw opium from the west of Yunnan. Wrapped into characteristic oil paper, 'bun opium' was mainly sold in Sichuan, Hubei and Shanghai. 'Opium cakes' (*gezi*) resembled home-baked cakes and were dark in colour. This third type reached its target markets of Guangdong, Hunan and Guangxi and retailed in bamboo containers padded with bamboo leaves. The most affordable category was 'brick opium' (*kuaizi*), red or yellow, wrapped into rough paper and particularly popular in Hubei and Guangxi. Once reconstituted into the form of liquid or paste, dates, sesame seeds or other local specialities could be admixed to all four categories, while cutting the opium with even cheaper varieties was also common.[90] Although these alterations generally increased the profit margin of retailers, they were also frequently dictated by consumer demand. For instance, arsenic was occasionally added to opium since it gave a pungent edge to the smoke. A special variety of green tobacco from Beijing produced a similar effect and was extremely popular with consumers who liked the flavour.[91] Despite the sophistication of China's internal opium culture, Chinese produce failed to make inroads into the Southeast Asian market. In British Malaya, Indian and Persian opium easily outsold Chinese varieties, at least unblended.[92]

'Taste' and 'quality', reflected in the range of prices, thus became markers of social distinction, much as beer and wine appealed to different social groups in Britain. The upper rank of opium consumers—Manchu aristocrats, high officials and wealthy merchants—generally preferred to smoke expensive imports as well as the best domestic produce from Yunnan. An intermediate rank of consumers normally smoked the less expensive opium from Sichuan, whereas the lower rank, including labourers, performers, prostitutes and beggars, would be resigned to smoking dross (*yanhui*), the residue left in the pipe after opium had been smoked. The outcome of this method was popularly known as 'dragon head dregs' (*longtou zha*) or 'dragon head water' (*longtou shui*). Though generally considered waste, it would be sold by most retailers to those who could not afford proper opium. Some-times dross was recycled several times to satisfy the desperately poor,[93] much as 'spent' tea leaves in poor English homes were dried and reused, and 'donkey tea' made of burnt bread was sometimes substituted.[94] Dross was so valuable that in opium houses in Sichuan customers were only allowed to recycle the ashes if they paid 50 per cent more than usual.[95]

Dross products accounted for nearly half of the opium smoked by weight during the second half of the nineteenth century, an indication of how vastly exaggerated some claims about opium addiction were. The exact morphine contents of dross, despised by connoisseurs as the opium for the poor,[96] cannot be ascertained. Dr O. Anselmino, who examined it for the League of Nations in the 1930s, was unable to reach a conclusion, since the content de-pended on smoking habits, the type of pipe used and the duration of each session. The longer the prepared opium was burnt in the pipe, the less morphine remained in the dross: 'As… it is scienti-fically unknown how much morphine is lost when prepared opium is smoked, it is not possible to indicate the average mor-phine content of dross.'[97] Dross was cheap and could often be found in opium houses for the poor, although even wealthy con-sumers preferred to blend stronger types of opium with ash in or-der to make the taste smoother. Chinese opium could be reused up to three times—this could not be done with Indian opium.[98]

Good quality opium underwent no major changes during sto-rage, except that it became gradually harder, whereas opium vari-eties that were too moist could become mouldy and lose their value. However, when kept free of impurities and well sealed in a cool place, opium paste could be stored for many years without losing its qualities.[99] When stored as a dense syrup in ceramic or clay jars sealed with cork and beeswax, it could even improve considerably with age due to a process of gradual fermentation. In Shanghai, for instance, the better opium houses used to season their opium for three years in porcelain jars, adorned with auspi-cious characters such as *shou* (longevity), *fu* (good fortune) or *xi* (happiness), before serving it to their customers.[100] The price that opium could fetch depended on its origin, taste, consistency and age. As the following citation by a high-ranking member of the British-Indian government shows, matured prime quality opium from north-eastern India was as sought-after in nineteenth-century China as a rare bottle of exceptional vintage in Europe: 'The flavor and delicacy of opium excite as much attention in the East, as those qualities in the wines of France and Spain in Europe. A connoisseur will tell at a glance whether the dark juice in its earthen vessel is the produce of the poppy of Mundisore or Rutlam... It is only opium of the best quality which is fit for the China market... China takes the new and fresh opium, which is used in a liquid form. In India, amongst the wealthy, old opium is valued as much as old port at home, and for the same qualities, mellowness and softness. Opium of a good season and vintage 20 or 25 years old commands a fabulous price, and is only to be had in the houses of the rich'.[101] Because good opium could improve with age, it was an excellent investment in periods of strong currency fluctuations, which were common in the nineteenth century.

THE MYTH OF THE OPIUM DEN

Social and economic differences between various consumer groups were expressed not only in terms of quality and price, but also through frequency, place and mode of consumption. Justus Doolittle, a medical missionary in Fujian, observed that 'officers, merchants, literary men, the wealthy, and generally all those who have their time at their leisurely disposal, buy the drug by the ball or in smaller quantity, and prepare it at their residences, where they smoke it whenever they please.'[102]

Whereas the wealthy sought solace in their private gardens and mansions, opium houses, alongside temples, theatres and teahouses, were the social venues for ordinary people. Opium houses were a far cry from the depraved and secretive 'dens' imagined by literary figures like Charles Dickens. W. Somerset Maugham, like so many other foreign travellers in search of the mystical East, was surprised to find that the opium house he visited was neat and bright, with clean matting in every room. Far from being the expected 'dope fiends', the customers were an elderly gentleman reading his newspaper, two friends chatting over a pipe and a family with a child. The atmosphere reminded him of 'the little intimate beerhouse of Berlin where the tired working men could go in the evening and spend a peaceful hour. Fiction', Maugham concluded, 'is stranger than fact.'[103] A League of Nations report dated 1930 observed that opium houses were often clean and tidy, failing to conform to the stereotype of 'the "opium den" as a breeding place for crime and immorality... scarcely, even at their worst, more repulsive than the localities where the corresponding classes of the Western peoples consume beer or stronger alcoholic beverages.'[104]

John Blofeld, who entered an opium house in Beijing during the Second World War, was also surprised to find that 'it was nothing like the sort of hell I had pictured':

The Te I Lou was a hotel outside the Ch'ien Men which owed to Japanese protection its immunity from visits by the police. Equipped with baths, telephones, majong tables and several sorts of cuisine, it had become a nest of small opium dens (one to each room) where some people were said to pass the whole of each day between rising at noon and returning home at dawn to sleep... we entered a number of rooms each furnished with padded divans and the six to eight lamps necessary to accommodate about thirty smokers per room each day... some of the customers we saw were busy cooking little pellets of opium over their lamps or inhaling clouds of smoke from their heavy pipes. Others sat or lay upon the divans talking to one another with the noticeable animation which opium-smoking produces in almost everyone. Those not ready yet for a smoke were seated at square tables playing majong or bending over delicious snacks brought in by hawkers or ordered from neighbouring restaurants. We saw very few people asleep or sleepy-looking; and only two or three elderly and undernourished men resembled my previous conception of 'dope-fiends'. In fact, I was disappointed to discover that, if the sour smell of beer could have been substituted for the sweet and all-pervading odour of opium, the atmosphere would have been very much indeed like that of a London pub on a Saturday night.[105]

The saloon in nineteenth-century America, rather than the pub in Victorian London, might have been a better comparison (Londoners, after all, had a choice of entertainment venues, from the theatre to the music-hall): in a world lacking cheap restaurants, public lavatories, libraries or meeting halls, the saloon was an oasis where prostitution, pornography, gambling, narcotics and local politics were all available to the male consumers.[106] Like the opium house, moreover, the saloon was an exclusively male preserve. Just as the saloon in America and the pub in Britain were important venues for male sociability, the opium house was a socially sanctioned place for male customers in search of recreation (*yuqing*) and leisure (*youxi*) in the second half of the nineteenth century.

Opium was rarely taken on its own. The paste was considered to be at the extreme *yin*-end of a balanced intake, and strong *yang* elements were ingested by customers to counterbalance it, mainly in the form of tea, food (meat, shellfish, mushrooms, pumpkin, plant oils) or herbal tonics (garlic, ginger, cinnamon, wolfberry and schisandra).[107] Opium and tea in particular were ideal partners, as the beverage would quench the thirst created by opium and clean the palate. Food was served in most opium houses, from elaborate meals to simple snacks. During the late Qing smokers in the opium houses of Hangzhou liked to eat sweets, fruit and dim sum, while every smoking couch in the better establishments offered cakes and candies. Up to 300 such opium houses existed in Hangzhou in the 1880s, most catering to merchants from Ningbo and Shanghai.[108] Even in the 1930s, when prohibition forced many opium houses underground, almond tea was served to smokers in the morning in Changchun, followed by soy milk, fried doughnuts, cured meat and baked bread. Congee, chicken soup, dumplings, smoked beef, pancakes, fruits and candy were among the other delicacies served during the day.[109]

Rock-bottom prices at the end of the nineteenth century meant that even the very poor could participate in narcotic culture. Reports from Hangzhou described the cheapest type of opium house as open round the clock, equipped in spartan fashion with iron couches and straw mattresses, and acting as a magnet for homeless migrants and roving gamblers. Such opium houses provided many of the poor with a temporary home, bath facilities and the opportunity to eat.[110] A good example from the twentieth century is the Heng Lak Hung in Bangkok, which in the 1950s was the largest opium house in the world: in this self-contained universe, 5,000 permanent boarders enjoyed their opium, accommodation and a frugal meal, all at less than half their normal day's pay; they left in the morning for work and returned in the evening, when they stripped to underpants and slippers for a couple of hours of leisurely smoke before falling asleep on the plain wooden floors of their cubicles.[111] Opium houses in the nineteenth century fulfilled a similar role, as the treaty ports began to benefit from foreign transport and banking, attracting a massive influx of labourers in search of a temporary home. On the other hand, the decline of the rural economy, a series of natural disasters which made millions homeless, and the impact of the mid-nineteenth century rebellions forced many displaced people to seek refuge in the burgeoning cities of the coast. When the opium houses were closed in the wake of the prohibition movement in 1906, many poor people lost their homes. In Shanxi province, Samuel Merwin noted that many of the poor were homeless: 'I was calling on one of the foreigners in Tai Yuan-fu and found a beggar lying on one of the door-steps, with his pipe and lamp all going... I asked him why he was there, and he told me he had nowhere else to go, now that the smoking-dens were all closed, and that he had to find some sheltered nook where he could have his smoke.'[112]

Opium houses were sites of male sociability, women generally smoking at home, although in much smaller numbers than men. There was no gender distinction where the medical uses of opium were concerned, and men and women alike intermittently resorted to the pipe as a palliative for a range of ailments. However, in wealthier circles smoking was an acceptable pastime for women gathered together, as demonstrated by Mrs Little, who visited a gentry house and observed that she was asked into the bedrooms of the ladies to smoke opium.[113]

OPIUM FOR THE PEOPLE

Even if the poor worker and the wealthy merchant both participated in a flourishing narcotic culture, the uses of opium could vary significantly from one social group to another. Social elites may have regarded opium houses as suitable locations for intimate chats or business meetings, but the poor often used them as cheap hostels to spend the night. Opium houses welcomed the many migrants of the later nineteenth century, providing not only affordable accommodation but also some relief from misery, diversion from boredom (*jiemen*) and escape from anxiety (*xinjiao*): 'When those who struggle to survive a life of hell are able to inhale a little opium, they immediately forget all the pains and miseries of life.'[114] Opium also provided an escape from the strains of working-class life in Victorian England: 'Men reverted to it to calm their fears of insecurity and poverty, to kill memories of long hours at the loom, the coal face or the plough. Women took it to numb the grinding poverty in which they lived and worked, struggling to raise a family and feed a husband.'[115]

Opium in China served as a refreshing tonic for hard-working men and women, including government runners, rickshaw pullers, factory workers, and female entertainers, often on the job for long hours throughout the night. Workers could take opium to stay awake (*tishen*) at night, while labourers throughout Southeast Asia used it for refreshment.[116] European travellers reported that after half a day's hard work Chinese coolies would rest and inhale a few puffs, then return 'refreshed' to work for several more hours.[117] Even in Shanghai the manager of a tannery employing 200 workers who were recruited indiscriminately and paid enough to afford opium noticed that they were never unfit to work.[118] Opium smoking was a habit carefully managed by users as an aid to hard work. Many prepared their pipes as a 'pick-me-up' before carrying on with their daily chores and enjoyed opium in moderation.[119] Even when their meagre earnings hardly sufficed to buy a meal, luggage carriers in Yunnan often preferred an invigorating whiff of opium to more food at the start of their long working day.[120] When opium smoking was effectively prohibited after 1906, thousands of poor salt miners were—at least temporarily—unable to continue with their work;[121] many had used opium either to induce sleep (*cuimian*) or to keep themselves awake in order to burn the midnight candle.

Opium was also used as a hunger-suppressant, akin to coca in Peru and Bolivia: it had the power to dull fatigue and silence hunger, and alleviated the misery felt by workers in strenuous occupations, from rickshaw pullers to miners.[122] In Canton opium smoking was one of the favourite and most affordable pastimes among rickshaw pullers, although many other labourers in the city also used it to lessen the pain of prolonged toil, keep the body warm and allay hunger.[123] As Virginia Berridge has noted about Chinese immigrants in London, 'opium smoking was an aid to hard work, not a distraction from it, and smokers managed to combine their habit with a normal working existence.'[124]

When the poor used opium to suppress hunger or kill pain, foreign observers critical of the substance often confused the symptoms of addiction with those of starvation, which marked the countless famished paupers produced by the mid-century rebellions. Many wealthy consumers, on the other hand, tended to smoke far more than the poor could ever afford, although they lived to a ripe old age. Some of the best studies which questioned popular notions of 'drug addiction' appeared in Europe and the United States during the first decades of the twentieth century. A captive prison population of drug users was closely examined for the effects of sudden withdrawal.[125] Dr Ayres, chief surgeon of the colonial administration in Hong Kong, had already used medical statistics from Victoria Gaol in 1889 to reveal that 'There were no deaths among them, and no cases of cholera occurred among them, enfeebled as though they are said to be by this said-to-be pernicious habit.' He charted the changes in body weight of all inmates during their time in gaol: habitual smokers reacted to the dietary regime in the same way as prisoners who had never used opium. Dr Ayres concluded: 'This habit in itself appears to me to be perfectly harmless. In conjunction with women, wine, late hours and gambling it is very possibly injurious, but in this case "it is not in it", to use a slang phrase.'[126] When opium was taken in excessive quantities, it was generally ingested deliberately to commit suicide.

OPIUM AND SUICIDE

Foreign medical experts such as William Lockhart observed that the swallowing of opium, along with more traditional methods such as hanging, drowning and the use of arsenic, had become one of the most popular ways of committing suicide in China.[127] Medical missionaries were well aware of the use of opium for such purposes, since it had topped the list of favoured suicide poisons in Britain in the second half of the nineteenth century.[128] Although opium poisoning had been known for many centuries in China, the vast expansion of narcotic culture in the nineteenth century transformed it into a relatively widespread means of suicide. Opium, in turn, was partially displaced by other products of modernity in suicide attempts by the end of the century, in particular rat poison, 'Ningpo Varnish', bed bug powder and phosphorus matches.[129] Several decades later, as the Lester Chinese Hospital observed in 1929, the number of patients using opium to commit suicide further decreased in a climate of opium prohibition, as many turned instead to synthetic drugs, including veronal, adalin and medinal, all comparatively cheap and easy to obtain: 'One can quite well prophesy that if and when opium is made really difficult to obtain, these other drugs will be so much more used that some form of legislation against them will be found necessary.'[130]

Specific case histories illustrate the range of motives behind suicide attempts with opium. One patient at a mission hospital in Shanghai had poisoned himself with a large dose of opium because he had lost all his money gambling and was too ashamed to face his partners. Apart from loss of face in business, family pressures were behind many suicides. One woman disliked her husband so much following an argument over the way she had trimmed the oil lamp that she took revenge by swallowing a large dose of opium.[131] Even housewives who were fully dependent economically would have the few coppers it took to purchase a potentially lethal amount of raw opium.[132] In October 1866 a Jiangsu widow refused to remarry after the death of her husband. Following intense pressure by her stepmother she took an overdose of opium to join him.[133] When Bao Tianxiao compiled his memoirs, he observed that in his native Suzhou those who killed themselves by eating opium were mainly married women. During an upsurge of opium poisonings in the 1870s and '80s, a charitable emergency service was specifically set up to deal with the problem.[134] Even among high officials and their families, suicide by taking opium was not unknown. A foreign medical officer reported a case involving the three sons of a former magistrate resident in Shanghai. After suffering the effects of financial recklessness, all three ended their own lives by swallowing raw opium.[135] As opium was also openly available in Europe, even Qing envoys would occasionally resort to it to kill themselves while on missions abroad. In 1886 while on a diplomatic visit to England a senior official, Kong Zhaogan, became increasingly jealous of his colleague Liu Qitong, and when the latter received orders to act as chief representative, Kong became estranged from the group, showed clear signs of madness and eventually swallowed half a jar of raw opium.[136]

Practitioners of traditional medicine in China were also familiar with accidental or intended opium poisoning and tried to develop antidotes. Imperial manuals recommended animal fluids and excretions to be forced down the victim's throat to induce vomiting. The body would then be drenched in cold water, the mouth forced open with the help of chopsticks and the patient left to recover protected from direct sunlight.[137] Medical missionaries used modern methods with the same objective but would resort to more 'scientific' means to achieve recovery: hot infusions of coffee and potassium permanganate as well as injections of atropine sulphate were administered to make the victim regurgitate the poison. Cold water, artificial respiration, washing out the stomach and the forced walking of patients were also common.[138] To the amazement of some foreign doctors, many of those who had been brought back from the clutches of death were far from grateful. Some refused to accept medical help: '[The victim] was much incensed at the trick that had been resorted to, and he thereupon flatly refused to assist me by swallowing water to wash out the stomach more completely.'[139]

Some smokers suffered health problems from the chemical substances blended into the opium paste. In order to maximise profits, wholesalers and retailers could mix opium with dross or herbs, jujube paste, pork rind, tobacco, arsenic and mercury.

Other adulterants were poppy heads and petals, dried fruit such as figs and apricots, turpentine, gum, stone, lead, clay, sand, soot, cow dung, flour, betel nut, powdered charcoal, dyes, liquorice, husk, and other mucilaginous, albuminous, farinaceous and saccharine substances.[140] Adulteration of opium also became a major problem in Victorian England, explaining why opiates often featured in the poisoning statistics.[141] On the other hand, reputable opium houses and private households in China often refined their own paste from raw opium purchased through a reliable supplier, not only to ensure that the smoking mixture was blended according to their consumers' requirements and tastes, but also to remove the adulterants which might have been added.[142] Patna opium was the exception: produced under government supervision to a standard degree of purity, it was famous for its consistent quality.

5

'THE BEST POSSIBLE AND SURE SHIELD': OPIUM, DISEASE AND EPIDEMICS (c. 1840–1900)

The last chapter noted that smokers generally controlled their intake and were unlikely to feel any involuntary compulsion to increase the quantity or frequency of their doses. Smoking was a complex social ritual with inbuilt restraints on the amount of opium which could be consumed, and had no serious consequences for the health or life expectancy of the vast majority of users. However, merely to argue that the physical consequences of moderate smoking were innocuous at best would not be sufficient to debunk the opium myth. Opium was primarily a painkiller. As Virginia Berridge noted for nineteenth-century England, opium was a medical panacea for many working people before modern synthetic medications became available.[1] The chief motive for smoking opium in China was self-medication: to reduce pain, fight fevers and suppress coughs. Opium was an effective costive, a respiratory depressant, an antitussive, an analgesic, an antispasmodic and a febrifuge. The lowering of the cost of opium in the nineteenth century allowed ordinary people to relieve the symptoms of endemic diseases such as dysentery, cholera and malaria and to cope with fatigue, hunger and cold. Nothing was more effective than opiates in treating diarrhoea.[2] 'Opium was our medicine, it was all we had', one ex-Guomindang soldier told interviewers in Thailand.[3]

Thomas Szasz has argued that the demonisation of opium was made possible only by the commercial production of acetylsalicylic acid (i.e. 'aspirin') in the 1890s.[4] However, aspirin remained beyond the reach of most working people in China well into the second half of the twentieth century, and opium retained its over-whelming importance as a painkiller. As an American delegate at the International Committee on Combating Drug Trafficking perceptively pointed out in 1934, 'China is a country which does not produce aspirin.'[5] While dependence on opium may have been problematic for a minority of smokers with personal or social pro-blems, its medicinal use was a considerable health benefit before the advent of affordable alternatives in the Second World War.

OPIUM AS A MEDICAL PANACEA

Opium has been used since antiquity as a panacea for common ailments, and is also thought to have been instrumental in sleep therapies.[6] Arab traders and scholars built on existing knowledge and helped popularise opium in India, China and medieval Eu-rope, where it was known under pseudonyms such as theriac, mithradatium or philonium. The physician Paracelsus (1493?–1541), who introduced the use of medications made from miner-als including sulphur, mercury, and antimony, popularised 'lauda-num', a solution of opium in water and alcohol. This became common in parts of Europe during the eighteenth and nineteenth centuries, in particular as a form of self-medication by those un-able to afford expensive medical fees.[7] Opium-based medications were used throughout England to treat a variety of illnesses and as a general tonic for working people. By the farming populations of the Fenlands around Norwich and Cambridge, where rheu-matism, pneumonia and 'miasmic diseases' were widespread, op-ium was used against the physical effects of pervasive damp. Medical opinion did not turn till the very end of the nineteenth century, coinciding with intense public pressure from the aboli-tionist movement.[8]

In imperial China sources usually refer to the opium poppy as *yingsuhua*, whereas the now commonly used name *yapian* is thought to be derived from the Arabic word *afiyun*.[9] As early as during the Tang (618–907), opium capsules were being imported on Arab ships and along the caravan routes linking China with

Central Asia and the Mediterranean. Travel accounts of that period bear witness to fields of the poppy plant (*yingsu*), while the poppy was mentioned in an official pharmacopeia (*bencao*) in 968.[10] During the Song (960–1279), capsules of the opium poppy (*yingsuke*) were used for curative purposes. The soup made from them was highly regarded for cleansing mouth and throat and for benefiting the lungs and digestion; it was also taken by the elderly and infirm.[11] Poppy soup was noted by travellers as a remedy against diarrhoea in Sichuan.[12] The opium capsule was cleaned, its outer skin removed, then dried in the shade, sliced and soaked in rice vinegar or honey. It was also used in the treatment of anal prolapse and coughs, as well as for the relief of pain.[13] The eleventh-century *Bencao tujing* (Illustrated materia medica) elaborated that the major medicinal property of opium was to alleviate 'bad heat' (*xiere*), treat stomach trouble (*fanwei*) and to relieve blockages in the respiratory system (*tanzhi*). However, opium could upset the functions of the bladder (*pangguang*) if taken in excess.[14] The Yuan (1279–1368) physician Wang Gui promoted a formula known as *doumen san* (combat powder), containing poppy capsules, Chinese angelica and root of sanguisorba, to treat infections, abdominal pains and diarrhoea, as well as heavy bleeding through dysentery or vaginal discharge.[15]

During the Ming (1368–1644), the *Yuyao yuanfang* (Collection of prescriptions from the Imperial Medicine Bureau) cited opium in nine different formulas, including pills against stomach problems (*huanchang wan*), soporifics (*anmian san*) and powders for soothing the lungs (*ningfei san*).[16] The *Yilin jiyao* (A collection of major medical treaties, 1488) by Wang Xi, a former military official posted in the empire's western fringes, gave a detailed account of the methods of producing opium, and among its medical merits cited its effectiveness against dysentery.[17] The opium poppy was further popularised through preparations such as the 'golden elixir pills', recommended in Li Shizhen's (1518–1593) *Materia medica* against bowel disorders and as a general tonic.[18] Li Shizhen also suggested that poppy capsules could be used to treat diarrhoea, anal prolapse, seminal emission, coughs and as an anodyne, while a late Ming account compares opium to the 'immortality medicines' (*danyao*) of Daoist alchemy.[19] Xu Boling traced the origins of medicinal opium in China to both the sea route via the coastal provinces and commerce along the trade routes of Central Asia:

A remedy known as *hefurong* has been produced in several countries overseas and in central Asia. It is also known in China as opium (*yapian*). It looks like myrrh, is dark yellow, pliable but strong like beef tendons [i.e. glue] and smells of horse. It is bitter, hot and can be poisonous. It is used as an aid to sex stamina (*zhu yangshi*), can strengthen the male fluid (*zhuangjing*) and restore the *qi*. Experts of esoteric arts and courtesans who practise the art of the bedchamber often take it. It can also cure chronic diarrhoea and deficiency of primordial *qi*. It should only be used occasionally and one should not exceed three doses. If taken in excess it can cause severe boils and crusty sores, as well as heat disorders. It is as lethal as sulphur and red lead, and can lead to more body heat and dryness than styrax liquidus. Opium is more powerful than many other drugs, including rhizoma curculiginis, herba cynomorii, hairy dear horn, dragon bones and dodder seed. During the nineteenth year of the Ming Xianzong period [1483], an imperial edict was issued ordering rich merchants to buy and collect the drug from overseas via Hainan, Fujian, Zhejiang, Sichuan, Shaanxi and areas bordering central Asia. It is as valuable as gold.[20]

Fang Yizhi (1611–71), on the other hand, remarked on the contemporary custom of preserving opium paste in jars sealed with paper. Once the privilege of the imperial clan, opium seems to have reached a wider market with the arrival of imports from India, mainly as a popular remedy against diarrhoea or as an alleged aphrodisiac (*fangzhong yao*).[21] Eighteenth-century manuals such as the *Jiyan liangfang* (A collection of good remedies, 1724) also listed opium preparations to cure typhoid fever (*shanghan*), plague (*wenyi*), heat stroke, headache, fever, vomiting and diarrhoea and stomach pains. Opium remedies were designed in accordance with medical tradition, e.g. for controlling 'bodily fluids' (*gujing*) and preserving 'vital energy' (*baoyang*), for 'warming' the organs, muscles and joints (*nuanshen buyaoxi*). The application of opium plasters to the navel could expel chills and prevent physical decay.[22] Qing scholar Shen Zhongyan even saw the poppy as the only comfort for hunger and misery.[23]

Even after the first Sino-British War (1839–42), opium continued to be classified as a 'medicine' (*yao*), for instance by the celebrated scholar Yu Zhengxie in his essay on the substance. Commenting on its important role in traditional medicine, Yu further observed:

[From] various translation of documents and from the Tongwenguan collections [we] know that in the Ming period... opium was a royal gift, as well as a popular medicine. In China opium has been known as *wuxiang* (black incense), or *wuyan* (black smoke), although originally it was known as *yapian, apian, yarong, afurong* or *hefurong*, terms common in a variety of texts from the Ming onwards.[24]

Opium was thus an important component of medical culture in imperial China, prescribed by experienced practitioners and popular for self-medication well before the spread of a smoking culture.

Some medical observers, however, also recognised its toxic properties, encapsulated by the term *du*, or 'poison'.[25] As early as 1515, the well-known physician Li Ting warned that opium ingested in its raw state 'can kill like a sword... and needs to be taken in moderation'.[26] According to traditional medicine, all medicinal herbs contained *du*, which was frequently used synonymously with *yao* (medicine).[27] However, for most of the late imperial period the benefits of opium were thought to outweigh its potential harm, which resulted from excessive use. The principle of moderation also applied to other 'poisonous' substances such as arsenic and mercury, commonly prescribed by physicians for pain relief and longevity. Furthermore, once a substance such as orange peel, black prunes, vinegar or honey had been added, it was thought that the toxic properties of opium could be effectively checked. The side effect of indigestion could be alleviated by blending the opium with the 'four noble medicines' of ginseng, atractylodes alba *(baishu)*, China-root and liquorice.[28]

The spread of affordable opium titrated in small quantities thanks to the sophisticated mechanism of the opium pipe allowed even the most dispossessed to benefit occasionally from the medical panacea in the nineteenth century. Even with the gradual spread of more modern medical facilities in the first half of the twentieth century, opium continued to be used for medical reasons by a majority of smokers. One of the few precise studies available indicates that digestive problems accounted for almost half of all the 359 cases of medical smoking examined in Taiwan in 1907–8 (44.3 per cent on average, but 88 per cent for women), followed by respiratory difficulties (30.4 per cent), and diseases affecting the genito-urinary organs (8.3 per cent), the nervous system (8.3 per cent), acute fevers (4.8 per cent), motor functions (3.1 per cent) and the circulatory system (0.9 per cent). People living in isolated parts of the island where no medical facilities were available would regularly resort to self-medication through opium smoking.[29]

Even in the large cities of China, opium often remained the cornerstone of self-medication in the absence of effective and affordable alternatives. The North Shanghai Addiction Treatment Hospital compiled statistics for 1,000 patients in 1935, of whom nearly 90 per cent cited health concerns as the main reason for taking opium or heroin. One in three took up opium smoking to relieve digestive problems, including gastric diseases and stomach pain. Coughs and haemoptysis (spitting blood) were also important reasons for reaching for the pipe; other studies mentioned stomach troubles, rheumatic pains, tuberculosis and malaria as the conditions for which opiates were most commonly taken. While poor health may have been regarded by some patients as a socially acceptable reason for smoking, the figures nonetheless reflect the overwhelming importance of opium as a painkiller, particularly in the absence of aspirin.[30] Experts in detoxification in Java acknowledged in 1930 that 80 per cent of smokers used it for medical reasons and further considered that total abolition was impractical 'because for the relief of suffering we have not yet been able to procure a substitute for opium and its derivatives'.[31]

PROPHYLACTIC SMOKE AND INFECTIOUS DISEASES

Among the medical reasons for the popularity of opium was its imagined or genuine efficacy against the infectious diseases which destroyed countless lives in late imperial China. Fevers[32] were endemic in the sub-tropical hills of southern China, and opium was considered an unrivalled remedy. A global epidemic of cholera (*huoluan*), causing painful diarrhoea and bowel disorders, also reached China between 1817 and 1822.[33] Cholera arrived in the wake of opium: from India via the Straits Settlements to Canton, and further inland following established opium trading routes.[34] It may be a mere coincidence that opium and cholera proliferated in China in the same period—both to some extent the result of a greater mobility of people and goods in an age of globalisation—but the use of opium by ordinary people was certainly encouraged by the epidemics which devastated parts of the country in the nineteenth century. Opium had long been recommended by European practitioners, such as Jacobus Bontius, a Dutch physician serving in Batavia, who wrote as early as in 1629 that the substance was indispensable in the treatment of cholera, as well as dysentery and tropical fevers.[35] Opium was also preferred by medical officers practising in India, despite long-running controversies over it, while local people took it as an antispasmodic to ease the cramps of cholera.[36] Some colonial medical officers with practical experience in India and China swore by ointments and infusions containing opium.[37] As late as 1927 several renowned medical journals in Britain argued that opium administered at an early stage often prevented the full eruption of cholera, and these reports were duly noted in China.[38]

These remedies were not restricted to medical missionaries and colonial authorities. In China, Zhu Mengmei noted, ordinary people saw opium as the only effective cure against cholera.[39] The use of opium in fighting the infectious intestinal disorder was even defended by ardent opponents of opium. Yu Fengbin, a keen crusader against narcotics in the 1920s, prescribed an alcoholic mixture containing opium, camphor and mint.[40] Combinations of opium, camphor and sugar were also commended by Chen Xingzhen in his popular *Self-Medication Against Cholera* (1926).[41] Besides its febrifugal qualities, opium's analgesic properties were widely appreciated, and the efficacy of opiates as a remedy for digestive disorders was recognised even in modern chemical handbooks used in anti-opium campaigns.[42]

Leprosy and typhoid were also common infectious diseases, and liable to be endemic in places where adverse climatic conditions and poverty coincided.[43] Even Shanghai, bastion of modernity during the late nineteenth century, was a hotbed for epidemics due to the combination of hygienic and climatic conditions. Perhaps unaware that much of contemporary Europe lived in similar conditions, Alexandre Duburquois, medical officer for the French navy, stated that Shanghai was 'not a place for European ladies and children', since it was built on the alluvial silt of the Yangzi, source of miasmic infection,[44] which accounted for more than 70 per cent of all deaths in the hospital of the French Concession in the 1860s.[45]

In such conditions foreign physicians also had recourse to local methods, including acupuncture and opium medications. Similar to laudanum and belladonna in contemporary Europe, opium was usually administered in combination with alcohol and aromatic oils or essences to combat fevers and dysentery.[46] Some foreigners also observed with interest the practice of inhaling opium, as prescribed by local physicians, against rheumatism and malarial fever (ague).[47] Both foreign and local practitioners commonly added arsenic to opium against malarial symptoms, for calming gastric and abdominal problems, and, ironically, to relieve the symptoms of arsenic poisoning.[48]

Opium was also administered to lepers in the nineteenth century, if only to alleviate the side effects of this chronic infectious disease. British colonial surgeons often transferred experience gained in India to the China field. N. H. Choksy, a medical officer in charge of the Homeless Leper Asylum in Matunga (Bombay), argued in the *China Medical Missionary Journal* that

none of the patients had taken the drug for mere luxury. The principal reasons assigned by them being—diarrhoea, dysentery, colic, chronic cough, fevers, pains of anaesthetic leprosy, and as a hypnotic. The drug, they said, had certainly prolonged their life and made their existence less miserable, besides acting as a prophylactic against bowel complaints. When admitted into the asylum, these opium habitués had a better physique than their less fortunate brethren in distress.[49]

Dr Choksy had few qualms about recommending the supervised eating of opium, since it alleviated the sufferings of the sick in his care, without any apparent problems. Soothing the suffering of potential converts had been one of the pillars of the medical missionary movement. For most of the nineteenth century, opium was therefore seen as a permissible, if not recommended, panacea for sufferers from a variety of debilitating diseases.

One of the most feared epidemics of the late imperial period was the bubonic plague, popularly known as the 'rat disease' (*shuyi*). Transmitted during the rice planting season in the south of China, the plague could also affect areas of the drier north, as it did Beijing in 1792–3. Plague spread in China during the nineteenth century, coinciding with the expansion of narcotic culture. By the end of the century a major epidemic had ravaged populations in Guangdong, Guangxi, Fujian and Yunnan.[50] The rapid spread of the plague was closely linked to the increased movement of soldiers and traders, who carried the bacterium along the interregional opium routes.[51] Even in the twentieth century smokers in some parts of the country thought that opium could protect against the plague. Wu Liande, the official head of the North Manchuria Plague Prevention Bureau, reported a widespread belief that opium acted as a prophylactic or a remedy against plague, so much so that some non-smokers were induced to take it during an epidemic. For example, an opium house kept by a Japanese woman in the Dalainor colliery was regularly visited in 1921 by miners to protect themselves against the plague.[52]

The smoke generated by the burning of incense, moxa, realgar, arsenic disulphate or trisulphide, opium and tobacco produced a considerable defence shield against the host of epidemics such as the plague. Belief in the prophylactic virtues of scent and smoke was widespread in imperial times, and sulphur was commonly burnt in pots to emit fumes against epidemics. During the late Qing solutions of carbolic acid were even pumped in diluted form from newly imported machines to saturate the air with its pungent smell (called *shidansuan*). In cases of plague, people would light fire-crackers in their courtyards, hoping that the smoke would drive away their invisible enemies.[53] More 'modern' ways of fumigation followed in the republican era, with coffins of plague victims being burnt in kerosene in order to expel 'scientifically' the plague demons.[54] However crude such defensive measures may seem to us, they may have helped in curbing the presence of insects and rodents. A puff of smoke in the evening was in itself a relatively effective measure against fleas and mosquitoes, as even staunch opponents of opium had to agree: the medical missionary W. H. Park, who considered opium a 'poison', conceded that he had never seen a case of malaria in an opium smoker.[55] The following paragraphs will examine more closely the link between malaria and opium.

OPIUM, NARCOTINE AND MALARIA

Humid, badly drained tracts of land had long been the object of health concerns in Europe. Roman observers visiting Britain noted the island's noxious 'humours', while Athenian surgeons commented on epidemics caused by heat, humidity and putrefaction. The naturalists of the Enlightenment drew on this classical knowledge in devising 'scientific' explanations for the diseases arising out of 'bad air' (*mal'aria*).[56] Following epidemics in Italy towards the end of the eighteenth century, this term was quickly adopted in the rest of Europe.[57] Malaria could be encountered in the rural tracts of Holland, Rhenish Germany and southern England,[58] but colonial expansion made the need for prophylactic medicines even more acute, since it was believed that Europeans in the colonies were more prone to malaria than the 'natives'.[59] This was partly explained as a consequence of perennial exposure to the most powerful types of malarial diseases, but also in part to the precautions taken by the indigenous populations against contagion. Popular prophylactics included fortified wine, juniper, mercury and arsenic, rivalled by the New World imports of coffee, tea, and tobacco.[60]

Tobacco also became popular in China as soon as it appeared in the late sixteenth century. The imperial army of the late Ming, during an expedition to Yunnan, was being reduced by marsh fevers—apart from one barrack block where all the soldiers were smoking tobacco. News of the medical properties of nicotine spread and prompted many ordinary people to start smoking.[61] In the hot, humid summers of the south, tobacco fumes were seen to be useful in fighting off 'miasmic diseases'. In Yunnan the local population used tobacco smoke and water to keep poison-ous snakes away. While their caravans rested at night, travelling merchants would light up water pipes filled with tobacco, and the remaining water would be spread around the site.[62] Tobacco was also widely used as a disinfectant, and its smoke was thought to have a beneficial influence on the mind.[63]

Before the advent of tobacco, betel nut was chewed by some population groups to ward off malaria. Zhu Gong, who served as a local official in southwest Hunan province in the eighteenth century, mentioned that the Miao chewed the leaves of the betel-pepper with the betel nut and lime as a recreational drug.[64] Tian Wen observed in the *Book of Guizhou*: 'When people encounter these conditions [of malaria] they hurriedly lie face-down on the ground, or chew betel nut, or else hold a piece of local sugar cane in their mouths, which gives them some chance of escaping.'[65] Du Zheng also recorded that travellers carried betel nut as a prophylactic.[66] Although evidence of the use of betel nut in the eighteenth and nineteenth centuries is lacking, it was probably superseded at least in part by tobacco and later opium in the fight against malaria.

Opium is a complex substance with dozens of alkaloids which have different pharmacological properties. Two in particular attrac-ted the attention of nineteenth-century physicians: 'morphine' and 'anarcotine', originally named 'narcotine' by its discoverer Derosne. While the former supplies the anodyne and hypnotic properties of the drug, narcotine is known to act as a palliative, abating the effects of malarial fever. The proportion of morphine and anarcotine varied according to specific types of opium. Turk-ish (Smyrna) opium was comparatively rich in morphine (12–15 per cent), whereas Indian (Bengal) opium had a higher percent-age of narcotine (4–8 per cent): both Patna and Benares, the most popular imports in China, had extremely low morphine content (2–3 or 4 per cent). Chinese opium also yielded low percentages of morphine (2.5 up to nearly 7 per cent), but in some cases contained up to 7.5 per cent of narcotine. The low morphine content of opium types affordable by the majority of smokers can be seen as one of the factors for the relatively low rate of dependence among them. Opium types with high yields of morphine were generally not imported into China (Turkish, Egyptian, French, German and American produce could contain as much as 20 per cent of morphine).[67] The smoking of narcotine-rich Indian opium in moderation was therefore highly commended by European observers such as H. N. Lay, formerly a customs official at Canton. Without it, Lay concluded, many water-bound populations would simply disappear.[68]

European physicians, clerics and public figures may well have questioned the tendency towards habit-forming, but the moderate use of opium was almost never queried.[69] Narcotine had gained a good reputation in India in the 1830s, when supplies of the potent anti-fever drug quinine were falling. Quinine, naturally present in the bark of the cinchona (also known as the 'Jesuit bark'), needed to be imported from the Andes, its only natural habitat, before being planted experimentally in the hills around Darjeeling.[70] Since the bark required costly processing, quinine was extremely expensive and could not be synthesised before the twentieth century.[71] The British medical administration therefore established experimental laboratories at Ghazipur and Patna, from which narcotine was despatched to medical depots throughout India.[72] Colonial surgeons preferred the remedial powers of the cinchona bark, and quinine soon became the preferred cure against malaria, cholera and other 'miasmic' diseases.[73] The rise of quinine shadowed the gradual decline of opium as the favoured remedy against fevers, the continued use of which among non-European peoples was observed with increasingly condemnatory comments.[74] However, this coincided with common practice in Europe: laudanum was openly available in shops in rural England, a business which provided trade for up to 26,000 shopkeepers.[75]

Until the first decades of the twentieth century opium would still have a staunch following among the medical community, being prescribed in particular 'in those wretched situations of combined poverty and disease, where wine cannot be purchased'.[76] European practitioners even conceded that the habitual opium eaters in Bengal enjoyed 'remarkable immunity from malarial infection'.[77]

Medical opinion was corroborated by medical practices among a variety of social categories in late imperial China, starting with government officials and the army. Malaria had long presented a serious threat to Qing officials posted in the south of the empire, and the high mortality rate for local representatives of the government was such a concern during the Qianlong period that magistrates who had survived an initial three-year post without any serious health problems were asked to extend their duties by another term. Similar preoccupations also existed in the army,[78] and soldiers often smoked opium before long marches to escape miasmic fevers.[79] Various reports and diaries from army officers suggest that opium was used by soldiers in southern China to relieve a whole range of illnesses.[80] It was also used in the imperial army to maintain morale on military campaigns.[81] In the provinces of Shanxi and Shaanxi, the imperial army was a major vector for the spread of opium smoking after the 1860s.[82]

Opium was also embraced by ordinary people as a fever suppressant in various parts of the country. In Hong Kong the local population was so convinced of the medical efficacy of opium that many would attach small plasters to their temples to act against headaches.[83] The same practice was reported by a senior medical official based in Xiamen.[84] Yan Shek-tsim, a shop owner in Canton and experienced smoker, even explained that the local farmers had extolled the virtues of the substance not only in alleviating rheumatism, but also in warding off malaria and fever.[85] One foreign resident in Canton was assured by his local friends that it was smoked not only 'for amusement' and 'to welcome guests', but also against malaria. Smoke was deemed all-important, and it was stated that 'Birdseye and manilla cigars have the same effect'.[86] According to vice-consul F. S. A. Bourne, opium was 'universally regarded as a prophylactic against malaria' in the south of China.[87] Alexander Hosie, travelling through Guangxi in 1883, took three teaspoons of quinine daily, while the locals smoked opium to protect themselves from malaria.[88] An anonymous French missionary who had lived in Canton for thirty years even remarked that opium smokers suffered less frequently from illnesses than those who abstained. Those who did not smoke ingested opiate-based pills instead.[89] Dr Alexander Rennie, a medical practitioner in Taiwan who was critical of recreational opium smoking, commended its use against feverish and rheumatic malaria. In cases where a painful death seemed certain, he thought it cruel to deny his patients the anodyne qualities of the drug.[90] It was generally assumed that labour-intensive work in rice paddies and sugar plantations in the malarial districts of the island was little short of impossible without opium—an argument opium proponents seized upon when the new Japanese rulers began to phase out its use.[91]

Even in the north of China opium was thought to have febrifugal and analgesic virtues. John Dudgeon, who had little direct experience of malaria, still observed that opium 'seemed prophylactic' and alleviated its symptoms, while 'in the absence of skilled physicians' it was used by a great number of commoners in Beijing to relieve pain.[92] Henry Cockburn, a British official in Beijing, commented on the similarities between smoking patterns in Europe and China. He concluded that the stronger nature of European tobacco made opium superfluous, while the Chinese faced the alternative between weak tobacco and the effects of opium.[93]

Chinese labourers earning their living in malarial regions of India or Southeast Asia usually took the habit of opium smoking as a prophylactic measure with them. Provided they remained physically active and well nourished, it was no immediate threat and could be regarded as a 'legitimate luxury'.[94] At least half of the labourers blazing the trail for the Burma Road during the early 1940s relied on opium smoking for its antispasmodic and analgesic effects.[95] Malnutrition, beri-beri, malaria and other subtropical diseases could immobilise up to one-third of the workforce, many of whom remained in a constant opium stupor. Whether to dull pain or to fight a range of illnesses endemic to this part of Asia, poor workers embraced opium with few qualms.[96] The opium smoked for self-medication complemented the official course of anti-malarial prophylactics (quinine pills containing atabrine) distributed by the company twice a week.[97] In the absence of the medical advances of the twentieth century—synthesised quinine, aspirin, penicillin—opium smoking continued to be simply 'the best possible and sure shield' against malaria.[98]

OPIUM AS A SOCIAL APHRODISIAC

Opium was described in the medical treatises of the late imperial period as 'medicine for the bedroom' (fangyao). This term is generally translated as 'aphrodisiac', meaning a substance capable of awakening or increasing sexual desire. However, available evidence indicates that opium was used less to stimulate or excite desire than to control and extend performance: after all, it is not an excitant but a sedative, and can be better described as an 'aid to sexual stamina' than as an 'aphrodisiac'. Opium is not even mentioned in the famous erotic novel Jin Ping Mei, suggesting that relatively few people used it for sexual purposes during the late Ming.[99] Li Shizhen (1518–93), on the other hand, reluctantly supported the claim that opium enhanced sex, noting that it was taken orally by some in the bedroom.[100] Medical treatises of the last third of the eighteenth century were much more explicit. According to Huang Guanxiu (1731–1818), writing in 1769, opium was used in the 'art of the bedroom' in an 'unrestrained and hasty way', whether or not any medical problem had been diagnosed. As we noted in an earlier chapter, the link between opium and sex probably contributed to the gradual shift after the 1760s from madak to pure opium. Although Huang did not specify whether the opium was eaten or smoked, his observation nonetheless reflected mounting concern from the end of the eighteenth century onwards over its use as an aid to sexual stamina.[101] Similar comments were made by medical contemporaries like Wu Yiluo (1704–66), who also mentioned the sale in the capital of a golden elixir (jindan) specifically designed for use in the bedroom.[102]

Opium's link to sex undoubtedly contributed to the success of narcotic culture in the nineteenth century. In China's more exclusive opium houses, it was often blended with other 'aphrodisiac' substances such as pearl powder and wild ginseng. For the male elite smoking utensils became sexual fetish objects, and these were often shaped like 'golden lily' feet or a woman's breasts. Opium houses also provided courtesans for smokers, while female entertainers in the many sing-song houses of the late Qing offered their customers the opium pipe. In Shanghai brothels were even called 'chambers of smoke and flowers' (*huayanjian* or *yanhuajian*).[103] Sex and opium also overlapped outside elite circles: the acting British consul at Danshui (Taiwan) estimated that around 70 per cent of ordinary smokers 'acquired the habit through associating with public women'.[104] Whether in the palace or the brothel, folk belief had it that opium impaired fertility and prolonged the performance.[105] Its habitual application in cases of syphilis and urological disorders further consolidated the sexual connotations of opium:[106] as late as 1935, more than 5 per cent of patients in a detoxification centre in Shanghai even claimed that smoking could cure spermatorrhoea.[107]

If opium became inextricably enmeshed with sex in elite and popular culture alike, most customers used it to calm rather than excite their desire. For inexperienced smokers who inhaled the fumes too quickly the result could be impotence. Moderate amounts, on the other hand, assuaged sexual desire and could enhance intercourse, either at home or in the brothel. Smokers were often aware of the sedative qualities of opium, using it to delay ejaculation and thus enhance pleasure.[108] In Europe too, writers such as Claude Farrère observed that 'opium calms virility and brings it under control'.[109] In some cases it could even be used to suppress desire altogether. The American surgeon Robert Coltman related the story of an old judge he had heard of when talking to local practitioners. Following the death of his wife, the judge had abstained from remarrying or taking a concubine and had kept his passions at bay for a decade by smoking opium, but having successfully abandoned his opium habit, his sexual desire returned with unprecedented violence. The story ends with the judge being so taken by the young courtesan he encountered along the way to the capital that he decided to marry her. If there is any truth in this story, opium has the property of counteracting sexual impulses.[110]

The sedative qualities of opium were confirmed by a report of the Royal Commission on Opium (1894–5) (discussed in much greater detail in the next chapter). While stressing that it could indeed increase male potency, the report also found that excess could lead to 'absolute sexual impotence after a brief period of super-excitation'.[111] When a group of Australian prostitutes expressed their views on opium and sex, all denied categorically that opium had been used by Chinese customers to dull their awareness ('A woman that smokes opium has always got her senses about her').[112] Asked about the alleged aphrodisiac qualities of opium, the women confirmed that Chinese customers tended to share the opium pipe with them. This did not so much stimulate as reduce sexual desire, if not completely killing it off: 'The man who has the opium habit is not like another man; he does not care for women.'[113]

The Commission's conclusion conforms to the available medical evidence, which indicates that opium has few harmful effects on the body, apart from inducing constipation and possibly impairing sexual capacity.[114] Heroin, another opiate substance, also reduces the level of sexual activity.[115] The aphrodisiac qualities of opium, in short, are more myth than fact. Peter Lee attacks the popular link between opium and sex:

Opium does not prompt the smoker to wild behaviour or extravagant sexual orgies, as many uninitiated Western commentators have reported. The mistaken view that opium works as a potent aphrodisiac probably stems from the fact that brothels in China often offered it to their customers on request, while many opium houses provided prostitutes to smokers who asked for them. In fact, men in brothels sometimes smoked a few pipes of opium before sex to cool the heat of their desire, so that they could better control themselves during the act, not to fire up their libidos.[116]

The author backs up this claim by referring to the reminiscences of individual smokers, such as the septuagenarian Laotian-Chinese owner of an opium establishment, who confessed that he first began smoking 'for sex... to play with young ladies'. 'Three pipes of opium', he concluded, were sufficient to have sex 'all night with the same girl, or with many different girls because it is very easy to control himself.'[117]

Customers in both dens and brothels, of course, could also gamble, although gambling would hardly be considered to be an 'aphrodisiac': historians have tended to characterise the activities which took place in these social spaces by reference to a single, stark and uncompromising word in English, namely 'sex', a tendency reflected in the use of such terms as 'aphrodisiac', 'prostitute' and 'brothel'. 'Sex', however, was not necessarily the only desired outcome for male customers, who may not have perceived it as an activity as discrete and distinct from other forms of leisure as the modern notion of 'sex' implies, although sexual intercourse undoubtedly played an important role in recreational activities. Female servants employed by brothels regarded the preparation of opium pipes as part of their work as much as massaging and the serving of tea—and they often enjoyed their regular smoke.[118] Social intercourse in a relaxed environment was the principal aim pursued in such activities as gambling, smoking, snacking or drinking, and female entertainers could help achieve these goals. Opium was a relaxant which could help male customers unwind in female company.[119]

The social anxieties projected on opium by political elites included fear of sexual license, attributing to the benign paste dark powers out of all proportion to its actual properties: some opium smokers keen to control their sexual performance better may well have shared this conviction. Late imperial China was awash with medical therapies designed to increase sexual power:[120] remedies to replenish the *yin* (*ziyin*), tonics to invigorate the *qi* (*yangqi*), prescriptions to nourish the kidney (*bushen*), medications to give tone to the blood (*buxue*): medical authors of the Ming and Qing constantly warned against abuse of tonics and indulgence in aphrodisiacs. Spermatorrhoea (*huajing*), premature ejaculation (*zaoxie*) and nocturnal emissions (*mengyi*) were some of the pathological categories constructed by medical discourse in order to enforce a message of restraint. In a patrilineal culture which revolved around the production of healthy sons, a disciplined practice of sexual intercourse and a balanced approach to food were deemed to have the potential to increase a person's generative power, prolonging life and multiplying one's descendants. By contrast, as health manuals continuously warned, over-indulgence and abuse would turn a potent weapon into a baneful force, leading to a depletion of vital forces, a waste of bodily substances, debilitating disorders, and ultimately to early death. Death of the self and death of the lineage: according to Wang Yanchang, aphrodisiacs (*chunfangyao*) were destructive and capable of killing a male and extinguishing a line of descent.[121] This alarmist rhetoric, as well as the alleged dangers of a whole range of aphrodisiacs, was also projected on to opium. In late imperial China sexual performance and generative power were overdetermined markers of social status, and it is not unlikely that they produced male anxieties which contributed to various sexual disorders, calling in turn for the use of opium: this hypothesis remains to be analysed by cultural historians.[122]

Regardless of the actual pharmacological properties of opiate substances, users might have profound faith in their sexual powers. Opium smoking by male customers in brothels should be seen as a social ritual which removed the customary restraints on sexual behaviour. As Michael Gossop has argued, the trust which consumers place in aphrodisiacs can be so strong that it effectively conditions them, some responses to placebos being more powerful than those to active drugs. Opium, like oysters, was no different.[123]

6

WAR ON DRUGS: PROHIBITION AND THE RISE OF NARCOPHOBIA (*c.* 1880–1940)

The previous chapters have questioned the image of China as the victim of a 'drug plague' by showing that opium was a culturally privileged intoxicant generally smoked in moderate amounts for recreational and medical reasons without any 'loss of control'. If smoking was a socially sanctioned practice with few adverse consequences, how could prohibition campaigns succeed in demonising it within such a short space of time? Rather than focus only on the pharmacological properties of psychoactive substances, historians should question the premises of narcophobic discourse and analyse the politics of prohibition. Until recently, in Europe as well as China, homosexuality was widely perceived as a medical aberration and a form of deviant sexual behaviour which threatened to undermine social order and corrupt young people, while masturbation was defined as a potentially lethal disease to be eradicated at all cost: the explanation for these anxieties cannot be found in the nature of these sexual preferences themselves, but in the social values and political choices which structure the discursive formations purporting to contain them.[1] As Thomas Szasz has argued, the difference between substance use and 'medical addiction' is not one of mere fact, but a matter of moral attitude and political strategy: with the decline of religious values, medical values instead are increasingly used to persecute individuals and social groups defined as 'unfit', 'unhealthy' or 'contaminated'.[2] 'War on drugs' allowed political leaders and social elites to invent a fictive enemy on to whom social anxieties could be projected: narcophobia created a scapegoat. Opium represented both the

enemy within—the morally depraved and physically weak addict—and the enemy outside—conniving foreign powers bent on
enslaving the country. Opium became the rallying point around
which social unity could be asserted, as both addicts and imperialists emerged as the ultimate alter ego against which national
identity could be defined. The addict literally embodied all that
was negative: physically decrepit, morally weak, a slave to both
opium and the imperialists who peddled it. Nationalism would
liberate the country from the oppression of foreign powers, and
nothing symbolised the iron grip of dependence under which the
country was alleged to have fallen better than opium.

The image of China as victim of an 'opium plague' spread
during the last decades of the nineteenth century as a variety of
interests intersected to replicate it in different social contexts: nationalists in China were eager to find a scapegoat in imperialism
and emphasised the catastrophic results of the opium trade, while
local missionaries and campaigning journalists published sensational reports portraying China as a victim of gunboat policy.[3] The
anti-opium movement also spread rapidly in Europe thanks to
notions of 'race' current by the end of the nineteenth century.
Opium was an Oriental poison behind the Chinese menace, as opium dens in Chinatowns in Britain and the United States threatened to contaminate the West, with young white girls being
ravished by sinister Orientals in these squalid places of sexual de-
pravity and degenerate racial mixing. China was infiltrating the
West, taking its revenge on its white persecutors by spreading the
drug plague. Opium became synonymous with the Yellow Peril.
Some of the first bans which appeared in the United States in the
1870s specifically prevented Chinese immigrants from using opium, as distinct from the rest of the population who were allowed
unrestricted access to it. In China, on the other hand, opium was
represented after 1895 as a racial poison spread by white people:
by turning the descendants of the Yellow Emperor into selfish addicts who lacked the will to stand up for their country, opium
smoking was leading to 'racial extinction' (*miezhong*). This image,
extrapolated from indigenous fears of 'lineage extinction' (*miezu*)
in a patrilineal culture which emphasised the need for male off-

spring, was seized upon by reformers after 1895: 'red barbarians' (*hongyi*) in America and other 'darker breeds' in the Pacific were seen as harbingers of racial decline.[4] The notion of race was also given legitimacy by the role of alcohol in the 'extinction' of native peoples in America: the idea that some societies could be destroyed by exposure to spirits gave credibility to the idea that China could be wiped out by opium.[5]

The disease theory of addiction further reinforced the movement towards prohibition. Before the 1870s excessive cravings were thought, in Europe as well as in China, to result from moral failure rather than chemical dependence: the excessive smoker was an opium sot rather than an 'opium addict'. The second half of the nineteenth century saw the rise of the medical profession, and newly-created medical associations sought moral authority and legal power by transforming opium from a folk remedy into a controlled substance. The germ theory in particular enabled medical experts to portray it as a dangerous poison which they alone were qualified to administer in controlled dosages. Medical associations vigorously pursued a monopoly over the opium supply, legal sanctions against opium trafficking and statutory rights to treat 'opium addicts', and addiction became a growth industry for the medical profession. New notions of an 'opium plague' and a 'drug contamination' also nicely dovetailed with the moral arguments advanced by anti-opium societies in the last third of the nineteenth century: the former enabled the latter to reach a much larger audience and obtain wider public support.[6] As Mike Jay has shown, while opium did not change in itself, the world around it gradually did, as the substance became a scapegoat in the politics of nationalism, a vector of racial anxieties, a bone of contention in a professional struggle against self-medication and the very foundation of a new disease theory of addiction.[7]

This chapter looks at the rise of anti-opium discourse and the image of the 'addict' among foreign missionaries and political elites in China, which culminated in the various prohibition laws passed between 1904 and 1935. Several studies have focused unilaterally on the prohibitionist arguments advanced by Protestant missionaries and anti-opium societies in Britain and America, as if opposition to the opium trade was a natural and inevitable development;[8] the first sections in this chapter highlight instead how different confessional communities in China came up with a considerable diversity of opinion. Moreover, the Royal Commission on Opium has hardly ever been mentioned by China scholars: set up in 1892 to lead a public inquiry into the opium question, its conclusions in favour of the trade demonstrate that even at the end of the nineteenth century, evidence in favour of the notion of an 'opium plague' in China was scattered at best. The next chapter looks at the concrete medical practices and legal structures put in place to 'cure' all smokers in the wake of prohibition. The history of the anti-opium movement has already received a disproportionate amount of scholarly attention;[9] this chapter and the following one do not focus again on questions of policy and implementation. They aim instead to provide a critical analysis of narcophobic discourse and an in-depth examination of the social costs of government attempts to police the bloodstream of the nation.

'THE HORRORS': MISSIONARY DEBATES ON PROHIBITION

The widespread use of opium for medical purposes up to the late nineteenth century left little scope for critical opinion. In Europe even recreational opium eating faced only occasional opposition.[10] An early opponent of the opium trade was R. Montgomery Martin, member of the Hong Kong Legislative Council in the 1840s. He spoke admiringly of the strict stance adopted by Qing officials, and compared their restrictive attitude to the laissez-faire spirit of Hong Kong.[11] Martin used customs statistics showing a steady increase in the tonnage of imported opium as evidence that China was falling victim to a foreign threat. In what became central to anti-opium discourse, he declared that 'Those who begin its use at twenty may expect to die at thirty years of age: the countenance becomes pallid; the eyes assume a wild brightness, the memory fails, the gait totters, mental exertion and moral courage sink, and a frightful marasmus or atrophy reduces the victim to a ghastly spectacle, who has ceased to live before he has ceased to exist.'[12] Martin was also the first to consider the slave trade 'merciful' in comparison with the opium trade, a view repeated by Karl Marx in 1858 and upheld by historians in the People's Republic of China to this day.[13]

Martin's views were not widespread, as most observers compared the trade in opium to that in strong spirits.[14] Some used the spectre of gin-infested London street life as an antidote to the perceived opium scare:

Let any unprejudiced European walk through the native towns of Java, Singapore or China', argued the botanist G. F. Davidson in the 1840s, 'and see if he can find a single drunken native… What he *will* meet with are numbers of drunken English, Scotch and Irish seamen, literally rolling in the gutter, intoxicated, not from opium, but from rum and other spirits sent all the way from England… I would recommend the well-intentioned persons who have of late been raising such an outcry on the subject of opium, to begin at home, and attempt to reform their own countrymen: they may then come to China with a clear conscience, and preach reform to the poor opium-smoker.[15]

Davidson concluded that 'the Chinese are just as capable of taking care of themselves as their would-be guardians are'. The view that opium smoking was a more benign equivalent of the drinking culture found in Europe remained prevalent until the last two decades of the nineteenth century.

Missionary societies became increasingly critical of the medical and recreational uses of opium during the second half of the nineteenth century. However, most of the existing scholarship has focused narrowly on Protestant missionaries from Britain and America: it is claimed that 'missionaries of the Catholic Church in China were generally not active in the anti-opium movement'.[16] Historians have discarded the vast archives left by other confessional denominations and mined the Protestant literature instead for evidence of opposition to the opium trade, portraying missionaries as enlightened crusaders leading the fight against the 'opium evil'. We show that some Protestant missionaries hardly ever mentioned opium at all while their Catholic counterparts expressed critical views as early as in the 1850s: missionary opposition to opium was not a natural and inevitable development, but the result of dispersed, ambivalent and sometimes contradictory attitudes which would crystallise only at the end of the century.

In an early petition to Rome, the missionary Angelo Argenti called for a stricter policy of prohibition in 1852, presenting an image of the opium addict which would become common a few decades later:

A pale and horribly emaciated expression deforms the faces of those who are in the grasp of the opium habit. Their senses are brutalised and eradicated, their memory becomes lost, leading to the greatest stupidity; the entire complexion becomes livid, the eyes languid and the appetite greatly reduced, except for very sugary food; sleep is neither refreshing nor cooling, because these poor wretches can only long for the feeling of fire and dryness in their guts during times of quietness, which only the opium can produce. If no opium can be procured, all willpower disappears completely, water begins to flow out of eyes and nostrils, the body is trembling with cold, chest and head hurting from horrendous pain. Soon this is followed by diarrhoea and—if no opium is available—often death after a few days. Such is the nature of the opium habit that… not even the most minute amount of work can be done, families cannot be sustained and therefore nothing but misery and crime come in consequence.[17]

While the first 'position paper' of the Holy See on opium already urged extreme caution on Catholic missionaries in 1830,[18] the latter continued to be marked by 'a plurality of opinion' even in the final quarter of the nineteenth century.[19] The 'instructions' of 1878 and 1891 called upon missionaries to be flexible towards all Christians involved in the opium trade, in particular poor farmers who relied on opium cultivation for their livelihood.[20] Mounting pressure towards prohibition yielded an official reaction from the Roman Catholic Church, which in 1892 convened a special Conference on Opium.[21] Having weighed the arguments of the prohibitionists and their opponents, the Conference decided to enact an earlier resolution of 1878, which called for 'vigilance' and defence of moral standards, while allowing priests to be lenient to parishioners who merely purchased opium for 'moderate' personal use.[22] Having devoted considerable attention to the 'uses' and 'culture' of opium during the late Qing, the clerical advisers did not fail to draw attention to the imperial prohibition (in particular the Guangxu edict of 29 December 1891) which was regarded as legally binding even though missionaries were not subject to local laws.[23] Nevertheless, despite a consensus in favour of a restrictive policy towards opium in areas dominated by Catholic missionaries, many participants seemed to share the opinion that opium was an integral part of social life and that in small quantities its possession and even commercial use could be condoned. Citing evidence from medical experts both at home and in China,[24] opium was regarded as 'a mild stimulant', the effects of which depended on the physical tolerance of the individual user.[25] Some clerics even objected to publication of the relatively tolerant resolution of 1878, fearing that local Christians would lose their respect for Rome's authority or abandon the Church altogether if outright prohibition were endorsed.[26]

Those advocating outright condemnation had to convince a sceptical audience that opium was qualitatively different from alcohol. Their main argument focused less on the physical damage allegedly caused by smoking than on the moral consequences of the habit—lethargy, lack of appetite and negligence of duties being cited as great social dangers.[27] A compromise emerged when the delegates decided to condemn dependence on opium rather than habitual use of it.[28] The conference also opposed the wholesale trafficking of opium, whether by foreign traders or by local merchants.[29] Although the conference prohibited any missionary from supporting the cultivation of poppies, the 'Rome Formula' specified that ordinary opium planters would still be entitled to receive the sacraments.[30]

The opium debate should not divert attention from the fact that throughout the late nineteenth century, missionary discourse continued to identify religious issues—superstition, apostasy and persecution—as topics of predominant concern, rather than malnourishment or the effects of habitual smoking. Even letters sent by Catholic missions from areas with a rich opium culture such as Sichuan rarely went beyond condemning social 'vices' occasionally reported in the context of the opium habit.[31] A letter by

Jacques Léonard Perocheau, titular bishop of Maxula and Apostolic Vicar of Sichuan, contained a detailed enumeration of China's vices, including idolatry, infanticide, brutality, materialism and greed, as well as indifference towards the poor and starving—but failed to mention opium even once.[32] Only occasionally did opium smoking create such concern among medical missionaries that the problem of physical dependence was publicly discussed. In sum, it is far from the truth to state that opposition to opium smoking was firm among foreign missionaries during the second half of the nineteenth century.

However, by the end of the century advocates of a more critical stance would soon become dominant among medical missionaries. China became a missionary battlefield, opium the chief enemy. The image of 300 million souls hopelessly enslaved by the 'pernicious drug' represented a powerful tool in legitimising missionary activities. The ubiquitous opium habit was seen as 'one of the devil's chief agents to bind the people to himself and blind their minds to the glorious gospel of Christ'.[33] Opium smoking was 'an extraordinary and most gigantic obstacle to the reception of the Gospel and the spread of it among the Chinese',[34] and when practised habitually was interpreted as a disease rooted 'deep down in the soil of the Chinese nature', which kept 'hundreds of millions of people bound in absolute slavery'. The only salvation, according to the missionary T. Windsor, was faith in Christ as the divine healer and belief in the Gospel as the 'ultimate panacea'.[35] The opium habit as a 'disease of the will' thus offered a useful vehicle for Christian proselytisation.

From the 1880s onwards a vocal faction of opponents increasingly portrayed opium as an agent of insidious compulsion to be eliminated at all cost. The China Medical Missionary Association was one that firmly attacked the 'immorality' inherent in the opium habit in 1889: 'Everyone who knows anything on the subject', the editors of the *Chinese Medical Missionary Journal* argued, 'cannot but condemn the habit as a vicious one, not only for its injurious effects upon the habitué himself, but also for the misery it brings upon others who are dependent upon the opium smoker for the necessaries of life. Even the "heathen Chinese" look upon the opium smoker with contempt.'[36] By marshalling evidence gathered by members of the association, the editors rejected the more permissive attitude of an older generation of doctors ('twenty or thirty years ago'), concluding that 'We have a good many hundreds of opium smokers pass through our hands, and, as far as our experience goes, there is no great danger to life from cutting off opium at once. It is followed, however... by great depression and restlessness, diarrhoea..., nausea, sometimes vomiting and anorexia, sleeplessness... seminal emission, and a general feeling of misery and wretchedness which is aptly called the "horrors".'[37] However, the views of medical missionaries found little support among the health authorities in foreign concessions. The Health Department of the Shanghai Municipal Council had to deal with many cases of death due to alcoholism among foreign residents. It concluded in 1901 that 'in comparison with Alcohol the evil wrought by indulgence in opium is trivial.'[38]

RESISTING CULTURAL IMPERIALISM: THE ROYAL COMMISSION ON OPIUM

In 1874 a group of Quaker reformers in London formed the Society for the Suppression of the Opium Trade to lobby the government for the complete prohibition of opium production and consumption in India.[39] Their campaign was soon joined by other dissenting churches, including Methodists, Presbyterians and Unitarians, all embracing the anti-opium cause, convoking meetings and organising mass petitions against what was perceived to be a pernicious substance. After the veteran W. E. Gladstone led the Liberal Party back to power in 1892, a Royal Commission was set up to lead a public inquiry into the 'opium question'. Seven British and two Indian members were appointed to it, including two pro-opium members with links to the Government of India and two avowedly anti-opium reformers. The Society for the Suppression of the Opium Trade was satisfied with its composition and even commented that it was 'as fair-minded and impartial a tribunal as we could have desired to hear our case'.[40]

The Commission gathered evidence from secular practitioners, medical missionaries, international traders and civil servants

with detailed knowledge of India and China. While the commissioners clearly sympathised with the more moderate opinions of
the older generation of practitioners, the papers they presented
show that they withheld any hint of a firm opinion. The privilege of expressing a binding verdict was reserved for the two
Houses of Parliament, to which the final evidence was presented.

Although the Commission intended to cover the entire sphere
of British influence in Asia, most of the evidence referred to India, where opium was ingested rather than smoked. The standard
reported effects of this practice were constipation, with bowel
movements down to once per week; emaciation, with body weight
reduced by about 10 kilos compared to non-consumers; starvation caused by the inability of the digestive tract to absorb nutrients and a generally weakened vitality—exposing the habitual
smoker to disease and exhaustion, and ultimately death.[41] Such
classifications coincided with alarmist calls against the perceived
opium evil by many missionaries, such as George T. Lay of the
British and Foreign Bible Society, who perpetuated the image of
the typical opium smoker 'with his lank and shrivelled limbs,
tottering gait, sallow visage, feeble voice, and death-boding glance
of the eye'[42]—a description dismissed as fantasy by visitors who
observed that the tendency to smoke often appeared among people who were already ill or physically exhausted.[43]

While the opinions of opium prohibitionists would eventually
prevail, supporters of the substance abound throughout the report. The medical officer Hunter Corbett summarised the main
reasons for smoking opium: 1, to relieve pain; 2, against depression and boredom; 3, for social diversion; 4, at home as a welcome
ritual; and 5, as 'fuel' at the brothel-dens so popular among young
men.[44] Timothy Richard, resident in China for two decades and
known as having liberal opinions, confirmed that social and medical reasons were behind the habitual smoking of opium, but was
adamant that for the poor it was a necessity: 'In Shansi, the poverty of the people is such that they try to live on very coarse food,
much of it being only fit for beasts.' Opium was indispensable to
deal with the consequential indigestion.[45] Even critical observers
commented that it was effective in reducing pain induced by

chronic ailments, such as dysentery and rheumatism.[46] Other foreign physicians and residents admired the effects of opium on ulcers, gangrene, diarrhoea, asthma and pneumonia.[47] Andrew Hosie, medical officer at Mhow in western Malwa, concluded that opium was 'the gift of God to man' for its many medical uses, but that misuse had turned it from 'a blessing to a curse'.[48]

When the commissioners met for their final meeting in Bombay they concluded that opium prohibition was neither necessary nor wanted by the Indians themselves, that the British government should not interfere in its production and consumption in the Indian princely states, and that its use in India did not cause any 'extensive moral or physical degradation': 'the habit is generally practised in moderation, and... when so practised injurious effects are not apparent.'[49] While the report was predictably attacked for bias in favour of the Government of India, two historians have recently analysed the mass of evidence presented to the Commission. John Richards believes that the conclusions reached by the Royal Commission (by and large identical to those of the Government of India) were more in tune with popular Indian opinion than the demands of the opium reformers. 'Ironically', the author concludes, 'the colonial government of India found itself resisting a virulent form of cultural imperialism from Britain.'[50] Richard Newman, in his meticulous research on the role of medical opium in colonial India, concludes that the anti-opium position of the medical missionaries was driven by ideological rather than scientific considerations, and that the Royal Commission's final opinion, that individual consumption patterns rather than the substance itself determined whether opium was problematic, was fundamentally correct.[51] Although both historians are specialists of India rather than of China, the region which the Commission was explicitly asked to examine, the evidence from China presented in the preceding chapters entirely endorses this view.

The conclusion of the Royal Commission on Opium was to be vigorously contested by a mounting tide of opinion in favour of prohibition. Under a new Liberal government a motion was passed in the House of Commons in 1905 stipulating that the trade in opium to China, which was 'morally indefensible', be brought to an end.[52] However, by this time opium had already become a scapegoat in the politics of nationalism in China.

NATIONALISM AND PROHIBITION IN LATE IMPERIAL CHINA

The disease model of addiction only appeared in Europe in the 1870s as part of the medical profession's search for moral authority, legal control and statutory power over pharmaceutical substances in their fight against a popular culture of self-medication: where 'opium sots' were previously seen to suffer from a moral flaw, 'opium addicts' were now increasingly described as hopeless victims in the grip of a chemical dependence which the medical professional only was entitled to cure. In China the notion of 'addiction' developed gradually during the late imperial period. Medical writers had always considered opium as no different from other potent medications: it had few harmful side effects when applied in moderation but could kill if used to excess. During the mid-Qing, however, the character *yin* started to denote a 'craving' or 'habit' as part of official concerns about the moral and fiscal dangers of opium. The notion that habitual opium smoking ruined individual health and family life can be traced back to the importation bans of the late eighteenth century. The renowned poet Yu Jiao (1796–1820) described *yin* as a craving for opium and as a chronic condition associated with habitual smoking:

There is no big harm if [opium] is smoked occasionally. However, if one smokes regularly, it will affect the heart and spleen. If one becomes ill after not smoking for a single day, this condition is called *yin*. When the *yin* comes, the nose and eyes start to run, whereas the hands and the feet become stiff and clenched. It feels like facing a dagger while a tiger is chasing one from behind—fearful yet unable to surrender. A chronic opium smoker ends up with shrunken shoulders and neck; his face becomes wan and he is without energy, just like a sick person.[53]

Another interesting reference to opium craving appeared at official level in an 1831 report to the Daoguang emperor. Liu Guangsan, an inspector from the Board of Military Affairs, referred to habitual smoking as *yin*: 'I hear that a long-term opium smoker tends to become ill, a condition called *yin*. He must take opium regularly to satisfy his *yin*. When deprivation brings on the *yin*, his body becomes weary (*weidun*), his eyes and nose start running (*tisi jiaoxia*), and he becomes absolutely desperate. Once he takes a few puffs, he immediately comes back to life and is full of spirit.'[54] Yu Jiao and Liu Guangsan used different characters to write the term *yin*, showing a semantic instability which would only disappear in the mid-nineteenth century. The lexicographer Lei Jin explained the confusion surrounding the term:

Smokers must resort to the pipe at regular times each day, otherwise their blood circulation stops and their limbs suffer. In severe cases their noses and eyes run constantly and they sneeze continuously. This is commonly referred to as having a 'craving' (*yin*). According to the *Jiyun* ('A collection of sayings'), '*yin* is a rash or lump on the skin'. It does not seem to have anything to do with opium smoking. The poet Wei Moshen mistakenly used the character *yin*, which according to the *Shuowen jiezi* means 'scars caused by wounds or sores'. Again, there seems to be no connection with the problems caused by opium smoking. The so-called 'opium craving' (*yanyin*) is of very recent coinage, hence the lack of a fixed written expression.[55]

The notion of 'craving' was closely connected to the politics of prohibition. Lin Zexu, as we saw in an earlier chapter, was one of the most prominent voices among a minority of government officials opposed to the opium trade. As the court envoy who initiated the first Sino-British War in 1839, he entrusted the medical expert He Qiwei (1774–1837) with the task of developing a theory which could account for opium craving:

Opium is a strong poison with a bitter and harsh taste, which enters… the liver and kidneys. Each inhalation makes it penetrate the flesh, meridian channels (*jingluo*) and bones; with each exhalation, it evaporates into the skin and hair, reaching every part of the human body, until… one eventually succumbs to it. Occasional use (*jian*) becomes regular (*chang*), and ultimately habitual (*shou*). Once dependent, all the internal organs and meridian channels and all the external parts of the body, including the eyes, the ears, the toes and the fingers, can only function through continued smoking. Without it, the kidneys become deficient and one starts to sneeze. Eventually, the liver becomes exhausted, the eyes and nose stream, and the lungs become ill and produce phlegm. Finally, the heart becomes weary, the body exudes perspiration… and if [opium smoking] is not abandoned, death becomes imminent.[56]

Similar theories rapidly spread during the Sino-British War, as opium emerged as a justification for war on foreign powers. Opponents of opium underlined the poisonous (*du*) nature of the substance which could culminate in incurable 'opium diseases' (*yingshuzhang*).[57] Yu Zhengxie (1775–1840), a major scholar noted for his strong interest in research and his liberal ideas, also hypothesised around 1830 that the craving was related to withdrawal from opium itself: 'Recently I learnt that medicinal opium can damage the lungs… which become overheated, causing the user to suffer from *yin*… When the smoke enters the liver and kidneys, it produces acid which can stop diarrhoea and reduce the appetite. When the smoke travels upwards, it changes its nature from *yin* into *yang*, thus lifting the spirit. After having penetrated the entire body, its effect is diminished. When used regularly, the smoker begins to feel exhausted—this is the so-called *yin* effect.'[58]

Yin could also be combined with *pi*, meaning a craving, a fondness, a propensity for a particular activity, whether book collecting or wine drinking: *shangyin chengpi* became the standard formula for translating the notion of 'addiction' from English into Chinese from the 1870s onwards. As in French, however, no clear medical equivalent existed for 'addiction', strong habits being described instead as 'cravings', 'habits' or 'dependencies' (dépendence, habitude, accoutumance). Even in English the terms 'opium habit', 'opium poisoning' or 'narcotic poisoning' continued to prevail well into the 1920s, even among the medical experts working in foreign hospitals in the international concession of Shanghai. In the Shanghai General Hospital the terms 'addict' and 'addiction' appeared for the first time in the annual report of 1934.[59]

While these early medical theories contributed to the stigmatisation of opium in political circles opposed to the opium trade in the decades following the first Sino-British War, few leading officials advocated an outright ban on opium before the country's defeat against Japan in 1894–5. After the devastation caused by the Taiping rebellion (1851–64) and other mid-century popular upheavals, opium taxation and a government monopoly were envisaged by a number of high officials as useful financial tools in reconstructing the countryside. Zhang Zhidong conceded that opium taxes could be used to finance a modernisation programme a few years after the disaster of the Boxer Rebellion (1900). Li Hongzhang consistently advocated opium taxation to finance special projects, from the repayment of loans in 1862 to the purchase of a steamship in 1891. Wang Tao, himself a smoker, adopted a policy of foreign opium taxation and increased poppy cultivation to enrich the country, whereas Zeng Guoquan switched from a call for total prohibition to the use of opium taxes for foreign policy initiatives by the late 1880s.[60] Considering the huge contribution of opium taxation to the national treasuries of some countries, and the extent to which official monopolies over opium or tobacco financed government institutions in yet other parts of the world, there can be little doubt that the course of China's history would have been profoundly different had it not switched towards a disastrous policy of strict prohibition after the Sino-Japanese War of 1894–5.

Chapter 3 showed how few government officials favoured a frontal attack on the opium trade in the decade before the first Sino-British War in view of the enormous practical problems of implementing such a policy. The reasons for the calamitous decision to wage war on opium was closely linked to internal court politics, in particular tensions between Han officials and Manchu aristocrats, as the former successfully turned opium prohibition into a political agenda. Confucian scholars not only saw it as their mission to express their concern over moral decay and an alleged breakdown in social order, but also hoped to regain the position of collective power and moral authority they had enjoyed before the conquest of the empire by the Manchus. A similar explanation lies behind the rhetorical switch towards rigid prohibition after the Sino-Japanese War of 1894–5: scholars viewed themselves as the moral vanguard alarmed at the fate of the empire in order to obtain influence at court, posing as the sole experts of foreign affairs capable of reforming the country. The reformers sought to overthrow the political leadership and moral authority of the traditional elites by appealing to foreign systems of knowledge: evolutionary theory, constitutional reform, human rights and industrial development were among the many ideas selectively appropriated by a number of leading scholars. Many of the most influential advocates of reform such as Liang Qichao (1873–1929) and Yan Fu (1853–1921) had failed to pass the traditional examination system and took the defeat against Japan as an opportunity to present themselves as the carriers of new knowledge more attuned to the needs of a new age. They briefly managed to implement a series of reforms with the support of the Guangxu emperor during the Hundred Days Reform of 1898 before the Empress Dowager seized control at the palace in Beijing. However, their ideas would became highly influential, disseminated by numerous reform journals in a new style of writing accessible to a much larger audience.

In search of wealth and power, the 1898 reformers aimed to eliminate what they viewed as imperial markers of 'backwardness', in particular opium-smoking and foot-binding.[61] Zheng Guanying thought that the poppy destroyed agriculture, while opium impoverished the commoner, depraved the official and weakened the farmer.[62] He depicted opium as a 'natural disaster' (*tianhuo*) and a 'chronic illness' (*guji*) undermining the nation.[63] Guo Songtao, a Qing diplomat who led a number of delegations to Europe, condemned smoking as a degenerate habit which inevitably encouraged its devotees to neglect their duties: farmers abandoned their fields, merchants cheated each other in commercial transactions, and young people were left rudderless, leading to destroyed homes and eventually the end of the country itself.[64] Yan Fu, the first scholar to introduce Darwin and Spencer to a Chinese readership in the 1890s, echoed these views. He regarded opium—together with female footbinding—as one of the principal reasons for the nation's weakness: if China was to be strong again, it had to reform and tackle the opium problem.[65] His ideas were widely shared by the social reformers and political elites who expressed concern over the fate of the empire in journals and newspapers such as the *Dongfang zazhi* (Eastern Miscellany) and the *Shenbao* (Shanghai News), which attacked opium as 'the poison (*du*), which weakens the country and drains the people's wealth. [China] is loosing its vitality by the day and is on the edge of extinction.'[66] The image of China as the 'sick man of East Asia' (*Dongya bingfu*) and the anti-opium discourse deployed by foreign missionaries were appropriated by modernizing elites to give their message of reform a sense of heightened urgency:

Since the opium poison began to flow throughout China's vast expanses, gentry and merchants, labourers and officials alike have been weakened to the extent that 60 to 70 per cent can no longer extricate themselves [from the habit]… Their lives fall drop by drop into the opium box, and their souls flicker away in the light of the opium lamp. Smoking scholars are unable to engage in academic pursuits. There is no prospect of defeating enemies as soldiers have taken to the pipe, while neither workers nor merchants who smoke can expect to prosper. Those entrusted with important duties struggle to stay alive. When stung, they feel no pain; when kicked, their wilted bones fail to rise. Since most of our countrymen wreck themselves by smoking opium, they represent our nation—a listless nation. In order to become a constitutional country and to unite our depleted people there is no alternative [but to prohibit opium]. To prevent worse to come, we have first to realise with sadness that in this world our race is the lowest.[67]

Peddled by imperialist powers, insinuating itself into the bloodstream of the nation, poisoning the minds and bodies of the country's millions, opium gradually emerged as a symbol of national weakness, the cause of a massive 'failure of the will'. It was the 'poison' used by the evil Other to destroy the 'race', and only its elimination could lead to a national revival: in 1906 the *Shenbao* stated that 'after opium is eliminated there will be a New China'.[68] Just as the missionary became the emblematic figure of a foreign religion, opium was the epitome of imperialist power.

The imperial reformers failed to secure the power necessary to implement their vision of change, but their demonisation of 'opium' as the principal cause of 'racial' decline and 'moral' turpitude became mainstream with the New Policies initiated after the Boxer Rebellion. The perceived inability to respond to the foreign domination of the opium trade, its effects—imagined or genuine—on the tottering Qing dynasty, and the increasing international pressure against the opium trade supported those parties that advocated a renewed ban. The Qing administration was far from inactive, negotiating separately with the foreign powers which had interests in China. A number of bilateral treaties were concluded after 1900, first with France in September 1900, followed by a Commercial Treaty with Britain in September 1902, an opium treaty with Germany in October 1903 and one regulating the opium trade with Portugal.[69] The Guangxu edict of 1906 prohibited the smoking of opium and paved the way to the Sino-British Ten Year Agreement of 1907, outlawing the importation of opium from overseas.[70]

The anti-opium movement has been interpreted as the only genuine success of the late Qing reforms by a number of recent historians, who have remained entirely oblivious of the medical and social consequences of prohibition, analysed in the following chapters.[71] The campaign aimed at the complete suppression of opium use by attempting to impose restrictions on both supply and demand. Poppy plantations were to be surveyed and reduced over a period of nine years to eliminate public availability. The market was attacked by a strict policy of closure of opium houses, the registration and licensing of habitual users and the participation of smokers under sixty years of age in replacement therapy.[72] Soldiers, officials and students all had to undertake to comply with the new legislation. Decrees were issued which gave regional officials extraordinary powers to implement the new policy. Particularly forceful campaigns against opium were led in Yunnan by Xi Liang and in Zhili by Yuan Shikai. By the end of the 1910s several provinces, including Shanxi, Shandong and Sichuan as well as Manchuria, reported significant progress in the eradication of poppy plantations.

China's anti-opium campaign unfolded well before similar policies were pursued in Europe and the United States: the Qing waged the world's first war on drugs, becoming the initial link in a chain of anti-drug campaigns which would gradually cover the globe in the twentieth century. In 1906 China formally declared a ten-year opium suppression plan with the support of the United States. The foreign powers were so impressed with the achievements during the initial test period that the ten-year agreement was renewed in 1911. The Qing administration, possibly with the Younghusband expedition to Tibet in mind, may also have realised that such an internationally prominent position would make the empire less vulnerable to further territorial encroachment.[73] The reinvigorated treaty gave Chinese officials the right to monitor—though not to veto—opium shipments in Calcutta. This concession was in tune with the change of public opinion in Britain, and also reflected the result of the trade's steadily decreasing financial returns. The importance of the successful campaign also became apparent when the Qing empire was invited to participate as an equal in the Shanghai meeting of the International Opium Commission in 1909.[74]

NARCOPHOBIA AND THE 'OPIUM PLAGUE' IN REPUBLICAN CHINA

After the collapse of the empire in 1911, the ratification of the second Hague Convention (1912–14) bound its signatories to regulate strictly the use of all natural and synthetic opiates.[75] The moral opposition and medical demonisation of opium was also pursued with great vigour in a profuse literature of propaganda. In the 1920s and '30s pamphlets on the 'opium problem', cartoons on opium addicts, tracts against the poppy, journals on prohibition and books on detoxification, all written in the name of science and for the sake of the nation, spread narcophobic discourse to all social levels. To condemn opium was an act of patriotism, to destroy the poppy a sign of national liberation against the pernicious forces of imperialist trade. Like countless others, the popular handbook entitled *Questions and Answers on Narcotics*, published by the National Anti-Opium Association in 1925, linked opiate addiction, racial strength and national revival in one breath:

To strengthen the country, we must first strengthen the race… at present, however, our country is weak and so are our people. What is the cause? The cause is the devastating evil of narcotics. We sincerely hope that the habitual users (*youcipizhe*) amongst us will abstain from this evil habit as soon as possible... Once narcotics are eradicated, our people will be strong again, a great prospect awaiting our nation and the whole world.[76]

Opium smokers were portrayed as hapless victims enslaved by powerful chemicals: once hooked, narcotics took possession of the addict, compelling him to take increasingly large doses to satisfy his craving. A state of euphoria (*shiwai taoyuan zhi xinjing*) was contrasted with the unbearable pangs caused by withdrawal symptoms, as an artificial paradise gave way to a living hell.[77] Addicts were seen as 'slaves' of addiction, the 'living dead' and 'walking corpses' in the permanent bondage of 'narcotics': their lack of willpower was treated as analogous to the weakness of the nation.[78] Dr Luo Yunyan, general secretary of the Anti–Narcotics Commission (Judu weiyuanhui), wrote: 'One can recognise addicts by their appearance: their faces are emaciated and sallow; their skin is parched and they grow old prematurely; their hair easily turns white and their eyes are hollow; their teeth are loose and their voices quiver. People disparage them as "opium ghosts" (*yangui*), a very accurate description indeed. Moreover, they also suffer from poor digestion, constipation, insomnia, heart problems, impotence in men and irregular menses in women.'[79] Thriving on eugenic ideas of racial degeneration, some propaganda pamphlets even claimed that many addicts suffered from 'low intelligence' or were beset by 'psychological defects'.[80] Clinical insanity, medical experts claimed, threatened to overtake the addict desperate for his dose.[81] Others classified 'addicts' into three categories: the mentally unfit, the physically decrepit and the uneducated.[82] 'Addicts' also destroyed the family, increased crime and caused rampant prostitution.[83] The relationship between opium and pauperism—a new topic for social investigation—was highlighted by social reformers, who decried the nefarious influences of smoking on the frail budgets of impoverished families: the typical smoker was seen to drag his dependants into poverty through his addiction. In a climate of public morality, opium-smoking was portrayed as personal failure, an egotistic act threatening to individuals, families and the nation.

Prohibition stigmatised the smoker by portraying the addict as a thief, a swindler or a beggar while opium houses were criminalised into dark places of deviant behaviour. Addicts were 'mean' (*linse*), 'slippery' (*diaohua*), 'heartless' (*guaqing*), 'greedy' (*zhongcai*), 'cruel' (*canren*) and 'shameless' (*wuchi*), ready to break family ties, treat their elders with disrespect and even sell their wives or become prostitutes to obtain their dose.[84] The opium house was transformed from a culturally sanctioned venue for male sociability into a site of perdition, a marker of uncivilised behaviour and 'barbarism' (*yeman*) where 'vulgar and despicable habits' (*yong'e loulie*) were leading the country to complete extinction (*wangguo*).[85] Mei Gongren, in his book *The opium plague leads to racial extinction* (1935), portrayed opium 'dens' as vectors of social contamination and racial poisoning: run by corrupt officials and traitors to the nation, they spread crime, sponsored gambling, promoted prostitution and harboured robbers. Evil warlords, corrupt officials, cunning landlords, local rascals, greedy merchants, degenerate playboys, communists, socialists, anarchists, gamblers, prostitutes, robbers, thieves: according to Mei, a close friend of Jiang Jieshi, all collaborated with imperialist powers to enslave the nation by peddling opium.[86]

In an age which gave a special status to women as guardians of the home and custodians of moral purity, fears of contamination and addiction multiplied, with images of 'addicted' women giving birth to 'addicted' infants—the innocent victims of drug addiction—while other vulnerable social categories such the elderly were also seen to be held in thrall to drugs.[87] Narcophobia was rooted in a more general fear of racial degeneration. For the modernising elites of republican China, individual sexual desire had to be disciplined and evil habits eliminated, and couples were to regulate their sexual behaviour strictly to help produce healthy offspring and bring about the revival of the nation.[88] Opium smoking was seen as leading to sexual impotence, reproductive failure and racial extinction. Medical writers such as Luo Yunyan, who wrote extensively on the 'narcotic problem', suggested that opium damaged the reproductive organs, addict families facing extinction within three generations. Female victims suffered from irregular periods and blocked breastfeeding, male smokers from impotence. When both partners were hooked, no offspring could be produced: 'From this we learn that narcotics have the power to destroy the country (*wang ren zhi guo*) and exterminate the race (*mie ren zhi zhong*). One must not regard this as mere words. How terrifying! How terrifying!'[89] 'Traditional' practitioners like Cao Bingzhang concurred, warning that addiction could lead to neurasthenia and infertility, two much-dreaded 'diseases' in republican China.[90]

The anti-opium movement culminated in a series of prohibition laws. Despite the financial gain to be made from the opium trade, successive governments in republican China moved openly against the use of opiates, rhetorically if not always in practice. Moreover, with the unfolding of a global movement towards drug prohibition official suppression campaigns were increasingly seen to be a vector of state legitimacy and moral authority. Failure to enforce prohibition became a symbol of government corruption, hypocrisy and national disunity: 'warlords' profited from the trade by allowing the opium plague to infect the nation. Opium merchants were transformed into 'traitor merchants' (*jianshang*), the 'running dogs' (*zougou*) of 'warlords' and slaves of imperialist powers.[91] By the end of the 1920s opium was officially viewed as an instrument of imperialist aggression and a cause of the demise of the country: Sun Yatsen (1866–1925), founder of the Guomindang and widely accepted as the 'father' of the nation in China and in Taiwan to this day, identified opium as the most dangerous enemy in his *Three principles of the people*, and this view was widely adopted during the Nanjing decade (1927–37): 'Opium has caused more harm than war, plague and famine in China for more than ten years.'[92] Mass meetings were organised during Anti-Opium Weeks, more than 30,000 people joining the Shanghai Citizens Anti-Opium Gathering in October 1927, while the last Sunday in September was declared an 'Anti-Opium Day'.[93] With the launch of the New Life Movement by Jiang Jieshi in February 1934, the public burning of confiscated drugs and smoking utensils during a commemoration of Opium Prohibition Memorial Day (3 June) elevated Lin Zexu to the status of national hero while the 'Opium War' became the founding myth of Chinese nationalism, as history was interpreted as a series of humiliating defeats against imperialist powers peddling an evil substance and reducing the country to a state of opium slavery:

Following our defeat in the Opium War, China had no right to stop the importation of opium and other narcotics. At the same time the Concessions and consular jurisdiction afforded protection to the transportation and storage of these poisonous drugs. Even though our Government had enacted all kinds of laws strictly prohibiting their consumption, opium smoking was still openly indulged in, as our jurisdiction could not extend to those areas. Furthermore, after the Russo-Japanese War the Japanese imperialists adopted the policy of poisoning our people as a weapon for the achievement of their territorial ambitions. Because of the unequal treaties, the Chinese Government had neither the means to prevent Japanese adoption of this iniquitous policy nor the power to check it after it had been put into effect. In the course of time, the method of poisoning our people became more and more serious.[94]

After passing a series of opium suppression laws from 1929 to 1934, the Guomindang launched a Six-Year Opium Suppression Plan which not only criminalised the trafficking of illegal drugs, but threatened habitual users who relapsed after treatment with punishments ranging from imprisonment to summary execution. The first half of the plan, intended to last from 1934 to 1940, but cut short by the Japanese invasion of 1937, saw an unprecedented degree of intervention by the state into the lives of opium smokers. They were forced to register publicly, and more than one million opium users were treated at detoxification centres created by local elites and government bodies: the next chapter will look at the social costs of these official policies. On the other hand, the new legislation pushed for a state monopoly over opium rather than for strict prohibition.

Edward Slack has used rich primary sources to analyse the rapidly changing policies which vacillated between prohibition and legalisation during the Nanjing decade. His approach sheds light on the crucial role of opium as a source of revenue for the Guomindang and examines the many tensions which appeared between pragmatic policies aimed at imposing a government monopoly over the distribution of opium and calls by nationalist elites for radical prohibition. Instead of morally condemning Jiang Jieshi's shift in 1935 from opium prohibition to the establishment of a government monopoly as an exercise in deception—a common strategy of contemporary critics and conventional historiography—he emphasises that his policies were inflected by practical determinants, including the enormity of the opium economy, the weakness of the central government, the existence of extraterritoriality and a global economic depression. The author rightly judges the Guomindang achievements to have been 'impressive, to say the least', contrary to others who describe Jiang Jieshi's attempts to regulate the opium trade in terms of a spectacular 'failure' to fully implement 'prohibition'. In light of the many problems engendered by 'war on drugs', which will be analysed in the following chapters, one could go further and judge the Guomindang to have successfully anticipated by more than half a century the drug policies pursued today by a number of governments critical of prohibition.[95] The destructive consequences of prohibition were fully understood even by specialists working for the League of Nations. According to John Farnham,

[I]t is the hordes of people addicted to the use of narcotic drugs who have created and maintained the constant illicit market. Therefore, any attempt to combat the situation through a method which regulates the supply and ignores the demand which creates the supply, is foredoomed to failure. Assume that the world's legitimate narcotic needs have been established and proportions of the required raw materials have been justly allocated to the producing countries. The result is obvious and inevitable. There remained two markets for the products, the legitimate medical market and the illicit addict market. The very nature of addiction, with its insatiate desire and, in many instances, necessity for the drug, make its price of little consequence. Therefore, much of the supply will be diverted from the lower priced legitimate market to the higher priced illicit market and the medical market will face the calamity consequent—a shortage. Accordingly there would be an increase of poppies and coca leaves allowed and the same diversion from proper channels would take place, and soon on in a vicious circle.[96]

While the notion of 'addiction' followed by an 'insatiable desire' is questionable, the following chapters show that John Farnham's observations about the consequences of prohibition were accurate. Cheap morphine flooded the market precisely when prohibition increased the price of opium. In the words of the International Anti-Opium Association: 'The trade in opium derivatives is in reverse ratio to the cultivation of poppy.'[97]

7

CURING THE ADDICT: PROHIBITION AND DETOXIFICATION (c. 1880–1940)

The preceding chapter dealt with the gradual emergence of anti-opium discourse and the rise of prohibition. Behind this shift was an unlikely alliance: puritanical missionaries who wanted to 're-turn China to the Lord' and nationalist elites concerned about the country's restoration to sovereignty. Though differing widely in their political outlook, both regarded the moral reformation and medical cure of the habitual smoker as their ultimate mission. This chapter deals with the spread of detoxification cures and the establishment of opium treatment centres from the late Qing to the start of the Second World War in Asia (1937). It shows that prohibition during the late Qing accelerated and broadened the use of opium in a variety of new applications, in particular as powders and as tinctures (laudanum). It also introduced consumers to new semi-synthetics like morphine and cocaine, which are analysed more closely in the following chapters. Toxic substances such as atropine, arsenic and strychnine were administered as part of opium replacement therapies, killing patients in some cases. 'The crowding of gaols, the banishment of numerous persons who are in no other way a danger to the Colony, the nourishment of a parasitic class of informers, the prevalence of blackmail, the corruption of government servants and the evils attendant on the inevitable system of payment of rewards to informers': these were but some of the disastrous consequences that the colonial government in Hong Kong believed would result from strict pro-hibition.[1] This chapter shows how uncannily accurate this pre-diction was, as otherwise law-abiding smokers were confined to overcrowded cells and died in disproportionate numbers of epidemics, while those deemed beyond any hope of redemption were simply executed. Corruption and a criminal underclass, on the other hand, thrived thanks to the opium suppression policies of the republican governments.[2]

FROM DROSS TO MORPHINE: MIRACLE CURES IN THE NINETEENTH CENTURY

Prohibition engendered a lucrative industry in opium cures, which more often than not contained large amounts of opium dross and had adverse medical consequences for their users. These already appeared in the wake of the anti-opium movement launched by Lin Zexu in Guangdong during the first Sino-British War (1839–42): Lin proposed the use of anti-acidic pills (*jisuanwan*) and restorative tonics (*buzhengwan*), consisting of a mixture of opium dross and a variety of herbs, to eliminate opium cravings (*yin*).[3] These medications were officially endorsed and openly sold in local drug stores, leading, in the region where Lin Zexu imposed a ban on opium, to long queues of prospective customers.[4] While the popularity of these remedies appears to point at an existing demand for detoxification treatment, most consumers may well have been more interested in buying legal remedies containing opium dross than in seeking medical help. Opium substitutes were not only legal but also proved to be cheaper. Far from curbing the use of opium in south China, Lin Zexu's campaign of prohibition may well have accelerated and deepened its proliferation, although this hypothesis requires more evidence to be substantiated.

The spread of opium substitutes, heralded as miracles cures, was also encouraged by foreign medical experts in the treaty ports. Between 1850 and 1895, large quantities of opium replacement medications were imported into the country. The exact amount is difficult to estimate, since before 1891 all drugs other than opium were collectively entered as 'medicines' (or 'foreign sundries') in the registers of the imperial customs.[5] Pills in particular became popular, leading to a shift away from opium smoking towards opiate ingestion among some consumers in parts of the country where prohibition was enforced. Their consumption frequently led to severe digestive problems, including abdominal pain and constipation, since opium was far more powerful as a costive when ingested rather than smoked. As prohibition exclusively targeted the practice of smoking, the health hazards caused by eating opiates went largely unacknowledged until the very end of the nineteenth century.

Having constructed an image of the opium smoker as a physically degenerate and morally depraved addict under the yoke of physical dependence, medical missionaries could proceed to rescue him, in particular by offering home cures which sought to counteract diarrhoea, the most frequent consequence of withdrawal. Astringents, such as pomegranate skin, combined with tonics, generous helpings of food and camphor pills, formed part of at least one nineteenth-century replacement therapy.[6] Other withdrawal aids included strychnine, quinine, capsicum, gentian and iron preparations.[7] Most opium cures contained liberal quantities of opium,[8] as well as emetics, intended gradually to wean patients off the habit. At the Williams' Hospital in Pangzhuang, Shandong, for instance, pills contained nux vomica, piperine, belladonna (7 per cent) and opium powder (23 per cent).[9] Sales boomed: 'The nostrums of the native doctors are innumerable, and anti-opium medicines presented by foreigners are eagerly sought for,' as one medical missionary commented in the early 1880s.[10]

In their renewed search for cures against the 'opium habit', foreign medical experts also praised the virtues of coffee. After chemical science succeeded in extracting caffeine—the alkaloid central to coffee and tea—from plants in 1820, it was immediately marketed as a new wonder drug. Because the 'passion' for opium had formed an obstacle to the conversion of the locals, Claude Chevenot, an entrepreneur from Dijon, proposed his 'coffee extract' as a remedy at the Catholic opium conference of 1892.[11] He drew on a recommendation by the Académie de Médecine, which suggested 'very strong coffee' as an antidote to the opium craving in France: potent infusions of coffee, with or without alcohol, were added to the panoply of methods devised by medical experts advocating the gospel of 'total withdrawal'. Since the coffee craze current in Europe had escaped China, Chevenot recommended that his specifically designed caffeine pills should be used there.[12]

From small beginnings in the 1890s, imports of caffeine increased until the 1920s, by which time caffeine had become a standard ingredient in opium replacement medicines. The China Medical Association mused why 'amounts … far greater than can possibly be required to meet the medical needs of China' were making their way into the country.[13] Figures suggest that imports peaked in 1923, at 19 tonnes, falling off dramatically over the succeeding years.[14] In 1938 Hong Kong alone imported some 7 tonnes, more than 80 per cent probably being intended for narcotic pill manufacture, as we see in the next chapter.[15] Some medical voices even suggested that the 'caffeine craze' was at the root of a new form of dependence,[16] a view questioned by the narcotic crusader Wu Liande. 'Even our national drink tea', Wu reasoned, 'has caffeine as its chief alkaloid.'[17]

Although caffeine did not succeed in becoming a viable alternative to opium, it would emerge as one of the principal ingredients of narcotic pills. Morphine, on the other hand, was far more successful as a substitute for the banned opium, and missionaries were a major factor in its spread. Having contributed more than others to the social construction of opium as a vector of insidious compulsion, missionaries enthusiastically joined the addiction treatment industry and proceeded to rescue the 'opium addicts' by distributing morphine free in their congregations. The Rev. C. H. Judd, of the Ninghai mission in Shandong, justified the administration of morphine-based opium cures as a means of obtaining 'followers of Christ and faithful upright citizens'.[18] Some Protestant mission stations even became popular centres for the distribution of semi-synthetics until morphine and heroin joined the ranks of prohibited drugs.[19] Akin to the earlier 'rice Christians', thousands of 'morphine Christians' filled the churches of the late Qing.[20] The replacement of opium by morphine was noted in 1894 by Dr R. A. Jamieson, a medical practitioner in

Shanghai since 1868 and, by then, consulting surgeon to the Imperial Maritime Customs and surgeon at St Luke's Hospital for Chinese:

The Chinese rarely, if ever, eat opium, except for the purpose of suicide. Opium-consumers have until lately smoked exclusively. Within the past few years, however, the so-called 'opium habit curing powders', which are nothing but morphia, have created a taste for morphia consumption, which I learn is rapidly spreading on account of its comparative convenience and cleanliness, and also on account of the secrecy with which the habit may be indulged. Still more recently, the hypodermic injection of morphia has been introduced, and this form of the habit is gaining ground with extraordinary rapidity. I am informed on excellent authority that the importation of hypodermic syringes from Europe, but especially from Japan, has already reached enormous proportions. … it may safely be predicted that it will prove far more hurtful and far more general than opium-smoking has ever been.[21]

After morphine was no longer portrayed as a miracle cure, some missionaries tried to detoxify their patients with cocaine. In Xiamen, for instance, medical missionaries were behind a huge increase in cocaine imports from 38 to 557 kilos between 1892 and 1902, mostly used for opium substitution. The use of cocaine peaked at 570 kilos in 1909, after which police action reduced its legal importation to negligible amounts.[22] The following chapters examine more closely how semi-synthetics spread in the wake of the prohibition movement.

MISSIONARY ASYLUMS AND THE 'OPIUM VICE'

The idea of establishing asylums as an effective means of curing 'addicts' of the 'opium vice' was first introduced by foreign missionaries around 1860, a decade before the first addiction clinic was founded in Europe (Levinstein's morphine treatment centre in Berlin).[23] Opium asylums would gradually appear along the coast during the last decades of the nineteenth century, in particular in the treaty ports. Even small surgeries would offer help in 'delivering' opium smokers from their habit, while most missionary hospitals had designated opium wards by the first decade of the twentieth century. Treatment centres were to offer moral support and a degree of confinement essential to endure the 'struggle necessary to give up the use of the enticing drug'.[24] Constant supervision and strict discipline was demanded over the 'inmates' who came to be cured, and contact with their families reduced to a minimum for the sake of therapeutic isolation.[25] At the opium treatment hospital of Suiding (near Yichang), patients even had to sign a form confirming their full consent to the treatment. Maintenance fees were low, usually sufficient to cover their basic diet. The patients were almost exclusively agricultural workers coming from a wide radius to find relief and security; once the harvest period began, the average of 120 patients fell to near zero.[26]

Canton emerged as a veritable laboratory for opium treatments during the 1860s. While detailed reports show that some patients were cured within a fortnight, others preferred to escape from the 'torture which necessarily followed the withdrawal of the intoxicating drug' and the 'fearful ordeal' of the strict hospital routine.[27] Tormented by terrible cravings, seized by severe pains and 'an indescribable feeling of prostration and distress [which] pervaded every part of the body', many were unable to sleep. The 'horrors' were claimed to peak around the third day or, in cases of exceptionally heavy use, by the sixth day.[28] By the eighth or tenth day patients were said to experience 'a sense of ease and relief'.[29] This observation was tempered by the discovery that many of the painful conditions which had at first caused smokers to resort to opium returned with a vengeance:[30] from the voluntary treatments proposed by medical missionaries during the late Qing to the compulsory confinement of opium smokers under republican governments, the medical reasons which prompted ordinary people to smoke opium in the first place were widely underestimated if not entirely ignored. Refusal to acknowledge the medical merits of opium led to the huge failure rates of treatment institutions and the opium cure industry. Dr G. Wilkinson, based in Fujian in 1911, observed that most of his patients had been introduced to the pipe in order to seek relief from relatively minor ailments, such as itching, dyspepsia or bronchitis: he was one of the few to suggest treating these diseases first.[31]

There was much debate among medical missionaries concerning treatment methods.[32] Medical discourse was dominated by proponents of either gradual or sudden withdrawal. Those who preferred sudden termination believed that it coincided with the goal of spiritual conversion they aspired to achieve. As Dr Osgood of the Zhuzhou mission hospital pointed out, the effects of the withdrawal caused patients to be in an 'impressionable mood', ready to listen to missionary sermons.[33] The Zhuzhou clinic near Hankou, to take another example, also adopted a policy of radical withdrawal and emphasised how the patient should undergo the treatment in all its terrifying aspects: opium cravings were assuaged by means of electric currents, hot water bags, sweat baths, massage and gramophone music.[34] Morphine and atropine were injected to reduce the pain building up towards the third day of treatment. Soporifics, antispasmodics and tonics, including arsenic, hydrochloric acid and strychnine, toxic substances far more dangerous than opium, were also administered in copious quantities to wean the patient off his habit.[35] Opponents of immediate suppression argued that the opium, laudanum and morphine given in small doses during the first days of treatment could convey the moral support necessary for the addicts to break an entrenched habit.[36] In Shanxi opium was reduced on a daily basis while stimulants such as strychnine or atropine were also administered.[37] Phased detoxification could also be difficult since some patients could trick their doctors into administering the substance to alleviate their 'horrors'.[38]

Little is known of the patients' reactions to these various treatments. However, in the opium refugee of the Suzhou hospital the following graffito was found: 'Opium took us to paradise; now we are tortured in hell'.[39] Overall numbers of patients voluntarily seeking treatment are difficult to estimate, but even in the St Luke's Hospital for Chinese in Shanghai, individuals admitted for the 'opium habit' represented no more than 2 to 4 per cent of the many hundreds of internal patients treated every year in the 1880s and '90s.[40]

The anti-opium campaigns during the late Qing did little to eliminate narcotic culture: opium replacement therapies instead accelerated and broadened the use of opium in a variety of new applications (powders and tinctures) and introduced consumers to new semi-synthetics like morphine and cocaine. Toxic substances such as atropine, arsenic and strychnine were also given to patients, leading to medical complications which far exceeded any harm which could possibly be caused even by heavy opium smoking: when these poisons would be injected during the republican period, many patients would die from their treatments. As the next sections show, opium rarely killed, but prohibition could be lethal when injecting poisons into the bloodstream of patients, confining smokers into overcrowded prisons rife with epidemics, or more simply by executing those deemed beyond any hope of redemption.

THE GREAT CONFINEMENT: THE PERSECUTION OF OPIATE USERS IN REPUBLICAN CHINA

Opium suppression was rigorously carried out in many parts of China from 1906 until the death of Yuan Shikai in 1916, despite widespread and sometimes armed opposition from farming communities.[41] The following decade has been critically described as the 'warlord period' in which selfish power struggles between regional militarists culminated in political fragmentation and national disunity. It is claimed that these 'warlords' needed substantial financial resources to fuel their machines of war, and these were found in opium trafficking. However, the assumption that 'warlord' involvement in the opium trade had devastating consequences is undermined by the abundant evidence—presented in the second half of this book—that the transition from a tolerated opium culture to a system of prohibition produced a cure far worse than the disease. By actively responding to consumer demand for opium, rather than persecuting 'opium addicts', some regional governors unwittingly impeded the spread of heroin and morphine and new modes of delivery like injection or snorting. As the following chapter shows, heroin smoking and morphine injection were most successful in provinces where prohibition was strictly enforced (Jiangsu, Hebei, Fengtian). These were generally in the east and north, while southern and western provinces (Guangdong, Yunnan, Sichuan)—usually seen to have fallen under the grip of 'warlordism' to a much greater extent—continued to be dominated by opium smoking. Moreover, the 'warlord period' did not see the disappearance of opium legislation: the opium trade remained technically illegal, even if national prohibition laws were often ignored by regional governments. Opium users were imprisoned in many parts of the country even in this period, a fact corroborated by specific archival evidence presented elsewhere.[42]

The criminalisation and persecution of opium smokers became official policy after the Guomindang overthrew a number of military governors and established a new capital in Nanjing in 1927. The opium suppression policies of Jiang Jieshi had obvious political advantages: they weakened opposition within his own party and undermined the main source of income for many of the independent military leaders who joined him after 1927 but continued to form a potential threat to his rule. The Opium Prohibition Act and Regulations passed in 1928 signalled a move towards complete prohibition as drug-related offences became one of the most important legal categories in the judicial system: in 1929 one third of all convicted criminals had been sentenced for possessing or selling drugs.[43] The enforcement of new anti-opium laws meant that opium smokers could no longer escape prison by paying a fine, and this led to an explosion in the prison population in coastal provinces like Jiangsu, where the number of inmates reached 20,000 by the end of the year. Many smokers, particularly those who relied on opium to control pain or alleviate serious diseases, became ill in prison and died in overcrowded cells.[44]

This trend increased over the following years: in 1931 the use or sale of opium emerged as the most common criminal offence, representing 27,000 out of 70,000 reported convictions throughout the country. While some still managed to escape prison by paying a fine, large numbers nonetheless ended up behind bars, lumped together with robbers, thieves and murderers.[45] Small county gaols in particular were ill-equipped to deal with the large numbers of sentenced opium smokers: two inspectors sent by the National Opium Suppression Commission reported that in the Jiangning county gaol, Jiangsu province, more than ten opium offenders were huddled together in cells designed for four. Left without any medical treatment, many died or underwent severe pain.[46] Large cities were no different: the courts in Shanghai alone sentenced more than 2,600 people for drug-related crimes in 1931. Thousands more paid fines, ranging from 1,000 to 2,000 yuan. The majority lived below the poverty line and were illiterate.[47]

In June 1934 Jiang Jieshi presented the Six-Year Opium Suppression Plan which aimed at the complete eradication of opium within six years. The military jurisdiction over opium prohibition in zones marked by communist activities since 1932 was drastically expanded, as military authorities were given complete control over drug-related matters in the municipalities of Nanjing and Shanghai. The result was an unmitigated disaster, as the judicial administration which nominally ran the penal system was overrun by thousands of 'addicts' arrested by the military and sent to prison without any regard for the logistical and humanitarian problems engendered by strict prohibition. In December 1934 the municipal police launched an operation against opium smokers in Nanjing, leading to an emergency conference aimed at discussing various ways of disposing of the new convicts.[48] The prison population exploded: the five principal prisons of Jiangsu, which had housed 2,788 inmates in 1928,[49] almost doubled their numbers to just under 5,000 in 1935. Jiangsu No. 2 and Jiangsu No. 3 Prisons respectively quadrupled and tripled their intake during the government's campaign against drugs. Even outside the two municipalities of Nanjing and Shanghai thousands of smokers were sent to prison: in counties like Rugao, local gaols, hospitals and poorhouses were all brimful by the end of 1934.[50]

The Nanjing Garrison Headquarters (*Nanjing jingbei silingbu*) overwhelmed the judicial authorities with drug felons from 1935 to 1937. The Jiangsu No. 1 Prison, for instance, protested that the number of drug-related prisoners had reached over 1,400 in the summer of 1937, more than twice the number of other inmates. As the winter approached, prisoners slept on the floor in overcrowded cells without bedding or uniforms, pressed shoulder to shoulder, sometimes fighting over space in the middle of the night as cold weather would freeze the weak ones to death. The simple task of feeding offenders sent to the prison by the military was a challenge, since their food allowance had not been paid by the municipal government for several months. According to a government inspector, some of the poor prisoners had no clothes at all, wrapping themselves in the thin sheets provided by the prison.[51] Control by the military authorities over drug-related offences, extended to nine provinces and other cities in April 1935, also led to a crisis in judicial administration in other parts of the country: according to a report compiled by the municipal government in Beijing that very month, more than 5,000 drug offenders lingered in prison, a huge number far exceeding the total capacity of the penal system.[52]

Disease and death were rampant in overcrowded prisons lacking adequate financial support and basic medical facilities. Inspection reports reveal the scope of penal problems caused by the war on drugs in the Nanjing decade. A report written in 1930 by an inspection team on the infamous Jiangsu No. 2 Prison at Caohejing, Shanghai, showed that it had more than doubled its maximum of 800 inmates, who were reduced to sharing crowded cells. Overcrowding was caused by the arrival of large numbers of opium smokers, and temporary shelters had to be built to accommodate more than 300 addicts.[53] The death rate was estimated at 10 per cent, a figure explained not only by the poor health of inmates but also by the absence of adequate medical facilities. Lack of fresh air, derelict buildings and poor food also increased mortality; walls were cracked and windows broken, while the cold from outside seeped into the cells to undermine the inmates' health still further.[54] While the situation in Jiangsu No. 2 Prison was extreme, other prisons too were ravaged by tuberculosis, dysentery, gastro-intestinal disorders and typhus in consequence of overcrowding.[55]

As neither the police nor the judiciary made any distinction between sick and healthy smokers, those afflicted with tuberculosis often ended up in the same cells as healthy convicts, thus contributing to the spread of epidemics.[56] Moreover, opium smokers were more likely than others to suffer from poor health, since many were dependent on opium for medical reasons. A Mrs Zhou took to opium to stop the pain caused by a miscarriage, only to fall victim to prohibition: she was arrested and given a two-year sentence.[57] The labourer Dai Xinsan, roaming Beijing in search of a job, resorted to opium to help his cough, and also ended up in prison.[58] If we accept that the majority of ordinary people used opium to manage a variety of ailments for which no effective medications were available, forced withdrawal could only be expected to precipitate medical problems. In Wuxi during the summer months of 1935, overcrowding and seasonal epidemics caused more than twenty deaths each month out of a total of over 700 prisoners, the majority being opium smokers.[59] As one journalist observed at the height of the prohibition movement, since opium was no longer available for self-medication, many habitual users simply died in prison.[60]

The bias of the penal system against the poor was reflected in the release of wealthy prisoners. In republican China fines could often be commuted to a custodial sentence; conversely, congestion sometimes resulted in the commuting of a prison sentence into a fee for the rich and influential. Beijing newspapers reported in September 1930 that the city's prisons were crowded beyond capacity. Prisoners who could afford to buy their freedom were released, and two of them, both leaders of drug-smuggling rings, apparently accepted the offer. One former chief of the Beijing Octroi Tax Bureau, who had been sentenced to thirty months in prison and a fine of 5,000 yuan, was required to pay an additional 5,000.[61] Of course, corruption was encouraged by the criminalisation of opium. Kong Molin, to give but one example, was the head of an anti-opium bureau in Shaanxi who encouraged his staff to blackmail and torture (*feifa kaoda*) opium users and arrest people at random, whether or not any evidence of drug use could be produced.[62] While social elites were generally able to avoid prison, their very wealth could made them a key target for the corrupt practices spawned by Jiang Jieshi's war on drugs. In Shanghai a wealthy merchant and resident of the

International Settlement was lured into Nandao, arrested by the local police, made to pay 2,000 yuan and confined for a month in a detoxification hospital, where he was forced to spend 200 yuan on detoxification treatment.[63]

PROHIBITION AND DETOXIFICATION

While opium treatment hospitals and refuges run by missionaries continued to function after 1911, they became less prominent in the republican period. Detoxification was largely carried out in police detention centres, health clinics and prisons, in conditions which varied significantly according to local facilities, circumstances and regulations. The Sichuan Model Detoxification Centre (*mofan jieyansuo*)—established in 1915—was one of the earliest institutions claimed as a success to be emulated by the rest of the country. Its administrative practices and institutional philosophy were inspired by the model prisons which had started to appear in the early republican period. The registration and identification of new arrivals followed rules and procedures similar to those in penal institutions: on admission all smokers were washed and changed into clean clothes, their personal belongings were impounded, and contact with their relatives was cut off until they were discharged. Discipline was inculcated and maintained by a strict routine that was closely modelled on that used in model prisons, from the uniforms and short hair to the orderly filing into the refectory. Donations were regularly encouraged from local merchants and voluntary associations to meet the costs of maintaining the centre.[64] The similarity between detoxification centres and penal institutions was further accentuated by overcrowding, as local reformatories (*jiaoyang gongchang*) and industrial training centres (*xiyisuo*) were regularly used as temporary shelters for patients.[65]

Detoxification centres spread after 1932 to deal with new legislation obliging opium smokers to register and undergo medical treatment. A proposal to establish detoxification hospitals and centres was first made in 1929 and approved at ministerial level in 1931.[66] The first official opium detoxification hospital was opened in Nanjing in 1934, designed as a model for the rest of the country.[67] Other detoxification centres were opened in cities like Shanghai and Beijing by the end of 1934.[68] The total number of addiction centres grew significantly after the adoption of the six-year plan, rising from less than 600 in 1934 to 1,160 in 1937.[69] By 1937, at the height of the prohibition movement, more than fifteen specialised hospitals and forty-six detoxification centres existed in Guangdong province, treating more than 90,000 registered opium users.[70] Even in the relatively poor provinces of the hinterland detoxification emerged as a national priority on the eve of the Sino-Japanese War in 1937: in remote Yunnan province, detoxification centres were planned for four cities,[71] while new hospitals specialising in opium replacement therapies appeared in Hubei to alleviate the logistical shortcomings of existing facilities.[72] Hundreds of thousands of ordinary people were forced to undergo treatment in these centres. In Jiangsu province alone, some 80,000 drug users went through a detoxification programme from August 1935 to February 1936.[73]

Much in the same way as the prison was seen as a moral space in which repentance could be instilled into criminals, detoxification centres represented addicts as misguided human beings in need of help: reformation rather than punishment was stressed. Such ideals were embodied by the model Nanjing Municipal Detoxification Hospital.[74] Patients were registered on arrival, bathed and shaved, and given uniforms. Discipline was key to 'correcting wrong ideas' among patients, 'changing their daily lives' and transforming them into 'morally good citizens'. *Ganhua*, 'moral reformation', undergirded the hospital's approach, as patients were to be reformed through moral lectures, formal education and wholesome leisure. Treatment was free for patients sent by the police or the courts and cost 3 yuan a day for others. According to the hospital's annual statistics, over 10,000 patients were treated in 1936, 80 per cent of whom were opium smokers, the others addicted to morphine or heroin.[75]

Nationalist elites during the republican period tried not merely to punish supposed 'addicts', but rather to mould them into model citizens who could contribute to the wealth and power of the nation. The Zhabei Anti-Opium Hospital most closely fulfilled this ambition and was hailed as a 'model institution' treating thousands of addicts. Converted from a silk factory early in 1935, renovated and fitted out with medical equipment, the hospital had discharged nearly 6,000 men a year later. There were four wards containing a total of 250 beds, and patients spent two to four weeks taking the cure, the majority being coolies sent by the police or the courts. Treatment was free. Female addicts were treated at neighbouring hospitals at Longhua and Nandao.[76] Similar to the admission procedures in a republican prison, each man registered on arrival, answered medical questions, was fingerprinted, weighed, bathed and shaved. His hair was cut, and his clothes taken away to be sterilised and laid aside until he was ready to leave the hospital. He was given a uniform and a bell-shaped metal disk with his number. His bed, eating utensils, medicine cups and everything else he used bore the same number. The staff segregated men suffering from serious diseases and tried to inculcate 'habits of cleanliness' in the patients, who were instructed to use spittoons. As the yearly report confidently noted, many had never before seen a modern lavatory, but 'a lot could be taught in two weeks'.[77]

The fragile boundary between medical and penal institutions was further eroded by compulsory work. Even in the model Nanjing Municipal Detoxification Hospital, patients who could not afford to pay for treatment were required to work eight hours every day for three months.[78] Forced labour was presented as vocational training, linked to the idea that institutional confinement would strengthen national wealth by transforming the poor and vagrant into a skilled workforce. Sociability and productivity were key notions that motivated official efforts to teach poor opium smokers a vocational skill: idleness would be swept off the streets, while responsible citizens would contribute to the national effort of economic revival.[79] The systematic conversion of 'addicts' into a productive workforce was first proposed in 1934 and actively implemented in Beijing the following year. After three weeks of detoxification treatment, reformed addicts were divided into teams of 150 assigned to either agricultural or construction work.[80]

The workers were given regular medical checks and any relapse into the opium habit was followed by immediate return to a detoxification centre. A police certificate was needed to discharge 'cured' opiate users.[81] The programme was heavily promoted by the Ministry of Internal Affairs in 1939, as dozens of Citizen-Strengthening Factories (*qiangmin gongchang*) were opened in Henan province.[82] Each factory was allocated eighty addicted paupers who were given medial treatment in exchange for work during their three- to six-month stay. Vocational training, including machine control, weaving, paper making, mining and milling formed the backbone of the factory system.[83]

'Addicts' were also given moral instruction against the evil of smoking in the factory system.[84] Throughout republican China, detoxification centres preached and practised the gospel of 'moral reformation' (*ganhua*)—the core principle of penal philosophy in republican China, with moral lectures, formal education and wholesome leisurely activities as its tool.[85] Dr Morinaka, practising in Shenyang, commented that 'the patient should be fully impressed with the awfulness of morphine poisoning by talking to him perhaps like a parson, who tearfully and with motherly heart, admonishes the prisoner before he is discharged from his imprisonment!'[86] Collective sermons on the importance of health and hygiene were central to this process of moral transformation, while anti-opium lectures invoked the words of Sun Yatsen and Lin Zexu. Physical exercise, in the form of *taijiquan*, was accompanied by the collective singing of anti-opium songs.[87] In the municipal detoxification centre of Tianjin, opened in February 1935, sermons were given in the morning to addicts on 'the harm of narcotics in destroying the country', while Jiang Jieshi's anti-opium speeches were carefully memorised by inmates who were further impressed with warnings about 'execution for reoffenders'.[88] In Jiangsu No. 2 Branch Prison, which had a special centre for treating opium smokers, the director summed up: 'You did not spend a penny in here, your habit is cured, the state provided you with meals, you were given an education and allowed to study, and you were even taught the good habit of rising early.'[89]

As the official 1929 proposal for the establishment of detoxification centres emphasised, addicts were criminals and should be treated as such, even if hospital rather than prison was the moral space in which self-renewal should take place.[90] Not surprisingly, many inmates tried to escape, indicating how 'addicts' rarely submitted voluntarily to opium cures. In Beijing patients at the principal detoxification centre, which opened in September 1934, had the words 'Undergoing Addiction Treatment' emblazoned on their uniforms to prevent escapes.[91] In parts of Shandong province, opium smokers were even tattooed with a 2-inch cross on the forearm from the summer of 1936 onwards (see illustration 10).[92] In Sichuan province too it was suggested that patients be tattooed when war broke out and the usual registration procedures no longer worked, but the proposal was rejected as 'barbaric' and 'inhumane'.[93]

Many detoxification hospitals were heavily guarded to prevent patients from escaping or rioting.[94] Violence, rather than controlled medical care and institutional discipline, often governed daily life. According to a report compiled by the Beijing Medical University, many addicts suffered serious psychological and physical problems during their treatment. Some would burst out with cries or suddenly start singing, while others were quarrelsome and shouted for no apparent reason. A few became violent and were difficult to restrain. The hospital staff were simply unable to manage the many problems created by forced treatment and relied on the police to keep control.[95]

Although hundreds of detoxification centres appeared in the Nanjing decade, the sheer number of smokers—occasional, intermittent, moderate and heavy—was such that only a fraction could possibly be coerced into undergoing treatment. The dynamics of social exclusion promoted by prohibition led to the discriminatory treatment of drug users by the state. Education, wealth and status were key determinants in a moral universe which viewed lack of education as a prime cause of crime: illiteracy was represented as immorality, and the war on drugs thus overwhelmingly targeted socially marginalised groups of young, poor and unemployed men. The wealthy inmates of a prison in Hebei were not only able to enjoy luxurious single cells and a large degree of freedom, but were even able to indulge their opium habit.[96] Social segregation marked almost all detoxification centres in the Nanjing decade, as the poor huddled together in overcrowded cells while wealthy smokers were allocated special wards to prevent any risk of their being contaminated by the great unwashed. In many parts of the country the prohibition campaign specifically targeted poor people, as opium smokers with social status and political connections were left largely undisturbed. An official report on anti-opium work carried out in Sichuan province from 1936 to 1938, at the height of the prohibition campaign, noted that wealthy 'addicts' were allowed to smoke at home, since only poor smokers were reported by the police and compelled to undergo detoxification treatment.[97] In 1940, in the middle of the six-year plan, the Second Army in Chongqing requested that the Ministry of Health give permission for a special provision of 100 *liang* of good opium from Yunnan, since the mother-in-law of a general had been suffering from high blood pressure. The request was granted without further ado.[98] Needless to say, the hundreds of thousands of poor people forced to undergo treatment had to work continuously for their living and for the support of their families: they could afford neither the time nor the expense of hospital treatment.[99]

Some smokers voluntarily sought medical help: Yan Fu is a good example. As we saw in the last chapter, he was one of the most prominent reformers who contributed to the portrayal of opium as a 'national problem' in the 1890s. He suffered from asthma and smoked moderately from 1880 onwards to alleviate his cough and tackle his insomnia. He repeatedly attempted to give up opium after 1907, tortured by feelings of guilt as well as by the breathing difficulties which ran in his family. Having finally succeeded in entirely abandoning the pipe in 1920, he died a year later from respiratory problems related to asthma.[100]

KILLING TO CURE: DETOXIFICATION TREATMENTS AGAINST 'ADDICTION'

Narcophobic discourse presented the 'addict' as a pale and emaciated creature with a wan complexion and languid eyes staring out of a grotesquely deformed face. Reality was rather different, as moderate users were entirely indistinguishable from the rest of the population, in particular from the poor and undernourished. Even heavy smokers showed none of the symptoms so eagerly described by anti-opium crusaders, provided they could afford regular sleep and a normal diet. Charles Terry and Mildred Pellens thus observed: 'There is a popular belief extant that practically anyone can detect the so-called "dope fiend", that he is a miserable, emaciated, furtive individual with pinpoint pupils, trembling hands, sallow complexion and characterized by a varied group of moral attributes... As a matter of fact, not even one of these characteristics need be present... The average physician, unaccustomed to dealing with the condition, might have difficulty in determining its existence.'[101] Other experts on detoxification agreed: a study conducted by A. B. Light and E. G. Torrance on behalf of the United States Committee on Drug Addiction demonstrated that it was impossible to detect any marked physical deterioration or impairment of physical fitness aside from the 'addiction' itself. They thus concluded that 'the existence of considerable emaciation in certain cases is caused by the unhygienic and impoverished life of the addict rather than by the direct effects of the drug.' The final verdict was that 'if the drug is used in sufficient amounts in relatively normal hygienic surroundings, the opium addict will escape detection for years and will not show any obvious physical deterioration or impaired physical fitness.'[102]

If 'addiction' was impossible to detect on the basis of a physical examination, how could smokers be convicted during the prohibition campaign? Besides denunciations from relatives, neighbours or colleagues, the mere possession of smoking utensils was considered a sign of guilt.[103] Urine tests were also used by doctors and chemists in the 1930s to testify against suspected addicts. However, reliance on medical evidence remained controversial. Lin Ji, the country's leading forensic scientist,[104] wondered as late as 1933 whether the chief constituents of opium such as morphine and meconic acid could actually enter the body with the opium fumes, since the smoking process was thought to reduce all vegetable matter to ash. Courts, government organisations and hospitals asked Lin to develop more reliable methods of determining opium addicts. There were technical shortcomings in most of the established methods, including insufficient sensibility of the reagents, but the key problem was lack of the most basic knowledge about the physiological changes during the smoking process. Lin Ji noted that the moisture and admixed impurities could cause the amount of 'toxic matter' in the body to vary significantly while the volume of each inhalation and the lapse of time between smokes was another important variant determining the quantity of opium in the blood. Experiments in his laboratories showed that only small amounts of morphine and meconic acid were absorbed, and appeared in the digestive tract. The widely-used urine analysis was described as an erroneous method for detecting the minute quantities released during the smoking process, and even after a hypodermic injection the amount in circulation was a mere 7 or 8 per cent, some of the opiates not passing into the urine at all. 'The urine may be perfectly negative when specimens are taken from addicts who are at that moment not excreting any of these bodies.'[105] Moreover, the testing of urine for the presence of morphine could only be done in hospitals or stations staffed by competent doctors. As a consequence, throughout the Nanjing decade the police would simply lock up suspects for an indeterminate period to watch out for any signs of withdrawal. These included yawning, running of the nose, restlessness and nervousness, loss of appetite, vomiting, diarrhoea and cramps.[106] Medical and judicial authorities also closely examined the general physical condition of suspects, including their facial appearance and state of their skin, teeth and lips, a practice which only deepened the longstanding confusion between the medical symptoms of the ailments against which opium was taken and the imagined physiological effects of 'addiction'.

Ignorance permeated the treatment given to those identified as 'addicts'. As Lawrence Kolb pointed out to the Bureau of Social Hygiene in the United States, almost nothing was known about the physiological changes brought about by opium addiction. The solution to 'addiction' was the 'creation of a drug that has the soothing properties of opium without its addicting properties', although he considered this an unrealisable dream.[107] Thus the medical treatment of addiction in China was haphazard: while opium smokers died in prison due to poor hygiene and over-crowding, many also suffered from the various methods tested on them in detoxification hospitals. Two methods of treatment in particular were widespread: the blister method (*choupao jieyanfa*) and the serum method (*zijia xueqing jieyanfa*). In the former, de-veloped by Polys Modinos, an irritant plaster was placed on the skin of the abdomen or thorax until a vesicle formed, the serous fluid being taken in a syringe and immediately injected subcuta-neously into the patient for three to four days. Modinos, director of the European Hospital in Alexandria, had treated rheumatism patients with serum since 1908, and he contended that antibodies present in the bloodstream appeared in a more active form in the vesicle fluid contained in a blister.[108] The use of blister fluid injec-tions spread in France and Italy in the 1910s and '20s, especially in the treatment of undulant fever, typhus and asthma. Tubercu-losis, gout, eye diseases and even cancer were treated by the me-thod known as autoserotherapy.[109] After Modinos noticed that one of his patients, who was also a morphine addict, developed an aversion to opiates, he further tested the method on cocaine and heroin addicts.[110]

As the Swedish health delegate to the League of Nations, Modinos circulated his method via the Advisory Committee on Traffic in Opium to a global audience in 1930.[111] Kwa Tjoan Sioe and Tan Kim Hong, physicians at a clinic in Batavia, immediately started applying this cure to opium smokers, using a large gauze pad smeared with a drawing substance (a cantharidin plaster) to produce a blister from which the liquid was tapped and injected intramuscularly as an anti-toxin: in their paper presented at a con-gress of the Far Eastern Association of Tropical Medicine in Bangkok in 1930, they described the method as 'startling', since it not only cured smokers without discomfort but also produced a phenomenon of 'hypersensitisation', with the mere smell of opium inducing dizziness, vomiting, profuse perspiration and dilated pu-pils. Although the authors were unable to explain this 'astound-ing phenomenon', they believed that the very simplicity of the cure made it the preferred method for 'mass treatment'.[112]

The blister method also appeared in China. Dr Lee S. Hui-zenga, a Dutch-born graduate of New York Medical College who was sent to China in the 1920s as a medical missionary by the Christian Reformed Church, experimented with the Modinos method after the gaol authorities of Rugao, Jiangsu province, asked him for assistance in curing opium smokers in 1934. Hui-zenga treated thirteen prisoners, some of them moderate opium smokers, others with a long history of frequent morphine injections, and reported the positive outcome of his experiments in the *Chinese Medical Journal*.[113] In response to letters of inquiry about the exact method to be followed, he published a short note in July 1935, observing that 'it has been suggested that normal blood might be used instead of serum'.[114] Others were thinking along similar lines: R. H. Mumford reported having tried taking an amount of blood from the arm for injection in a few cases in Quanzhou, since the whole blood had the same virtues as blister serum. Blood was also used in the Elizabeth Blake Hospital in Suzhou in 1934.[115] The 'serum method' did not require a blister, although both approaches were adopted by many detoxification centres in China in the following years (see illustration 11).

Throughout the period of treatment, urine tests were also made in most detoxification centres to determine the level of opium in the system. Diminishing doses of opium or morphine-based tinctures were sometimes given for about a week until all symptoms disappeared.[116] A reduction of the daily opiate intake needed to show flexibility, since the constitution as well as the state of mind of each individual patient had to be taken into account. Withdrawal symptoms were reduced by means of potassium bromide, veronal, bromural, luminol, antipyrin or aspirin. Scopolamine or atropine were also widely used as they acted on the nervous system during abstinence, although some doctors attributed no effect to these subsidiary drugs.[117] The blister treatment was particularly popular,[118] and was criticised by at least one detoxification expert for inducing extreme pain and mental anguish without any noticeable benefits.[119] While research into the history of detoxification methods is scarce, the Colorado State Penitentiary apparently announced in 1938 that it had developed a 'new cure' called the 'serum method' to treat opiate 'addicts'.[120] The treatment was exactly the same as the one used in China in earlier years, suggesting that medical expertise in addiction treatment circulated widely: however, the main contribution came from Asia, as the direction of the flow of knowledge about 'addiction' turned back towards the West.

In their search for a single therapeutic procedure or a magical chemical substance which would 'cure the addict',[121] other inventions were also proposed. Ma Wenzhao, based at the Central Hospital in Nanjing, located craving at the level of the cell, having observed in experiments with morphinised rats and human addicts that the absence of lipoid in body cells caused withdrawal symptoms. He developed the 'lecithin cure' (*luanlinzhi jieyanfa* or *danhuangsu jieyanfa*), consisting either of a chemical mixture of soy beans and egg yolks or of pure lecithin, since the substance was claimed to mimic some of the effects of opium in the bloodstream, effectively reducing the craving for drugs.[122] The widely advertised 'miracle cure' resulted in successful treatment after only a few days, without the usual withdrawal symptoms, weight loss, bowel irritation, sleep deprivation and 'horrors'.[123] Some specialists had reservations about the lecithin cure, which appeared to be based on medications already used in the treatment of neurasthenia,[124] although the method seemed much less painful than the growing of a blister and the repeated injection of serum.

Other 'miracle cures' were also tried out on patients in the model Nanjing Municipal Detoxification Hospital. A medication called Black Sea Star (*Heihaixing*) was used experimentally on thirty-seven patients in 1936, inducing diarrhoea and constant vomiting without any apparent benefit. Another restorative given to 100 patients caused variously nose bleeding, constipation, loss of appetite, tiredness, vomiting and diarrhoea: all of the subjects described the treatment as unbearable. Other opium smokers were used to test a mixture containing calomel, a mercury compound: the negative reactions were such that even the hospital had to admit that it had only managed to increase pain in patients.[125] The Nanjing Municipal Detoxification Hospital was a model institution: far more bizarre experiments were carried out in the hinterland, including the use of human urine or goat droppings. The 'goat shit cure' developed by Luo Lebin, a medical expert from Nanning, Guangxi province, was based on the chemical reaction between goat faeces and liquorice, to be administered for six days to opium addicts. His approach was heralded as a medical breakthrough by the local police.[126]

'Spiritual cures' (*jingshen jieyan fa*) were to supplement the use of modern pharmaceuticals, according to yet other self-proclaimed experts in detoxification. These included incantations, incense and talismans. Xia Shenchu required patients to practise sitting quietly (*jingzuo*) in the presence of two priests chanting the name of the Buddha. A ritual of presenting incense and receiving tea—seen as a pure and natural substance—was to be repeated twice daily over three days.[127] The Philosophical Study Centre of Gao'an county, Jiangxi province, even experimented exclusively with 'spiritual cures'. Abstaining from opium replacement pills and medical treatment altogether, the 'addicts' rose each morning at five to practise *taijiquan* for one hour, followed by readings from the Diamond Sutra and meditation. In their spare time, patients listened to the radio, performed music, played chess and read books. Each night they participated in Buddhist worship and recited from the Heart Sutra. The method, which was painless and cheap because smokers only had to pay for their food, was claimed to be popular.[128]

Opium smokers died in detoxification centres either because the medical authorities failed effectively to treat the ailments for which opium was taken in the first place or because replacement treatments were poorly conceived and badly administered. Plenty of archival evidence exists to illustrate how patients died within the first few days of treatment. One Han Zeng took advantage of an amnesty granted to volunteers, but died on the first day of a fever: none of his relatives could be traced to collect his body.[129] Song Jitang was welcomed at a detoxification centre in Beijing in April 1915 suffering from severe diarrhoea, and although given essential oil (*caomayou*) to treat it, he died two weeks later.[130] These cases date from the 1910s, but an abundance of other examples exist that show how patients continued to die in clinics throughout the republican period. In May 1946 Lu Quanbao was sent to the detoxification hospital in Wu county, Jiangsu province. Lu was aged sixty-two and suffering from a heart problem: he died five days later. The following month, seventy-three-year-old Luo Bangshi, who had relied on opium to control severe gastro-intestinal problems, was compelled by the local court in Jiangsu province to follow treatment, and he died in hospital on the second day of his replacement therapy.[131] These were not isolated cases: out of 12,105 addicts registered in Henan province, 290 were reported to have died during treatment; all but five were from the poor.[132] On the other hand, some hospitals felt compelled to prescribe opiates to the very same smokers they were treating if they suffered from a severe cough or spitted blood: at the heart of the prohibition campaign, opium remained the best available palliative for the commonest ailments, tuberculosis in particular, a simple truth recognised even by anti-opium institutions.[133]

CAPITAL CRIMES: THE JUDICIAL KILLING OF 'ADDICTS'

The judicial killing of ordinary people defined as 'addicts' started with the military jurisdiction over opium prohibition in communist areas in 1932. Military control of drug-related matters was extended in June 1934 to the municipalities of Nanjing and Shanghai and again in April 1935 to encompass nine provinces and other cities. In general only serious drug traffickers were given the death penalty, but this was extended also to opiate users: a twenty-eight-year-old barber from Linzheng, Anhui province, thus became one of the first relapsed heroin users to be executed under new government legislation in November 1934 as a warning to others; his use of heroin was the only charge against him.[134] During the narcotics suppression campaign in early 1935 more were executed: five on charges of 'drug addiction', two for trafficking, five for wrongly inculpating others and two for administering morphine injections; several others were still awaiting execution in April.[135] Patients who relapsed after having been cured also faced the firing squad,[136] as the example of the poor fisherman Shi Fenglou showed. Caught stealing a watermelon in the summer of 1935 in Nanhui, he was found to have already undergone compulsory treatment, but had continued to inject morphine after his release. Reported to the military authorities, he was paraded through the city and shot in public as a lesson to other morphine users.[137] By the end of 1935 over 800 drug offenders had been executed, the majority in Shandong (620) and Shanxi (106), but also in cities like Nanjing (58), Hankou (15) and Shanghai (3). Over 1,100 executions were carried out in Shandong, Zhejiang, Nanjing, Weihaiwei and Hebei the following year.[138]

In February 1936 the National Opium Suppression Commission announced that anybody with a narcotic habit could face up to seven years in prison and would have to undergo compulsory treatment. Second-time offenders could face execution;[139] opium smokers relapsing after treatment 'will be shot without further ceremony'.[140] The new legislation was put into practice in many parts of the country: in April 1936, eight men and one woman were sentenced to death in Xian, paraded through the streets in rickshaws and publicly executed before thousands of spectators.[141] The marching of addicts and dealers through the streets on their way to the execution ground became a common sight in Hangzhou,[142] while in Beijing dealers were shot following public burning of illegal drugs.[143] In June 1936 the Provisional Anti-Opium Law further included strict measures against relapsed smokers, whereas even the keeping of smoking appliances as collectors' items was subject to prison sentences, forced labour or heavy fines.[144] Foreign observers were not impressed, and the Municipal Council in Shanghai even considered that 'the penalty of death for such an offence is no more defensible than hanging for sheep stealing': it refused to be party to these draconian regulations in the foreign-controlled areas of Shanghai.[145]

Harsher punishments were accompanied by the issuing of rehabilitation certificates to registered opium smokers who would be cured in detoxification centres according to a plan which envisaged the gradual elimination of all opium by 1940.[146] The certificates could be used to buy opium from wholesale shops and

retail outlets accredited by the government under opium monopoly legislation until all smokers were successfully rehabilitated.[147]
While a policy of gradual suppression under a government monopoly would have avoided many of the problems created by
strict prohibition, it was never fully implemented: the outbreak
of the war with Japan in July 1937, the failure of the government
to control all opium held by the public and establish a state monopoly, and lack of institutional coordination in drug suppression
after the resignation of Jiang Jieshi as General Supervisor of Opium Prohibition in March 1938 undermined the entire campaign.[148] Evidence also shows that the 'public opium' sold under
government control to licensed smokers was too expensive for
many poor workers: the municipal authorities in Chongqing,
for instance, were obliged to issue extra licences for forty opium
shops to sell local produce, because the existing fifty-eight outlets
only retailed Yunnan opium, which was beyond the means of
the poor coolies who turned to cheaper morphine instead.[149]

Institutional fragmentation also led to abuse of the death penalty, as different organs set up to carry out prohibition work applied existing legislation haphazardly. While the offences of most
of those convicted were manufacturing, transporting or selling
semi-synthetics, some who were no more than opium smokers
were also put to death. In parts of the country where local authorities had insufficient funds to establish detoxification centres,
execution could be seen as a handy shortcut in opium suppression. In Yunnan, where the easy availability of opium prevented
the spread of morphine and heroin, opium smokers were executed as a solution to 'the opium problem'.[150] In Fujian province
alone forty opium smokers were shot in 1938.[151] In the capital
Nanjing, where there were reportedly hundreds of executions of
opiate users by the military authorities every month in 1937, some
were carried out in response to the congestion problems experienced by the Jiangsu No. 1 Prison, showing how judicial killing
was used to solve organisational problems encountered during
the prohibition movement: the military admitted that innocent
people were being shot.[152] Even after the government was forced
to abandon the coastal provinces during the war and establish a

new capital in Chongqing, the shooting of drug users continued: in 1940 fourteen were sentenced to death in Sichuan and the following year twenty were executed out of a total of 2,785 drug-related offenders.[153]

While most of the executed 'addicts' used 'dangerous narcotics' such as morphine or heroin, the military authorities did not differentiate between different semi-synthetics and their various modes of delivery. In May 1937 several people in Shaanxi were arrested and one was executed for using red pills.[154] However, as the next chapters show, a world of difference existed between the injection of strong morphine and the smoking of weak pills which often contained little if any heroin.

8

PILLS AND POWDERS: THE SPREAD OF
SEMI-SYNTHETIC OPIATES (*c.* 1900–1940)

In the wake of the anti-opium movement large quantities of semi-synthetics began to be imported into China. This chapter looks at the spread of morphine and heroin in modern China, examining the reasons for their popular appeal. Heroin has been demonised by narcophobic discourse as the very epitome of addiction and the squalid descent to certain death of the social dropouts who inject it. However, during the first decades of the twentieth century morphine and heroin were widely smoked in moderate quantities by a variety of social categories, and some of the heroin pills taken for recreational purposes contained only a very small proportion of alkaloids and were often based on lactose or caffeine. Morphine and heroin had few concrete drawbacks, and a number of practical advantages which persuaded many opium smokers to switch: pills were convenient to transport, relatively cheap, odourless and thus almost undetectable in police searches, and easy to use since they no longer required the complicated paraphernalia and time-consuming rituals of opium smoking. Heroin pills enabled consumers to replicate the smoking culture created around opium while avoiding most of the practical constraints produced by prohibition: they allowed narcotic culture to be reproduced in a different legal context. Morphine and heroin could be ingested, smoked or injected: a later chapter looks more closely at the syringe, a new tool which would create a range of serious medical problems for the very poor who could no longer afford to smoke.

1. Opium paraphernalia (Wellcome Library).
2. A teahouse in Hong Kong, *c.* 1870.

3. Wealthy opium smokers, end of Qing (Archibald Little, *The Land of the Blue Gown*, 1902).

4. Wealthy opium smokers displaying a variety of pipes, end of Qing (Wellcome Library).

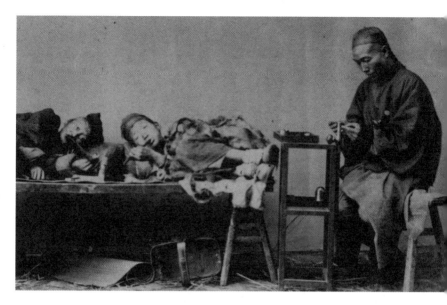

5. Poor opium smokers in an opium house, 1900 (Franklin and Bertha Schweinfurth Ohlinger Papers, Yale Divinity Library).

6. Poor opium smokers in an opium house, 1939 (Wellcome Library).

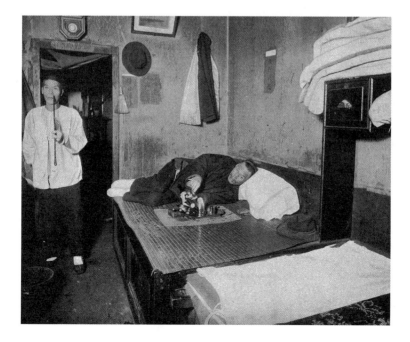

7. Anti-opium propaganda, 1932 (*Lunyu half-monthly*, October 1932).

8. Anti-opium propaganda, 1936 (*Jinyan banyuekan* [Anti-Opium half-monthly], 3 June 1936).

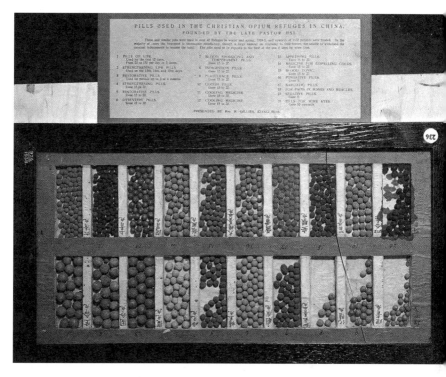

9. Anti-opium pills, 1904-5 (Wellcome Library).

10. Tattoo on an opium smoker in Beijing, 1936 (*Jinyan banyuekan*, 3 June 1936).

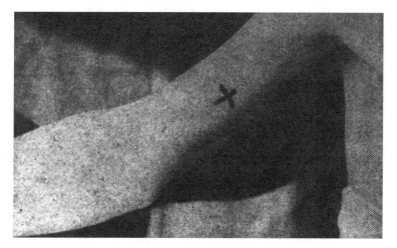

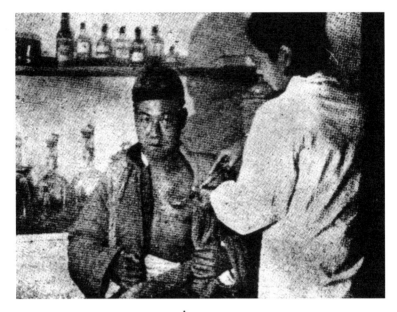

11. A patient being given the blister method treatment, 1936 (*Jinyan banyuekan*, 3 June 1936).

12. A government detoxification centre, 1930s (*Jinyan banyuekan*, 3 June 1936).

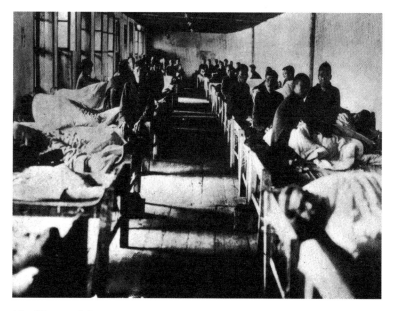

13. The ward for poor patients at a detoxification centre in Hunan, 1936 (Jinyan banyuekan, 3 June 1936).

14. The ward for wealthy patients at the Nanjing detoxification hospital, 1936 (Jinyan banyuekan, 3 June 1936).

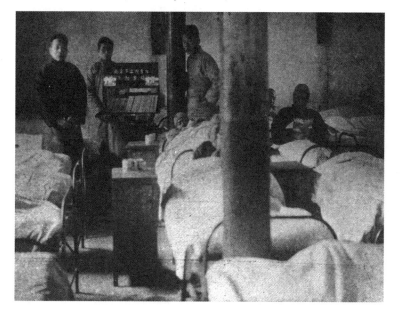

15. Red pills (C.P. Fairchild, 'The rise and fall of the pink pill', ms.
16. Drug-user Ding Yuting before being executed in Qingdao, 1936 (Jinyan banyuekan, 3 June 1936).

扎成篩孔　痛苦難堪

17. Itinerant doctor curing rheumatism by sticking needles into patients (Paul Monroe, *China: a nation in evolution*, New York: Macmillan, 1928, p. 284).

18. Image of a drug injector, 1930s (Lang Xiaocang, Duhuojian [The harm of drugs], 1934).

19. A drug user being injected, 1930s (Lang Xiaocang, Duhuojian, 1934).

20. Two habitual morphine users in Manchuria, 1930s (Zhonghua yixue zazhi, 6, 2, June 1920, p. 62).

THE NEW PANACEA: MORPHINE

Morphine was isolated in Europe as the active agent of opium in the early decades of the nineteenth century. First produced by the pharmacist Friedrich Wilhelm Sertürner (1783–1841) between 1803 and 1805, the crystalline white substance was christened morphium—after the god of sleep, Morpheus. The potential benefits of the isolated alkaloid were rapidly recognised in medical circles, and in 1827 Heinrich Emanuel Merck produced morphine commercially in his chemical laboratories. Pharmacists and practitioners, writers such as Jules Verne, the statesman Otto von Bismarck and the political adventurer Georges Boulanger were among those who found morphine attractive. Medical experts appreciated it for its predictable therapeutic action since, unlike opium, it was unadulterated and could be measured exactly. It was widely distributed to Prussian soldiers during the war against France in 1870, and its use spread rapidly throughout Europe, particularly in France and Germany in the following decades.[1] By the end of the nineteenth century morphine, whether injected, ingested or taken in suppository form, was popular against insomnia, neuralgia, painful conditions such as peritonitis or tetanus, or incurable diseases and cancers. While considered more modern, precise and effective to administer than opium, it fulfilled the same medical functions.[2]

Morphine appeared in Bengal in 1881, its use gradually increasing up till the end of the nineteenth century. Taken as pills or dissolved in water but rarely in an alcoholic solution, it was at first only available on prescription. Opium eaters began to take morphine pills instead, though rarely more than three times a day. Excessive use of morphine, in the opinion of Dr Ram Moy Roy, medical officer in Calcutta, led to complaints of insomnia and loss of appetite.[3] When it reached Singapore around 1890, it became so popular that imports of opium declined significantly, although it regained some of its commercial position two years later.[4] Morphine use gradually spread throughout Asia in the first decades of the twentieth century, some alarmed observers even noting that 'morphinomania' had become widespread in parts of India and the Malay peninsula by 1915.[5]

Smokers started adding medical morphine to opium in Hong Kong in the early 1890s to increase strength at the expense of flavour. Experienced smokers recruited for experimental purposes by a local hospital described the mixture as 'coarse' and neutral in taste.[6] Morphine also appeared in mainland China, and was listed for the first time as a separate item in the Imperial Customs annual report in 1891. Xiamen was one of the major ports of entry, where it was repackaged for wholesale distribution, shops in the region advertising the morphine as an effective opium cure. The increase of morphine in Xiamen, as elsewhere, coincided with a decrease in opium.[7] As a contemporary journalist observed, morphine, either injected or taken as pills, 'follows in the footsteps of opium'.[8] Morphine started to move up the Yangzi river in the 1890s, being widely advertised as a 'remedy for foreign smoke'.[9] Morphine pills, powders and solutions were also available in cities along the coast, including Beijing, Tianjin, Jinan, Hankou, Nanjing, Suzhou, Ningbo and Fuzhou.[10] The pills had the advantage of being instantly disposable and more portable, easily spreading from the coastal region to the hinterland. Between 1892 and 1901 morphine imports increased from just under 450 kilos a year to 3.25 tonnes.[11]

The preceeding chapter noted how morphine pills were used by medical missionaries as part of detoxification cures during the late Qing. Japan also played an important role in the distribution of morphine, in particular after the fall of the empire in 1911. In the wake of the Hague Convention morphine appeared in southern ports like Shantou and in Shandong province in which Japanese traders were active after 1915. Foreign post offices in the principal cities of China were used for mailing narcotic products and remained beyond the control of the Chinese government because of extraterritorial rights.[12] The restrictive measures introduced by several European governments following the Hague Convention were easily circumvented, while the outbreak of the First World War impeded effective international action against the flow of morphine. The two prime manufacturers before the war were Germany and Britain; blockaded trade routes and declining domestic production in Germany entailed a drastic increase in British exports after 1915; the main importer of British morphine was Japan, a pattern which continued despite international opposition to the trade. During the late 1910s alkaloids were purchased directly from the manufacturer and sent out undeclared with other goods, no longer appearing in the trade returns. In 1920 morphine could thus be legally ordered in England, shipped to Kobe via New York, passing through the customs in bond to San Francisco, and transhipped on arrival in Kobe without entry in the customary trade returns, for distribution in China.[13]

In Japan the morphine was packaged into little packets or small bottles labelled 'pure morphine', 'white powder', 'soothing medicine', 'dreamland elixir' and other brand names before being exported openly or smuggled into China.[14] Whereas only Britain and Germany possessed the necessary equipment for manufacturing morphine before the First World War, Japan soon established laboratories and factories in Taiwan, Osaka and Dalian.[15] Morphine was imported from Japan via the ports of Qingdao, Dalian, Andong, Hong Kong, Macau and Canton. Figures based on customs seizures and published by the health official Wu Liande showed a marked increased in morphine imports during the 1910s. Between the fall of the Qing and the Paris Peace Conference imports increased from under 60,000 kilos a year to some 280,000 (see following table).[16]

	kilos
1911	59,121
1912	78,408
1913	115,145
1914	142,890
1915	170,100★
1916	170,100★
1917	226,800★
1918	226,800★
1919	283,500★

★ approximate

Many Japanese subjects used their extraterritorial privileges to pursue the morphine trade in China, and Japanese pharmacists, pawnbrokers, peddlers and shopkeepers were notorious for supplying semi-synthetic drugs. This trade developed unabated during the decades before the Second World War. In 1930, for instance, around 100 morphine outlets existed in the immediate vicinity of Japanese dispensaries or residences. The number of Japanese-sponsored morphine huts in some cities was rumoured to vary between 500 (Mukden) and 1,500 (Changchun), said to be operated by Koreans, Japanese and naturalised citizens of Japan.[17] The Nanjing government, and later the communist authorities, repeatedly claimed that drug trafficking formed an integral part of Japan's colonial ambitions. By 'poisoning the Chinese people' and 'destroying the Chinese race' with morphine, cocaine, heroin and opium, Japan was intent on breaking the nation's spirit of resistance. While the factual details of such allegations may not be unfounded, anti-Japanese propaganda by Chinese nationalists no doubt helped shape an image of criminal trafficking by the Japanese enemy.

Spurred by prohibition, morphine thrived on the illegal market, the dimensions of which swamped public authorities, as specific cases from archival material show. Between 1920 and 1925, the Jinan police confiscated packages of morphine products ranging in size from a few grams to 2 kilos, while in Qiu county pillmaker Wang Luoshan made daily sales of 500,000 pills, aided by a small army of peddlers. Shandong labourers would divide their daily ration of morphine pills into three parts, eating two during the day, and smoking the third at leisure in the evening.[18] Nearly three quarters of a million dollars were imposed in fines during 1924 in seventy-five counties of the metropolitan province of Zhili (largely corresponding to modern Hebei), where morphine consumption was considered lower than in Shandong, Henan or Manchuria. Contraband activities could be organised on a small-scale basis—such as in 1915 in Lingyuan county (Liaoning), where a Japanese subject sold morphine marketed as opium cure medicine, complete with hypodermic needles.[19] The trade could involve powerful networks, utilising banks, post offices and army posts which even the local criminals as well as the police were loath to take on.[20] Small-scale pill makers, on the other hand, could churn out half a million pills daily, flooding country towns in the provinces north of the Yangzi river. Widespread smuggling, often by respectably-clad gentlemen and female bootleggers along the railway routes, contributed to the proliferation of morphine pills. Observers thought the situation there 'deplorable', not hesitating to point out that 'opium is almost innocent when compared with morphia'.[21] Even Chinese subjects based in London—to the dismay of the local Overseas Chinese Association—made their fortune by selling opium, morphine and other narcotics via Paris.[22] Much of the morphine reached Chinese ports in European cargo consignments, usually in French or British ships. Twenty-five tins of morphine despatched from Liverpool, each containing 500 grams, were 'closely packed with eight tins of lobster paste in a trunk which was practically new, with brass corners and leather handles'. Smuggled morphine was also hidden in coal recesses, among fruit cases or in wardrobe trunks.[23]

During the 1920s morphine pills were known by various names in different parts of the country, and were transported as wholesale items in white cotton bags containing 10,000 pills. A growing number of users preferred the morphine pill to the ever more expensive opium, while many dreaded the abscesses caused by the syringe. The morphine pill 'presents every element which appeals to the Chinese worker, it is cheap, effective and secretive'.[24]

MEDICAL CULTURE, MIRACLE CURES AND MAGIC PILLS

Medical morphine imported from Britain was advertised in the *Shenbao* as early as 1874 as a miracle cure less crude than opium or dross,[25] and as noted above it was used by medical missionaries in opium remedies during the 1890s. Shrewd entrepreneurs also marketed countless opium remedies in a medical culture which placed great faith in foreign medicines. Huang Chujiu (1872–1931) was a prime example of those who made a fortune out of this trade. The son of a herbal doctor who had never left his native region, Huang moved to Shanghai and hawked medicines as a street peddler before opening a traditional drugstore. In 1890 he moved his business to the French Concession and converted his shop into a modern pharmacy, selling its own patent 'modern' medicines, including morphine-based 'natural pills for breaking the opium habit' (*tianran jieyanwan*). This pill alone generated an annual profit of more than 100,000 yuan.[26] Other commercial dispensaries also benefited from selling opium remedies based on morphine. Patent medicines with morphine were commercialised as powders, liquids, cakes or pills. Some of the cures—known as 'powders against craving' (*duanyinsan*), 'white medical powders' (*baiyaofen*) or 'white crystal powders' (*baijingfen*)—even included codeine.[27] By the early 1930s over fifty anti-opium pills containing morphine were listed by Cao Bingzhang, a traditional physician and author of a treatise on addiction cures. These came in glass jars or bottles, tin containers, paper boxes, wraps, tubes or envelopes, mostly manufactured by Japanese or Chinese companies.[28] 'Tranquillity' (*caizhi feilei ping'an yaosu*), marketed in bottles of 4 fluid ounces (c. 115 ml) in Shanghai, included morphine and meconic acid.[29] Even the officially licensed opium cure 'Body Builder' (*jieyan jianshen wan*) from Sichuan, marketed all over China, was discovered to comprise morphine.[30] Countless others appeared in the 1930s, and the Chongqing police bureau uncovered twelve samples of the most popular opium replacement cures, eight of which were shown on being tested to contain morphine—the remaining four were not examined, having been damaged in transit. A similar situation prevailed in Chengdu, where the government inspector Xiao Zhiping urged the Central Prohibition Office to regulate and restrict the sale of all anti-opium medicines, arguing that they had become a 'serious obstacle' in the implementation of official opium suppression plans.[31]

The use of morphine, besides being cheap and effective, was also seen as a 'modern' statement: like opium in the late eighteenth century, its foreign origin conferred status, respect and prestige. Its consumption was also part of a more general craze for things foreign. The watch, the bicycle and the syringe were prestige symbols which conferred social status and a cultural cachet—this made them attractive regardless of their original purpose.[32] However, the rapid growth in unlicensed 'modern' medications led to frequent misdiagnoses. In search of a miracle cure patients often switched doctors and tried out a mixture of incompatible remedies bought from 'modern' dispensaries rather than from local hospitals, resulting in confusion if not death.[33] Morphine-based medications could be contaminated or adulterated with poisonous substances. To increase profits manufacturers often cut the product, mixing it with iron filings, exhausted dross or even extracts of pork rind (*zhupi liao*).[34] In 1919 the government laboratory issued a health warning concerning the drug 'Body Calmer' (*anti yaopian*), manufactured by the Yangzi Pharmaceutical Company in Shanghai. These pills contained large amounts of morphine, codeine, nicotine and nitric acid. The widely advertised tonic 'Life Endower' (*shengzhiling*), to take another example, harboured the poisonous substance yohimbine, and was also singled out for withdrawal from the market.

In the absence of a system of patenting, testing and regulating medicines, harmful substances, widely advertised as cures for every imaginable ill, were not only important sources of economic loss, of prolonging illness or giving false hopes, but could also lead to narcotic habits in some patients. When Woo Tsenzung, manager of a Chinese dispensary in Hangzhou, was arrested in the autumn of 1916, the Shanghai municipal authorities concluded that the 'quinine pills' marketed by his firm and smuggled into Shanghai in the hulls of commercial ships contained nearly three times more morphine than quinine, 'sufficient to kill a child'. Woo's pills also contained a large amount of strychnine, which would have an adverse effect even on adults accustomed to morphine.[35] Foreign travellers in late 1918 reported with bewilderment that 'Western doctors' in Hankou sold medicines clearly labelled 'Corrosive Sublimate' in English and containing enough strychnine to kill a dog.[36] Successive governments during the republican period thus not only had a difficult task in attempting to regulate access to semi-synthetics, but also more generally in controlling all pharmaceuticals.

As a consequence of weak regulation and strong market demand, opium, morphine and heroin figured prominently in many popular brands of patent medicines, which were widely available on the market. These ranged from cough syrups, vaccines against epidemics and pills for bowel syndromes to remedies against venereal diseases and soporifics. The *Chinese Medical Journal* even concluded rather dramatically in 1933 that China was 'the only country in the world that can be flooded with all kinds of worthless medicines.'[37]

Lin Yutang—professor of literature, journalist and writer of popular books—concurred by observing that China was the ideal place for unscrupulous practitioners who advertised their shoddy products in the countless 'medical supplements' which thrived in the modern print culture of republican China.[38] According to a contemporary observer, 'Practically every newspaper of this country derives its main financial support from the patent medicine vendors, as any reader of the Chinese press may quickly ascertain. The gullibility of the general public is proverbial in any country, but in China this takes on an extreme form, for both the educated and the uneducated readily swallow all the lies and exaggerations which appear in print.'[39]

The rampant spread of quack medicine, of course, was equally widespread in other countries, including England and the United States,[40] and in their search for professional autonomy and moral authority their medical associations relentlessly attacked charlatans and self-styled clinics.[41] Members of the Chinese Medical Association launched their campaign to restrict folk remedies and medical advertising as early as in 1909.[42] Their organ, the *China Medical Journal*, believed that Pure Food and Drug laws as well as clear labelling on medicines would drive out the opiates from the home market.[43] A draft law restricting the sale of semi-synthetics and licensing all pharmacies was unsuccessfully proposed in March 1920 by Wu Liande, a medical administrator for the central government.[44] He approached the government again in 1929, describing many of the new patent medicine as 'harmful luxuries' and criticising the 'general public' for readily accepting all the false claims made by drug manufacturers.[45] The acting Minister of Health Liu Ruiheng issued a Proposed Regulations Governing Patent and Proprietary Medicines a year later, whereby all

medicines had to be properly tested, registered, labelled and packaged, and medical advertising had to be free of any false claims.[46]
Although the regulations were attacked by the Shanghai New
Medicine Trade Association (*Shanghaishi xinyao shangye tongye
gonghui*), Huang Chujiu being one of its firmest lobbyists,[47] it was
finally passed by the government by the end of 1932.[48] A vast
amount of unlicensed medications nonetheless continued to flood
the market, leading the government to promulgate a new Patent
Medicine Law in January 1937.[49] However, in a country where
the vast majority of ordinary people had no access to a modern
health infrastructure many had no alternative but to rely on morphine pills—especially in a culture with a long tradition of self-
medication.[50]

HEROIN: THE GENTLE DRUG

Diacetyl morphine was first discovered in 1874 in St Mary's Hospital, London, and traded after 1899 by Bayer under the trade
name 'Heroin'. This was a more powerful painkiller than morphine, yet in the early twentieth century it was still considered a
gentle medicine to be used mainly against respiratory symptoms.[51]
In Europe it was initially heralded as a chemically pure, non-
addictive anaesthetic, and was also widely used as an effective
remedy for morphine addiction. In the 1900s heroin was widely
applied hypodermically as a non-addictive substitute for morphine
by doctors in Europe and the United States.[52] Pharmaceutical
companies marketed it as a cure for numerous diseases, including
infantile respiratory ailments, coughs and bronchitis. Its recreational
use spread quickly in the United States until it was outlawed in
1914, but this did not happen in Europe with its established tradition of opium use.[53] Heroin was also popular during the 1920s
and '30s in Egypt. Produced almost entirely by three factories
near Istanbul, it was smuggled into Alexandria in the cargo bays
of steamships and in the luggage of individual travellers. The
United States, China and Egypt opted for an uncompromising
war against illegal drugs,[54] and these policies exacerbated the very
problems they were designed to contain.

'RED TERROR': THE MYSTERIOUS RED PILLS

Heroin arrived in China after the turn of the century as a 'gentle' anaesthetic drug, more effective and with fewer side effects than either opium or morphine. As one medical expert commented, it was a 'safe, reliable analgesic, one which can be repeated if necessary without producing habit or doing harm in any way.'[55] As an alternative to opium, heroin pills and powders only appeared on the market after the fall of the empire. Although the main ingredient was heroin, these narcotic substances could include caffeine, quinine and occasionally also cocaine to suit the predilections of different consumer groups.[56] The red pill in particular was unique to China, where it allowed users to replicate a smoking culture without the practical constraints associated with opium.

The first red pills entered the narcotic market around 1912 as opium replacement cures.[57] The heroin pills took their name from the infamous 'red pills' prescribed in 1620 to the Guangzong emperor, who died soon after taking the drug. The name may also have been linked to 'the red lead magic drug' (*hongqian qiyao*), rumoured to contain the first menstrual blood of a virgin.[58] Red pills resonated with red cinnabar, a time-honoured ingredient of Daoist alchemy. In parts of northern China heroin was even referred to as 'cinnabar' (*dansha* or *danliao*).[59] Whatever their original connotation, red pills, like opium in previous centuries, were given an imperial cachet by ordinary users: just as 'modern' medications were endowed with quasi-magical properties, the names of the semi-synthetic drugs purveyed a sense of continuity with the medical tradition of the imperial past.

Resembling small and slightly unripe lychees, red pills consisted of heroin or morphine, caffeine, quinine or other cinchona alkaloids, a trace of strychnine, cane sugar or lactose, gum, flour or starch and colouring agents.[60] The pills were often pink, carmine or pale purple. The ingredients used for the pill mass varied widely, depending on the quality of their ingredients (*liao*). 'Refined' (*xi*) pills contained pure morphine or heroin, with added cocaine at times. At 0.065 grams each, 'Fairy Horse' pills were based on caffeine (8 per cent) and quinine (2.2 per cent), as well as heroin (1.3 per cent). Unusually, they were not uniformly coloured, but white inside with a bright pink coating.[61] Some consumers preferred the dearer morphine as the main ingredient, purer in taste than the often adulterated heroin. A pill with added morphine was the most expensive variety, a luxury akin to attaching a filter to a cigarette.[62] 'Less refined ingredients' (*zhongliao*) normally consisted of caffeine, quinine or other cinchona alkaloids. Caffeine was often listed together with dye in the composition list, and may have been considered less a stimulant than a substance adding dimension to the pill, not unlike mild spices and natural dyes, counteracting the influence of 'rustic ingredients' (*culiao*).[63] Given the extremely low narcotic content of these pills, it may well be that some users actually craved for caffeine,[64] and since this could be obtained legally from any pharmacy the possibility of caffeine 'addiction' was largely ignored in the official discourse. Other additives included perfumes such as rose essence, sugar and sweetened milk powder, substances that induced memories of scented opium.[65] On the other hand, a sweet tooth among consumers may have been the reason why pills were sweetened: some recalled that their sugary taste was preferable to the lingering bitterness left by opium smoking.[66] However, since a distinct smell could lead to police detection, many preferred the odourless white powder: morphine and heroin were immune to olfactory recognition.[67]

Consumer demand also guided the colour and shape of pills— for example, extremely small ones were preferred in Henan and pearl-like ones in the lower Yangzi valley.[68] Pills could be sold in any quantity, with consumption ranging from sixteen to 100 pills per day, depending on size and strength.[69] Like opium, different categories of red pills commanded a range of prices, most being widely available from local shops. Commonly known as 'anti-opium pills' (*jieyanyao*), a variety of brands vied for consumer attention, the most famous being 'VIP' (*shangdaren*), 'Tiger Boy' (*huzai*), 'Golden Coin' (*jinqian*) and 'Three Peaches' (*santao*). Regional products also thrived. Competing for a niche in the provincial market of Zhejiang, brands such as 'Single Dragon', 'Double Phoenix' and 'Number Eleven' sold for 105 to 130 yuan for 10,000 pills.[70]

Contemporary observers were uncertain how much actual harm was caused by red pills, most portraying heroin as insidious and leading to certain death. The Shanghai Municipal Council warned that the effect of the pills was 'similar to indulgence in opium, but [they are] more harmful'.[71] Local crusaders against opium also viewed opiate pills with great alarm. The *North China Daily News* stated in 1925: 'It is true that as an "anti" opium pill, the new product serves its purpose. It does in most cases lead to the abandonment of opium, but for the reason that the new "smoke" is more attractive, more potent in its effect as a stimulant, and, in its effect on the system of the smoker, more deadly.' Another expert estimated that 'the average life of an addict to the new habit can only be about four years.'[72] Others commented on the 'beggar–addicts' of Shanghai's slums, where 'a piece of tinfoil, charred on one side' revealed the use of heroin use. 'Addicts' were described as 'scarcely notic[ing] the strangers within the walls. Their gaze is fixed, their greyish skin is set in a horrible sardonic mask. Most of them are drug addicts,'[73] 'slaves of the lethal drug heroin… victims of the cheapest and most destructive narcotic known to man'.[74] The National Anti-Opium Association even demonised red pills as the 'red terror spreading across China, endangering the Chinese race.'[75]

On the other hand, in a study commissioned by the League of Nations, Dr Knaffl–Lenz of Austria concluded in 1926 that the pills (weighing on average 0.25 grams) contained a negligible amount of heroin (2.76 per cent) but 6.87 per cent caffeine; all contained at least 66 per cent lactose and 22 per cent sugar. In a number of contraband consignments reaching Hong Kong in 1930, heroin pills made in Canton and Macau contained no heroin at all. None of the intoxicating ingredients were found to have passed into the smoke, which contained as much as 40 per cent of caffeine.[76]

Another report by the Hong Kong authorities concluded that the main sensation after inhalation was a dull, sugary feeling, produced by the incinerated lactose. The heroin in red pills was characterised as 'very imperfectly acetylated', rendering it into nothing but unconverted morphine. It was estimated that 140 kilos of strychnine and some 900 of caffeine were imported into China each month uniquely for the manufacture of red pills.[77] Many smokers in the crown colony's opium divans even shunned heroin as an 'unnecessary refinement for the unsophisticated', often preferring smoking pills which contained no other substances besides caffeine, begging the question whether smokers simply craved a 'caffeine kick'. With red pills increasingly being manufactured locally, Hong Kong imported some 5,160 kilos of caffeine in 1936.[78] Heroin nonetheless found a ready consumer market in Hong Kong's smoking establishments, particularly after the outbreak of hostilities in 1937 brought a rising number of refugees to the colony from the mainland. Official estimates for late 1937 put the number of smoking houses where opium only was consumed (with fragrances and additives such as caffeine) at 800, to be matched by an equal number of 'divans' where both opium and heroin were smoked.[79] However, despite the onslaught of red pills opium remained the dominant drug in Hong Kong as well as in other European colonies in Asia: thanks to a colonial monopoly over its legal sale and distribution from 1914 to 1943, it persisted as the most cost-effective and convenient drug, a situation brought to an end by American pressure to eliminate all opium monopolies during the Second World War.[80]

Red pills were smoked like opium, requiring a pipe, a needle and a lamp. The pill pipe was made of a bamboo stem, about 30 centimetres long, with a porcelain bowl, resembling a small vase into which the stem was inserted. The side was pierced, so that a small pill could be balanced for smoking. The authorities in Macau related in 1933 to the League of Nations a brief document outlining other methods of smoking the pills, among the most common being the use of an ordinary china jar, or a liquor flask with the spout removed, with a pill-sized hole. Having heated the pill, the smoke was inhaled via a bamboo tube, simply placed above the open jar.[81] The smoke was described as 'very pleasant on the lungs', characterised by an exceptional aroma. Smokers purportedly used it to purify their breath, while it also acquired a reputation as a laxative.[82] Brothels supplied the pills to their customers for 'relaxation' (*xiaoqian*).[83]

A report from Hong Kong indicated that most smokers were poor coolies, but some also belonged to the well-to-do classes. Pills were considered cleaner to handle and smoke, while the operation was comparatively quick so that the smoker could return to his job. Finally, they were cheap, 10 cents to buy three to five being enough.[84] These factors may help explain why by the late 1930s millions of red ('pink') pills were consumed in Hong Kong alone, and more than half a million illegally imported or produced pills were seized by the colony's law enforcement agencies (600,000 in 1937).[85] In an interesting reversal of the global stream of psychoactive substances, heroin pills were even exported to Europe and North America in the 1930s, before gradually disappearing during the Second World War.[86] However, in the 1970s authorities in Amsterdam noticed that heroin cut with strychnine and caffeine was arriving on the black market: this granular heroin was prepared for smoking purposes in Hong Kong but had 'escaped' into those illicit markets where intravenous injection was the usual method of use, thus increasing the risk of strychnine poisoning among heroin injectors.[87]

Following the Hague Convention red pills were officially listed in China as illegal drugs, together with opium, morphine, cocaine and heroin.[88] While red pills were less cumbersome to consume than opium, the mere fact that a specific type of lamp and pipe were required made smokers liable to police detection. Heroin powder, on the other hand, could be smoked in a number of ways, often blended with tobacco and smoked in very small pipes which could easily be hidden. The appearance of alternative heroin products is explored in the following section.

GOLDEN ELIXIRS AND WHITE POWDERS

'Golden elixir' (*jindan*) appeared on the market as an alternative to red pills in the aftermath of the Hague Convention. Golden elixir pills, named after the 'immortality pills' of Daoist alchemy, were dark yellowish and oval in shape, although improved methods of production later resulted in white, red, yellow, purple and other colours, the pills being round and slightly bigger than a pea.

Some were even sold in bottles as a government-sanctioned opium cure (*jieyanyao*) at modern drug stores in Tianjin and Shanghai. Sales figures of golden elixir pills were in the millions per week during the early 1920s, suggesting a burgeoning consumer market for heroin products.[89]

Heroin pills were widely used by poor people as a substitute for the more expensive opium. They could be as cheap as one yuan for seventy to eighty pills, a similar measure of opium costing five times more: always alert for a good deal, smokers started stuffing their pipes with heroin instead of opium or tobacco.[90] Golden elixir soon spread inland and became common in North China, particularly in the provinces of Shanxi and Henan, appealing to individuals across the social spectrum.[91] Specific cases from archival sources highlight the popularity of 'immortality pills' in Shanxi: in 1919–20, for instance, 191 criminal cases were related to heroin pills compared to only forty-eight to opium.[92] The three counties of Lingchuan, Fenxi and Yangcheng alone had a total of over 8,500 heroin users, ranging from government officials to poor beggars.[93] The British diplomat John Jordan commented in 1919 that opiate dealers in northern Henan were also 'doing a roaring trade', describing the use of narcotic pills as 'very great'.[94] Hebei too was a big market for heroin: in 1928 large numbers of pills were confiscated by the local government. Consumers came from all walks of life, ranging from farmers to policemen.[95]

'White pills' (*baiwan*) were a variant of golden elixir. Resembling sorghum grains, they became known as 'the white drug of the immortals' (*baiyao xian*), and were popular in the army of Yan Xishan. The resonance between heroin and alchemy was so strong that a journalist even boasted that heroin 'immortality pills' had imbued the youth of Shanxi with 'an immortal spirit and a Daoist body' (*xianfeng daogu*).[96] A detailed study of 'immortality pills' in Biancheng county, Hebei, revealed that ordinary customers used these pills in the same way as traditional alchemical drugs.[97] Alchemical substances, often known under the umbrella term *jindan*, were commonly used in imperial China for the treatment of snake bites, various pains, inflammation of the joints, ulcers, digestive problems, hypothermia and even partial paralysis.[98] Heroin pills, just like red pills, thus thrived on their popular affinity with alchemy.

White pills also came in powdered form, the substance being simply known as 'white powder' (*baimian*) in the north and 'old sea' (*laohai*), a popular pun on 'heroin' (*hailuoyin*), along the coastal regions. White powder was frequently smoked in a small bamboo pipe mixed with tobacco, or added to the end of a cigarette after the removal of a small amount of tobacco. The latter method was referred to as 'anti-aircraft gun', because the tip of the cigarette would point upwards. After only one puff, the end of the cigarette would be torn off and the process repeated.[99] Heroin could also be sold as 'machine-guns' (*jiqibang* or *jiqipao*) in the shape of a cigarette or a pen.[100] This variety was also known as the 'ratt-ta-tatt' (*kuaishangkuai*) of machine-gun fire, referred to in Hong Kong as 'firing the ack-ack [anti-aircraft] gun', since it was easy to use and yielded immediate effect.[101] Smoked in pipes, rolled into cigarettes, or simply snorted as powder, the 'machine-gun' was particularly popular in southern Shanxi and parts of Hebei. Marketed in appealing colours, from pink to bright blue, there were even sugar-coated varieties (*tianwan*) which were as sweet as candies.[102]

Heroin could also be sprinkled on a piece of tin foil which was then held over the flame of a candle or a match, the fumes being sucked up via a trumpet-shaped instrument.[103] In Hong Kong this method was known as 'chasing the dragon' (*zhuilong*), as the liquidised heroin would be gently tilted from one end of the foil crease to the other. This was necessary because fine heroin powder has a tendency to compact into a single mass over a flame.[104] In the early 1930s snorting heroin also became popular: a user would simply crush the pill into fine powder and snort it through a nostril, and follow up by inhaling warm water. According to tabloid gossip, this method was apparently introduced by Yan Xishan's army, as moisture during field campaigns frequently made the matches useless, depriving the soldiers of the heroin without which they could not muster the courage and energy they needed to go into battle.[105]

However, smoking was the most popular mode of consumption in Manchuria, the north of China and most cities along the coast from Tianjin to Shanghai. Just as more refined opium houses had done in the past, sophisticated heroin pill divans catered to the various needs of wealthy customers, also providing tit-bits to eat and entertainment.[106] In remote areas of Shandong white powder functioned as a substitute for expensive opium, its consumption by local elites indicating social status and wealth. Ordinary villagers, who used to give their guests a cup of tea, also offered a puff of heroin as a sign of respect, smoking being a major recreational activity. The same was true in urban China, for example in Shanghai. The *North China Daily News* reported in 1936 that the poor in Shanghai preferred to smoke heroin, which was cheaper at about 20 cents per small packet and more potent—some even considered it eight times stronger than the popular red pills.[107] The Annual Report of the Shanghai Municipal Council reasoned that the habit of smoking heroin in the end of cigarettes or blended into the tobacco of a normal pipe had sounded the death-knell for the secret opium houses. Poorer consumers often had to be satisfied with negligible amounts of heroin, the pills often containing less than 0.25 mg. (or some 2 per cent) of heroin, and at times as little as 0.07 mg. (or 0.1 per cent).[108] Narcotic consumers were thus quite able to manage their intake instead of being forced to slide into a 'state of dependence' by dark chemical forces of compulsion. Given the very low heroin content in many pills, they may well have acted as placebos, yet another indication of the importance of psychological expectations as well as pharmacological properties in the use of psychoactive substances.

As noted above, heroin pills were widely used by poor people as a replacement for more expensive opium, especially during anti-opium campaigns. In parts of Shandong province during the 1920s consumers gradually replaced the expensive opium from licensed shops with white pills and heroin powders.[109] Immortality pills and white powder were also common in Shanxi, although opium retained some of its popularity in the west of the province.[110] To the east of the Qiantang river in Zhejiang province, it was claimed that local people spent more than 2 million yuan on pills each year.[111] Consumption of pills increased steadily after 1922 to become 'prevalent to such a degree that it exceeded the smoking of opium itself'.[112] In Shanghai and Wuxi heroin pill houses (*duwanchu*) attracted the urban poor who could no longer afford their opium.[113]

Apart from the comparatively low cost of heroin, pills and powders were much faster and less complicated to use.[114] Even for the wealthy, the changing pace of work in the bustling city meant that time was money: workers and professionals alike sought more immediate stimulation than the opium pipe could offer.[115] Foreign journalists noticed that opium smoking was already regarded as old-fashioned in Shanghai by the mid-1930s and conjectured that it was only a matter of time before the practice would completely disappear: meanwhile, heroin and morphine pills spread as more convenient and modern alternatives.[116]

Even in cities where the pace of life was less intense, opium houses increasingly gave way to heroin houses, which took over many of their social functions. In Beijing clandestine heroin houses were situated in private courtyards or secret locations advertised in pawnshops through cryptic references to dispensaries of patent medicines. A typical establishment would consist of the owner or manager, his wife, a waitress and a 'boy'. The owner normally looked after the business outside, while the wife or waitress sat by the till selling the goods. The 'boy' took care of rich patrons while keeping an eye on poor customers. He also administered injections. For those wishing to smoke the powder the commonest way was to blend some heroin with tobacco for smoking in the typical small bamboo pipes.[117]

The link between anti-opium policies and the increased use of semi-synthetics was even noted by the National Anti-Opium Association of China in 1929: 'We are quite taken by surprise by the fact that inversely as the evil practice of opium smoking is on the decrease through the united effort of the people, the extent of illicit trade in, and use of, narcotic drugs, such as morphine, heroin and cocaine, is ever on the increase.'[118] The association noted that in the provinces of Shandong and Shanxi, where opium was effectively prohibited, an unexpected expansion in the volume of morphine, heroin and cocaine trading was taking place in the late 1920s. Similar observations were made by members of the association based in other provinces where new regulations were being rigidly enforced, in particular in Fujian, Zhejiang, Jiangsu, Hubei, Anhui, Hebei, Jehol and Fengtian.[119] Foreign experts in alkaloid drugs also noted how opium suppression encouraged heroin use. Dr K. Morinaka observed that morphine intoxication in the rest of the world was often due to dependence on or misuse of medical drugs, while in China the main motive was the search for cheaper alternatives to the opium available on the black market or through government monopolies.[120]

Government officials made similar observations. Tang Liangli, for instance, questioned the efficacy of anti-opium measures, noting that the use of narcotics tended to develop precisely in the very provinces in which the suppression of opium had been most severely applied. Strict prohibition thus encouraged opium smokers to become morphine injectors. Opium smokers required bulky paraphernalia, such as the pipe and lamp, which were difficult to conceal. Smokers were also easily detected by their smell, and opium took up more space than morphine. Heroin mixed with tobacco, either in a pipe or in cigarettes, could be smoked openly without attracting undue attention.[121] 'By enforcing drastic measures against the use of opium the Chinese Government would run the risk of increasing the number of drug addicts,' Tang warned in 1935, in approval of the draconian Six-Year Opium Suppression Plan.[122]

HEROIN AS A GLOBAL COMMODITY

After modest beginnings, heroin imports of European and Japanese origin reached Shanghai, Tianjin and Dalian at a monthly rate of five tonnes by the early 1920s, sufficient for thirteen million doses.[123] Ten years later, the League of Nations narcotics report for 1936 concluded that 'morphine, heroin and morphine pills, have become more common, especially along the coast and in the northern provinces... constituting a greater menace to the country.'[124] To this amount the output of factories in Manchuria had to be added. Owing to an excessively narrow definition in the Hague Convention,[125] many of the esters of morphine, e.g. benzylmorphine, continued to be imported from Europe, and were bought up by Japanese importers, contributing to a fall in the price per kilo from £100–120 sterling in 1926 to £60 three years later.[126] When the legal loophole was closed with the enforcement of the 1924–5 Geneva conventions, Turkey began to replace the former European producers.[127]

Drug raids, such as the seizure by Shanghai customs officials of opium, morphine and heroin in November 1930, illustrated the global implications of the contraband traffic. Quantities hitherto unheard of had been smuggled aboard the steamers *Lloyd Triestino* and *Cracovia*, possibly destined for the west coast of the United States. Concealed among dried fruits, raisins, jams, dyes, kerosene, varnish and wax were small packets of prime quality heroin.[128] Along the waterways of China, especially on the lower Yangzi river, narcotics could be transported in British and American oil tankers. Heroin, for instance, was also wrapped into white cloth and openly posted into Shanghai as powdered Fritillary Bulb, a Chinese herbal cough medicine.[129]

Despite the large volume of heroin imports, semi-synthetics were increasingly produced locally during the 1930s. When police officers of the French concession in Shanghai raided a red pill factory in North Chekiang Road, 350,000 pills were seized, stitched into silk bags, together with valuable equipment. Strainers, driers, pill-shaping machines, mortars and chemicals all suggested the sophistication of heroin manufacturing in China.[130] The clandestine manufacturing of heroin was encouraged by the incorporation of the 1925 League of Nations Convention into Chinese law in 1928.[131] This made its importation increasingly hazardous, and dealers reacted by mass-producing heroin locally, providing a seemingly unlimited quantity for the market. At first the manufacturing methods were unsophisticated and accomplished by unskilled labourers. Heroin pills were rolled and cut on hand-operated machines common in the pharmaceutical industry and rounded manually before being dried on trays heated by a earthenware stove or in drying cabinets.[132] Even the hinterland boasted heroin factories, although the local product was far from being as pure or effective as that of metropolitan or imported origin.[133]

Backyard factories existed in almost every region, and entire hamlets in Jiangsu specialised in the manufacture of heroin pills.[134] A clandestine factory in Guanglin county (Sichuan) even employed 2–3,000 workers round the clock, as well as Japanese scientists who were put in charge of its chemical laboratory.[135] The production of heroin in China before the 1935 Six-Year Opium Suppression Plan reached astounding proportions, making it over 20 per cent more economical than the cheapest product offered by European rivals: the global flow of narcotics to China went into reverse towards the West. Affordability and availability thus not only stimulated local consumption, but also fuelled the global trade in illicit substances.[136] A statement by the International Missionary Council of 1933 confirmed this:

China, instead of a consuming country victimised by the overproduction of high power narcotic drugs in the West, is now a producing country herself. The cheapness of raw material and labour, the technical assistance of Japanese experts, the backing of local military authorities make it possible for China to turn out the immense amount of morphia and heroin at a very low cost... she is now exporting to other countries, especially America... Factories have now been established in Hopei, Honan, Hupeh, Szechuan and Kiangsu and the number is no less than a dozen. It is believed that at least eight factories of this kind exist in the province of Szechuan under various local warlords.[137]

The scale of production reached industrial levels. Between 1933 and 1934 a dozen clandestine factories were stormed by the police in the International Settlement of Shanghai, and 21.8 kilos of different heroin products were seized in one plant alone, ranging from heroin hydrochloride to crude heroin and purified powder. Other chemicals were also uncovered, including huge quantities of carboys containing nitrates and chloroform, spirits and soda ashes.[138] Production methods were sophisticated. One factory raided by the police in August 1934 revealed the existence of elaborate equipment, including electric motors, suction pumps, condensing apparatus, drying trays, retorts, and distilling and filtering equipment. Chemicals and gas masks were also found in the raid. Divided into four units, the factory was designed to produce heroin and red pills with great efficiency.[139] A similar haul in May

1935 by the French Municipal Police in Shanghai confirmed the popularity of red pill production.[140] The demand for heroin products could take on truly bizarre dimensions. In September 1929, sophisticated chemical equipment was uncovered in an empty house in the British Concession of Tianjin, which, it was claimed, would have enabled dealers to extract heroin hidden in floor polish. A Russian was arrested as the mastermind of a smuggling operation linking Tianjin with a heroin laboratory in France.[141]

Intelligence gathered in 1934 by American authorities testified to the fact that Sichuan province, Greater Shanghai, Beijing, Dalian and the leased territory in Guandong were the principal centres for the clandestine manufacturing of morphine and heroin in East Asia, Manchuria only ranking as the second most important contributor.[142] According to a report by Sir Malcolm Delevingne, the 20 kg (44 lb) of morphine seized in Hong Kong in 1933 came from China.[143] Chengdu was also one of China's biggest hubs for narcotics: large quantities of morphine and heroin were transported there from the province's many chemical factories, and distributed to metropoles in occupied China.[144] While morphine went east, the local opium was transported to Canton, to be sold on to American or British troops desperately short of medical drugs. Local warlords used the proceeds to purchase weapons.[145]

The main participants in the contraband traffic were either Koreans (who held Japanese passports), White Russians or Chinese.[146] Garfield Huang, secretary of the China's National Anti-Opium Association, believed that Japanese citizens—often Koreans and Chinese from Taiwan—exploited extraterritoriality to escape the clutches of China's law enforcers. Using the foreign concessions of Shanghai, Tianjin, Dalian, Shenyang, Beijing, Qingdao, Jinan, Hankou, Fuzhou and Xiamen as entrepots, the smugglers would seek local Japanese traders, such as the Yamamijo firm in Jinan, with whom to deposit their wares.[147] Traffickers sometimes also disguised themselves as medical practitioners, as in Shanhaiguan in 1930.[148] Alternatively, semi-synthetics also arrived in postal parcels, frequently from Switzerland or Germany. In one such case, some 120 parcels of heroin (piloline) from

Hamburg were discovered by the Chinese Post Office of Liaoning, with a total value of more than 60,000 US dollars.[149]

Many of the clandestine factories were owned by high-ranking officials or powerful local potentates. The ones in Beijing, Henan and Tianjin were mostly run by local officials and military governors.[150] In Shanghai many were run by gangster associations; in November 1933 the police raided a clandestine factory in the South Market belonging to the notorious gangster Du Yuesheng, seizing morphine and red pills with an estimated worth of 5 million dollars.[151] While Du Yuesheng was behind many of these enterprises in Shanghai,[152] his companion Ye Qinghe had factories producing narcotics in faraway Sichuan. Benefiting from abundant local opium, Shanghai equipment and Japanese chemists, Sichuan province was transformed into a narcotic paradise.[153] Liu Yushan, known in Shanghai as the 'king of morphine', bought military equipment from the Japanese and made a fortune transporting it to Chongqing on British or French ships. Opium-producing regions, such as Dianjiang, Fengdu, Dazhu and Lingshui, had numerous morphine plants, and as a result produced powerful local leaders, such as Xie Chunfeng in Dianjiang. Xie began by engaging in petty smuggling, and used the profits to open his own plant. The morphine it produced was of the best quality, its production supervised by Japanese chemists.

Morphine plants mushroomed in other regions too. Many warlords in Hunan and Yunnan were involved in narcotic manufacture, their plants being often referred to as 'chemical factories'. Tang Jiyao, strongman of Yunnan in the early 1930s, hired Japanese experts. Further north, especially in Henan, there were even more clandestine factories, and the huge illegal plants of Bo'ai county produced golden elixir. Most were set up in the early 1920s and all employed small armies of armed guards. The situation in Shanxi was similar: Taiyuan, Wenshui and Yicheng all ran golden elixir plants, often made viable by low-interest loans from the local government to purchase pill-making machines. While the equipment and know-how came from the cosmopolitan cities of the north and east (and sometimes from Japan), the raw ingredient—opium—was obtained from the southwestern provinces, mainly Sichuan. One clandestine factory even operated within the Legation Quarter of Beijing, and sold into Taiyuan and Shijiazhuang.[154]

The production and transportation of heroin in the republican era provided the basis for new uses by the narcotic consumer, either for self-medication or as a cheaper alternative to the now prohibited opium. Heroin could be liquefied and injected, crushed and smoked, or simply swallowed; compared to the elaborate rituals of opium smoking, only lighting a cigarette was a more trouble-free procedure than heroin use. However, in many parts of the country opium persisted throughout the republican period.

THE RESILIENCE OF OPIUM SMOKING

Morphine and heroin, as well as other narcotic products, flooded the market during the first decades of the twentieth century, but in many parts of the country opium remained important. It was far from being marginalised by modern drugs, even if consumption patterns were profoundly affected by prohibition and the availability of cheaper and more convenient alternatives. The purpose of this section is not to provide a comprehensive overview of the use of opium in republican China, which largely followed patterns analysed in the earlier chapters, but to highlight how it remained a highly desirable product in many parts of China, particularly in the provinces which cultivated the poppy, namely Gansu, Guizhou, Sichuan and Yunnan.[155]

In Manchuria, as in Japanese-controlled Guandong, tens of thousands of opium smokers prevailed despite the flourishing market for morphine in the late 1920s. In other cities under Japanese control, such as Yingkou, Fengtian, Changchun and Andong, morphine and opium also coexisted, the former being more widespread among the poor. In Harbin, according to American estimates, around 1,000 illegal opium houses were supplied by Persian consignments of opium and Japanese supplies of synthetic drugs.[156] In Canton opium houses known as 'chat rooms' (*tanhuashi*) still catered to a diverse clientele in the 1930s.[157] Contrary to the trend in large cities, opium smoking also remained popular with coolies and soldiers in Fujian, where over 700 licensed opium houses and many unregistered dens served the local population in the mid-1920s.[158] In Guangxi opium smoking was not only popular among the business community, but even with the flotsam on the streets: sources scarcely mention morphine or heroin at all. This was the case too in Hubei, where opium smoking remained the most important recreational activity. In Hanyang a mere ten people were known to have received morphine injections, and only four or five shops were discovered selling red pills in Yichang in 1927. In Anhui coolies, teachers and business people smoked opium, while red pills were making inroads in the east of the province. In Jiangxi the local economy relied heavily on the opium trade and local consumption remained considerable. Heroin pills were only discovered in Lichuan.[159]

Opium remained even more popular further away from the coastal regions in the poorer hinterland, notably in provinces which had traditionally thrived on poppy cultivation. In Hunan and Shaanxi local produce provided most of the opium smoked, although in Gansu province, only about 10 per cent of the annual production was earmarked for local consumption: the rest was sold to Shaanxi and Sichuan. Ningxia province was thought to shelter over 100,000 smokers, mostly labourers, including many women who occasionally blew smoke into the mouths of their babies to stop them crying. In Guizhou too, poppy production and opium consumption were openly encouraged by the provincial government as a source of revenue. The cities of Zunyi and Songtao boasted hundreds of opium houses, each tailored to its specific clientele, from local officials and merchants to coolies and vagrants. Since the entire province had only one public hospital with ten beds before the 1940s, self-medication through opium was the only effective solace for pain and disease.[160]

In Yunnan opium was inextricably enmeshed with the local economy. Soldiers often preferred the more expensive mountain varieties (*shantu* or *shanyan*), coolies smoked dross and ashes, and farmers used their own abundant produce.[161] In the town of Malipeng opium was the most stable currency in 1935, five grams changing hands for a pound of salt or half a bowl of buckwheat.[162]

In Sichuan too local opium was smoked by ordinary people, although wealthy consumers often preferred imported produce from India and Yunnan. Well into the 1930s peddlers would carry baskets of opium around cities like Chengdu in search of smokers, well aware that such transactions were technically illegal. On the steamers between Chongqing and Luzhou boys would offer both tea and opium. Even at the famous Buddhist pilgrimage site on the Emei mountain, monks organised themselves to sell opium to pilgrims, tourists and coolies.[163] The poor could only afford dross, smoked in shacks consisting of one big room with bare floorboards. Smokers were supplied with a cushion and a straw mat.[164] Opium smoking rooms were fixed features in many hotels, much like in-house restaurants or cafés; even bathhouses in Chongqing had special smoking rooms, although their opium was more expensive. Customers also expected to be served opium in the city's many brothels, showing again the resilience of opium culture in the hinterland even during the 1930s and '40s. At home opium remained an essential treat: if the opium lamp was not lit when guests arrived, it was taken as a social affront.[165] In most of these provinces, morphine and the needle remained relatively rare thanks to the lacklustre efforts made at opium suppression by local governments.

9

NEEDLE LORE: THE SYRINGE IN CHINA
(*c.* 1890–1950)

The last chapter shows how narcotic substances flooded the market in modern China as pharmaceutical companies responded to consumer demand by producing a variety of psychoactive substances which competed favourably with opium in a climate of prohibition. This chapter examines the reasons why the syringe became a popular way of administering drugs: not only was it cheap and effective, but it also encountered relatively few cultural obstacles since an existing needle lore endowed the hypodermic with positive attributes. Recent research has highlighted how in China biomedicine was selectively appropriated from Europe by cultural intermediaries.[1] The appropriation of the syringe equally needs to be explained with reference to specific cultural, social and political variables. This chapter analyses a variety of factors which contributed to the successful inculturation in China of an object still viewed with fear by many Europeans. It explores the almost magical properties attributed to the syringe in both elite medical culture and popular drug consumption in modern China.

The injection of morphine represented a major shift away from the hitherto dominant mode of narcotic consumption, namely opium smoking. As opium increasingly became the subject of anti-opium campaigns in the early twentieth century, imports of morphine offered poor consumers a competitive and convenient alternative. However, as in other parts of the world, the syringe also produced problems: needles were often dirty, were rarely disinfected when shared, and contained contaminated water used to make the morphine solutions.[2] This was all the more true in

China where the vast majority of morphine users came from the bottom of the social scale. In contrast to Europe and the United States, where the first generation of 'genteel addicts' in the late nineteenth century was generally confined to the middle classes, morphine users in China were overwhelmingly drawn from the poor who could no longer afford the price of opium. Prohibitive government policies were a major factor in this trend, as opium was outlawed in the early twentieth century while morphine remained on sale openly until the First World War.

NEEDLE CULTURE

The syringe was introduced in Europe in the 1850s and became a therapeutic staple in medical circles a decade later. Sulphates of quinine and strychnine, as well as saline solutions, water and even human blood were routinely injected to combat diseases such as cholera.[3] As Patricia Rosales underlines in her history of the syringe, the rapid action of the hypodermic allowed it to become embedded in various aspects of medical culture. This was despite its initial unpopularity: it was new and intimidating, the thickness of some needles generated anxiety, and patients were haunted by fears of punctured veins or slipping syringes. Injections also collided with holistic medicine in America, which emphasised the 'surroundings' of an individual, as well as mind and body, as the key components of health: any imbalance between these elements could lead to illness. Diet, climate, occupation, environment, cleanliness and housing were seen as being more effective agents of good health than drugs, which only fulfilled an ancillary role in orthodox practice in the mid-nineteenth century.[4] An important shift away from these negative perceptions resulted from the fruitful partnership between morphine and the needle, as the hypodermic administration of the drug proved rapid and potent; it was also economic since it could measure precise amounts capable of bypassing the digestive tract. Used at first by medical practitioners to relieve pain and abate insomnia, hypodermic morphine became an increasingly popular tool in other medical interventions such as the reduction of mucous secretions. The syringe thus broadened the appeal of morphine, which became a cure-all, while conversely morphine consolidated the hypodermic practice.

However, during the last quarter of the nineteenth century the medical practitioner needed significant additional skills and detailed knowledge of chemical properties in order to use the syringe. The preparation of hypodermic solutions demanded extreme patience and precise knowledge of the various ingredients; moreover, syringes could be highly corrosive and fragile; glass barrels cracked, leather pistons deteriorated within days, and needles could break.[5] Improvements in the manufacture of syringes, advances in the pharmaceutical field, the industrial production of tablets and ampoules containing accurately measured dosages for hypodermic injection, the multiplication of hypodermically delivered drugs including therapeutic agents such as mercury, heroin, cocaine, codeine—by 1900 these developments had contributed to a widespread diffusion of injections. The syringe appeared in China during the last decade of the nineteenth century, precisely after therapeutic preparations had already been simplified. While technological innovations help to explain the success of the hypodermic in China, a long-standing needle lore must also be taken into account. The curative power of the injection captured the imagination of different constituencies in China, many being already accustomed to the use of needles in local medical practices involving acupuncture.

Acupuncture, consisting of the implantation of a series of fine needles to different depths at a number of points on the surface of the human body, was an ancient therapeutic technique in China.[6] The earliest needles were made of stone, bone and bamboo, later to be replaced by metal needles. Needles came in many types and sizes, the medical classic *Huangdi neijing* (second century bc) recording nine different ones, namely 'arrow-headed, blunt, puncturing, spear-pointed, ensiform [shaped like a sword-blade], round, capillary, long and great'. They came in various lengths, and could be used for scratching the skin, pricking and bleeding, and piercing deep-lying tissues—the last-named being the commonest thanks to thread-like metal needles. These were inserted into the flesh to a greater or lesser depth, or could be driven in with a blow from a light hammer. The point of insertion, the direction of their rotation, the number of needles and the depth of the puncture all depended on the severity of the case in hand.[7] Although historians of medicine are still debating the origins of the practice,[8] there is no doubt that the use of needles to treat illnesses was popular in the late imperial period, as itinerant doctors, local physicians and religious healers all catered to the medical needs of ordinary people, even if the practice was banned in 1822 by the imperial medical college.[9] Elite scholars may have viewed the practice with increasing suspicion during the Ming and Qing, but hot or cold needles several centimetres long could be stabbed into the skin and underlying tissues by popular practitioners, sometimes with great force. Acupuncture was popularly considered a magic cure, and seen to be especially effective against cholera, colic, coughs, rheumatism, sprains, swollen joints, and deep-seated pains of all kinds. Chen Boxi typifies the condemnatory attitude of elite circles, reflecting on the use of needles during the last years of the Qing: 'Many quacks practised what was known as the "magic needle" (*shenzhen*). This method was very brutal and without regard for the life of the patient... During the summer and autumn seasons, cholera became endemic as the result of poor sanitation. It was commonly known as *shahuan*. The victims would ask barbers who had no [medical] knowledge to insert needles randomly into their bodies until their veins became covered with purple spots. This therapy was called *tiaosha* (pricking out disease), and was very popular in the Suzhou and Shanghai area.'[10]

The spread of the syringe in modern China was thus facilitated by a popular needle lore, which regarded the insertion of needles into the body as a therapeutic practice. As in Europe and the United States, its popularity also hinged critically on a powerful association with morphine.

HYPODERMIC MORPHINE AND THE MAGIC NEEDLE

Hypodermic morphine was first introduced into Hong Kong in the late nineteenth century by disciples of the medical missionary

Norman Kerr before spreading to mainland China. Implemented on a small scale in 1892, such replacement therapy centres mushroomed throughout the crown colony, where the morphine solution was administered with small hypodermic syringes to each patient who volunteered. Within weeks habitual opium users discovered that it was far more economical to have morphine injected directly than to smoke opium—often it reduced the costs by more than 80 per cent. The popularity of this new, radically cheaper form of morphine consumption quickly caused the habit to spread to inns and gambling houses, causing many casualties as well as a rapid decline of the older opium houses.[11] The Hong Kong government analyst who visited an indigenous surgery where injections had become common noted:

I entered and observed three men asleep on mats, and about twelve or fifteen standing in the verandah. There were numerous puncture scars on their arms. The quantity used depended on the amount of opium the patients had been in the habit of smoking.[12]

In contrast to mainland China, however, the colonial authorities in Hong Kong had an economic incentive in the sale and distribution of opium: the government quickly launched a Morphine Ordinance in 1893 specifically prohibiting the unauthorised sale and administration of a dangerous drug.[13]

As the new mode of delivery spread rapidly to the rest of China, several medical missionaries witnessed the sale of morphine solutions and the use of the syringe in Hangzhou, Suzhou and Shanghai at the close of the century. William Park reported that morphine peddlers in Suzhou, with hypodermic syringes and morphia solutions up their sleeves, would frequent tea shops, giving injections for a few coppers apiece. Their customers stood in a row, each getting his allowance like 'coolies being vaccinated on an emigrant steamer.' The syringes were never cleaned, and when the solutions ran out, they prepared a fresh supply using dirty water found in the tea shop and mixing it in unwashed cups. Injections often produced ulceration. When scars completely covered the arms, injections were extended to the shoulders and chest.[14] Returned emigrants from Singapore to Shantou also introduced the hypodermic use of morphine, which spread rapidly into Fujian. However, people in Canton seemed rarely to resort to needles.[15]

Morphine and the needle became fashionable in the coastal cities at the turn of the century not only as a cure against opium but also as a 'Western' medicine, its foreign origin conferring status, respect and prestige. Moreover, the hypodermic use of morphine may well initially have been understood by analogy as a new way of treating the opium 'poison': by injecting morphine into the blood, it would spread quickly to the entire body and counteract the poison of opium. In Europe and the United States too, morphine was used at first to break the opium habit, although 'morphine addiction,' 'morphinism' and 'morphinomania' were increasingly observed by medical practitioners in the 1880s.[16] These reservations were only partly shared in China, where both foreign and local doctors continued to use morphine injections in a political context of mounting prohibition against opium. Although evidence about popular beliefs is often missing from the historical record, a police officer, Ding Yongzhu, proposed a ban on morphine injections used in detoxification treatments in Shanghai as late as in 1906.[17] Despite these injunctions, hospitals and detoxification centres injected a variety of alkaloids into drug 'addicts,' including morphine, throughout the republican period. For instance, in 1930 somnifen and paraldehyde were injected at a convalescent hospital in Shanghai to induce sleep—known as the 'sleeping method', this approach was reported to have cured fifty patients of the drug habit within half a year (however, two also died in the process). In the same hospital the hyscin method, involving the injection of hyscin hydrobromate or philcaprin, was used to 'calm the nerves' (anshen) of sick patients. Patients were also regularly injected with morphine to keep them calm. Zhang Tianhui, a regular morphine user, expressed his satisfaction with the 'sleeping method' combined with an occasional morphine shot, and reputedly left the hospital without any craving for drugs.[18] These medical practices also appeared outside an institutional context: thirty-seven-year-old Song Liang, to take but one example, injected morphine specifically in order to stop the opium habit, unaware that morphine was far more potent than opium.[19]

Whether used as a cure against opium or as a remedy against such illnesses as sleeplessness or nervous tension, it can scarcely been doubted that morphine injections became an essential part of medical culture in China at the beginning of the twentieth century. Morphine offered immediate relief from pain and fever, and for many patients also induced a euphoric state of well-being. However, for some customers its use had little to do with medical needs, since it appeared as a substitute for opium when the prohibition campaigns started to take effect. And, in all cases, the limited quantity of syringes imported and the shortage of distilled water meant that injection was restricted to a small number of urban users in the first decade of the twentieth century. The government soon discovered that regulating the importation of morphine and of syringes was a sizeable source of revenue, and legislation was passed in 1909 to tax both and restrict morphine injection to medical cases supervised by doctors.[20] Concern about hypodermic addiction, as in the United States, thus encouraged official restrictions on the use of the syringe, as the needle emerged as a symbol of the medical profession and of the doctor's power to heal. Nonetheless, the explosion in pharmaceutical products and the shift from opium smoking to morphine injection meant that after the fall of the empire the syringe would become ubiquitous in medical culture and narcotic circles alike.

SYRINGES, VACCINES, PATENTS AND QUACKS

As the power of the syringe to administer drugs became more widely accepted, a whole range of patent medicines became available in the 1910s and '20s. Needles were used for administering a variety of products offered by new pharmaceutical companies, from vitamins to tonics against coughs and headaches. Drugs could be injected intravenously (*jinmai zhushe*) and hypodermically (*pixia zhushe*)—or 'sticking the vein' (*zhaguan*) and 'sticking the skin' (*zhapi*), as they were popularly known. Many patent medicines came in handy ampoules (*anbu*), bulb-shaped glass containers which were sterile and instantly available, greatly simplifying and shortening the injection process.

Immunogens and insulin were injected. Coagulen, manufactured by Ciba as a haemostatic, was taken intravenously. Remogland, for the treatment of sexual weakness, premature ejaculation, general neurasthenia and hypochondria in men, and frigidity, amenorrhoea and neurasthenia in women, was taken intramuscularly and sold in ampoules (the tablets could also be orally administered). Vita spermin, for men and women, was aimed at a similar range of disorders and also injected to fight the symptoms of detoxification (Dr Zhu Peizhang personally injected masturbators, who suffered from sexual neurasthenia as a consequence of their habit, with spermin).[21] Trypaflavine was injected for leucorrhoea, gonacrine for gonorrhoea. Transpoin, containing camphor and quinine, was used hypodermically to treat lung infections. Entodon was injected in the arm ('without any pain'). Pantocain, containing tetracaine chlorhydrate and produced by Bayer as a replacement for cocaine, was taken by injection. Bayer also produced tutocain as a substitute for cocaine.[22] Cafaspin, also by Bayer, contained aspirin and caffeine and was useful against headaches and hangovers. Omnadin, prolan, gono-yatren, phage, campolon, livemin, pasuma, melubrin, novalgin, rivanal, hygytol, secartin, anaptol, narcopon and countless other pharmaceutical products were injected. Most were available both in ampoules and as tablets, although advertisers emphasised their hypodermical use, for instance by using pictures of a syringe or a young lady elegantly inserting a needle into her arm: injection was not only 'scientific,' it was chic. Tonics, vitamins and body-builders were injected.[23] Although many of these pharmaceutical products came from foreign companies, local factories started manufacturing injectable products from the early 1920s onwards. Before the start of the war in 1937, just under sixty pharmaceutical companies in Shanghai alone produced 120 medical substances designed for hypodermic application, turning out over 300,000 ampoules each month.[24]

Popular manuals on injection, with precise instructions and illustrations of intravenous, subcutaneous and intramuscular use, appeared throughout the republican period, one example being Zhang Jian's *Newest Treatment by Injection* (1925), reprinted many times up till 1939: as the author commented, 'injections penetrate

wonderfully, hence a dedicated handbook is necessary.' He nonetheless warned that too many consumers injected medicines out
of pure curiosity or changed from one product to another without adequate knowledge.[25] Other manuals included an *Encyclopaedia on the Hypodermical Treatment of Various Diseases* (1926), an
Introduction to Injections (1933), published as part of the popular
'Small Medical Self-Study Series,' *Various Treatments by Injection*
(1936) and *Injection Methods and Injected Medications* (1941).[26] Some,
like the *Treasure Raft of Injected Treatments* (1930), were published
by local pharmaceutical companies like the Haipu firm.[27] Large
medical compendiums, compiled by companies like Bayer as useful guides to their products for both doctor and layman, also provided detailed instruction on the various ways of inserting a
needle. Star Brand, a local company which sold many varieties of
drugs, included drawings of the human body with arrows indicating the best points for injection.[28]

An important development which contributed to the popularity of the syringe was the development of a diphtheria anti-
toxin in the 1890s, as immunity was increasingly understood by
medical practitioners to be a component of the blood which could
be transferred from one person to another by means of the syringe.[29] Bacterins appeared in Europe after 1904 in sterile salt solutions, and were believed to promote immunity to infection; in
the hypodermic administration of drugs patients, as much as doctors, determined the choice of syringe. As Peter Keating observed
in his article on the history of vaccine therapy, 'There is no doubt
that at the time and, in some respects, even today, a subcutaneous
injection of anything appeared to be scientific and was more
impressive to patients than doing nothing at all. Given that the
vaccines were harmless, it is quite likely that vaccine therapy
functioned as a placebo for both doctor and patient.'[30] The spread
of the syringe also depended on the popularity of vaccines in
China. Vaccines appeared against typhus, cholera, meningitis,
gonorrhoea, pneumonia and typhoid, among other conditions.
From the 1920 onwards anti-cholera and anti-rabies injections,
and inoculations against whooping cough, were promoted regularly in greater Shanghai. At the height of the epidemic season,

injections were often compulsory and urban citizens were required to obtain a certificate stating that they had received them. Smallpox and diphtheria were also effectively treated with the needle. Serums against tuberculosis, bubonic plague, diabetes and dysentery were injected. The British physician H. G. W. Woodhead, practising in Shanghai, put it in a nutshell: 'It [the syringe] is employed, as everyone knows, not only for the injection of narcotic drugs, but also for preventing rabies, and for curing a range of illnesses… [this provides] an indispensable part of a doctor's equipment.'[31]

In many countries around the world, the needle became especially popular in alleged cures for sexually transmitted diseases. A crucial development was the discovery of salvarsan, or '606', synthesised by Paul Ehrlich in his search for a magic bullet against syphilis. Although at first the arsenic compound was complicated to administer, since intravenous delivery was a technique involving surgical procedures which few medical practitioners mastered, neosalvarsan, or '914', was less toxic and introduced with greater success.[32] In China preparations with arsphenamine such as salvarsan made rapid inroads during the 1910s, although even neosalvarsan initially struggled to take the place of mercury.[33] In Harbin, 200 self-proclaimed 'hospitals' derived their main income from injecting patients with salvarsan or substitute solutions, as was noted with alarm in 1927.[34] Some clinics for the treatment of sexually transmitted diseases also injected narcotic substances.[35] Imports of salvarsan could even be used to smuggle opium, as happened when fifty tubes of medical liquor mixed with opium were found by the police in Beijing: all were sealed and imported as salvarsan from Germany.[36]

Historians of Africa have also argued that the development of salvarsan for the treatment of syphilis made injections popular, as external symptoms were rapidly cured even when a course of treatment was incomplete.[37] Injections became the cure of choice of many Africans, a popularity which astonished medical missionaries and government observers alike. By the 1920s, while surgery was feared, injections seemed to hold a mysterious fascination for the many: injections were accorded a magical respect, being regarded almost as fetishes. On the other hand, in India local people were less than enthusiastic about the use of 'one yard long needles', which were rumoured to cause impotence, sterility and death.[38] But in China, as in Africa, injections assumed magical dimensions in the eyes of many ordinary people, with an unequalled effectiveness against a range of diseases.

The anthropologist Francis Hsü even observed how the local gentry in Yunnan donated equal amounts of money to the prayer meeting and the hospital which administered anti-cholera injections during an epidemic in the 1940s. Although they were firm believers in the efficacy of injections, they also thought it necessary to appease the local spirits. A student from the local middle school who was particularly enthusiastic at the prayer meeting boasted that he had received two free injections at the local hospital:

He told me that the hospital only gave one injection and that he knew the college infirmary gave three. He believed that the hospital was being economical and that one injection alone would be ineffective, so he insisted on having two, by telling the hospital people that he would pay for the second one if he was refused it free. He thought that injection was the only way to prevent one from getting cholera, but working in the prayer meeting gave him a good time. 'Besides,' he said 'my parents want me to be at the prayer meeting.'[39]

While some parents refused injections for themselves and their children, local priests specifically asked for them, many regarding syringes and prayers as equally effective in the fight against epidemics.[40]

Quack doctors were quick to capitalise on the popular belief in the efficacy of injecting medicine, and operated on ignorant people or gave them medicine without adequate qualifications or training. Barbers, for instance, not only cut hair but also performed nursing tasks such as cleansing the ears, treating the eyes and beating the back. Many used unclean instruments which could lead to infection. Traditional practitioners of medicine also killed patients through infected needles or excessive doses of dangerous medications.[41] Tuberculosis, which was widespread in China, attracted unscrupulous practitioners as the market was flooded with new medications, including solutions to be administered hypodermically. These were advertised as the 'TB-Busting Needle' (*pilaozhen*) or 'Lung-Tonic Needle' (*bufeizhen*), and had to be applied dozens of times without any benefit to the patient. In one case a patient was injected daily with sodium cacodylate—today classified as a poison which can cause irritation of the respiratory tract, skin and eyes, damage nerves and the lungs, and affect the liver—causing uncontrollable nervous spasms after three months.[42] In another case about forty casualties were reported in 1927 at the Fenzhou hospital, Shanxi, resulting directly from injection of a toxin against whooping cough. Some of the survivors suffered from paralysis while others were covered in running sores and erythaemia (excess of oxygen in the blood); all carried streptococci in the blood. The case was investigated by the health authorities in Beijing, who carried out laboratory tests on mice. The results showed that the drug itself was safe to use, indicating that the infections were caused by needles which had not been thoroughly sterilised.[43] The misuse of needles was so great in Beijing that in 1942 traditional practitioners were forbidden to give injections without official authorisation.[44] This indicated the widespread medical problems caused by dirty needles, but was also part of a strategy of assault on traditional practitioners who were disparaged by modern doctors. Folk medicine was feared in modernising nations for several underlying reasons: the need for medical science to be accepted by the public and achieve professional integrity, competition over the shifting allegiance of certain sectors of the public, the emergence of new social norms of behaviour, and the spread of general education.

NARCOTIC CULTURE AND THE SYRINGE

Within a medical culture which endowed the syringe with quasi-magical attributes, narcotic substances were eagerly injected. Workers initially injected their solution, usually very dirty, with a hypodermic syringe made of glass or metal, or even consisting of a hollow bamboo.[45] After-care drugs were also injected into the veins of opium smokers in early detoxification centres, thus introducing many patients for the first time to the syringe and contributing to the banalisation of injection. Morphine was commonly applied hypodermically in morphine houses (*mafeiguan*) in the 1910s and '20s, while heroin houses (*baimianguan*) also provided customers with a syringe. In most provinces in north China drug peddlers sold both morphine and needles to customers in the 1910s.[46] The needles were in high demand, and some morphine users financed their habit by mending broken needles. In Beijing, for instance, Liu Wentong regularly repaired needles for acquaintances to earn some extra money.[47]

In the 1930s a journalist visiting a heroin house in Shanghai noted that some hypodermics were made from ordinary eye-droppers or pipettes and the more expensive ones from copper. Porcelain spoons were used for heating a mixture of heroin and strychnine dissolved in water.[48] Even in local gaols, crude hand-made syringes circulated to inject shots bought for a mere ten coppers.[49] Heroin, morphine and other drugs were usually dissolved in a small cup in distilled water (*zhengliushui*), or sometimes just in water considered pure (*qingshui*). The mixture was then administered to customers either intravenously or hypodermically with the help of a syringe. As neither the syringe nor the customer's skin was systematically disinfected, sepsis and even death as the result were not uncommon. This risk increased with intravenous injections. Some observers noted that in Tianjin most needles were never sterilised, often being the principal vector in the spread of syphilis. Others contracted lung infections, blood poisoning or nephritis through needle infection.[50] In Shanghai a journalist witnessed several men in a den with hundreds of marks on their legs, abdomens and arms, the spots having in a few cases become infected; one man was covered with sores. Although needles were not necessarily shared, no attempt was made to clean the equipment between injections.[51] Many medical problems among drug users were caused not so much by the drugs themselves as by lack of sufficient medical skills, resulting in the sharing of dirty needles.[52] Those suffering from a swollen chest and muscular dystrophy often continued regularly to inject morphine.[53]

As in other countries, the punctured skins of narcotic users became a cultural marker of addiction, as a body covered in sores represented the ultimate physical degeneration to which craving for chemical substances could lead. Some detailed case-studies were published in medical journals. The Cambridge-educated Wu Liande wrote a rare study of two unusual cases, the first being a blind fortune-teller who had been addicted to the morphine habit for thirteen years, the second a beggar guide persuaded by the former to become an 'habitué.' The first, Leng Shazi, was thirty-four and came from a petty merchant family in Jinchou, Manchuria. He was described as inclined to laziness, taking to the opium habit early and induced in 1907 by a Japanese drug seller to experiment with morphine injection, following enforcement of the opium prohibition laws. He took up the profession of fortune-telling in Niuzhuang to earn a living, and became so popular that he could increase his doses of morphine. His body was covered in old injection spots, made septic by dirty needles and suppuration (see illustration 20). Whereas his injection spots were blueish-green and not particularly prominent, those of the beggar guide were raised and clearly visible. Leng could withstand extreme cold, and even in winter temperatures of 10 degrees below zero still wore his summer gown of plain cotton. His companion had used morphine for six years and presented no striking features beyond his beggarly appearance. Thus even poor morphine users could vary considerably in how they looked.[54]

Despite the frequency of medical problems caused by dirty needles, the number of users injecting drugs constantly increased. While opium was outlawed during the late Qing, the government only imposed a tax on the importation of morphine in 1909, which continued to be widely on sale for 'medical' purposes in the foreign concessions until banned in 1914.[55] The restrictions imposed on the sale of needles also faltered. According to a customs report, the number of syringes illegally imported rose from 940 in 1924 to 3,892 in 1927, and 13,402 morphine needles (*mafeizhen*) being smuggled into the country were seized between 1924 and 1928.[56] From south China to northern Manchuria, the hinterland to the costal regions, the injection craze spread ever more widely. Between 1927 and 1928, morphine injections were given to 20,000 people in Zhaoxian, a small town outside Beijing, and they became particularly popular in Manchuria, where many of its users were jobless or homeless.[57] Like the heroin houses (*baimianguan*) in Beijing, countless morphine houses (*mafeiguan*) were scattered across Manchuria. Heroin and morphine products could be smoked or injected in dens, catering mainly to the poor. In Harbin impoverished Chinese and Russians preferred injections, which were very cheap at 1 *jiao* a shot. According to a journalist, one district alone counted more than 600 Chinese and Russian beggars who regularly received morphine injections. The total number of drug users in this city during the 1920s and '30s was estimated at 10,000 Russians and 50,000 Chinese, making it one of the biggest narcotic markets in East Asia.[58] A foreign resident observed:

During the winter months, anywhere from five to a dozen human bodies, morphine addicts, are picked up frozen on the streets of Harbin and are carried away as so much refuse… These people began as opium addicts and ended up with morphine. It is now so easy to obtain morphine injections and these injections may be had for such a small sum that these poor, weak, dejected people take to the use of morphine as a duck takes to water.[59]

Wu Liande, based in Harbin during his fight against a plague epidemic, also observed how thousands of morphine victims died every year of neglect, starvation and septicemia caused by dirty needles. In the cities of Harbin, Changchun and elsewhere in Manchuria the public health services had to bury hundreds of bodies found by the road with injection marks.[60] He noted that many morphine victims ended up in prison, half of the inmates in Harbin having injected narcotics.[61] This observation is corroborated by archival evidence, as between a quarter and a half of most prisons in Manchuria were filled with drug users, many injecting morphine.[62] Based at the Manchuria Medical College of Shenyang (Mukden), Dr K. Morinaka found in 1929 that opium smoking had quickly been replaced by morphine injection, cases of morphine intoxication being much more frequent and common than ever before.[63] Many former opium users who could no longer afford their smoking habit had switched to injecting morphine. Foreign observers noted that in Mukden, Changchun, Jinan, Tianjin and other cities

numerous 'dope' huts are operated under Japanese consular protection in open defiance of Chinese suppression acts. In the Japanese concession in Mukden, these huts number some two hundred, the owners of which pay regular cumshas to the Japanese police in return for protection. Some one hundred morphine shops are also found to have existed and these are situated either in the neighbourhood of Japanese dispensaries or in the rear of Japanese residences. In a single shop, about forty to fifty persons come to receive injections every day, the number of morphine addicts in the Japanese concession alone being found to be in the vicinity of 500.[64]

Most of these consumers used morphine shots to relieve physical pain, and one thirteen-year-old orphan had done so to overcome the grief at the death of a relative.[65]

Chilling accounts also appeared of poor people who had no other means of survival than selling their blood—after the transaction they were kept alive by morphine injections. Morphine would sometimes be injected in the same spot where the blood had been drawn, a method popularly known as 'one needle out, the other one in.' About 15 yuan was paid for each tube of blood, and half of it was spent on morphine.[66] While such reports often came from anti-opium associations which could be suspected of exaggeration for political purposes, the *Shanghai Times* also observed in 1937 that 'hundreds end their lives like this in Manchuria daily.'[67]

The situation was similar in Shanghai, where many poor customers survived on morphine injections, which cost a third of the average pipe of opium. Some were covered with a 'honeycomb' of scars (*fengwo*) all over their arms, legs and chests.[68] Rumour had it that some paupers would beg the owner of a morphine den to let them inject the residual blood from a previous injection, since a certain amount of blood always seeped into the syringe.[69] These accounts clearly point at the addictive qualities of injected narcotics, although the social and psychological dimensions still need to be considered by the historian. Drug users can crave the needle as much as the substance itself. American practitioners observed the potent action of morphine as well as the 'pleasurable punctures' which defined the role of the syringe. Some users maintained the habit in order to experience the puncture of the needle, as a slight prick or intense stab was in itself 'the most pleasurable part of an injection.'[70] Bingham Dai, in his 1937 study of opiate consumption in Chicago, noted that morphine users were fascinated by the hypodermic and obsessed by the sight of their own blood.[71] Like opium smoking, opiate injection was structured by elaborate rituals, even in highly negative situations, as the following quotation from a present-day heroin user shows: 'It's not only a question of kicks. The ritual in itself, the powder in the spoon, the little ball of cotton, the matches applied, the bubbling liquid drawn through the cotton filter into the eye dropper, the tie round the arm to make a vein stand out, the fix often slow because a man will stand there with the needle in the vein and allow the level of the eye-dropper to waver up and down, up and down... all this is not for nothing; it is born of a respect for the whole chemistry of alienation.'[72]

By the end of the 1920s morphine injection was also reportedly popular in Fujian, parts of Jiangsu and the south of Anhui.[73] In certain areas of Shandong consumers gradually replaced the expensive opium from licensed shops with white pills and other heroin products. In several counties near Jinan, there were about 60,000 consumers. In Jiangsu heroin pills were popular, morphine injections finding particular appeal among the working class in Nanhui and Nantong. In Nantong alone some 400 people regularly received morphine injections, using up to 800 liang (30 kilos) of morphine annually. Most had switched to injecting morphine because they could no longer afford smoking opium. Heroin and morphine were less popular in Zhejiang, where a relatively affluent local population continued to enjoy traditional opium.[74] In Hubei province consumers generally also preferred the opium pipe to the needle. In Hanyang there were said to be only about ten people who received morphine injections, all rickshaw pullers.[75] In Xiamen, Fujian province, rickshaw pullers were also the most loyal customers of the city's morphine dens. The following account explains why:

> The rickshaw pullers in Xiamen spend half of the money they make through hard labour in the morphine den. But the puzzling thing is that they often enter completely exhausted, seemingly on the verge of death, yet on their way out they look like tigers, brimming with energy, or like defeated soldiers who, having been comforted and encouraged by their kind mothers, have fully recovered... Following the injection they fall asleep. Lying on the dirty and damp floor, they breathe in the mildew and rotten air, snore like pigs, wave their hands and mutter unintelligible words.[76]

Their bodies were covered with thousands of injection marks, resembling from a distance a shrunken sponge or a leper. They were depicted by their contemporaries as having 'ghostly looks', with 'thin faces', 'lank with shrivelled limbs' and 'swollen bellies'. However, as medical studies show, these signs were more likely to be linked to malnutrition, abscesses and general debility than to the use of drugs.[77] Few contemporary observers cared to distinguish between the signs of 'addiction' and the symptoms of the many diseases against which narcotic products were used in the first place: they couched their observations in the morally loaded language of anti-opium campaigns, which represented alkaloids as active agents and human beings as their passive victims.

The syringe represented many things to many people, from an object of fear to a potent symbol of healing power, an emblem of medical authority or a marker of drug addiction. Its ability to deliver minute yet precise dosages rapidly deep inside the body transformed it into an indispensable tool in medical circles, although injection also captured the imagination of lay audiences, who attributed to the needle quasi-magical properties. In a context dominated by prohibition against opium smoking, moreover, the syringe offered a quick, economic and odourless, hence relatively safe, alternative to the pipe: it attracted the many millions who could no longer afford opium. By the 1930s, as Tang Liangli observed, the use of injected drugs threatened to do far more damage than could possibly be caused by opium smoking, as the problem of morphine and heroin had supplanted opium in gravity.[78] The replacement of opium smoking by morphine injection, of course, was not unique to China. In Korea, the Japanese colonial authorities progressively prohibited opium between 1910 and 1914: injected morphine use surpassed opium smoking and became the predominant form of drug use soon afterwards, as John Jennings has demonstrated.[79] A similar pattern has been observed for countries in Southeast Asia after the Second World War, as anti-opium measures caused a shift towards injected heroin.[80] In Hong Kong, on the other hand, the legalisation of opium succesfully prevented the emergence of an injection culture: in 1909 only one prisoner in the crown colony was found to have injection scars, in contrast to other places in East Asia. After the colonial authorities could no longer withstand international pressure against the opium trade and abolished the state opium monopoly in 1943, most smokers switched to heroin in less than ten years.[81] While morphine never entirely replaced opium in China, the evidence presented in the last few chapters amply demonstrates that prohibition against opium contributed to social exclusion, drove drug consumption down the social ladder, and led to the replacement of opium smoking by drug injections among the poor: to a significant extent, government policies purporting to contain opium actually resulted in creating a 'drug problem'.

10

CHINA'S OTHER DRUGS (c. 1900–1950)

'Drugs' is a rather stark and uncompromising term for psychoactive substances which can vary hugely in their pharmacological properties. Moreover, the distinction between illegal 'drugs' and legal 'medicines' was far from clear in the republican era, a period marked by constant innovation, rapid growth and aggressive marketing of pharmaceutical products. Pharmaceutical companies, foreign and local, flooded the market with a broad range of semi-synthetics which required expert knowledge in their medical applications. Just as morphine and heroin were heralded at first as miracle cures only to be demonised later as profoundly addictive substances, numerous products were developed which first found widespread medical use before being classified as dangerous drugs. The very notion of drug control was based on a questionable distinction between medical and recreational use, drawing an even finer line between pain and pleasure: drugs to manage pain were legitimate, drugs to enhance pleasure were not. Although medical associations and government bodies tried to regulate the market, consumers ultimately decided which substances they wanted to buy: as the last chapters have emphasised, the criminalisation of particular commodities such as morphine and heroin did not prevent their spread, and may even have encouraged it.

FROM DIONINE TO METHADONE

In a narcotic culture concerned with the control of pain, opium derivatives were especially popular. Semi-synthetics like dionine were openly on sale in the drug stores of coastal cities like Fuzhou.[1] Dionine, also known as ethylmorphine, was similar to codeine in its properties and although accompanied by greater toxicity, was particularly effective as a cough sedative. Both were opium derivatives, requiring ample amounts of raw opium as a basis for pharmaceutical production: whereas dionine was comparable to heroin (850 and 880 kilos of opium respectively per 100 kilos), no less than 1,000 kilos of raw opium were required to produce 100 kilos of codeine.[2] Besides its use against coughs, codeine was also effective as an analgesic and a sedative. League of Nations experts argued that it should be submitted to exactly the same legal framework (chapter III of the Geneva Convention) as morphine and heroin, despite most countries not regarding it as habit-forming. The argument for prohibition was that codeine was being used as a substitute for banned semi-synthetics, making the trade and distribution of licensed alkaloids of opium very difficult. Shrewd entrepreneurs could claim that they used medical morphine for the manufacture of legal codeine, when in reality it was being sold on the black market for recreational use: this controversy shows how easily successful pharmaceutical products could elude strict legal and medical definitions. The same problems of control and definition also applied to eukodol and dicodide, both recognised as habit-forming substances, as well as cocaine.[3]

Other preparations available in republican China—often intended as opium replacement drugs—were pantopon, papaverin, eukodol and scopoliae, all including alkaloids which medical experts thought conducive to addiction.[4] Pantopon was a remedy for pain, colic, spasms, cough and anxiety introduced by Roche in 1909. It contained opium alkaloids in a standardised form free of inert material (it is still available in a few countries, making it Roche's longest-selling product). Papaverine, one of opium's active alkaloids, was a vasodilator, which caused blood vessels to expand and muscles to relax. This medicine was used to treat problems resulting from poor blood circulation. Eukodol was a chemical derivative many times stronger than codeine (William Burroughs was one of the more famous drug users who injected it). Administered subcutaneously to allay pain and relieve coughs, it was reported by the League of Nations in 1928 to have properties similar to morphine and that it too should be controlled.[5] Anticholinergics or antispasmodics, a group of medicines that included the natural belladonna alkaloids, were also used as complementary products in detoxification cures.[6] Extracts of the leaves and roots of belladonna, also called deadly nightshade, contained the alkaloids atropine, scopolamine and hyoscyamine, which dilated the pupils and were used as cosmetics by women in Europe. Eaten in times of famine in medieval Europe, it caused 'men to become crazy and wild, and similar to those possessed', and has been used since ancient times as a poison and a sedative.[7] Hou Guangdi, to give a specific example, injected opium addicts with atropine for two to four weeks in a branch hospital of the Red Cross.[8]

Yu Fengbin (1881–1930), president of the prestigious Chinese Medical Association in the early 1920s, noted that codeine and dionine entered China in postal parcels, just like morphine and heroin.[9] While many of these preparations were legally on sale in drug stores, some were even recommended as 'home remedies' by self-proclaimed 'experts in detoxification' (*jieyan zhuanjia*). A dazzling array of tonics, stimulants, fortifiers and vitamins, from spermin to chloral hydras, and from aspirin to atropine were also prescribed, in particular to reduce opium withdrawal symptoms.[10] A report issued by the Ministry of Health in 1931 showed that no less than twenty-four popular opium cures contained a semi-synthetic.[11] Two years later the Bureaux of Public Safety and of Public Health in Shanghai jointly called upon the mayor to scrutinise the potential danger of 'medicines purporting to cure the opium habit', since many had been proved to contain 'poisons'.[12]

Coinciding with global breakthroughs in modern pharmacology, many new synthetic drugs flooded into China during the Second World War.[13] By 1944 drug shops from Shanghai to Baotou were selling pavinol and procaine (novocaine), pethidine (demerol) and amphetamines.[14] Demerol was synthesized in Germany, presumably in response to a war-time shortage of morphine. Similar to heroin and morphine, demerol was originally celebrated as a non-addictive substance. On the other hand, amphetamines were stimulants of the central nervous system whose actions resembled those of adrenaline. First introduced in the 1930s as a remedy for nasal congestion, amphetamines were manu-

factured in China for the Japanese army and often given to soldiers and workers in military factories to increase their alertness
and prevent fatigue.[15]

After the war with Japan ended in 1945, other synthetic substances such as amidone appeared on the market. Amidone (methadone) is believed by some historians to have been commissioned
by Hitler as a substitute for scarce opiates at the end of the war. In
reality amidone was discovered accidentally by chemical engineers
of I. G. Farbenindustrie. It lacked any resemblance to known com-
pounds, and its narcotic and analgesic properties were unantici-
pated. Despite a severe morphine shortage, amidone was only
used in Europe as an analgesic in the post-war period.[16] It reached
the market in China roughly at the same time, although its use
appears to have remained confined to the cities.[17]

THE STIMULANTS: COCAINE AND EPHEDRINE

The leaf of the erythroxylon coca was used in the Inca empire
before gradually spreading throughout the colonial world. Cocaine was isolated in the 1850s, but spread only slowly because it
was expensive and the leaves decayed relatively quickly. Coca seeds,
on the other hand, travelled well, could be wrapped up as ordinary postal parcels and kept moist by a little added soil, and could
be grown almost anywhere. Experimental stations and commercial
plantations spanned the globe, from its original home in Peru, via
London (Kew Gardens), Lagos, Assam and Darjeeling, Southeast
Asia, China and Japan.[18] By the end of the nineteenth century, cocaine replaced opium and morphine as the favourite anaesthetic
of the surgical profession.[19] A wide range of remedies containing
cocaine became available in the early twentieth century, not only
at chemists and local shops but also bought by post and hawked
from door to door. Cocaine tonics and powders were marketed
for self-medication against conditions such as headache, toothache,
asthma, haemorrhoids, impotence and diseases of the blood.[20]

Before the First World War, cocaine also became a recreational
drug for the urban chic. In France the 'divine coco' of artists and
writers spread from the clubs of Montmartre and Montparnasse

to the poorer environs of Paris.[21] Small quantities were used for nasal inhalation, as additives to alcoholic drinks and as cigarette filters. Alternatively, it could be injected, or its solution soaked into cotton swabs which would then be inserted into one nostril.[22] The increase in the price of alcohol between 1917 and 1920 in France and Germany meant that cocaine spread to the working classes.[23] American surgeries and hospitals were also instrumental in the proliferation of cocaine, using more liberal quantities as an anaesthetic for operations. The prohibition of alcohol in the 1920s meant that in the United States cocaine was cheaper than whisky, generating millions of regular users—although many would subsequently switch to heroin.[24] By the 1920s cocaine was increasingly prohibited and driven underground, while synthetic substitutes like novocaine supplanted it in medical practice.[25]

If British colonial administrators in India had contributed more than others to the spread of opium in Asia, Dutch officers in Java anticipated the global demand for cocaine. They were eager to repeat the success of the cinchona and coffee plantations there, and believed that coca plants were well suited to the local climate and could contribute to the colonial economy. Coca leaves were exported for chewing as a mildly intoxicating tonic, while coca wine and coca beef were successful in North America.[26] When the demand for Javanese coca finally took off in the 1890s, the plantations became the base for a soaring Asian market. By appropriating the latest German technology—no bilateral treaty protected the German patent—the Nederlandsche Cocainefabriek opened in 1900 in Amsterdam to become the world's largest producer of chemically manufactured cocaine.[27]

The virtual monopoly of the Nederlandsche Cocainefabriek was challenged by Japan in the First World War. Once Japan had mastered the manufacturing process and cultivated coca plantations, imports from Java plunged. The coca leaf was a hugely successful substitute for sugarcane in Taiwan, then a Japanese colony, since sugar exports to Europe and North America declined drastically during the First World War;[28] as a cash crop in global demand, the coca leaf became a vital export commodity. First cultivated in 1916, coca leaves from Taiwan supplied a growing cocaine industry in Japan, with pharmaceutical companies such as San-kyo, Dai Nippon and Hoshi competing with German, Swiss and American firms.[29]

While the coca leaves cultivated in Asia had the strength nec-essary for refinement into cocaine, the less potent leaves imported from Peru were used for producing Coca-Cola and other coca tonics.[30] The cocaine produced in Japan with coca from Taiwan was exported to many countries, India being the principal market after the First World War.[31] Many users of cocaine in India were already familiar with opium and cannabis, and added it to their repertoire of recreational drugs: they generally swallowed the powder or chewed it with betel leaves and lime.[32] Thanks to the extremely high alkaloid content of coca from Taiwan, the Japa-nese brand names printed onto the 700-gram containers used in the wholesale trade would become as familiar in Bombay, Singa-pore and Shanghai as they were in Tokyo.[33] Some entrepreneurs faked the label of the pharmaceutical giant Boehringer or of 'Oo-long Tea' from Taiwan. Cocaine seized in Bombay was wrapped into rubber ice sacks, the characters for 'ice bag' clearly visible.[34] According to official League of Nations estimates, coca produc-tion more than doubled between 1926 and 1928 to 129 tonnes. The plantations and factories in Taiwan yielded large amounts of cocaine estimated at 892 kilos in 1937 and some 205 in 1944.[35] These figures did not include the considerable contraband traffic, some of which found its way to mainland China.[36]

According to a customs report, however, only an estimated 2.9 kilos of cocaine were (illegally) imported into Shanghai in 1916, followed by little more than half a kilo in 1917.[37] Varying amounts of cocaine could be found hidden in the cargo bays of Shanghai-bound ships during the 1920s,[38] and although the League of Na-tions report covering the second half of that decade could not of-fer any complete figures for China, it did mention that 'the illicit traffic in narcotic drugs such as… cocaine has been increasing': legal imports, mainly from France, Britain and Germany, stood at roughly 100 kilos a year.[39] Smaller amounts were also legally im-ported into Hong Kong and the Japanese territory of Guandong.[40] Although cocaine was also smuggled into China, mainly as Japanese and Russian contraband, customs reports show that it appeared to be in much smaller quantities than the huge amounts of morphine and heroin.[41]

The earliest certified use of cocaine in China was by foreign doctors in extremely painful surgical operations, especially on the eye and the nose.[42] One of the favourite uses of cocaine, according to the medical press, was to kill the pain during an amputation of the penis.[43] Cocaine was also used for recreational purposes, and was a component of golden elixir,[44] while customers could go to Korean drug houses to buy 'coke'.[45] A letter of June 1924 to the editor of the *North China Herald* suggests that 'coke' was widely used by the 'unfortunate women' of Shanghai. According to the anonymous correspondent, cocaine was also available, despite its prohibition, in many of the cafés frequented by foreigners.[46] The market for it nonetheless seemed to be rather limited, which illustrates how popular demand shaped the narcotic economy despite the easy availability of this excitant produced in Taiwan. As a popular painkiller, for instance, morphine was far more economical than cocaine—which only removed pain locally, producing a euphoric effect which lasted a shorter time than opiates. The fact that it was more complex to refine than opiates may also have impeded its spread in mainland China.[47]

Just as derivatives of opium appeared on the market, synthetic substitutes for cocaine also found their way into China. In cities along the coast novocaine and other derivatives were openly on sale in modern drug stores. Most were not classified as narcotic substances in China and therefore not subject to any official restrictions.[48] Joseph Oscar Thomson, medical missionary employed by the Canton Hospital between 1910–41, observed that novocaine was readily available for surgical anaesthetics. Spinal and tropical novocaine apart, intestinal avertin and intravenous evipan sodium were also deemed useful, while chloroform was 'safe', since it evaporated swiftly in the subtropical temperatures of the Chinese south.[49]

If cocaine was produced in Japan with the coca leaf from Taiwan, ephedrine, a synthesised version of the herbal drug *mahuang*, was specific to mainland China. Marketed globally by the German firm Merck as ephetonin, its precise origins are unclear, although by the end of the 1920s it had spread sufficiently to become the subject of international enquiries. As a local researcher reported to Johns Hopkins University's pharmacology department, ephedrine could be without any palpable effect, although negative symptoms could consist of 'palpitation, tremor, weakness, sweating, feeling of warmth, chilly sensation, dizziness, nausea, vomiting, extrasystoles, and tonal arrhythmia', without producing 'exhilaration or pleasurable intoxication'.[50] The Austrian scientist Knaffl-Lenz noted the chemical proximity of ephedrine to adrenaline, the synthetic alkaloid being used therapeutically for asthma and circulatory disturbances.[51]

Ephedrine was soon produced on an industrial scale in western China, where the herb *mahuang* grew in abundance. Between 1926 and 1928, ephedrine exports to the West exploded from under 4 to 216 tonnes. Since ephedrine was not included in any international narcotics legislation, it became a legal substitute for cocaine, which was difficult to tell apart from ephedrine.[52] As we see in the conclusion, the fortunes of ephedrine would be dramatically revived by the end of the twentieth century with a global shift away from sedatives towards stimulants.

CHINA'S NON-PROBLEM: CANNABIS

Cannabis (*cannabis sativa, dama* in Chinese)[53] also failed to become part of narcotic culture in modern China. It was widely grown locally and had been known as a medicinal herb for nearly 2,000 years, although the most common use of the hemp plant in late imperial China was as a source of rope and textile fibre. Cannabis was also believed to lead to demon possession and insanity.[54]

The medical uses were highlighted in a pharmacopeia of the Tang, which prescribed the root of the plant to remove a blood clot, while the juice from the leaves could be ingested to combat tapeworm. The seeds of cannabis, reduced to powder and mixed with rice wine, were recommended in various other materia medica against several ailments, ranging from constipation to hair loss.[55] The Ming dynasty *Mingyi bielu* provided detailed instructions about the harvesting of the heads of the *cannabis sativa* plant (*mafen, mabo*), while the few authors who acknowledged hemp in various pharmacopoeias seemed to agree that the resinous female flowering heads were the source of dreams and revelations. After copious consumption, according to the ancient *Shennong bencaojing*, one could see demons and walk like a madman, even becoming 'in touch with the spirits' over time.[56] Other medical writers warned that ghosts could be seen after ingesting a potion based on raw seeds blended with calamus and podophyllum (*guijiu*).[57]

The generally negative connotations of cannabis were replicated during the republican period, when government authorities claimed that smoking cannabis could cause nervous dysfunction and madness.[58] Such official attitudes must have reflected popular beliefs, since very little concrete evidence exists concerning the use of cannabis even in the large coastal metropoles. In Shanghai not a single case of cannabis use was discovered during the 1930s.[59] With the exception of the Uyghurs, the popular perception of the smell of smoked cannabis as 'foul' (*chou*) also impeded its spread.[60] On the other hand, the extraction of hemp oil was widespread in Shanxi, Mongolia and Manchuria. Although most of it appears to have been used for lighting and to lubricate cart wheels, its narcotic powers may have been understood by the local farmers.[61]

Cannabis also met with mixed success in other parts of the world. The Spanish cultivated it in their colonies from the sixteenth to the nineteenth centuries, mainly as fibre for the manufacture of naval rigging. However, Angolan slaves brought cannabis to the sugar plantations of Brazil, where Indian and rural mestizos adopted it for social and medicinal reasons, a clear example of how one substance could be used for radically different purposes by different social groups. Regarded as the opium of the poor, it shifted towards the Caribbean between the late nineteenth and early twentieth century, as planters imported indentured labour from India after the abolition of slavery.[62]

Large quantities of opium were imported from India before the poppy was cultivated locally in China. However, cannabis failed to find a social niche and cultural meaning, although it was widely used recreationally and medicinally in South Asia. Foreign observers of nineteenth-century India noted that it was reputed to induce a voracious appetite.[63] British authorities in India only started to condemn it in moral and medical terms in the 1870s, reflecting deeper political anxieties about local populations who used the substance. It was viewed in asylums as a cause of insanity, and linked by the colonial authorities to sexual immorality, infanticide, suicide, chronic indolence, and violent and disorderly behaviour, in particular the uprising of 1857 and attacks on missionaries. As these views spread to British medical journals, cannabis became the subject of parliamentary hearings in 1890, followed by legal restrictions on its use and sale in India.[64] Similar views also appeared in the Middle East, notably in Egypt where the first law prohibiting the use of hemp came into effect in 1879.[65] By contrast, cannabis was not able to generate either consumer demand, medical approval or political opposition in China: in his comprehensive overview of narcotic products Luo Yunyan dismissed it as an unknown quantity.[66] This lack of interest made it socially insignificant, which further reinforces the view that the favourable reception of opium was conditional upon cultural and social variables rather than political, economic or even pharmacological factors. However crucial government restrictions on opium and the international war on drugs may have been in the shaping of narcotic culture in China, consumers rather than suppliers continued to determine patterns of intoxication: in their search for a panacea against pain, hunger and cold and a lubricant for social intercourse, they opted for sedatives like opium, morphine and heroin rather than stimulants like cocaine and caffeine or hallucinogens such as cannabis.

A MARKER OF MODERNITY: THE CIGARETTE

Despite the spread of morphine and heroin as alternatives to opium, the commodity that benefited most from prohibition was the cigarette. Already in the nineteenth century, a shrewd observer noted that 'one always talks about opium, of its harmful

effect on the Sons of Han, but one tends to forget that the abuse
of tobacco, so widespread in China, is debilitating in the extreme, and nobody has ever paid any attention to this.' He concluded that 'the Chinese smoke excessively'.[67] Tobacco spread
even further with opium prohibition: much as the nineteenth
century was dominated by opium, the cigarette defined the twentieth century in China. Within half a century the ready-made
cigarette superseded not only opiates but also other forms of tobacco smoking, including the water pipe and hand-rolled native
produce: cigarettes were light and palatable, easy to store and
handy to use, capable of delivering nicotine straight to the lungs
as the smoke could be inhaled deeply in a short span of time perfectly attuned to the faster pace of industrial life. As one editorial-
ist wrote in the United States, 'Short, snappy, easily attempted,
easily completed or just as easily discarded before completion, the
cigarette is the symbol of a machine age in which the ultimate
cogs and wheels and levers are human nerves.'[68] The vast majority of workers surveyed by the Shanghai Bureau of Social Affairs
in the 1930s, to take but one example, smoked cigarettes, and
only 3 per cent resorted to native tobacco.[69] By the end of the
twentieth century China would become the largest market for
cigarettes and the world's leading producer of tobacco, the cigarette having largely taken over the social functions of opium
within a thriving smoking culture which appeared impervious to
the harmful effects of nicotine.

Cigarettes were imported into China for the first time in the
1890s. Travelling on foot just before the downfall of the Qing,
Edwin Dingle witnessed how the foreign cigarette was sold at
wayside stalls by vendors of monkey nuts and marrow seeds. According to his observations, no trade prospered so much in Yunnan
as that in foreign cigarettes, as garish posters advertising them appeared on the walls of temples, private houses and official residences. The common cigarette was smoked by high and low, rich
and poor, and also by women and children, especially with the
spread of the anti-opium movement. It was offered at small cele-
brations, while a packet of cigarettes instead of a whiff of opium
was offered when people called upon high officials in Kunming.[70]

During the same period the missionaries Fullerton and Wilson, travelling by mule cart through Shanxi, also noticed that cigarettes were widely advertised on city walls throughout northern China.[71] The cigarette became an even more ubiquitous feature in the 1910s, even in the remote interior, as hand-painted advertisements adorned pagodas, street corners and city walls.[72] Although the number of people who substituted cigarettes for opium is impossible to calculate, one observer was struck in 1915 by the 'astonishingly rapid' spread of cigarette smoking among men and women 'of all classes and ages, from ten years up'.[73]

The number of cigarettes legally imported into China multiplied nearly tenfold between 1915 and 1924 to some 7 billion.[74] In 1915 the Life Extension Institute in New York, a supporter of medical missions, claimed that 'the Anglo-American Tobacco Company is distributing tens of millions of cigarettes free for the avowed purpose of planting the habit in the wake of the opium habit'.[75] British American Tobacco's greatest success was indeed in China, where an integrated system of mass distribution and production was created between 1905 and 1922, including modern factories and camel trains fanning out across the hinterland. Native slogans and bright placards appeared in advertising campaigns throughout the country; a huge clock sign touting Ruby Queen Cigarettes was built in Shanghai with ten-foot-square neon characters. The company prided itself on combining business with humanity by 'weaning the Chinese… from opium and teaching them to smoke North Carolina cigarettes.'[76] Delivered in tin-lined wooden cases, cigarette imports grew to almost half a billion a month in a number of provinces in the north by the 1930s.[77]

It is not surprising that the American government should have been a shrill opponent of opium and other psychoactive substances in which it had no stake, although it had few reservations about the growing cigarette industry from which it stood to gain fiscally. The cigarette, unlike opium, had few enemies in China either: if opium was decried as poison, cigarettes were promoted as a healthy and modern consumable. Even renowned medical publications denied any health hazards,[78] and opposition to cigarette smoking stemmed mainly from a minority of foreign temperance activists.[79] One exception was Herbert Lamson's *Social pathology in China* published in Shanghai in 1935. This referred to opium in one sentence but condemned nicotine as the real poison, since it tended to raise blood pressure, decrease powers of prolonged exertion and increase the habit of spitting.[80] Consumers, on the other hand, thought that foreign cigarettes were elegant to smoke, convenient to carry and fashionable to display: they also enjoyed their refreshing taste.[81] With the huge population movements in the republican period, cigarettes were marketed as 'the best companions of modern travellers'.[82] The ready-made cigarette, in a context of increased geographical and social mobility, made the habits of sociability fostered by opium smoking even more popular: as a sign of conviviality, friendship and gratitude, it was shared in a ritual of exchange which transcended the practical as well as the social constraints of opium smoking. As opium pipes were increasingly depicted as vehicles of diseases in an age marked by new regimes of moral and medical hygiene, accused of spreading syphilis, tuberculosis or pyorrhea,[83] the cigarette was seen as 'hygienic' (*weisheng*).[84]

The match further facilitated the spread of the cigarette. Before its advent, fire was obtained by striking a steel blade on flint.[85] The first match appeared in China in 1865, 2–3,000 boxes being imported in the following years to reach 100,000 in 1891 as the country rapidly became the world's biggest market for matches: by 1928 almost 200 different brands were competing for consumer attention.[86] Two types of matches were popular in the republican period: safety matches (*anquan huochai*), which had to be struck across a special surface, and phosphorus matches (*liuhualin huochai*), which would ignite when drawn across any rough surface. The first were in demand in central and southern China, where humidity prevailed, while the second were sold mainly in the north, where the climate was much drier. Matches came in all sorts of sizes and packs, most of them being sold in boxes of 75, 100 or 115, the shorter varieties being considered to be better than the longer ones. Matches could be bought cheaply at just over 5 cents for a pack of ten boxes; in the 1920s rag-pickers in Beijing went from door to door collecting old cloth, giving away small boxes of matches in exchange.[87] Lighters also appeared in the republican period, some producers even including one with each pack of cigarettes as a marketing ploy. The cigarette, the match and the lighter thus emerged as the new technologies of smoking culture and the symbols of a desirable modernity.[88] The opium utensils, once considered highly desirable collectables, were seen as cumbersome and old-fashioned. In an age of advertisements, the sets of picture cards which were enclosed, one or two at a time, in cigarette boxes, were the popular collectables.[89]

With the advent of the Chinese Communist Party, the cigarette would become the official intoxicant, as committee meetings of party delegates were held amid clouds of smoke, the floor covered in cigarette butts. Smoking came to symbolise the relentless sequence of struggle sessions, deliberations and resolutions, while in the war films of the early 1950s decisive action by political leaders was often expressed by the energetic throwing of burning cigarettes on the ground. Smoking culture had finally completed its revolution, as the cigarette had come to take over the social functions of opium. Penicillin, which appeared in the 1940s, took care of its medical uses.

11

CONCLUSION

'China was turned into a nation of opium addicts by the pernicious forces of imperialist trade'. We have systematically questioned this image on the basis of extensive primary sources, showing that opium had few harmful effects on either health or longevity, that most smokers used it in moderation without any fatal 'loss of control', and that it was prepared and appreciated in highly complex rituals with inbuilt constraints on excessive use. Opium was an ideal social lubricant in a culture of restraint which emphasised decorum and composure, and became a major vector of male sociability in late imperial China. Contrary to received knowledge, most smokers were generally able to determine the quantity and quality of the opium they wished to consume, and could curb their use for personal and social reasons or even stop smoking altogether without too much difficulty. The notion of an irresistible compulsion towards ever-increasing doses ignores the overwhelming evidence that the majority of smokers used the substance in moderation. Occasional, intermittent or moderate smokers were probably unaware of any undesirable effects, since smoking was a more wasteful mode of delivery than oral ingestion.

While the morphine content of imported opium from India and of the locally cultivated varieties was relatively low, smoking had numerous medical advantages. The most common reason for smoking was self-medication: to ease pain, combat fevers and suppress coughs. Opium was a panacea which provided relief against the symptoms of cholera, malaria and tuberculosis and helped counter-act fatigue, hunger and cold. In a climate marked by frequent and sometimes lethal dysentery, no remedy was more effective than opium.

As Andrew Sherratt has noted, 'different kind of drugs are appropriate to different sorts of society', and in late imperial China opium was a culturally privileged intoxicant which fulfilled a variety of social and medical roles.[1] If opium was medicine as much as recreation, this book also provides plentiful evidence that the transition from a tolerated opium culture to a system of prohibition produced a cure which was far worse than the disease. Ordinary people were imprisoned and died from epidemics in crowded cells, while those deemed beyond any hope of redemption were simply executed. On the other hand, the opium suppression policies of the modern period engendered corruption, a black market and a criminal underclass. They also assisted a shift in consumption patterns: heroin and morphine were snorted, smoked, chewed or injected in the wake of the anti-opium movement, often in conditions far more harmful than opium smoking. Although heroin pills were smoked at all social levels in relatively small and innocuous quantities, some hardly containing any alkaloids, the dirty needles shared by the poor caused lethal septicemia and transmitted a range of contagious diseases: prohibition spawned social exclusion and human misery, and encouraged—however inadvertently—the very problems it was designed to contain.

Ironically, the only region in China where semi-synthetics failed to displace opium was the British crown colony of Hong Kong. As a result of colonial commitment to a government monopoly over the sale and distribution of opium from 1914 to 1943, the paste remained more cost-effective and convenient than heroin and morphine (more research may show that a similar stability in established patterns of intoxication characterised other colonial regimes in Asia between the two World Wars, notably Java under the Dutch Opium Regie and British India). After the colonial authorities were no longer in a position to withstand American opposition to the opium trade and were obliged to eliminate state monopolies, most opium smokers switched to heroin within less than ten years.[2] Harold Traver suggests that the example of Hong Kong shows not only that opium prohibition generally encourages the spread of heroin, but that governments may be more successful when it comes to actively promoting drugs—whether alcohol, tobacco or opium—than in striving against all odds to prohibit them.[3]

The Chinese Communist Party actively participated in the lucrative opium trade during their fight against the Guomindang: opium was one of the most important financial resources of the party, allowing it to overcome a number of fiscal difficulties and build an alternative state in the hinterland.[4] After their takeover of the country in 1949, however, it took the party a mere three years radically to eliminate all illegal substances: a dense network of police institutions, resident committees and mass organisations were used to crush drug offenders, some even being denounced by their own family members. Public trials and mass executions dealt a final blow to narcotic culture, while tens of thousands of offenders were sent to prison, often for life.[5] 'Opium', like 'prostitution', was portrayed as evil incarnate and the communists spared no effort in suppressing these symbols of capitalist decadence brutally and massively.

While it is a major tenet of the opium myth that the communists 'successfully' eliminated the 'drug plague', with complete disregard for the human cost of their crusade, medical and social variables were as important in the long-term decline of narcotic culture as political factors. Penicillin appeared in the 1940s as the first antibiotic successfully to treat a whole range of diseases which had previously been managed with opiates. Discovered in 1928 by Sir Alexander Fleming, penicillin became widely available in various forms for medical use in China after the Second World War, playing an important role in treating pneumonia, rheumatic fever, scarlet fever and other diseases. Antibiotics took over the medical functions of opiates. The social status of opium was already on the decline in the 1930s, abstinence being seen as a mark of pride and a badge of modernity among social elites, very much as the rising middle classes elsewhere started to 'free' themselves from morally reprehensible 'drugs'. In Java the number of opium smokers dropped drastically during the 1920s without any forceful prohibition under the Opium Regie, opium being regarded increasingly as a sign of the uncivilised: cigarette smoking took off instead.[6] Betel chewing was also gradually replaced in Java by cigarette smoking, a habit seen by new professional groups as more appropriate in an age of modernity.[7] Similar social differentials were also prevalent in China as opium went out of fashion: Emily Hahn noted in the 1930s that the 'modern, Westernised Chinese of Shanghai frowned on smoking opium—not on moral grounds but because it was considered so lamentably old-fashioned.' Her friends wore long gowns and were deliberately 'reactionary', and opium smoking was part of that: 'Opium was decadent. Opium was for grandfathers.'[8] Even the *Shanghai Times* confidently stated in 1937 that 'opium-smoking is doomed in China' as the practice was not 'in keeping with modern habits and outlook of life'.[9] Jean Cocteau put it more succinctly: 'Young Asia no longer smokes because "grandfathers smoked".'[10]

The cigarette, on the other hand, was fashionable and modern, in Java as in China. British American Tobacco thrived in republican China, selling half a billion cigarettes a month in a number of provinces in the 1930s,[11] and its sophisticated system of mass distribution and production was transferred to the Chinese government by Mao Zedong in 1952.[12] Tobacco cultivation and cigarette production were vigorously promoted by the CCP, as the cigarette was allowed to take over the everyday rituals and social roles of opium within a thriving smoking culture which appeared impervious to the deleterious effects of nicotine. Cigarettes evoked power and prestige and were promoted by the top leadership: Deng Xiaoping even expressed his gratitude to the cigarette as the reason for his longevity.[13] By the end of the twentieth century China would emerge as the largest market for cigarettes and the world's leading tobacco producer.

However crucial government restrictions on opium and the international war on drugs may have been in shaping narcotic culture in China, consumers rather than suppliers generally determined patterns of intoxication: in their search for a panacea against pain, hunger and cold as well as a lubricant for social intercourse, they opted for sedatives like opium, morphine and heroin rather than stimulants like cocaine and caffeine, or hallucinogens such as mescaline or cannabis. However, opium should also be understood as part of a much wider culture of intoxication based

on the inhalation of smoke: as Europe took to alcoholic and caffeinated drinks from the sixteenth century onwards, China developed a sophisticated smoking culture, starting with tobacco in
the seventeenth century, followed by madak in the eighteenth,
opium in the nineteenth, and cigarettes in the twentieth. The habit
of smoking crossed all social divides and included women and
children, supported by the invention of ingenious smoking technologies, the opium pipe being a prime example. The advent of
the cigarette in the twentieth century thus completed the smoking revolution, which had started and now ended with tobacco.

Tobacco, of course, is a stimulant, and the gradual replacement
of opium by the cigarette in the twentieth century has heralded a
much larger shift in global patterns of consumption away from
sedatives towards new stimulant drugs. Some observers have noted
how the illicit consumption of narcotics has reappeared in the
PRC with the economic reforms of the 1980s, making the country a major transit point in the international heroin traffic.[14] However, experts underline that amphetamine-type stimulants (ATS),
in particular methamphetamines ('ice'), are far more widespread
than the more traditional opiates: in Shanghai, Hong Kong, Manila,
Bangkok, London and New York ecstasy, amphetamines and crack
cocaine have become the most popular recreational drugs. Narcotic culture is well and truly dead, as consumers the world over
seek designer drugs more attuned to new patterns of work and
leisure.[15]

China, once again, is at the centre of this global trend. As we
saw in chapter 9, ephedrine, which is only found in its natural
form in China, was already produced on an industrial scale during
the republican period: used to manufacture 'ice' as well as other
new stimulant drugs, it is smuggled in large quantities to other
parts of the world today, despite legal controls introduced between
1992 and 2000.[16] In December 1998 a Notice on Issues Pertain-
ing to the Strengthened Control of the Export of Ephedrine-
typed Products was issued, attempting to control the export of
twelve saline products, semi-finished products, derivatives and single preparations of ephedrine. The following year, over 16 tonnes
of 'ice' were seized in China, compared to 5 tonnes of heroin.[17]

This trend has increased in the twenty-first century, as demand for amphetamine ecstasy, known as 'head-shaking pill' (*yaotou-wan*), is moving from coastal areas to inland provinces.[18] Amphetamines, it should be noted, can be administered in a variety of ways in Asia. While relatively little is known about ATS consumption in China, smoking, sniffing and fume inhaling are common in Thailand and the Philippines, as consumers replicate a widespread smoking culture which started with tobacco many centuries before.

The core of the opium myth is the image of China as a passive victim on the international market, but as this book sets out to demonstrate, consumers in all social categories actively shaped narcotic culture: they took smoking further than anybody else, developed the sophisticated mechanism of the opium pipe, enthusiastically embraced the products offered by the pharmaceutical industry, eagerly appropriated the syringe, diversified the uses of heroin and rapidly took to the cigarette: new designer drugs, ephedrine in particular, have now placed them at the very centre of a global shift towards excitants.

NOTES

Chapter 1   Introduction

1. John K. Fairbank, 'The creation of the treaty system' in Denis Twitchett and John K. Fairbank (eds), *The Cambridge history of China*, Cambridge University Press, 1978, vol. 10, part 1, p. 213.

2. The most recent contribution to this myth is W. Travis Hanes III and Frank Sanello, *The Opium Wars: The addiction of one empire and the corruption of another*, Naperville, IL: Sourcebooks, 2002.

3. Mike Jay, *Emperors of dreams: Drugs in the nineteenth century*, Sawtry: Daedalus, 2002, pp. 71–2.

4. Richard K. Newman, 'Opium smoking in late imperial China: A reconsideration', *Modern Asian Studies*, 29, no. 4 (Oct. 1995), pp. 767–9; another critical voice is Mark Elvin, in Caroline Blunden and Mark Elvin (eds), *Cultural atlas of China*, Oxford: Phaidon Press, 1983, pp. 148–9, as well as a remarkable chapter in Virgil K. Y. Ho, 'The city of contrasts: Perceptions and realities in Canton in the 1920s and 1930s', doctoral dissertation, Oxford University, 1995, pp. 79–123; Jack Gray, *Rebellions and revolutions: China from the 1800s to the 1980s*, Oxford University Press, 1990, is exemplary in his refusal to uncritically reproduce the stereotypes of dominant historiography; one of the earliest opponents of the opium myth was the sinologist Herbert Giles, *Some truths about opium*, Cambridge: Heffer, 1923.

5. Martin Booth, *Opium: A history*, London: Pocket Books, 1997, p. 63.

6. John F. Richards, 'Opium and the British Indian empire: The Royal Commission of 1895', *Modern Asian Studies*, 36, part 2 (May 2002), pp. 406–8.

7. Newman, 'Opium smoking in late imperial China', pp. 776, 779–80.

8. John A. Turner, *Kwang Tung, or five years in south China*, Hong Kong: Oxford University Press, 1988 (1st edn 1894), p. 43.

9. Virginia Berridge, *Opium and the people: Opiate use and drug control policy in nineteenth and early twentieth century England*, London: Free Association Books, 1999.

10. Joseph Westermeyer, *Poppies, pipes and people: Opium and its use in Laos*, Berkeley: University of California Press, 1982, p. 285.

11. Berridge, *Opium and the people*, p. 192.

12. Richard L. Miller, *The case for legalizing drugs*, New York: Praeger, 1991, p. 4; see also Ted Goldberg, *Demystifying drugs: A psychosocial perspective*, Houndsville: Macmillan, 1999, pp. 22–8.

13. Peter Lee, *The big smoke: The Chinese art and craft of opium*, Bangkok: Lamplight Books, 1999, p. 121.

14. Jean Cocteau, *Opium: Diary of a cure*, London: Icon, 1957, p. 20.

15. Berridge, *Opium and the people*, p. 193.

16. Michael Gossop, *Living with drugs*, London: Ashgate, 2000, p. 16.

17. Oden Meeker, *The little world of Laos*, New York: Scribner's, 1959, pp. 133–4.

18. Westermeyer, *Poppies, pipes and people*, p. 86.

19. A. de Mol van Otterloo and A. Bonebakker, 'Over de doeltreffenheid van de ontwenningskuur volgens Modinos voor opiumschuivers', *Geneeskundig Tijdschrift voor Nederlandsch-Indië*, vol. 79 (1931), p. 870.

20. Richard Hughes, *Foreign devil: Thirty years of reporting from the Far East*, London: Deutsch, 1972, p. 254.

21. Lee, *The big smoke*, p. 115.

22. Cocteau, *Opium*, pp. 10–12 and 26.

23. James R. Rush, 'Opium in Java: A sinister friend', *Journal of Asian Studies*, 44, no. 3 (May 1985), p. 555.

24. Jon Boyes and S. Piraban, *Opium fields*, Bangkok: Silkworm Books, 1991, p. 60.

25. An excellent introduction to questions of supply and policy appears in Edward R. Slack, *Opium, state, and society: China's narco-economy and the Guomindang, 1924–1937*, Honolulu: University of Hawai'i Press, 2000; other recent studies, in alphabetical order, include Alan Baumler, *Modern China and opium: A reader*, Michigan: University of Michigan Press, 2001; Alan Baumler, 'Playing with fire: The Nationalist government and opium in China, 1927–1941', doctoral dissertation, University of Illinois, 1997; Timothy Brook and Bob T. Wakabayashi (eds), *Opium regimes: China, Britain, and Japan, 1839–1952*, Berkeley: University of California Press, 2000; Dong Yiming, 'Étude sur le problème de l'opium dans la région du sud-ouest de la Chine (pendant les années 1920 et 1930)', doctoral dissertation, Paris: École des Hautes Études en Sciences Sociales, 1997; P. W. Howard, 'Opium suppression in Qing China: Responses to a social problem, 1729–1906', doctoral dissertation, University of Pennsylvania, 1998; Lin Manhong, 'Qingmo shehui liuxing xishi yapian yanjiu: Gongjimian zhi fenxi (1773–1906)' (A study of opium consumption in late Qing society: A supply-side analysis [1773–1906]), doctoral dissertation, Taipei: National Normal University, 1985; Joyce Madancy, 'Revolution, religion and the poppy: Opium and the rebellion of the "Sixteenth Emperor" in early republican Fujian', *Republican China*, 21, no. 1 (Nov. 1995), pp. 1–41; Thomas D. Reins, 'Reform, nationalism and internationalism: The opium suppression movement in China and the Anglo-American influence, 1900–1908', *Modern Asian Studies*, 25, no. 1 (Feb. 1991), pp. 101–42; Carl A. Trocki, *Opium, empire and the global political economy: A study of the Asian opium trade 1750–1950*, London: Routledge, 1999; Zhou Yongming, *Anti-drug crusades in twentieth-century China: Nationalism, history, and state-building*, Lanham, MD: Rowman and Littlefield, 1999.

26. David Lenson, *On drugs*, Minneapolis: University of Minnesota Press, 1995, p. 60.

27. In his pioneering article on the history of opium in China, Jonathan D. Spence pointed out the diverse types of opium, although it is unfortunate that his otherwise exquisite piece invariably describes every smoker as an 'addict'; see Jonathan D. Spence, 'Opium smoking in Ch'ing China' in Frederic Wakeman and

Carolyn Grant (eds), *Conflict and control in late imperial China*, Berkeley: University of California Press, 1975, pp. 143–73.

28. A welcome exception is the pioneering article by Harold Traver, 'Opium to heroin: Restrictive legislation and the rise of heroin consumption in Hong Kong', *Journal of Policy History*, 4, no. 3 (1992), pp. 307–24.

Chapter 2　The Global Spread of Psychoactive Substances (*c.* 1600–1900)

1. David T. Courtwright, *Forces of habit: Drugs and the making of the modern world*, Cambridge, MA: Harvard University Press, 2001, pp. 2–3.

2. Some classic works include R. S. Dunn, *Sugar and slaves*, Chapel Hill: University of North Carolina Press, 1972; W. H. McNeill, *Plagues and peoples*, London: Penguin, 1979; and Eric R. Wolf, *Peasants*, Englewood Cliffs, NJ: Prentice-Hall, 1966.

3. John Burnett, *Liquid pleasures: A social history of drinks in modern Britain*, London: Routledge, 1999, pp. 49–69; for a general history of tea, see also Paul Butel, *Histoire du thé*, Paris: Éditions Desjonquères, 1989.

4. Courtwright, *Forces of habit*, pp. 22–23.

5. Burnett, *Liquid pleasures*, pp. 70–92.

6. B. A. Weinberg and B. K. Bealer, *The world of caffeine: The science and culture of the world's most popular drug*, London: Routledge, 2001, pp. 83–94.

7. Courtwright, *Forces of habit*, p. 23.

8. Sidney Mintz, *Sweetness and power: The place of sugar in modern history*, Harmondsworth: Penguin Books, 1985, pp. 109–11, as well as Courtwright, *Forces of habit*, p. 25; see also William Gervase Clarence-Smith, *Cocoa and chocolate, 1765–1914*, London: Routledge, 2000, pp. 19–27 and 66–77.

9. Courtwright, *Forces of habit*, p. 25; Clarence-Smith, *Cocoa and chocolate*, pp. 15–16 and 24–28.

10. Burnett, *Liquid pleasures*, pp. 185–7, and Clarence-Smith, *Cocoa and chocolate*, pp. 10–11.

11. Fernand Braudel, *The structures of everyday life: Civilisation and capitalism, 15th to 18th century*, New York: Harper and Row, 1979, pp. 236–41.

12. Burnett, *Liquid pleasures*, p. 217.

13. Braudel, *The structures of everyday life*, pp. 241–4.

14. On the boom in gin distilling during the eighteenth century, see Patrick Dillon, *The much-lamented death of Madam Geneva: The eighteenth-century gin craze*, London: Review, 2002.

15. Burnett, *Liquid pleasures*, pp. 160–6.

16. Yong Yap Cotterell, *The Chinese kitchen: A traditional approach to eating*, London: Weidenfeld and Nicolson, 1986, pp. 32–5; Wang Lihua, *Zhonggu Huabei yinshi wenhua de bianqian* (The changes in eating and drinking culture in the north of China during the ancient and medieval periods), Beijing: Zhongguo kexue chubanshe, 2000, pp. 255–6.

17. Feng Erkang and Chang Jianhua, *Qingren shehui shenghuo* (Everyday life in the Qing dynasty), Shenyang: Shenyang chubanshe, 2002, p. 195.

18. John Barrow, *Travels in China: Containing descriptions, observations, and comparisons*, London: Cadell and Davies, 1804, p. 152.

19. Robert Coltman, *The Chinese: Their present and future*, London: Davis, 1891, pp. 122–4.

20. Frank Welsh, *A borrowed place: The history of Hong Kong*, New York: Kodansha International, 1993, p. 168.

21. Zhang Deyi, *Hanghai shuqi* (Travels abroad), Changsha: Yuelu shushe, 1985, p. 456.

22. Stephen Braun, *Buzz: The science and lore of alcohol and caffeine*, New York: Oxford University Press, 1996, pp. 34–5.

23. Burnett, *Liquid pleasures*, pp. 120–35.

24. Braudel, *The structures of everyday life*, pp. 254–5.

25. Ibid., pp. 236–41.

26. On the uses of opium in early modern England, see Liza Picard, *Dr Johnson's London: Life in London, 1740–1770*, London: Phoenix Press, 2000, p. 172 and Matthew Sweet, *Inventing the Victorians*, London: Faber and Faber, 2001, pp. 23–28.

27. A detailed analysis appears in Amédée Dechambre, *Dictionaire encyclopédique des sciences médicales*, Paris: Lahure, 1881, vol. 16, pp. 149–51.

28. Virginia Berridge, *Opium and the people: Opiate use and drug control policy in nineteenth and early twentieth century England*, London: Free Association Books, 1999, pp. 8, 34–5, 292–3.

29. Ibid., pp. 11–13 and 15.

30. Ibid., pp. 22–31.

31. George Lefevre, 'On poisonous drugs: The danger of their indiscriminate use, and their remedies', *The Lancet*, 1 (29 June 1844), p. 443.

32. Cited in Marek Kohn, *Narcomania: On heroin*, London: Faber and Faber, 1987, p. 47.

33. Berridge, *Opium and the people*, pp. 30–48.

34. 'The opium habit in children', *China Medical Missionary Journal*, 14, no. 1 (Jan. 1900), p. 16.

35. Berridge, *Opium and the people*, p. 8.

36. Arnould de Liedekerke, *La Belle Époque de l'opium*, Paris: Éditions de la Différence, 2001, pp. 184–97.

37. J. M. Scott, *The white poppy: A history of opium*, London: Heinemann, 1969, p. 8. See also Antonio Escohotado, *Historia de las drogas*, Madrid: Alianza Editorial, 1989, vol. 1, pp. 253–62.

38. Escohotado, *Historia de las drogas*, vol. 1, p. 259.

39. Courtwright, *Forces of habit*, p. 96.

40. Berridge, *Opium for the people*, p. 4.

41. Richard Davenport-Hines, *The pursuit of oblivion: A social history of drugs*, London: Phoenix Press, 2002, p. 12.

42. Scott, *The white poppy*, p. 11.

43. LoN, C171(1)/M88(1)/1922/XI, *Summary of answers to the opium questionnaire, 1921*, 1 June 1922, p. 8.

44. Richard K. Newman, 'Opium as a medicine in nineteenth-century India' in Sanjoy Bhattacharya and Biswamoy Pati (eds), *Imperialism, medicine and South Asia (1800–1950)*, Hyderabad: Orient Longmans, 2004.

45. This paragraph draws on John F. Richards, 'Opium and the British Indian empire: The Royal Commission of 1895', *Modern Asian Studies*, 36, part 2 (May 2002), pp. 401–5 and 419.

46. R. M. Dane, 'Historical memorandum' in Royal Commission on Opium (ROC), vol. VII, *Final report of the Royal Commission on Opium*, part II, *Historical appendices; together with an index of witnesses and subjects, and a glossary of Indian terms used in the evidence and appendices. Presented to both houses of Parliament by command of Her Majesty*, London: Eyre and Spottiswoode, 1895, pp. 31–2.

47. For a general introduction to the Arab and early European periods of commercial influence, see Wang Gungwu, 'The Nanhai trade: A study of the early history of Chinese trade in the South China Sea', *Journal of the Malayan Branch of the Royal Asiatic Society*, 31, part 2 (June 1958), pp. 74–112; K. N. Chaudhuri, *The trading world of Asia and the English East India Company, 1660–1760*, Cambridge University Press, 1978; Carl A. Trocki, *Opium, empire and the global political economy: A study of the Asian opium trade, 1750–1950*, London: Routledge, 1999; John F. Richards, 'Indian empire and peasant production of opium in the nineteenth century', *Modern Asian Studies*, 15 (1981), pp. 59–82; as well as Roderich Ptak (ed.), *China and the Asian seas: Trade, travel, and visions of the other (1400–1750)*, Aldershot: Ashgate Publishing, 1998, in particular pp. 29–59 and pp. 65–88.

48. For the eighteenth century, see Weng Eang Cheong, *The Hong merchants of Canton: Chinese merchants in Sino-Western trade*, Richmond: Curzon Press, 1997, pp. 280–1.

49. For the wider background of the Dutch engagement in the Pacific, see W. P. Groeneveldt, 'De eerste bemoeiingen om den handel in China en de vestiging in de Pescadores (1601–1624)', *De Nederlanders in China*, The Hague: Martinus Nijhoff, 1898. On the Dutch East India Company, see John E. Wills, *Pepper, guns and parleys: The Dutch East India Company and China, 1622–1681*, Cambridge, MA: Harvard University Press, 1974, pp. 17–25; see also Dane, 'Historical memorandum', pp. 34–5.

50. Chang T'ien-tse, *Sino-Portuguese trade from 1514 to 1644: A synthesis of Portuguese and Chinese sources*, Leiden: E. J. Brill, 1934, pp. 62–3.

51. James B. Lyall, 'Note on the history of opium in India and of the trade in it with China' in Royal Commission on Opium, vol. VII, *Final report of the Royal Commission on Opium*, part II, *Historical appendices; together with an index of witnesses and subjects, and a glossary of Indian terms used in the evidence and appendices. Presented to both houses of Parliament by command of Her Majesty*, London: Eyre and Spottiswoode, 1895, pp. 7–9.

52. For the meandering course of negotiations between Indian princes, British tax and excise officials and diplomats see Richards, 'Opium and the British Indian empire', pp. 375–8; see also Richard Connors, 'Opium and imperial expansion: The East India Company in eighteenth century Asia' in Stephen Taylor, Richard Connors and Clyve Jones (eds), *Hanoverian Britain and empire: Essays in memory of Philip Lawson*, Suffolk: Boydell Press, 1998, pp. 248–66.

53. Trocki, *Opium, empire and the global political economy*, pp. 37–52 and 62–4.

54. Dane, 'Historical memorandum', p. 51.

55. The quantity and price of Bengal opium can be seen to be representative of a general trend in India. See the statistical tables compiled by R. M. Dane for the period 1787–1841 in his 'Historical memorandum', pp. 61–2.

Chapter 3   Opium before the 'Opium War' (*c.* 1600–1840)

1. Alexander von Gernet, 'Nicotian dreams: The prehistory and early history of tobacco in eastern North America' in Jordan Goodman, Paul E. Lovejoy, Andrew Sherratt (eds), *Consuming habits: Drugs in history and anthropology*, London: Routledge, 1995, pp. 67–74.

2. Jacob M. Price, 'Tobacco use and tobacco taxation: A battle of interests in early modern Europe' in Goodman, Lovejoy and Sherratt, *Consuming habits*, pp. 165–81; see also Jordan Goodman, *Tobacco in history: The cultures of dependence*, London: Routledge, 1993.

3. Thurstan Shaw, 'Early smoking pipes: Africa, Europe, and America', *Journal of the Royal Anthropological Institute of Great Britain and Ireland*, 90 (1960), pp. 279–87, as well as John Edward Philips, 'African smoking and pipes', *Journal of African History*, no. 24 (1983), pp. 303–19.

4. Anthony Reid, 'From betel-chewing to tobacco smoking in Indonesia', *Journal of Asian Studies*, 44, no. 3 (May 1985), p. 536.

5. Barney T. Suzuki, *The first English pipe smoker in Japan. Le premier fumeur de pipe anglais au Japon: William Adams, the pilot and the English trade house in Hirato (1600–1621)*, Paris: Académie Internationale de la Pipe, 1997, pp. 5–11; see also Aoki Yoshio, '"Drinking" tobacco: The customs and aesthetics of smoking in early modern Japan', paper presented at the *Beverages in early modern Japan and their international context, 1660s–1920s: A conference organised by the Sainsbury Institute for the Study of Japanese Arts and Cultures*, London: School of Oriental and African Studies, 9–11 March 2001, pp. 1–2.

6. Aixinjueluo Yingsheng and Yu Runqi, *Jingcheng jiusu* (Old customs of Beijing), Beijing: Yanshan chubanshe, 1998, p. 148.

7. Wang Shizhen, *Xiangzu biji* (Travel notes) in *Siku quanshu* (Complete library of the four treasuries), Shanghai: Shanghai guji chubanshe, 1987, 870:469.

8. Yuan Tingdong, *Zhongguo xiyan shihua* (A history of smoking in China), Beijing: Shangwu yinshuguan, 1995, pp. 83–96.

9. Archaeological research seems to suggest an earlier date; see Zheng Chaoxiong, 'Cong Guangxi Hepu Mingdai yaozhi nei faxian ci yandou tanji yancao chuanru woguo de shijian wenti' (The question of the timing of the spread of tobacco in China discussed on the basis of the discovery of clay pipes in Hepu, Guangxi province), *Nongye kaogu*, no. 2 (1986), pp. 383–7 and 391. The account book of the Jesuit missionary François de Rougemont contains the oldest references to tobacco discovered in Western sources to date, predating the observations of Louis Lecomte, *Nouveaux mémoires sur l'état présent de la Chine*, Paris: Jean Anisson, 1696; see Golvers, *François de Rougemont*, pp. 511–12.

10. Victor G. Kiernan, *Tobacco: A history*, London: Hutchinson, 1991, pp. 69–70.

11. L. C. Goodrich, 'Early prohibitions of tobacco in China and Manchuria', *Journal of the American Oriental Society*, no. 58 (1938), p. 652.

12. He Lingxiu, 'Qingchu jingshi xiyanfeng deng jige wenti' (Some questions regarding the craze for smoking in the capital during the early Qing), *Qingshi luncong* (Essays on Qing history), Beijing: Hebei jiaoyu chubanshe, 1999, p. 382.

13. G. Cordier, *La province du Yunnan*, Hanoi: Imprimerie Mac-Dinh-Tu, 1928, pp. 184–5.

14. Yao Lü, *Lushu* (A journal of travels and customs), 1628–44 edition, *juan* 10, no page number.

15. Wang, *Xiangzu biji*, 870:410.

16. Ye Mengzhu, *Yueshi bian* (Collected notes), Shanghai: Shanghai guji chubanshe, 1981, p. 167.

17. Li Zhiyong (ed.), *Zhang Jingyue yixue quanshu* (The medical treatises of Zhang Jingyue), Beijing: Zhongguo zhongyixue chubanshe, 1997, p. 1546.

18. Fang Yizhi, *Wuli xiaoshi* (Knowledge regarding nature), Taipei: Shangwu yinshuguan, 1974, p. 237. For contemporary medical opinions, see Goodrich, 'Early prohibitions of tobacco', pp. 648–9 and 653.

19. Goodrich, 'Early prohibitions of tobacco', p. 651.

20. Wang Ang, *Bencao beiyao* (Essential materia medica), orig. 1694, Taipei: Shangwu yinshuguan, 1955, p. 122.

21. Zheng Tianyi and Xu Bin, *Yan wenhua* (Smoking culture), Beijing: Zhongguo shehui kexue chubanshe, 1992, p. 62.

22. Ibid., p. 2.

23. Tian Wen, for instance, observed in the *Book of Guizhou:* 'When people encounter these conditions [of malaria] they hurriedly lie face-down on the ground, or chew betel nut, or else hold a piece of local sugar cane in their mouths, which gives them some chance of escaping.' See Mark Elvin, *The retreat of the elephants: An environmental history of China*, New Haven: Yale University Press, 2004.

24. Section 25 of the *Seng shilüe*, translated in Peter N. Gregory and Daniel A. Getz (eds), *Buddhism in the Sung*, Honolulu: University of Hawaii Press, 1999, pp. 43–5. See also James Legge, *Li Chi: Book of rites*, New York University Books, 1967, vol. 1, p. 443. For further discussion see Albert Welter, 'A Buddhist response to the Confucian revival: Tsan-ning and the debate over *wen* in the early Sung' in Gregory and Getz, *Buddhism in the Sung*, pp. 43–5.

25. He Yumin and Zhang Ye, *Zouchu wushu conglin de Zhongyi* (Magic and Chinese medicine), Shanghai: Wenhui chubanshe, 1994, pp. 97–99 and 102.

26. Moxa is a downy substance from the dried leaves of medicinal plants which is burnt on the skin as a counterirritant. See Li Shizhen, *Bencao gangmu* (Materia medica), Beijing: Renmin weisheng chubanshe, 1957, vol. 2, p. 848–50; for further reading, see He and Zhang, *Zouchu wushu conglin*, pp. 97–9 and 102; Yuan, *Zhongguo xiyan shihua*, p. 25.

27. J. L. Cranmer-Byng, *An embassy to China: Being the journal kept by Lord Macartney during his embassy to the emperor Ch'ien-lung 1793–1794*, London: Longmans, 1962, p. 225.

28. Archibald John Little, *Through the Yang-tse gorges or Trade and travel in western China*, London: Sampson Low, 1898, p. 195.

29. Xu, *Zhongguo yinshi shi*, vol. 3, pp. 376–83, 399–401.

30. See James Benn, 'Temperance, tracts and teetotallers during the T'ang: Bud-
    dhism, alcohol and tea in medieval China', MA dissertation, School of Oriental
    and African Studies, University of London, 1994, pp. 42–3. A comparison with
    Edo Japan can be found in Ogawa Kooraku, 'Sencha and Japanese literati', pa-
    per presented at the *Beverages in early modern Japan and their international context,
    1660s–1920s: A conference organised by the Sainsbury Institute for the Study of Japa-
    nese arts and cultures*, School of Oriental and African Studies, 9–11 March 2001,
    pp. 3–9.
31. See the rhetorical confrontation between 'Mr Wine' and 'Mr Tea' in the *Chajiu
    lun* (A dialogue between tea and alcohol) in Benn, 'Temperance, tracts and tee-
    totallers', pp. 47–50; see also Lu Yu, *Chajing* (The tea canon), translated by
    Francis Ross Carpenter, Boston: Little, Brown, 1974.
32. Xu, *Zhongguo yinshi shi*, vol. 3, pp. 399–401.
33. The work of Wang Fu and Du Fu, celebrated poets of the Tang, vividly illus-
    trates the important place of alcohol in the life of the scholarly elite; on early
    poetry devoted to wine and inebriation, see Poo Mu-Chou, 'The use and
    abuse of wine in ancient China', *Journal of the Economic and Social History of the
    Orient*, 42, part 2 (May 1999), pp. 126–8.
34. See Frédéric Obringer, *L'aconit et l'orpiment. Drogues et poisons en Chine ancienne
    et médiévale*, Paris: Fayard, 1997, pp. 145–52. For a recent study on the Five
    Stone Powder, see also Li Ling, *Zhongguo fangshu xukao* (Supplementary studies
    on the esoteric arts in China), Beijing: Dongfang chubanshe, 2000, pp. 341–9
    and Rudolph Wagner, 'Lebensstil und Drogen im chinesischen Mittelalter',
    T'oung Pao, 59, 1973, pp. 79–178.
35. Obringer, *L'aconit et l'orpiment*, p. 146.
36. Anthony R. Butler, 'A treatment for cardiovascular dysfunction in a Dunhuang
    medical manuscript', unpublished paper, pp. 2 and 7.
37. Obringer, *L'aconit et l'orpiment*, pp. 182–3.
38. Medical powders flourished between the seventh and twelfth centuries, though
    many recipes, e.g. by Huangfu Mi and He Yan (Imperial Secretary of Cao Wei,
    240–49), stretched back into early imperial times; see Obringer, *L'aconit et
    l'orpiment*, pp. 153–61.
39. Wu Zhihe, 'Mingdai sengren, wenren dui cha tuiguang zhi gongxian' (The
    contribution of monks and scholars to the spread of tea during the Ming),
    Mingshi yanjiu zhuankan, no. 3 (Sept. 1980), pp. 1–74.
40. Xu, *Zhongguo yinshi shi*, vol. 4, pp. 713–4.
41. Lu, *Chajing*, p. 167, note 138.
42. K. H. Li, 'Public health in Soochow', *Zhonghua yixue zazhi*, 9, no. 2 (June
    1923), p. 124.
43. 'Xi'an tongxun' (Correspondance from Xi'an), *Judu yuekan*, no. 90 (Aug. 1935),
    p. 17.
44. Wu, 'Mingdai sengren', pp. 15–16, 56–9.
45. Xu, *Zhongguo yinshi shi*, vol. 5, pp. 135–7; see also Wu Zhihe, *Ming Qing shidai
    yincha shenghuo* (Tea culture during the Ming and Qing), Taipei: Boyuan
    chuban youxian gongsi, 1990.
46. Yuan, *Zhongguo xiyan shihua*, p. 48.

47. Qian Gechuan, 'Yanjiu yu pengyou' (Alcohol, tobacco and friends) in Lao Pin, *Mingjia bixia de yanjiuchadian* (Famous people talking about tobacco, alcohol, tea and dim sum), Beijing: Zhongguo guoji guangbo chubanshe, 1994, p. 341.

48. Goodrich, 'Early prohibitions of tobacco', p. 654.

49. Engelbert D. Kaempfer, *Amoenitatum exoticarum: politico-physico-medicarum—quibus continentur variae relationes, observationes, et descriptiones. Rerum persicarum et ulterioris asiae multa attentione in peregrinationibus per universum orientem, collectae ab auctore Engelberto Kaempfero*, Lemgo (Lippe): Heinrich Wilhelm Meyer, 1712, vol. 5, fasc. 5, p. 650.

50. Louis Dermigny, *La Chine et l'Occident. Le commerce à Canton au XVIIIe siècle, 1719–1833*, Paris: S.E.V.P.E.N., 1964, vol. 3, p. 1255 and D. E. Owen, *British opium policy in China and India*, New Haven: Yale University Press, 1934, pp. 15–16.

51. Dane, 'Historical memorandum', p. 33. For a study on late imperial trade connections, see James R. Rush, *Opium to Java: Revenue and Chinese enterprise in colonial Indonesia, 1860–1910*, Ithaca: Cornell University Press, 1990, pp. 84–6.

52. Huang Shujing, *Taihai shichai lu* (Journal of a mission to Taiwan), orig. 1736, Shanghai: Shangwu yinshuguan, 1935, p. 40; Zhu Shijie, *Xiao liuqiu manzhi* (Account of a voyage to Taiwan), orig. 1765, Taipei: Datong shuju, 1960, p. 54.

53. Joseph Edkins, 'Historical note on opium and the poppy in China' in Royal Commission on Opium, *First Report of the Royal Commission on Opium with minutes of evidence and appendices*, London: Eyre and Spottiswoode, 1894, vol. 1, p. 153 pp. 153–6.

54. Lan Dingyuan, *Luzhou chuji* (First impressions of Taiwan), orig. 1722, in *Siku quanshu* (Complete library of the four treasuries), Shanghai: Shanghai guji chubanshe, 1987, 1327:590.

55. Yu Zhengxie, 'Yapianyan shixu' (An essay on opium), *Guisi leigao* (Collection of notes), 1884 ed., Shanghai: Shangwu yinshuguan, 1957, p. 521, also reprinted in Zhongguo shixue xuehui (ed.), *Yapian zhanzheng* (Historical documents on the Opium War), 1954, Shanghai: Shenzhou guoguangshe, pp. 309–10.

56. 'Guangdong jieshi zongbing Su Mingliang zouchen yanjin fanmai yapian yizheng mingsheng zhe' (Memorial by the governor of Guangdong Su Mingliang concerning the prohibition of opium), *Gongzhongdang* (Imperial Archives), *Zhupi zouzhe*, 1728, *juan* 36, p. 136, reprinted in Ma Mozhen (ed.), *Zhongguo jindu shi ziliao* (Archival materials on the history of drug prohibition in China), Tianjin: Tianjin renmin chubanshe, 1998, p. 4.

57. Feng Erkang, Xu Shengheng and Yan Aimin, *Yongzheng huangdi quanzhuan* (Complete biography of the Yongzheng emperor), Beijing: Xueyuan chubanshe, 1994, p. 293.

58. See Susan Naquin, *Shantung rebellion: The Wang Lun uprising of 1774*, New Haven: Yale University Press, 1981, pp. 198–9.

59. Dermigny, *Le commerce à Canton*, p. 1255, citing the *Encyclopädie van Nederlandsch Indië*, vol. 3, pp. 102–111; on Dutch trade in opium, see also Ewald Vanvugt, *Wettig opium: 350 jaar Nederlandse opiumhandel in de Indische archipel*, Haarlem: In de Knipscheer, 1985.

60. Ch'ü T'ung-tsu, *Local government in China under the Ch'ing*, Stanford University Press, 1969, pp. 28–29.

61. Matthew H. Sommer, *Sex, law, and society in late imperial China*, Stanford University Press, 2000.

62. Edicts were issued in England in 1604, Japan in 1607 and 1616, by the Sublime Porte in 1611 and the Persian Shah around the same time, by the Mughals in 1617, the kings of Sweden and Denmark in 1632, the Tsar in 1634, the Pope in 1642 and a number of other kingdoms after 1640; see Goodrich, 'Early prohibitions of tobacco', pp. 655–6.

63. 'Fujian xunfu Liu Shiming zou Zhangzhoufu zhifu Li Zhiguo chajin yapian cuohun shixing guru renzui zhe' (Commissioner of Fujian Liu Shiming's memorial to the governor of Zhangzhou concerning opium restriction) in *Gongzhongdang*, Zhupi zouzhe, 1729, reprinted in Ma, *Zhongguo jindu shi ziliao*, p. 5.

64. H. B. Morse, *The chronicles of the East India Company: Trading to China 1635–1834*, Oxford: Clarendon Press, 1926, vol. 1, pp. 215 and 288.

65. R. Alexander, *The rise and progress of British opium smuggling and its effects upon India, China, and the commerce of Great Britain: Four letters addressed to the Right Honourable Earl of Shaftesbury*, London: Seeley, Jackson and Halliday, 1856, p. 2; also also James Bromley Eames, *The English in China: Being an account of the intercourse and relations between England and China from the year 1600 to the year 1843 and a summary of later developments*, London: Isaac Pitman, 1909, p. 233.

66. Morse, *The chronicles of the East India Company*, vol. 2, pp. 76–8.

67. Dermigny, *Le commerce à Canton*, vol. 3, p. 1266, and F. S. Turner, *British opium policy and its results to India and China*, London: Low and Marston, 1876, p. 103.

68. Zhao Xuemin, *Bencao gangmu shiyi* (A supplemented edition to the Materia Medica), orig. 1765, Shanghai: Shangwu yinshuguan, 1954, vol. 2, p. 35.

69. Yu Jiao, *Mengchang zaji* (Notes from a dreamy cabin), Beijing: Wenhua yishu chubanshe, 1988, p. 154.

70. Zhao, *Bencao gangmu shiyi*, p. 34.

71. Zhu, *Xiao liuqiu manzhi*, p. 54.

72. Xiao Yishan, *Qingdai tongshi* (A general history of the Qing), Taipei: Shangwu yinshuguan, 1962, vol. 2, pp. 907–8.

73. Wang Hongbin, *Jindu shijian* (Historical evidence about the prohibition movement), Changsha: Yuelu shushe, 1997, pp. 17–19.

74. Ernest Watson, *The principal articles of Chinese commerce*, Shanghai: Chinese Maritime Customs, 1930, pp. 475–6.

75. The main part of the Indian opium reached the islands of Southeast Asia, where it was smoked as madak; Morse, *The chronicles of the East India Company*, vol. 1, p. 215.

76. George Staunton, *An historical account of the embassy to the emperor of China undertaken by order of the king of Great Britain*, London: Stockdale, 1797, p. 278.

77. Ibid., p. 326.

78. Clarke Abel, *Narrative of a journey in the interior of China, and of a voyage to and from that country in the years 1816 and 1817*, London: Longman, 1818, pp. 214–5.

79. H. B. Morse, *International relations of the Chinese empire*, London: Longmans, 1910, vol. 1, p. 173.

80. Morse, *The chronicles of the East India Company*, vol. 2, p. 365.

81. Virginia Berridge, *Opium and the people: Opiate use and drug control policy in nine-teenth and early twentieth century England*, London: Free Association Books, 1999, p. 292.

82. Dermigny, *Le commerce à Canton*, vol. 3, pp. 1267–68.

83. Ibid., pp. 1269–74.

84. Dian H. Murray, *Pirates of the South China Coast, 1790–1810*, Stanford University Press, 1987, p. 87.

85. Eames, *The English in China*, pp. 233–6.

86. Martin Booth, *Opium: A history*, London: Pocket Books, 1997, pp. 112–5.

87. Weng Eang Cheong, *The Hong merchants of Canton: Chinese merchants in Sino-Western trade*, Richmond: Curzon, 1997, p. 15.

88. Robert Alexander, *The rise and progress of British opium smuggling, and its effects upon India, China, and the commerce of Great Britain*, London: Seeley and Jackson, 1856, pp. 22–3 and 44.

89. Richard Davenport-Hines, *The pursuit of oblivion: A social history of drugs*, London: Phoenix Press, 2002, pp. 49–50.

90. Watson, *The principal articles of Chinese commerce*, pp. 520–2; see also S. A. M. Adshead, 'Opium in Szechwan, 1881–1911', *Journal of Southeast Asian History*, 7, no. 2 (Sept. 1961), p. 96.

91. Jack Gray, *Rebellions and revolutions: China from the 1800s to the 1980s*, Oxford University Press, 1990, p. 30.

92. David Bello, 'Opium in Xinjiang and beyond' in Timothy Brook and Bob T. Wakabayashi (eds), *Opium regimes: China, Britain, and Japan, 1839–1952*, Berkeley: University of California Press, 2000, pp. 127–151.

93. Joseph Fletcher, 'The heyday of the Ch'ing order in Mongolia, Sinkiang and Tibet' in D. Twitchett and J. K. Fairbank (eds), *The Cambridge history of China*, Cambridge University Press, 1978, vol. 10, part 1, pp. 375–85.

94. Dermigny, *Le commerce à Canton*, vol. 3, pp. 1341–3.

95. George W. Cooke, *China: Being 'The Times' special correspondence from China in the years 1857–58*, orig. 1858, Wilmington, Delaware: Scholarly Resources, 1972, p. 184.

96. Richard von Glahn, *Fountain of fortune: Money and monetary policy in China, 1000–1700*, Berkeley: University of California Press, 1996, pp. 6, 254–6.

97. James Polachek, *The inner Opium War*, Cambridge, MA: Harvard University Press, 1991, p. 103. Some of the edicts and petitions are reprinted in Shanghai shi dang'anguan (ed.), *Qingmo minchu de jinyan yundong he wanguo jinyanhui* (The opium prohibition movement during the late Qing and early Republic and the anti-opium meetings of the League of Nations), Shanghai: Shanghai kexue jishu wenxian chubanshe, 1996, pp. 2–15.

98. Polachek, *The inner opium war*, pp. 132–5, 282–3.

99. Accounts of the war appear in Peter Ward Fay, *The Opium War, 1840–1842: Barbarians in the Celestial Empire in the early part of the nineteenth century and the war by which they forced her gates ajar*, New York: Norton, 1976; Michael Greenberg, *British trade and the opening of China 1800–42*, Cambridge University Press, 1951; Brian Inglis, *The Opium War*, London: Hodder and Stoughton, 1976; Tan Chung, *China and the brave new world: A study of the origins of the Opium War*

(1840–42), Durham, NC: Carolina Academic Press, 1978; Frederic E. Wakeman, *Strangers at the gate: Social disorder in south China, 1839–1861*, Berkeley: University of California Press, 1997.

100. Morse, *The international relations of the Chinese empire*, vol. 1, p. 254, note 177.

Chapter 4   Opium for the People: Status, Space and Consumption (*c.* 1840–1940)

1. Anon., *China as it was, and as it is: With a glance at the tea and opium trades*, London: Cradock, 1842, p. 57.

2. Richard K. Newman, 'Opium smoking in late imperial China: A reconsideration', *Modern Asian Studies*, 29, no. 4 (Oct. 1995), pp. 791–3 and Jonathan D. Spence, 'Opium smoking in Ch'ing China' in Frederic Wakeman and Carolyn Grant (eds), *Conflict and control in late imperial China*, Berkeley: University of California Press, 1975, p. 168.

3. Alexander Hosie, *Three years in western China: A narrative of three journeys in Ssuch'uan, Kuei-chow, and Yün-nan*, London: George Philip, 1890, p. 17.

4. S. A. M. Adshead, 'Opium in Szechwan, 1881–1911', *Journal of Southeast Asian History*, 7, no. 2 (Sept. 1961), p. 97.

5. Isabella L. Bird, *The Yangtse Valley and beyond: An account of journeys in China, chiefly in the province of Sze Chuan and among the Man-Tze of the Somo territory*, London: John Murray, 1899, p. 506.

6. Hosie, *Three years in western China*, p. 84.

7. See the calculations by Mr Finlay, Secretary to the Government of India, 11 April 1882, Royal Commission on Opium, *Royal Commission on Opium*, London: Eyre and Spottiswoode, 1894–5, hereafter ROC, vol. 2, p. 384. Finlay's estimates are based on the conditions in Sichuan, where he spent four months examining the province's opium industry.

8. FO, 228/665, E. L. Oxenham, 'Report on opium', 13 July 1880, f. 179.

9. Bird, *The Yangtse Valley and beyond*, p. 506.

10. Archibald John Little, *Through the Yang-tse gorges, or Trade and travel in western China*, London: Sampson Low, 1898, p. 195.

11. Three according to Gervais Courtellemont, *Voyage au Yunnan*, Paris: Plon, 1904, p. 188, eight after Louis Pichon, *Un voyage au Yunnan*, Paris: Plon, 1893, p. 91.

12. Hosie, *Three years in western China*, p. 17.

13. For a detailed description, see ibid., pp. 287–90.

14. Ferdinand von Richthofen, *Tagebücher aus China*, Berlin: Reimer, 1907, vol. 1, pp. 566–7.

15. Samuel Merwin, *Drugging a nation: The story of China and the opium curse*, New York: Fleming Revell, 1908, pp. 90–1.

16. These advantages also made opium appealing to the hill tribes in Southeast Asia; Joseph Westermeyer, *Poppies, pipes and people: Opium and its use in Laos*, Berkeley: University of California, 1982, p. 44.

17. For examples from Yunnan, see Dong Yiming, 'Étude sur le problème de l'opium dans la région du sud-ouest de la Chine (pendant les années 1920 et 1930)',

doctoral dissertation, Paris: École des Hautes Études en Sciences Sociales, 1997, p. 48; see also Hosie, *Three years in western China*, pp. 168–9 (Yunnan) and 208 (Sichuan).

18. Courtellemont, *Voyage au Yunnan*, pp. 187–8.

19. See evidence by Secretary Finlay, 11 April 1882, RCO, vol. 2, pp. 387–8. See also the communication by S. E. J. Clarke, Bengal Chamber of Commerce, RCO, vol. 2, p. 444.

20. Edward R. Slack, *Opium, state, and society: China's narco-economy and the Guomindang, 1924–1937*, Honolulu: University of Hawai'i Press, 2000, p. 3.

21. Newman, 'Opium smoking in late imperial China', pp. 770–3.

22. Ibid., pp. 770–1.

23. Ernest Watson, *The principal articles of Chinese commerce*, Shanghai: Chinese Maritime Customs, 1930, pp. 475–6.

24. FO, 228/780, 'Commercial report on the trade of China for the year 1884', f. 365, 26 May 1885.

25. Newman, 'Opium smoking in late imperial China', pp. 772–3.

26. See the letter by T. W. Duff, merchant in China for thirty years, read out before the House of Lords, Westminster, 16 Sept. 1893, RCO, vol. 1, p. 112.

27. YDL, International Missionary Council Archive, RG 46/6, 'Report of the National Anti-Opium Association of China to the International Missionary Council', 1 Jan. 1931, p. 3.

28. William Lockhart, *The medical missionary in China: A narrative of twenty years' experience*, London: Hurst and Blackett, 1861, p. 385, referring to the listings of imports in the *China Mail* (edition unspecified).

29. 'The opium hulks', *North China Herald*, 29 May 1901, p. 1025.

30. Newman, 'Opium smoking in late imperial China', p. 770.

31. See, for instance, the figure of 'two thirds of one per cent' computed by the Royal Customs official W. W. Myers, based in Taiwan but speaking for the whole of the empire; RCO, vol. 5, p. 324. China Inland missionary Marcus Wood put his figure at 60 per cent. See his evidence before the House of Lords, Westminster, 13 Sept. 1893, RCO, vol. 1, p. 50.

32. On the tendentious portrayal of information concerning opium, see Newman, 'Opium smoking in late imperial China', p. 766.

33. The problem of statistical reliability is discussed in Dong Yiming, 'Étude sur le problème de l'opium', pp. 7–11.

34. Ibid., pp. 12–14.

35. Newman, 'Opium smoking in late imperial China', pp. 776–8.

36. The questionnaire was sent to foreign traders in nineteen treaty ports and foreign concessions along the coast and up the Yangtse river. See Robert Hart, *China Imperial Maritime Customs: II. Special Series: No. 4 Opium*, Shanghai: State Department of the Inspectorate General, 1881, pp. 1–3.

37. Newman, 'Opium smoking in late imperial China', pp. 785–6.

38. Ibid., pp. 786–8.

39. Hart, *China Imperial Maritime Customs*, p. 2.

40. Ibid., question 12: 'The habit of smoking is not easily given up after smoking xx [years or months]'.

41. H. Libermann, *Les fumeurs d'opium en Chine. Étude médicale*, Paris: Victor Rozier, 1862, pp. 4 and 9.

42. Eugen Wolf, *Meine Wanderungen (I). Im Innern Chinas*, Stuttgart: Deutsche Verlags-Anstalt, 1901, pp. 124–5.

43. Robert Coltman, *The Chinese: Their present and future*, London: Davis, 1891, pp. 125–7.

44. Ibid, p. 130.

45. FO, 228/700, 'Annex to enclosure in Mr. Spence's No. 4 of 20 April 1882: Native opium', f. 186 (V), 1882.

46. LoN, C635/M254/1930/XI, Commission of Enquiry into the Control of Opium-Smoking in the Far East, *Report to the Council*, Nov. 1930, vol. 1, p. 25.

47. 'Donghe zongdu Wen Chong zouqing jiang cengjing xiyapian zhi qianzong He Yongqing chigepian' (The governor general of Donghe requests the dismissal of official He Yongqing for using opium), *Junjichulu fuzouzhe*, 23 Aug. 1840, reprinted in Ma Mozhen (ed.), *Zhongguo jindu shi ziliao* (Archival materials on the history of drug prohibition in China), Tianjin: Tianjin renmin chubanshe, 1998, p. 209.

48. RCO, vol. 5, p. 244.

49. Quoted in Newman, 'Opium smoking in late imperial China', p. 779.

50. Ding Shaoyi, *Dongying shilüe* (A brief account of the eastern seas), orig. 1873, Taipei: Zhonghua shuju, 1957, p. 35.

51. Cited in Slack, *Opium, society, and state*, p. 41.

52. Richard Hughes, *Foreign devil: Thirty years of reporting from the Far East*, London: Deutsch, 1972, p. 254.

53. Merwin, *Drugging a nation*, p. 16.

54. Wang Penggao, 'Yapian texie' (Special feature on opium), *Judu yuekan*, no. 97 (March 1936), p. 14.

55. RCO, vol. 5, p. 305.

56. Newman, 'Opium smoking in late imperial China', p. 781.

57. 'Sichuan zongdu Bao Xing zou weizunzhi nahuo bing shenni yanfan zhe' (Memorial by Bao Xing, Governor General of Sichuan regarding the arrest and interrogation of opium offenders), 19 Nov. 1841, reprinted in Ma, *Zhongguo jindushi ziliao*, pp. 235–7.

58. Zhou Zhaoxi, private correspondence, 9 Oct. 2001.

59. Shushan, 'Yapian yu zuojia' (Opium and writers), *Lunyu banyuekan*, no. 30 (Dec. 1933), pp. 278–9.

60. Peter Lee, *The big smoke: The Chinese art and craft of opium*, Bangkok: Lamplight Books, 1999, p. 121.

61. Jean Cocteau, *Opium: Diary of a cure*, London: Icon, 1957, p. 20.

62. Virgil K. Y. Ho, 'The city of contrasts: Perceptions and realities in Canton in the 1920s and 1930s', doctoral dissertation, Oxford University, 1995, p. 112.

63. Lockhart, *The medical missionary in China*, pp. 385–7.

64. Ibid., p. 387.

65. P. L. McAll, 'The opium habit', *China Medical Missionary Journal*, 17, no. 1 (Jan. 1903), pp. 3–4.

66. Westermeyer, *Poppies, pipes and people*, p. 58.

67. O. Anselmino, 'ABC of narcotic drugs', *Opium and other dangerous drugs*, Geneva: League of Nations Publication, 9, 1931, pp. 20–1.

68. McAll, 'The opium habit', pp. 3–4.

69. Xiaoliu, 'Xianzi shou' (Opium sous-chefs), *Judu yuekan*, no. 85 (Feb. 1935), p. 24.

70. Léon Rousset, *À travers la Chine*, Paris: Hachette, 1886, p. 289.

71. Lee, *The big smoke*, p. 46–7.

72. J. B. Clair, 'Causerie sur l'opium', *Annales de la Société des Missions Étrangères et de l'oeuvre des partants*, no. 67 (Jan. 1909), p. 18.

73. Lee, *The big smoke*, pp. 68–75; see also Jerry Wylie and Richard E. Fike, 'Chinese opium smoking techniques and paraphernalia' in Priscilla Wegars (ed.), *Hidden heritage: Historical archaeology of the overseas Chinese*, Amityville, NY: Baywood, 1993, p. 259–67.

74. Emily Hahn, 'The big smoke', *Times and places*, New York: Thomas Cromwell, 1970, p. 3.

75. Rousset, *À travers la Chine*, p. 288.

76. See Patrick J. Maveety, *Opium pipes, prints and paraphernalia*, Stanford: Stanford University Museum of Art, 1979.

77. See the opinion of Claude Farrère, *Fumée d'opium*, Paris: Mille et Une Nuits, 2002, pp. 16–23.

78. Lee, *The big smoke*, p. 138.

79. John Burnett, *Liquid pleasures: A social history of drinks in modern Britain*, London: Routledge, 1999, p. 50.

80. Bing Miao, 'Yanxia zhuiyu' (Embellished words for smoking clouds), *Jinyan zhuankan* (Special publication on opium prohibition), Shanghai: Shanghai jinyan weiyuanhui, 1935, p. 28.

81. Yu Jiao, *Mengchang zaji* (Notes from a dreamy cabin), Beijing: Wenhua yishu chubanshe, 1988, p. 372.

82. Zhang Changjia, 'Yanhua' (On opium) in A Ying (ed.), *Yapian zhanzheng wenxue ji* (Collection of literary writings on the Opium War), Beijing: Guji chubanshe, 1957, vol. 2, pp. 755–78.

83. Lu Geting, 'Chunxilu shang de "xiaojinku"' (Money spending holes on Chunxi Street) in Feng Zhicheng, *Lao Chengdu* (Old Chengdu), Chengdu: Sichuan wenyi chubanshe, 1999, pp. 133–5.

84. 'Hangzhou tongxun: Qingmo Hangzhou' (Correspondence from Hangzhou: Hangzhou during the late Qing), *Judu yuekan*, no. 98 (April 1936), p. 6. See also Craig Clunas, *Superfluous things: Material culture and social status in early modern China*, Cambridge: Polity Press, 1991, pp. 114–15 and 147–52.

85. Luoluo jushi (Zhong Zufen), 'Zhao yinju' (The charm of living in seclusion) in A Ying, *Yapian zhanzheng wenxue ji*, vol. 2, pp. 645–55.

86. Rousset, *À travers la Chine*, pp. 288–9.

87. Coltman, *The Chinese*, p. 127.

88. See Sun Jiazhen, *Xiaoxiang haishang fanhuameng* (The vanity fair of Shanghai with portraits), Shanghai: Shangwu yinshuguan, 1915 and Sun Jiazhen, *Xu Haishang fanhuameng* (Sequel to the vanity fair of Shanghai), Shanghai: Jinbu

shuju, 1916; also Chen Songfeng, *Yanshi wenjianlu* (Stories on tobacco), Beijing: Zhongguo shangye chubanshe, 1989, p. 152.

89. Yu Zhao, *Beijing jiushi* (Old Beijing), Beijing: Xueyuan chubanshe, 2000, p. 393.

90. Qin Heping, *Yunnan yapian wenti yu jinyan yundong: 1840–1940* (The problem of opium in Yunnan and the anti-opium movement), Chengdu: Sichuan minzu chubanshe, 1998, pp. 15–16.

91. Lockhart, *The medical missionary in China*, pp. 60–1.

92. YDL, International Missionary Council Archive, RG 46/6, 'Report of the National Anti-Opium Association of China to the International Missionary Council', 1 Jan. 1931, p. 3.

93. De Mei, 'Shanghai xiacheng shehui jianying yiye' (A reflection on the life of the lower classes in Shanghai), *Judu yuekan*, no. 101 (July 1936), pp. 36–8; see also Qin, *Yunnan yapian wenti*, p. 100.

94. Burnett, *Liquid pleasures*, p. 56.

95. FO, 228/698, Alexander Hosie, 'Forwarding a memorandum on native opium', 11 Oct. 1882, ff. 259–60.

96. Lee, *The big smoke*, p. 38. See also LoN, C635/M254/1930/XI, Commission of Enquiry into the Control of Opium-Smoking in the Far East, *Report to the Council*, Nov. 1930, pp. 34–5.

97. Anselmino, 'ABC of narcotic drugs', pp. 20–1.

98. Newman, 'Opium smoking in late imperial China', p. 773.

99. As farmers discovered in Shanxi when they stumbled upon a hoard of earthen opium paste jars in October 2001; see Jiao Yang, 'Yaodong "chutu" yapiangao' (Opium paste unearthed from cave), *Chengdu shangbao*, 12 Dec. 2001, special supplement, p. B9.

100. Lee, *The big smoke*, pp. 41 and 53.

101. H. D. Daly, *Report on the political administration of the territories within the Central India Agency for the year 1873–74* [Selections from the Records of the Government of India, CXIV], Calcutta: Foreign Department Press, 1874, pp. 6–7.

102. Justus Doolittle, *Social life of the Chinese*, New York: Harper, 1865, vol. 2, p. 352.

103. W. Somerset Maugham, *On a Chinese screen*, London: William Heinemann, 1922, pp. 60–1.

104. LoN, C635/M254/1930/XI, Commission of Enquiry into the Control of Opium-Smoking in the Far East, *Report to the Council*, Nov. 1930, p. 33.

105. John Blofeld, *City of lingering splendour: A frank account of old Peking's exotic pleasures*, London: Hutchinson, 1961, pp. 151–2.

106. C. G. Murdock, *Domesticating drink: Women, men, and alcohol in America, 1870–1940*, Baltimore: Johns Hopkins University Press, 1998, pp. 12–14. A debate on the desirability of women to demand equal access to opium houses can be gleaned from the (all-male) First Opium Conference, Geneva, LoN, C684/M244/1924/XI, *Minutes and Annexes*, 3 Nov. 1924–11 Feb. 1925, pp. 68–71.

107. Lee, *The big smoke*, pp. 80–81 and 139.

108. FO, 233/14, Alexander Hosie, 'Report of a journey from Wenchow to Hangchow', 11 Nov. 1883.

109. 'Weidu yanshi pianxia' (A sketch of the opium market in Changchun), *Judu yuekan*, no. 96 (Feb. 1936), pp. 2–4.

110. 'Hangzhou tongxun', p. 6.

111. Hughes, *Foreign devil*, pp. 249–53.

112. Merwin, *Drugging a nation*, p. 91.

113. Archibald Little, *Intimate China: The Chinese as I have seen them*, London: Hutchinson, 1899, p. 179.

114. 'Hangzhou tongxun', p. 9.

115. Martin Booth, *Opium: A history*, London: Pocket Books, 1997, pp. 60–1.

116. Luoluo jushi, 'Zhao yinju', p. 655.

117. C. Trocki, 'Drugs, taxes and Chinese capitalism' in Timothy Brook and Bob Tadashi Wakabayashi (eds), *Opium regimes: China, Britain, and Japan, 1839–1952*, Berkeley: University of California Press, 2000, p. 87.

118. RCO, vol. 1, p. 109.

119. Robert Fortune, *Three years' wandering in the northern provinces of China, including a visit to the tea, silk, and cotton countries: With an account of the agriculture and horticulture of the Chinese, new plants, etc.*, London: John Murray, 1847, p. 240.

120. Hosie, *Three years in western China*, pp. 40 and 58.

121. *Correspondence Respecting the Opium Question in China*, London: His Majesty's Stationary Office, 1908, p. 37.

122. A general theme in S. H. Alatas, *The myth of the lazy native: A study of the image of the Malays, Filipinos and Javanese from the 16th to the 20th century and its function in the ideology of colonial capitalism*, London: Frank Cass, 1977.

123. Virgil K. Y. Ho, 'The city of contrasts: Perceptions and realities in Canton in the 1920s and 1930s', doctoral dissertation, Oxford University, 1995, pp. 90–1.

124. Virginia Berridge, *Opium and the people: Opiate use and drug control policy in nineteenth and early twentieth century England*, London: Free Association Books, 1999, p. 202.

125. In 1916 one of the first studies found no fatal casualties among the 12,000 opiate users who withdrew from their habit in prison over a twelve-year period of observation; see Richard L. Miller, *The case for legalizing drugs*, New York: Praeger, 1991, p. 6.

126. 'Dr. Ayres on opium smokers in the Hongkong Gaol', *China Medical Missionary Journal*, vol. 3, no. 4 (Dec. 1889), p. 134. The same article was reprinted in the *China Mail*, 9 Dec. 1892.

127. Lockhart, *The medical missionary in China*, 1861, pp. 50–6.

128. Berridge, *Opium and the people*, pp. 80–1 and 121.

129. SH, U1/16/914, 'Poisons and poisoning', 1923, pp. 2, 4–8 and 96, as well as Coltman, *The Chinese*, p. 149. Only in 1925 would China join a growing number of states adhering to the Berne Convention of 1906, which called for the abolition of phosphorus in the match industry; see SH, U1/16/914, 'Memorandum concerning a special regulation to be issued by the Municipal Council, Shanghai, re Prohibition of the manufacture and sale of white phosphorus matches', 1933, pp. 4–8, as well as pp. 12 and 45 for concrete examples; see also Charles T. Maitland, 'Phosphorus poisoning in match factories in

China', *China Journal of Science and Art*, 3, nos 2–3 (Feb. and March 1925), pp. 103–13, 169–78.

130. Lester Chinese Hospital, *Annual report of the Lester Chinese Hospital*, Shanghai: Lester Chinese Hospital, 1930, pp. 16–17.

131. Lockhart, *The medical missionary in China*, pp. 50–6.

132. 'Opium poison', *North China Herald*, 1 June 1894, and 'Opium suicide', *North China Herald*, 16 Oct. 1896.

133. Xu Ke, *Qingbai leichao* (Fictitious history of the Qing), Shanghai: Shangwu yinshuguan, 1984, pp. 3113–4.

134. Bao Tianxiao, *Chuanyinglou huiyilu* (Memoirs from Chuanying mansion), Hong Kong: Xianggang daohua chubanshe, 1971, p. 79.

135. V. P. Suvoong, 'Observations on opium', *China Medical Missionary Journal*, 7, no. 3 (Sept. 1893), p. 173.

136. Xu, *Qingbai leichao*, pp. 3531–2.

137. Wu Liande, 'The ancient Chinese on poisoning', *China Medical Journal*, 30, no. 3 (May 1916), p. 177.

138. See various earlier reports in the *China Medical Missionary Journal*, for example J. M. Swan, 'Opium poisoning treated with atropia-sulphate', *China Medical Missionary Journal*, 3, no. 4 (Dec. 1889), pp. 46–8.

139. See Norton Downs, 'Opium-poisoning treated with potassium permanganate', *China Medical Missionary Journal*, 9, no. 4 (Dec. 1895), p. 246, and also the anonymous contribution 'Permanganate of potassium in opium-poisoning', *China Medical Missionary Journal*, 10, no. 3 (Sept. 1896), pp. 150–1. A reference to the possibility of treating morphine addiction with the same substance can be found in 'Potassium permanganate as an antidote for morphine', *China Medical Missionary Journal*, 9, no. 2 (June 1895), p. 108.

140. Watson, *The principle articles*, p. 474.

141. Berridge, *Opium and the people*, pp. 87–93.

142. A description of the boiling process can be found in Clair, 'Causeries sur l'opium', pp. 13–14; see also Lee, *The big smoke*, pp. 34–5.

Chapter 5 'The Best Possible and Sure Shield': Opium, Disease and Epidemics (*c.* 1840–1940)

1. Virginia Berridge, *Opium and the people: Opiate use and drug control policy in nineteenth and early twentieth century England*, London: Free Association Books, 1999, pp. 35–8.

2. Robert M. Julien, *A primer of drug action*, New York: Freeman, 1996, p. 247; Alexandre Duburquois, *Notes sur les maladies des Européens en Chine et au Japon*, Paris: Faculté de Médecine, 1872, pp. 12–13, concerning hospitalisation rates for dysentery and diarrhoea in Shanghai during the mid-nineteenth century.

3. Jon Boyes and S. Piraban, *Opium fields*, Bangkok: Silkworm Books, 1991, p. 64.

4. Thomas Stephen Szasz, *Ceremonial chemistry: The ritual persecution of drugs, addicts and pushers*, London: Routledge and Kegan Paul, 1974, pp. 143 and 149.

5. SH, U1/4/2690, 'Minutes of the 13th meeting of the League's Drugs Commission', May 1934.

6. Joseph Edkins, 'Historical note on opium and the poppy in China' in Royal Commission on Opium, *First Report of the Royal Commission on Opium with minutes of evidence and appendices*, London: Eyre and Spottiswoode, 1894, vol. 1, p. 147.

7. Marek Kohn, *Narcomania: On heroin*, London: Faber and Faber, 1987, pp. 43–5.

8. Berridge, *Opium and the people*, pp. 22–4, 38–48 and 97–109.

9. From the 1550s onwards the transliteration *afuyong* was also used; see Edkins, 'Historical note', pp. 148–50; see also Zhu Di, *Pujifang* (Collection of popular remedies), Harbin: Heilongjiang kexue jishu chubanshe, 1996, p. 606.

10. Edkins, 'Historical note', p. 148.

11. Su Zhe, *Su Zhe ji* (A collection of Su Zhe's work), orig. twelfth century, Beijing: Zhonghua shuju, 1990, vol. 3, p. 1203.

12. Fang Shao, *Bozhai bian* (Collected work from years of wandering), orig. c. 1125, Beijing: Zhonghua shuju, 1983, p. 47.

13. G. A. Stuart, *Chinese materia medica*, Taipei: Southern Materials Center, 1987, p. 307.

14. Su Song, *Bencao tujing* (Illustrated materia medica), orig. 1062, Hefei: Anhui kexue jishu chubanshe, 1994, p. 26.

15. Wang Gui, *Taiding yangsheng zhulun* (A treatise on nurturing life), orig. 1338, Jinan: Yuelu shushe, 1996, p. 15.

16. Xu Guozhen, *Yuyao yuanfang* (Prescriptions issued by the Imperial Medicine Bureau), orig. 1267, Beijing: Renmin weisheng chubanshe, 1991, pp. 78, 79–82, 88 and 129.

17. Yu Ende, *Zhongguo jinyan faling bianqian shi* (The changing history of opium prohibition in China), Beijing: Zhonghua shuju, 1934, p. 5.

18. Li Shizhen, *Bencao gangmu* (Materia medica), Beijing: Renmin weisheng chubanshe, 1957, vol. 2, p. 1132.

19. Xu Hongzu, *Xu Xiake youji* (The travels of Xu Xiake), orig. 1638, Shanghai: Shanghai guji chubanshe, 1980, vol. 2, p. 636.

20. Xu Boling, *Yinjingjuan* (The works of Xu Boling) in *Siku quanshu* (Complete library of the four treasuries), Shanghai: Shanghai guji chubanshe, 1987, 867:139. The passage was later cited by the acclaimed Jiangsu scholar Lei Jin, active during the late Qing and early republican period; Lei Jin, 'Rongcheng xianhua' (Gossip from the kingdom of opium), *Wenyi zazhi*, nos 1–12 (1917), reprinted in *Yapian zhanzheng shiliao huibian* (Compendium of historical material on the Opium Wars), Shanghai: Shenzhou guoguang chubanshe, 1954.

21. Fang Yizhi, *Wuli xiaoshi* (Knowledge regarding nature), orig. 1664, Taipei: Shangwu yinshuguan, 1974, pp. 232–3.

22. Nian Xiyao, *Jiyan liangfang* (A collection of good remedies), n.p., 1724, pp. 1–2, quoted in Gong Yingyan, *Yapian de chuanbo yu duihua yapian maoyi* (The spread of opium and the opium trade with China), Beijing: Dongfang chubanshe, 1999, pp. 102–3.

23. Sun Shu'an, *Yonghua shipin* (A annotated collection of poetry on flowers), Nanchang: Jiangxi renmin chubanshe, 1996, p. 330.

24. Yu Zhengxie, 'Yapianyan shixu' (Essay on opium) in *Guisi leigao* (Collection of notes), Shanghai: Shangwu yinshuguan, (1884 edition) 1957, p. 521, also republished in Zhongguo shixue xuehui (ed.), *Yapian zhanzheng* (Historical

documents on the Opium War), Shanghai: Shenzhou guoguangshe, 1954, pp. 309–12.

25. On 'poison', see Ma Boying, *Zhongguo yixue wenhua shi* (A history of medical culture in China), Shanghai: Shanghai renmin chubanshe, 1994, pp. 198–203.

26. Li Ting, *Yixue rumen* (Introduction to the study of medicine), orig. 1575, Tianjin: Tianjin kexue jishu chubanshe, 1999, vol. 1, p. 378; see also Edkins, 'Historical note', p. 150.

27. Frédéric Obringer, *L'aconit et l'orpiment. Drogues et poisons en Chine ancienne et médiévale*, Paris: Fayard, 1997, pp. 25–6; Ma, *Zhongguo yixue wenhua shi*, pp. 198–203.

28. Edkins, 'Historical note', p. 149.

29. K. Morinaka, 'Chronic morphine intoxication', *Zhonghua yixue zazhi*, 15, no. 6 (Dec. 1929), pp. 764–94.

30. Shanghai shili hubei jieyan yiyuan (ed.), *Shanghai shili hubei jieyan yiyuan nianbao fuce* (Annex to the yearly report of the Zhabei anti-opium hospital), Shanghai: Shanghai shili hubei jieyan yiyuan, 1935, pp. 2–12.

31. Kwa Tjoan Sioe and Tan Kim Hong, 'The mass treatment of drug addiction by the Modinos' phlycten method' in Phya Damrong Baedyagun and Luang Suvejj Subhakich (eds), *Transactions of the eighth congress of the Far Eastern Association of Tropical Medicine*, Bangkok Times Press, 1931, p. 53.

32. The terminology for epidemic diseases during the eighteenth and nineteenth centuries in both Chinese and European sources varied enormously and was often imprecise by modern standards. The Chinese general term *yi*, for instance, was listed in gazetteers to encompass any type of epidemic, whereas *zhangqi* referred to diseases caused by foul 'climate'. European practitioners, meanwhile, struggled to define the difference between malaria and cholera. The epidemic diseases referred to in this chapter are therefore based on the perception of contemporaries rather than on current medical knowledge.

33. Dong Lu, Xi Ma and François Thann, *Les maux épidémiques dans l'empire chinois*, Paris: L'Harmattan, 1995, pp. 59–61 and Katz, *Demon hordes and burning boats*, p. 45; see also Yu Yunxiu, 'Liuxingxing huoluan yu Zhongguo jiu yixue' (Cholera epidemics and Chinese traditional medicine), *Zhonghua yixue zazhi*, 29, no. 6 (Dec. 1948), pp. 273–88.

34. J. W. H. Chun, 'An analysis of the cholera problem in China with special reference to Shanghai' in Wu Lien-teh (ed.), *Transactions of the ninth congress of the Far Eastern Association of Tropical Medicine*, Nanjing, 1935, vol. 1, pp. 399–400.

35. See R. M. Dane, 'Historical memorandum' in Royal Commission on Opium, *Final report of the Royal Commission on Opium*, London: Eyre and Spottiswoode, 1895, vol. 7, part 2, p. 32.

36. William Brooke O'Shaughnessy, *On the preparation of the Indian hemp, or gunjah, (Cannabis Indica), their effects on the animal system in health, and their utility in the treatment of tetanus and other convulsive disorders*, Calcutta: Bishop's College Press, 1839, p. 28. The habitual use of opium against cholera is attested in the statement by Atool Krishna Datta, medical practitioner in Calcutta, given 29 Dec. 1893, Calcutta, RCO, vol. 2, p. 312. See also the observation by Ernest Bridge, tea planter in Darrang, that the biggest opium eaters escaped the effects of

cholera in times of epidemics; 28 Dec. 1893, Calcutta, RCO, vol. 2, p. 295. A 'placebo' character of opium for the treatment and as a prophylactic against cholera is indicated in the witness statement by Surgeon-Lieutenant-Colonel J. McConaghey, employed as civil surgeon of Allahabad and superintendent of the city's district gaol, 8 Jan. 1894, RCO, vol. 3, p. 65; see also Richard K. Newman, 'Opium as a medicine in nineteenth-century India' in Sanjoy Bhattacharya and Biswamoy Pati (eds), *Imperialism, medicine and South Asia (1800–1950)*, Hyderabad: Orient Longman, 2004.

37. David Allan, *Notes on the treatment of spasmodic cholera: As successfully employed in many instances that occurred in India and China*, Edinburgh: Stillies Brothers, 1832, p. 4. Similar observations could be made about medical circles in most of Europe well into the middle of the nineteenth century. See for instance F. Toussaint, *Description du choléra-morbus, suivi de considérations topographiques*, St Nicolas: Trenel, 1835, pp. 49–51.

38. 'Treatment of cholera', *Zhonghua yixue zazhi*, 13, no. 5 (Oct. 1927) p. 419.

39. Zhu Mengmei, *Huoluan yufang fa* (Preventive measures against cholera), Shanghai: Shangwu yinshuguan, 1919 (3rd edn 1926), pp. 17–18.

40. Yu Fengbin, *Huoluan congtan* (Notes on cholera), Shanghai: Yu Fengbin, 1922, pp. 8–9.

41. Chen Xingzhen, *Huoluan zizhifa* (Self-medication against cholera), Shanghai: Wenming shuju, 1926, pp. 32–5.

42. Gu Xueqiu, *Yapian* (Opium), Shanghai: Shangwu yinshuguan, 1936, pp. 87–8.

43. Lu, *Les maux épidémiques*, pp. 77 and 93–4.

44. Duburquois, *Notes sur les maladies des Européens en Chine et au Japon*, pp. 7–9 and 78–9.

45. Ibid., pp. 9–13, and an earlier report from the Chinese Hospital in the *North China Herald*, 1, no. 1 (3 Aug. 1850), p. 3.

46. W. Haslewood and W. Mordey, *History and medical treatment of cholera, as it appeared in Sunderland in 1831*, London: Longmans, 1832, p. 35.

47. Lockhart, *The medical missionary in China*, p. 383.

48. Ibid., pp. 58–60 and 224.

49. N. H. Choksy, 'The opium habit among lepers', *China Medical Missionary Journal*, 8, no. 1 (March 1894), p. 18.

50. Lu, *Les maux épidémiques*, pp. 55–9.

51. On trade routes, see Carol Benedict, *Bubonic plague in nineteenth-century China*, Stanford University Press, 1996, pp. 59–60.

52. Wu Lien-teh, *Plague fighter: The autobiography of a modern Chinese physician*, Cambridge: Heffer, 1959, p. 120.

53. Wu, *Plague fighter*, pp. 13 and 31.

54. *Ha'erbin (Fujiadian) zhuanjia xianfang yi cuoying* (View of Harbin [Fujiadian] taken during the plague epidemic December 1910 to March 1911), Shanghai: Shangwu yinshuguan, 1911, p. 9.

55. W. H. Park, 'Opium smoking in China', *China Medical Missionary Journal*, 19, no. 3 (May 1905), p. 80.

56. William Aiton, *Dissertations on malaria, contagion and cholera*, London: Longmans, 1832, pp. 17–19 and Thomas Wilson, *An enquiry into the origin and intimate nature of malaria*, London: Renshaw, 1858, *passim*.

57. See *Discorso sopra la mal'aria, e le malattie che cagiona principalmente in varie spiaggie d'Italia e in tempo di estate,* Rome: Luigi Perego Salvioni, 1793.

58. See C. A. Steifensand, *Das Malaria-Siechthum in den niederrheinischen Landen. Ein Versuch in der medizinischen Geographie,* Crefeld: Funcke and Müller, 1848, and Andrew Ure, *The general malaria of London and the peculiar malaria of Pimlico; investigated, and the means of their economical removal ascertained,* London: William Orr, 1850.

59. Carl Schwalbe, *Beiträge zur Kenntnis der Malaria-Krankheiten,* Zürich: Meyer, 1869, pp. 52–3, and Aiton, *Dissertations on Malaria,* pp. 28–30.

60. Steifensand, *Malaria-Siechthum in den niederrheinischen Landen,* pp. 201–3; John Macculloch, *Malaria: An essay on the production and propagation of this poison and on the nature and localities of the places by which it is produced,* London: Longmans, 1827, pp. 280–1. Also J. Bierbaum, *Das Malaria-Siechthum vorzugsweise in sanitäts-polizeilicher Beziehung,* Wesel: Bagel, 1853, pp. 171–2.

61. Li Zhiyong (ed.), *Zhang Jingyue yixue quanshu* (The medical treatises of Zhang Jingyue), Beijing: Zhongguo zhongyiyao chubanshe, 1997, p. 1546.

62. Zheng Tianyi and Xu Bin, *Yan wenhua* (Smoking culture), Beijing: Zhongguo shehui kexu chubanshe, 1992, p. 15; see also G. Cordier, *La province du Yunnan,* Hanoi: Imprimerie Mac-Dinh-Tu, 1928, pp. 184–185 and W. W. Rockhill, *Diary of a journey through Mongolia and Tibet in 1891 and 1892,* Washington: Smithsonian Institution, 1894.

63. Sun Jiazhen, *Tuixinglu biji* (Scattered essays), orig. 1925, Shanghai: Shanghai shudian, 1996, p. 92.

64. Mark Elvin, *The retreat of the elephants: An environmental history of China,* New Haven: Yale University Press, 2004.

65. Ibid.

66. Ibid.

67. Ernest Watson, *The principal articles of Chinese commerce,* Shanghai: Chinese Maritime Customs, 1930, p. 479.

68. RCO, vol. 1, p. 86.

69. AME, 'Kouy-tcheou: Question de l'opium', 1852–94, vol. 549S, ff. 416–17, citing Alphonsus Maria de S. Lignori, *Theologica Moralis* (1755).

70. Experiments also took place at Kew Gardens as well as in Java; see Steven B. Karch, 'Japan and the cocaine industry of Southeast Asia, 1864–1944' in Paul Gootenberg, *Cocaine: Global histories,* London: Routledge, 1999, p. 147. Martin Wall, *Clinical observations on the use of opium in low fevers and in the synochus,* Oxford: Clarendon Press, 1786, pp. 11 and 17 mentions the use of the 'Peruvian Bark' as an additional means of abating typhoid fevers, though not being as effective as opium in 'calming the agitation of the spirits, in moderating the heat, in abating the quickness of the pulse, relieving pain and headache, inducing calm refreshing sleep, and shortening the paroxysm'.

71. Patricia Ann Rosales, 'A history of the hypodermic syringe, 1850s–1920s', doctoral dissertation, Harvard University, 1997, pp. 54–5, and W. H. Brock, *The Norton history of chemistry,* New York: Norton, 1993, chapter 8.

72. William Roberts, 'Anarcotine: A neglected alkaloid of opium', *China Medical Missionary Journal,* 9, no. 4 (Dec. 1895), p. 288.

73. Aiton, *Dissertations on malaria*, pp. 37–39, C. A. Steifensand, *Die asiatische Cholera auf der Grundlage des Malaria-Siechthums*, Crefeld: Funcke, 1848, pp. 30–4.
74. Ludwig Martin, *Aerztliche Erfahrungen über die Malaria der Tropen-Länder*, Berlin: Springer, 1889, p. 17. Among the suggested alternatives to laudanum was also the infusion of concentrated coffee; see 'The use of coffee in the treatment of Asiatic cholera', *China Medical Missionary Journal*, 9, no. 2 (June 1895), p. 155.
75. Berridge, *Opium and the people*, p. 25.
76. D. E. Owen, *British opium policy in China and India*, Hamden, CT: Archon Books, 1968, p. 62.
77. Roberts, 'Anarcotine', p. 288; see also Aiton, *Dissertations on malaria*, pp. 22 ff.; Dr Percy Mathews, Shanghai, 7 March 1894, found opium a 'sound physiological basis for the treatment of … malaria'; RCO, vol. 5, p. 330.
78. Erhard Rosner, '"Gewöhnung" an die Malaria in chinesischen Quellen des 18. Jahrhunderts', *Sudhoffs Archiv*, 68, no. 1 (1984), pp. 47–48.
79. F. S. A. Bourne, Vice Consul at Canton, reminiscing on the expedition of a Chinese army form Sichuan across Yunnan in the spring of 1885, 24 Feb. 1894, RCO, vol. 5, p. 216.
80. See, for example, 'Donghe zongdu Wen Chong zouqing jiang cengjing xishi yapian zhi qianzong He Yongqing chigepian' (The governor general of Donghe requests the dismissal of official He Yongqing for using opium), 23 Aug. 1840, reprinted in Ma Mozhen (ed.), *Zhongguo jindu shi ziliao* (Archival materials on the history of drug prohibition in China), Tianjin: Tianjin renmin chubanshe, 1998, p. 209, see also 221–2, 235–6; Zhang Jixin, *Zhang Jixin riji* (Diary of Zhang Jixin), Beijing: Zhonghua shuju, 1981, pp. 420–1.
81. Zhang, *Zhang Jixin riji*, pp. 328–9, 341–2; 420–1.
82. Ibid., pp. 341–2; 420–1.
83. RCO, vol. 5, p. 198.
84. RCO, vol. 5, p. 316.
85. RCO, vol. 5, p. 226.
86. RCO, vol. 5, p. 227.
87. RCO, vol. 5, p. 216.
88. FO, 233/14, Alexander Hosie, 'Account of a journey to Yülin and back', 27 March 1883.
89. RCO, vol. 5, p. 220.
90. RCO, vol. 5, p. 217.
91. 'Opium in Formosa', *North China Herald*, 28 Feb. 1896, p. 308.
92. William Roberts, 'Anarcotine: A neglected alkaloid of opium', *China Medical Missionary Journal*, 9, no. 4 (Dec. 1895), pp. 287–90, and RCO, vol. 5, p. 230.
93. RCO, vol. 5, p. 233.
94. Following the opinion of the Commissioner of Excise in British Burma, Copleston, cited in G. H. M. Batten, 'The opium question', RCO, vol. 1, pp. 141–2.
95. RA, RGI, series 601, box 44, folder 364, 'Reports (of the American Medical Commission) of malaria condition', Jan. 1942, pp. 1–2.
96. Ibid., and, on Siam, see also the letter by the Home Office to Lawrence B. Dunham of the Rockefeller Foundation, 8 July 1932, kept at RA, Bureau of

Social Hygiene, series III–I, box 4, folder 133, 'Narcotics', May–Dec. 1932, pp. 1–2.

97. Victor H. Haas (Chief of American Medical Commission to China), 'Mosquito threatens China's lifeline: U.S. lease-lend aid takes form of medicines; Paris green, spray pumps and 16 corps of public health specialists to fight malaria pest', RA, RG1, series 601, box 44, folder 363.

98. RCO, vol. 5, p. 247.

99. Gong Yingyan, *Yapian de chuanbo yu duihua yapian maoyi* (The spread of opium and the opium trade with China), Beijing: Dongfang chubanshe, 1999, p. 81.

100. Li, *Bencao gangmu*, vol. 2, p. 1132; Su, *Zhongguo dupin shi*, p. 38.

101. Huang Guanxiu, *Bencao qiuzhen* (Authentic materia medica), orig. 1769, Shanghai: Shanghai kexue jishu chubanshe, 1959, p. 57.

102. Wu Yiluo, *Zhenzhu bencao congxin* (New materia medica), orig. 1757, Shanghai: Shanghai guangyi shuju, 1953, p. 193.

103. Christian Henriot, *Prostitution and sexuality in Shanghai: A social history, 1849–1949*, Cambridge University Press, 2001, pp. 80–1.

104. RCO, vol. 5, p. 321; also William Muirhead, Shanghai missionary for forty-six years, RCO, vol. 5, p. 243.

105. RCO, vol. 5, p. 337.

106. RCO, vol. 4, pp. 244–5.

107. Shanghai shili hubei jieyan yiyuan (ed.), *Shanghai shili hubei jieyan yiyuan nianbao fuce* (Annex to the yearly report of the Zhabei anti-opium hospital), Shanghai: Shanghai shili hubei jieyan yiyuan, 1935, pp. 2–12.

108. Lee, *The big smoke*, pp. 99–101 and 107.

109. Claude Farrère, *Fumée d'opium*, Paris: Mille et Une Nuits, 2002, p. 34; see also Nguyen Te Duc, *Le livre de l'opium*, Paris: Éditions de la Maisnie, 1979, p. 7.

110. Robert Coltman, *The Chinese: Their present and future*, London: Davis, 1891, p. 127.

111. Dr R. A. Jamieson, surgeon in Shanghai for twenty-six years, RCO, vol. 5, p. 245.

112. RCO, vol. 1, pp. 167–8.

113. Ibid., p. 167.

114. Cynthia Kuhn, Scott Swatzwelder and Wilkie Wilson, *Buzzed: The straight facts about the most used and abused drugs from alcohol to ecstasy*, New York: Norton, 1998, p. 176.

115. Michael Gossop, *Living with drugs*, London: Ashgate, 2000, p. 144.

116. Lee, *The big smoke*, p. 99.

117. Ibid., pp. 168–169.

118. Ibid., p. 64.

119. The effects on libido are examined in H. Libermann, *Les fumeurs d'opium en Chine: Étude médicale*, Paris: Victor Rozier, 1862, pp. 48–9.

120. Frank Dikötter, *Imperfect conceptions: Medical knowledge, birth defects and eugenics in China*, London: Hurst; New York: Columbia University Press, 1998, pp. 42–3.

121. Wang Yanchang, *Wangshi yicun* (Writings of Wang Yanchang), orig. 1871, Hangzhou: Jiangsu kexue jishu chubanshe, 1983, p. 50, quoted in Dikötter, *Imperfect conceptions*, p. 43.

122. The link between patrilinear culture, reproductive health and sexual disorders is explored in Dikötter, *Imperfect conceptions*, pp. 16–63.

123. Gossop, *Living with drugs*, pp. 21–6 and 32.

Chapter 6   War on Drugs: Prohibition and the Rise of Narcophobia (*c.* 1880–1940)

1. See Frank Dikötter, *Sex, culture and modernity in China: Medical science and the construction of sexual identities in the early republican period*, London: Hurst; Honolulu: University of Hawaii Press, 1995, pp. 137–45, 165–79.

2. Thomas S. Szasz, *Ceremonial chemistry: The ritual persecution of drugs, addicts, and pushers*, London: Routledge, 1975, p. 54; see also Robert I. Moore, *The formation of a persecuting society: Power and deviance in Western Europe, 950–1250*, Oxford: Blackwell, 1987.

3. Mike Jay, *Emperors of dreams: Drugs in the nineteenth century*, Sawtry: Daedalus, 2002, pp. 71–2.

4. On the prevalence of racial discourse in China after 1895, see Frank Dikötter, *The discourse of race in modern China*, London: Hurst; Stanford University Press, 1992.

5. Jay, *Emperors of dreams*, p. 224.

6. Virginia Berridge, *Opium and the people: Opiate use and drug control policy in nineteenth and early twentieth century England*, London: Free Association Books, 1999, pp. 193–4.

7. Jay, *Emperors of dreams*, p. 69.

8. For instance K. S. Lodwick, *Crusaders against opium: Protestant missionaries in China, 1874–1917*, Lexington: University Press of Kentucky, 1996.

9. See, among others, Alan Baumler, 'Opium control versus opium suppression: The origins of the 1935 six-year plan to eliminate opium and drugs' in Timothy Brook and Bob T. Wakabayashi (eds), *Opium regimes: China, Britain, and Japan, 1839–1952*, Berkeley: University of California Press, 2000, pp. 270–91; Thomas D. Reins, 'Reform, nationalism and internationalism: The opium suppression movement in China and the Anglo-American influence, 1900–1908', *Modern Asian Studies*, 25, no. 1 (Feb. 1991), pp. 101–42; Edward R. Slack, 'The National Anti-Opium Association and the Guomindang state, 1924–1937' in Brook and Wakabayashi, *Opium regimes*, pp. 248–69; Judith Wyman, 'Opium and the state in late-Qing Sichuan' in Brook and Wakabayashi, *Opium regimes*, pp. 212–27; Zhou Yongming, *Anti-drug crusades in twentieth-century China: Nationalism, history, and state-building*, Lanham, MD: Rowman and Littlefield, 1999.

10. Most notably Thomas De Quincey, *The confessions of an English opium eater*, orig. 1822, London: Bodley Head, 1930.

11. R. M. Martin, *China: Political, commercial, and social*, London: James Madden, 1847, vol. 2, pp. 186–7.

12. Ibid., p. 179.

13. Karl Marx, 'Trade or opium?', *New York Daily Tribune*, 20 Sept. 1858, reprinted in Karl Marx and Friedrich Engles, *On colonialism*, Moscow: Progress Publishers, 1959, pp. 215–21.

14. G. F. Davidson, *Trade and travel in the Far East; or recollections of twenty-one years passed in Java, Singapore, Australia and China*, London: Madden and Malcolm, 1846, p. 240.

15. Ibid., pp. 37 and 242.

16. Lodwick, *Crusaders against opium*, p. 52; the author bases her assessment not on an examination of the available evidence, but on the opinion of a rival Protestant community in the *Chinese Recorder*, vol. 23 (Nov. 1892), p. 541.

17. AME, 'Kouy-tcheou: Question de l'opium', vol. 549S, ff. 581–3.

18. Ibid.

19. AME, 'Conferentia de opio', vol. 549S, 1894–95, f. 3.

20. Ibid., f. 5.

21. The Conferentia de Opio is documented at length in AME, 'Kouy-tcheou: Question de l'opium', vol. 549S.

22. Ibid., ff. 620–621 and 498–500. For a summary of the debate around 1870, see the 'Questions proposées aux vicaires apostoliques de la Chine', AME, vol. 549T, f. 77 *et passim*, and ff. 685–9.

23. AME, 'Kouy-tcheou: Question de l'opium', ff. 504–5.

24. H. Libermann, *Les fumeurs d'opium en Chine. Étude médicale*, Paris: Victor Rozier, 1862, and Walter Henry Medhurst, *The foreigner in far Cathay*, London: Edward Stanford, 1872.

25. AME, 'Kouy-tcheou: Question de l'opium', vol. 549, ff. 11–12.

26. Ibid., ff. 807–11.

27. Report by bishop T. M. Guichard, 29 Jan. 1885, AME, vol. 549T, vol. 2, ff. 393–4.

28. AME, 'Kouy-tcheou: Question de l'opium', vol. 549, ff. 13, 18–19 and 25–6.

29. Ibid., Appendix, ff. 541–2.

30. AME, 'Kouy-tcheou: Question de l'opium', vol. 549T, f. 79.

31. The relevant documents are AME, 'Lettres de la Chine', 1836–57, vol. 450, and AME, 'Sichuan', 1843–56, vol. 527.

32. Letter to M. de Bessé in Lyon, AME, 'Se-tchouan', vol. 527, ff. 33–6, 5 Sept. 1843.

33. YDL, Yale Divinity School Archive, Miner Searle Bates Papers, RG 10, II, box 11, f. 196, T. Windsor, 'Opium: Methods of rescue', 1899, p. 184.

34. Justus Doolittle, *Social life of the Chinese*, New York: Harper, 1865, vol. 2, p. 358.

35. YDL, Yale Divinity School Archive, Miner Searle Bates Papers, RG 10, II, box 11, file 196, T. Windsor, 'Opium: Methods of rescue', 1899, p. 184.

36. 'Dr. Ayres on opium smokers in the Hongkong Gaol', *China Medical Missionary Journal*, 3, no. 4 (Dec. 1889), p. 136.

37. Ibid., p. 138.

38. Arthur Stanley, *Health department annual report*, Shanghai Municipal Council, 1902, p. 40.

39. J. B. Brown, 'Politics of the poppy: The Society for the Suppression of the Opium Trade, 1874–1916', *Journal of Contemporary History*, 8, no. 3 (July 1973), pp. 97–111; see also Barry Milligan, *Pleasures and pains: Opium and the Orient in nineteenth-century British culture*, Charlottesville: University Press of Virginia, 1995.

40. This paragraph draws on John F. Richards, 'Opium and the British Indian empire: The Royal Commission of 1895', *Modern Asian Studies*, 36, part 2 (May 2002), pp. 375–420.

41. These arguments are summarised in the representative statement by Dr Maxwell, secretary of the Medical Missionary Association, London, 8 Sept. 1893, in RCO, vol. 1, pp. 18–19.

42. Quoted in G. E. Morrison, *An Australian in China*, London: Cox, 1895, pp. 37 and 45–6.

43. Archibald John Little, *Through the Yang-tse gorges or trade and travel in western China*, London: Sampson Low, 1898, p. 125.

44. RCO, vol. 5, pp. 285–6.

45. RCO, vol. 5, p. 257.

46. P. L. McAll, 'The opium habit', *China Medical Missionary Journal*, 17, no. 1 (Jan. 1903), p. 2.

47. RCO, vol. 5, pp. 288 and 342.

48. Alexander Hosie, *Three years in western China: A narrative of three journeys in Ssu-ch'uan, Kuei-chow, and Yün-nan*, London: George Philip, 1890, p. 290.

49. A view reported and violently contested in P. B. Cousland, 'Some observations on the opium habit', *China Medical Missionary Journal*, 10, no. 1 (Jan. 1896), p. 20.

50. Richards, 'Opium and the British Indian empire', p. 420.

51. Richard K. Newman, 'Opium as a medicine in nineteenth-century India' in Sanjoy Bhattacharya and Biswamoy Pati (eds), *Imperialism, medicine and South Asia (1800–1950)*, Hyderabad: Orient Longman, 2004, p. 13.

52. John F. Richards, 'Opium and the British empire', Kingsley Martin Lecture, Cambridge University, 23 May 2001, p. 21.

53. Yu Jiao, *Mengchang zaji* (Notes from a dreamy cabin), Beijing: Wenhua yishu chubanshe, 1988, p. 154.

54. 'Bingke geishizhong Liu Guangsan zouqing zhuojia shi yanpianyan zuiming deng qingzhe' (Military officer Liu Guangsan requests a more severe punishment for opium smokers), 15 May 1831, reprinted in Ma Mozhen (ed.), *Zhongguo jindu shi ziliao* (Archival materials on the history of drug prohibition in China), Tianjin: Tianjin renmin chubanshe, 1998, p. 30.

55. Lei Jin, 'Rongcheng xianhua' (Gossip from the kingdom of opium), *Wenyi zazhi*, nos 1–12 (1917), reprinted in *Yapian zhanzheng shiliao huibian* (Compendium of historical material on the Opium Wars), Shanghai: Shenzhou guoguang chubanshe, 1954, p. 322.

56. 'Hu Guang zongdu Lin Zexu zoufu Huang Juezi sailou peiben zhizhe bing zhouyi jinyan zhangcheng liutiaozhe' (Lin Zexu's reply to Huang Juezi's memorial regarding the silver drain and six articles on opium legislation), 19 May 1838, reprinted in Ma, *Zhongguo jindu shi ziliao*, p. 69; see also He Shutian, *He Shutian yizhu sizhong* (Four medical treaties by He Shutian), Shanghai: Xuelin shushe, 1984, pp. 57–9.

57. Huang Jiqing, 'Yingshuzhang' (The opium disease) in A Ying (ed.), *Yapian zhanzheng wenxue ji* (Collection of literary writings on the Opium War), Beijing:

Guji chubanshe, 1957, vol. 1, p. 197; Luoluo jushi (Zhong Zufen), 'Zhao yinju' (The charm of living in seclusion) in ibid., vol. 2, pp. 645–55.

58. Yu Zhengxie, 'Yapianyan shixu' (An essay on opium), *Guisi leigao* (Collection of notes), Shanghai: Shangwu yinshuguan, (1884 edn) 1957, also reprinted in Zhongguo shixue xuehui (ed.), *Yapian zhanzheng* (Historical documents on the Opium War), 1954, Shanghai: Shenzhou guoguangshe, p. 311.

59. Shanghai General Hospital, *Report of the Shanghai General Hospital*, Shanghai General Hospital, 1934, p. 14.

60. Reins, 'Reform, nationalism and internationalism', pp. 105–7.

61. Xia Tiandong (ed.), *Zheng Guanying ji* (Collected writings of Zheng Guanying), Shanghai: Shanghai renmin chubanshe, 1982, vol. 1, pp. 395–9 and vol. 2, pp. 1177–8; Yan Fu, 'Yuanqiang' (The origins of strength), *Yan Fu ji* (Collected writings of Yan Fu), Beijing: Zhonghua shujiu, 1986.

62. Xia, *Zheng Guanying ji*, vol. p. 71 and pp. 395–404.

63. Xia, *Zheng Guanying ji*, vol. 1, p. 395.

64. Guo Songtao, *Guo Songtao riji* (The diaries of Guo Songtao), Changsha: Hunan renmin chubanshe, 1982, vol. 4, pp. 255–7, 318–22 and 364–6.

65. Yan Fu, 'Yuanqiang', pp. 28–9.

66. 'Yichu yandu shuo' (Discourse on eradicating the opium poison), *Shenbao*, 12 Feb. 1906, reprinted in Ma, *Zhongguo jindu shi ziliao*, p. 381. See also Kequan, 'Gailiang fengsu lun' (On reforming popular customs), *Dongfang zazhi*, 1, no. 8 (Aug. 1904), pp. 153–8; Peiqing, 'Lun Zhongguo shehui zhi xianxiang jiqi zhenxing zhi yaozhi' (The current situation of Chinese society and the key to its restoration), *Dongfang zazhi*, vol. 1, no. 12 (Dec. 1904), pp. 279–80.

67. 'Lun jieyan yu lixian zhi guanxi' (The link between opium prohibition and constitutionalism), *Shenbao*, 6 Oct. 1906, reprinted in Ma, *Zhongguo jindu shi ziliao*, pp. 395–6.

68. Ibid.

69. Reins, 'Reform, nationalism and internationalism', pp. 104–5.

70. For a translation of the edict see H. B. Morse, *The trade and administration of the Chinese empire*, London: Longmans, 1908, pp. 434–9; see also Alan Baumler, *Modern China and opium*, pp. 66–71 and William McAllister, *Drug diplomacy in the twentieth century: An international history*, London: Routledge, 2000, pp. 24–7.

71. Zhou Yongming, *Anti-drug crusades in twentieth-century China: Nationalism, history, and state-building*, Lanham, MD: Rowman and Littlefield, 1999, pp. 25–6; see also Joyce Madancy, 'Revolution, religion and the poppy: Opium and the rebellion of the "Sixteenth Emperor" in early republican Fujian', *Republican China*, 21, no. 1 (Nov. 1995), pp. 1–41 and Judith Wyman, 'Opium and the state in late Qing Sichuan' in Timothy Brook and Bob Tadashi Wakabayashi (eds), *Opium regimes: China, Britain, and Japan, 1839–1952*, Berkeley: University of California Press, 2000, pp. 216–23.

72. 'The abolition of opium smoking', *North China Herald*, 23 Nov. 1906, p. 451.

73. Reins, 'Reform, nationalism and internationalism', p. 102.

74. Zhou, *Anti-drug crusades in twentieth-century China*, pp. 27–32.

75. The first Hague Convention, convened by the United States in September 1909, had been obstructed by Britain's refusal to discuss any existing treaties

between Britain and China. The second Hague Convention was concluded on 9 July 1913, followed by a third convened in June 1914, and delayed by the outbreak of the World War. On all Hague Conventions, see International Anti-Opium Association, *The war against opium*, Tianjin: Tientsin Press, 1922, pp. 22–4.

76. Zhonghua quanguo jidujiao xiejinhui judu weiyuanhui, *Duji wenti* (Questions and answers on narcotics), Shanghai: Zhonghu guiming judu hui, 1925, p. 1.

77. Luo Yunyan, *Dupin wenti* (The problem of narcotics), Shanghai: Shangwu yinshuguan, 1931, p. 17.

78. Mei Gongren, *Wangguo miezhong de yapian yanhuo* (The opium plague leads to racial extinction), Beijing: Minyou shuju, p. 22.

79. Luo, *Dupin wenti*, p. 19.

80. Guomindang zhongyang zhixing weiyuanhui (ed.), *Jinyan xuanchuan zhuankan* (Special publication on opium prohibition), Nanjing: Zhongguo Guomindang zhongyang zhixing weiyuanhui, 1929, p. 44; on eugenics, see Frank Dikötter, *Imperfect conceptions: Medical knowledge, birth defects and eugenics in China*, London: Hurst; New York: Columbia University Press, 1998.

81. 'Jieyan zhuanhao' (Special edition on addiction treatment), *Judu yuekan*, no. 84 (Feb. 1935), pp. 31–2; Zhejiang sheng minzhengting (ed.), *Jinyan xiaoce* (A small handbook on opium prohibition), Hangzhou: Zhejiang sheng minzhengting, 1933, p. 23.

82. 'Judu de di sandao fangxian' (The third problem concerning opium prohibition), *Judu yuekan*, no. 57 (June 1932), pp. 34–5.

83. 'Yapian zhi hai' (The evil of opium), *Judu yuekan*, no. 80 (Oct. 1934), p. 24.

84. Wang Jingming, 'Dupin manyan yu nongcun shehui' (The spread of narcotics and agricultural society), *Judu yuekan*, no. 43 (Sept. 1930), p. 22.

85. Peiqing, 'Lun Zhongguo shehui zhi xianxiang jiqi zhenxing zhi yaozhi', p. 279.

86. Mei, *Wangguo miezhong de yapian yanhuo*, pp. 30, 230–5, 287.

87. Cai Jinjun, 'Shanghai shi jinyan wenti' (Problems with the suppression of opium in Shanghai), *Yiyao pinglun*, 7, no. 9 (1935), pp. 19–20.

88. Dikötter, *Sex, culture and modernity in China*.

89. Luo, *Dupin wenti*, p. 22.

90. Cao Bingzhang, *Yapianyin jiechufa* (Opium detoxification methods), Shanghai: Zhongyi shuju, 1931, vol. 2, p. 3.

91. *Judu yuekan*, no. 14 (June 1927), p. 18.

92. Sun Zhongshan, *Sun Zhongshan quanji* (The complete works of Sun Yatsen), Beijing: Zhonghua shuju, 1982, p. 569.

93. Zhou, *Anti-drug crusades in twentieth-century China*, p. 67; Slack, *Opium, state, and society*, p. 59.

94. Jiang Jieshi, *China's destiny*, with notes by Philip Jaffe, London: Dobson, 1947, pp. 73–4.

95. Slack, *Opium, state, and society*, pp. 104–10.

96. RA, Bureau of Social Health, series IV–I, box 1, file 558, 'John D. Farnham's note on narcotic problem', pp. 5–6.

97. International Anti-Opium Association, *The war against opium*, p. 45.

Chapter 7   Curing the Addict: Prohibition and Detoxification
              (*c.* 1880–1940)

1. Richard Davenport-Hines, *The pursuit of oblivion: A social history of drugs*, London: Phoenix Press, 2002, p. 215.

2. The links between prohibition and crime are explored in Jonathan Marshall, 'Opium and the politics of gangsterism in Nationalist China, 1927–1945', *Bulletin of Concerned Asian Scholars* 8, no. 3 (July 1976), pp. 19–48; Frederic Wakeman, *Policing Shanghai 1927–1937*, Berkeley: University of California Press, 1995; Brian G. Martin, *The Shanghai Green Gang: Politics and organized crime, 1919–1937*, Berkeley: University of California Press, 1996.

3. 'Fu: Jieyanfang' (Supplement: Anti-opium cures), reprinted in Ma Mozhen (ed.), *Zhongguo jindu shi ziliao* (Archival materials on the history of drug prohibition in China), Tianjin: Tianjin renmin chubanshe, 1998, p. 69.

4. 'Hu Guang zongdu Lin Zexu zoubao Chu sheng chana yanfan shoujiao yanju geqing zhe' (Memorials by Lin Zexu to the throne on the situation of investigating and arresting opium traders and confiscating smoking utensils in Hunan), 2 Aug. 1838, reprinted in Ma, *Zhongguo jindu shi ziliao*, p. 85; 'Hunan xunfu Qian Baoshen zouwei Hunan sheng yanxing jinyan qingxing zhe' (Imperial inspector for Hunan Qian Baoshen's memorials to the throne on the opium prohibition situation in Hunan), 1 Aug. 1838, reprinted in Ma, *Zhongguo jindu shi ziliao*, p. 84.

5. 'The spread of morphia', *North China Herald*, 25 April 1900, pp. 725–6.

6. William Lockhart, *The medical missionary in China: A narrative of twenty years' experience*, London: Hurst and Blackett, 1861, pp. 384–5, 390–1.

7. Robert Coltman, *The Chinese. Their present and future: medical, political, and social*, London: Davis, 1891, p. 129.

8. Free medication in pill form, probably containing opium dross, was already a feature of missionary munificence before the end of the nineteenth century; see letter by L. C. Delamare, 16 October 1855 to the Missions Étrangères de Paris, AME, vol. 527 (*Sichuan* 1843–1856), f. 1041.

9. A. P. Peck, 'The antidotal treatment of the opium habit', *China Medical Missionary Journal*, 3, no. 4 (Dec. 1889), pp. 49–51.

10. YML, Peter Parker Collection, *Report of the Ophthalmic Hospital in Canton*, 1881, p. 19.

11. Report of 12 Aug. 1889 and letter of 8 October 1898, AME, 'Kouy-tcheou: Question de l'opium', 1843–56, vol. 549S, ff. 672 and 1050–1.

12. The businessman presented his goods by means of a letter sent on 1 April 1887 to a friendly cleric; AME, 'Kouy-tcheou: Question de l'opium', vol. 549, *Question de l'opium*, ff. 507–8.

13. 'Coffee and strychnine', *China Medical Journal*, 40, no. 12 (Dec. 1926), pp. 1245–6.

14. 'Imports of caffeine into China', *China Medical Journal*, 41, no. 1 (Jan. 1927), p. 99.

15. United Nations Office for Drug Control and Crime Prevention, 'The mysterious heroin pills for smoking', *Bulletin on Narcotics*, no. 2 (1953), pp. 50–1.

16. 'Editorial', *China Medical Journal*, 40, no. 12 (Dec. 1926), pp. 1245–6; see also Graham Aspland, 'Abuse of the drugs caffeine and strychnine', *China Medical Journal*, 41, no. 2 (Feb. 1927), p. 180.

17. Wu Lien Teh, 'Note by Dr. Wu Lien Teh', *China Medical Journal*, 40, no. 12 (Dec. 1926), p. 1248.

18. RCO, vol. 5, p. 288.

19. See the testimony by Dr Lalcaca, an Indian working as a surgeon in Shanghai, RCO, vol. 5, p. 254.

20. Léon Rousset, *À travers la Chine*, Paris: Hachette, 1886, pp. 251–2.

21. RCO, vol. 5, p. 244.

22. J. A. Otte, 'Treatment of the opium habit', *China Medical Journal*, 24, no. 4 (July 1910), pp. 237–8.

23. *Report of the Ophthalmic Hospital in Canton*, 1862, p. 9. On the confinement of addicts in nineteenth-century Europe see Virginia Berridge, *Opium and the people: Opiate use and drug control policy in nineteenth and early twentieth century England*, London: Free Association Books, 1999, pp. 164–70.

24. *Report of the Ophthalmic Hospital in Canton*, 1862, p. 9.

25. *Report of the Ophthalmic Hospital in Canton*, 1864, p. 19.

26. 'Hospital reports', *China Medical Missionary Journal*, 19, no. 3 (May 1905), p. 122.

27. *Report of the Ophthalmic Hospital in Canton*, 1868, p. 21.

28. *Report of the Ophthalmic Hospital in Canton*, 1873, p. 16; see also Elliott J. Osgood, 'Some experiences with patients breaking opium', *China Medical Missionary Journal*, 17, no. 2 (March 1903), p. 55.

29. *Report of the Ophthalmic Hospital in Canton*, 1873, p. 16.

30. Osgood, 'Some experiences with patients breaking opium', p. 56.

31. G. Wilkinson, 'Among the small-tooth comb makers', *Mercy and Truth*, 15, no. 170 (Feb. 1911), pp. 52–4.

32. W. H. Park, *Opinions of over one hundred physicians on the use of opium in China*, Shanghai: American Presbyterian Mission Press, 1899, pp. 49–53.

33. Osgood, 'Some experience with patients breaking opium', p. 56.

34. On the merits of hot baths, see also the 'sudden withdrawal' method advocated by Otte, reporting on his treatment experience in Xiamen; Otte, 'Treatment of the opium habit', p. 241.

35. Osgood, 'Some experience with patients breaking opium', pp. 55–6.

36. H. T. Whitney, 'The medical missionary and the opium habitué', *China Medical Missionary Journal*, 5, no. 2 (June 1891), pp. 86–7; see also Arthur Morley, 'The opium cure: A plea for gradual withdrawal', *China Medical Missionary Journal*, 4, no. 3 (Sept. 1890), pp. 250–2; P. L. McAll, 'The opium habit', *China Medical Missionary Journal*, 18, no. 1 (Jan. 1903), pp. 6–8.

37. Samuel Merwin, *Drugging a nation: The story of China and the opium curse*, New York: Fleming Revell, 1908, pp. 92–3.

38. *Report of the Ophthalmic Hospital in Canton*, 1881, p. 19.

39. Park, *Opinions of over one hundred physicians*, p. 88.

40. St Luke's Hospital for Chinese, *Annual reports*, 1887–1900.

41. Lucien Bianco, 'The responses of opium growers to eradication campaigns and the poppy tax, 1907–1949' in Timothy Brook and Bob T. Wakabayashi (eds), *Opium regimes: China, Britain, and Japan, 1839–1952*, Berkeley: University of California Press, 2000, pp. 292–319.

42. Frank Dikötter, *Crime, punishment and the prison in modern China*, London: Hurst; New York: Columbia University Press, 2002, pp. 77, 84, 97–9, 123–7 and 130.

43. Sifa xingzhengbu (ed.), *Sifa tongji (1929 niandu)* (Judicial statistics: 1929), Nanjing: Sifa xingzhengbu, 1931, pp. 180–1, 292–312.

44. NJ, 2/1/1392, 'Sifa xingzhengbu qing zai gedi cheshe yanfan jieyan yiyuan ji jieyansuo' (The Ministry of Judicial Administration requests the establishment of detoxification hospitals and centres in various regions), 1929–32.

45. Sifa xingzhengbu (ed.), *Sifa tongji (1931 niandu)* (Judicial statistics: 1931), Nanjing: Sifa xingzhengbu, 1934, pp. 150–1.

46. NJ, 2/1376, 'Jinyan weiyuanhui niding sheli shoudu jieyan yiyuan ji bianju jingfei linshi yusuanshu' (The National Opium Suppression Commission's plan of setting up a detoxification hospital in the capital and its costing), 1931.

47. 'Shanghai gonggong zujie zhuohuo yanfan zhi yanjiu' (A study on the drug criminals in the Shanghai International Settlement), *Judu yuekan*, no. 54 (April 1932), pp. 10–13.

48. Edward R. Slack, *Opium, state, and society: China's narco-economy and the Guomindang, 1924–1937*, Honolulu: University of Hawai'i Press, 2000, pp. 105–7.

49. JS, 1054/2/291, 'Sheng gaoyuan sifabu guanyu huibao ge xinjian yuebao deng biao' (The provincial high court on the compilation of monthly reports by the new prisons), 1927–8, pp. 13 and 135.

50. 'Jukao suppresses opium', *North China Herald*, 5 Dec. 1934, p. 370.

51. NJ, 12/775, 'Jiangsu diyijian gonghan gei Nanjing jingbei silingbu junzhengbu' (Official letter from the Jiangsu Number One Prison to the headquarters of the Nanjing Military Police Department), 1937; NJ, 7/571, 'Jiangsu Wuxian difang fayuan chengsong zhixing wunian weiman tuxing anjian yilanbiao de wenjian' (Documents on criminal sentences under five years passed by the Wu county court).

52. *Jinyan jinian tekan* (A special edition on the anti-opium movement), Nanjing: Neizhengbu jinyan weiyuanhui, June 1935, p. 156.

53. NJ, 2/1/1392, 'Sifa xingzhengbu qing zai gedi choushe yanfan jieyanyiyuan ji jieyanshuo' (The Ministry of Judicial Administration requests to set up opium detoxification hospitals and centres in various regions), 1929–1932; NJ, 7/1102, 'Jiangsu gaodeng fayuan suoshu di'er jianyu fengxian xian jianfang deng xiushan kuojian wenti de youguan wenshu' (Documents regarding the expansion of Jiangsu Number Two Prison), 1931–1934.

54. Zhao Chen, *Jianyuxue* (Penology), Shanghai: Shanghai faxue bianyishe, 1948, new edition (1st edn 1931), pp. 136–7; Zhao Chen's observations are confirmed by an inspection report contained in JS, 1047/41 baogao/845, 'Shicha jiansuo baogao' (Prison inspection reports), 1930, pp. 1–5.

55. Dikötter, *Crime, punishment and the prison*, pp. 276–80.

56. Shanghai shili hubei jieyan yiyuan (ed.), *Shanghai shili hubei jieyan yiyuan nianbao* (Yearly report of the Zhabei anti-opium hospital), Shanghai: Shanghai shili hubei jieyan yiyuan, 1935, pp. 2–12.

57. SC, 58/283, 'Qianjiang xian zhengfu panjueshu' (Verdict reached by the Qianjiang county government), Sept. 1942.

58. BJ, J181/23/202, 'Dai san deng xishi yapian an' (Smoking opium by Dai and three others), 1935.

59. Li Jianhua, *Jianyuxue* (Penology), Shanghai: Zhonghua shuju, 1936, p. 6.

60. 'Opium addicts help to build roads', *North China Herald*, 26 May 1937, p. 318.

61. 'Peking prisoners and freedom', *North China Herald*, 2 Sept. 1930, p. 348.

62. NJ, 12/2/358, 'Shaanxi sheng 1936 nian 9 yue 1937 nian 12 yue jinyan jindu gongzuo baogao' (Report on anti-opium work in Shaanxi from Sept. 1936 to Dec. 1937), 1937.

63. SH, U1/4/2695, 'Narcotics and drugs: Chinese government measures', 1936, p. 18.

64. Yu Ende, *Zhongguo jinyan faling bianqian shi* (The changing history of opium prohibition in China), Beijing: Zhonghua shuju, 1934, pp. 281–4.

65. 'Sichuan sheng shixing jinyan xize' (Opium suppression regulations of Sichuan in detail), *Zhengfu gongbao*, 8 Feb. 1915, no. 989, reprinted in Ma, *Zhongguo jindu shi ziliao*, p. 647.

66. NJ, 2/1376, 'Jinyan weiyuanhui niding sheli shoudu jieyun yiyuan ji bianju jingfei linshi yusuanshu' (The National Opium Suppression Commission's plan of setting up a detoxification hospital in the capital and its costing), 1931.

67. Nanjing shi jieyan yiyuan (ed.), *Nanjing shi jieyan yiyuan ershiwu nian gongzuo nianbao* (1936 report of the detoxification hospital in Nanjing), Nanjing: Nanjing shi jieyan yiyuan, 1936, p. 1.

68. 'Nanking's campaign against opium', *North China Herald*, 19 Dec. 1934, p. 448.

69. 'China battle opium on long front', *North China Herald*, 19 Aug. 1936, p. 338.

70. NJ, 12/2/347, 'Guangdong sheng gexianshi yanmin dengji jieyan yiyuansuo ji yijie yanmin shu yi lanbiao' (General statistics on registered opium users, opium treatment hospitals and centres, and cured addicts in Guangdong province), 1937.

71. NJ, 12/2/349, 'Yunnan sheng 1937 nian 6 yue zhi 1938 nian 1 yue jindu gong-zuo baogao' (Report on anti-narcotic work in Yunnan from June 1937 to Jan. 1938), 1938.

72. NJ, 12/2/345, 'Hubei tepaiyuan jinyan baogao' (Report by the opium suppres-sion inspector for Hubei), 1937; NJ, 12/2/344, 'Hubei sheng 1936 nian 7 yue zhi 1937 nian 11 yue jinyan jindu gongzuo baogao' (Report on anti-narcotic work in Hubei from July 1936 to Nov. 1937), 1937.

73. *Jieyan banyuekan* (The Anti-Opium Bi-Weekly), 3 June 1936, appendix.

74. NJ, 2/1376, 'Jinyan weiyuanhui ni sheli shoudu jieyun yiyuan ji bianju jingfei linshi yusuanshu' (The National Opium Suppression Commission's plan of set-ting up a detoxification hospital in the capital and its costing), 1931.

75. Nanjing shi, *Nanjing shi jieyan yiyuan ershiwu nian gongzuo nianbao*, pp. 3, 5, 11, 27–9 and 34.

76. Shanghai shili hubei jieyan yiyuan (ed.), *Shanghai shili hubei jieyan yiyuan nianbao* (Yearly report of the Zhabei anti-opium hospital), Shanghai: Shanghai shili hubei jieyan yiyuan, 1935.

77. 'Shanghai shili ge jieyan yiyuan zhuyuan guize' (Regulations for inmates of all Shanghai detoxification hospitals), *Jinyan zhuankan*, Shanghai, Dec. 1935, p. 49.

78. Nanjing shi, *Nanjing shi jieyan yiyuan ershiwu nian gongzuo nianbao*, p. 29.

79. 'Xidufan jiechuhou de shanhou wenti' (Relevant issues following the treatment of addicts), *Jinyan jinian tekan*, Nanjing: Neizhengbu jinyan weiyuanhui, 1935, pp. 155–6.

80. Ibid., p. 157.

81. Ibid., p. 160.

82. Neizhengbu, 'Ge shengshixian chouban qiangmin gongchang banfa' (Regulations concerning the establishment of Citizen-Strengthening Factories in various provinces, cities and counties), *Jinyan jinian tekan*, Chongqing: Neizhengbu, 1939, 12–3 and 83.

83. YN, 11/11/147, 'Henan sheng liunian jinyan zongbaogao' (General report on opium suppression work in the past six years in Henan), 1937.

84. Ibid.

85. Ibid.; BJ, J5/1/1090, 'Beiping shi waisanqu yandu jiechusuo yanmin xundao kecheng biao' (Lectures for addicts in the detoxification centre of the outer third district in Beijing), 1946; on moral reformation in republican penal philosophy, see Dikötter, *Crime, punishment and the prison in modern China*, pp. 144–62.

86. K. Morinaka, 'Chronic morphine intoxication', *Zhonghua yixue zazhi*, 15, no. 6 (Dec. 1929), p. 794.

87. YN, 11/11/147, 'Henan sheng liunian jinyan zong baogao' (General report of opium suppression work in the past six years in Henan), 1937.

88. 'Jinshi jieyansuo yipie' (A glance at the detoxification centre in Tianjin), *Judu yuekan*, no. 87 (May 1935), p. 16.

89. SH, Q177/1/105, 'Jiaohui jiaoyu weisheng' (Matters relating to moral instruction, basic education and hygiene), 1931.

90. NJ, 2/1376, 'Jinyan weiyuanhui niding sheli shoudu jieyun yiyuan ji bianju jingfei linshi yusuanshu' (The National Opium Suppression Commission's plan of setting up a detoxification hospital in the capital and its costing), 1931.

91. T'ang Leang-li, *Reconstruction in China*, Shanghai: China United Press, 1935, p. 123.

92. NJ, 12/1121, 'Weihaiwei gongshu ji Zhongshan xian niban lejie yandufan ciji' (Weihaiwei public police control area and Zhongshan county start tattooing narcotic offenders), 1936–7.

93. NJ, 12/2/350, 'Sichuan sheng 1936 nian 9 yue 1938 nian 12 yue jinyan jindu gongzuo baogao' (Report on anti-opium and anti-narcotic work in Sichuan from Sept. 1936 to Dec. 1938), 1937.

94. YN, 11/11/147, 'Henan sheng liunian jinyan zong baogao' (General report on opium suppression work in the past six years in Henan), 1937.

95. BJ, J5/1/67, 'Weishengju guanyu mianfei shijie deng ling' (The Bureau of Health on free detoxification treatments), 1935, pp. 5–6.

96. 'Hebei jianyu', *Judu yuekan*, no. 91 (Sept. 1935), p. 12.

97. NJ, 12/2/350, 'Sichuan sheng 1936 nian 9 yue to 1938 nian 12 yue jinyan jindu gongzuo baogao' (Report on anti-opium work in Sichuan province, Sept. 1936 to Dec. 1938), 1938.

98. NJ, 41/412, 'Di'er jituanjun zhu Yu banshichu gonghan' (Official letter of the Chongqing office of the No. Two Army), April 1940.

99. LoN, C76/M31/1938/XI, *Annual reports by governments for 1936, China*, Feb. 1938.

100. Huang Kewu, 'Yan Fu de yixing qingyuan yu sixiang jingjie' (Yan Fu's emotional and intelllectual life) in Huang Kewu (ed.), *Sixiang, zhengquan yu shehui liliang* (Knowledge, politics and social power), Taipei: Zhongyang yanjiuyuan jindaishi yanjiusuo, 2002, pp. 112–17.

101. Charles E. Terry and Mildred Pellens, *The opium problem*, New York: Committee on Drug Addiction, 1928, p. 2.

102. RA, Bureau of Social Hygiene, IV–I, box 4, f. 147, 'Opium addiction and physical fitness: Investigators unable to detect any marked deterioration from its use', *New York Times*, 1 July 1929.

103. 'Capital punishment for addicts: New anti-opium laws come into force', *North China Herald*, 10 June 1936, p. 447.

104. On Lin Ji and forensic medicine in China, see Dikötter, *Crime, punishment and the prison*, pp. 215–16.

105. Lin Ji, 'Jianyan yanfan yijian' (Opinions on the examination of opium addicts), *Zhonghua yixue zazhi*, 19, no. 3 (June 1933), pp. 362–6.

106. LoN, C76/M31/1938/XI, *Annual reports by governments for 1936, China*, Feb. 1938.

107. RA, Bureau of Social Hygiene, IV–I, box 1, f. 554, 'Opinions by Lawrence Kolb, etc.', 1928.

108. RA, Bureau of Social Hygiene, III–I, box 4, f. 134, W. D. Reddish, 'The treatment of morphine addiction by blister fluid injections', pp. 1–9, n.d.

109. Daniel Albespy, *Du traitement du cancer par l'autosérothérapie*, Sens: Société Générale d'Imprimerie, 1921; Georges Bonnet, *Sur l'autosérothérapie intramuqueuse dans l'asthme et ses équivalents*, Paris: Masson, 1934; Joseph Rohmer, *De l'autosérothérapie en ophthalmologie*, Angers: Grassin, 1913; Jean Lauze, *Contribution à l'étude de l'autosérothérapie de l'ascite*, Montpellier: Imprimerie Générale du Midi, 1911; Xavier Soubigou, *Contribution à l'étude du traitement de la tuberculose par une méthode d'autosérothérapie*, Bordeaux: Imprimerie de l'Académie et des Facultés, 1930.

110. Polys Modinos, *Le traitement des toxicomanes par la phlycténothérapie*, Paris: Baillière, 1932; Polys Modinos, 'La guérison des toxicomanes par le sérum du vésicatoire', *Revue Pratique des Maladies des Pays Chauds*, vol. 10 (Feb. 1930), pp. 68–77; see also Kwa Tjoan Sioe and Tam Kim Hong, 'Opiumontwenningskuren met blaarserum', *Geneeskundig Tijdschrift voor Nederlandsch-Indië*, vol. 79 (1931), pp. 138–51; A. de Mol van Otterloo and A. Bonebakker, 'Over de doeltreffenheid van de ontwenningskuur volgens Modinos voor opiumschuivers', *Geneeskundig Tijdschrift voor Nederlandsch-Indië*, vol. 79 (1931), pp. 862–72.

111. LoN, OC 1188, Advisory Committee on Traffic in Opium and other Dangerous Drugs, 'The curing of drug addicts by vesicatory serum method of Dr Modinos', 21 March 1930.

112. Kwa Tjoan Sioe and Tan Kim Hong, 'The mass treatment of drug addiction by the Modinos' phlycten method' in Phya Damrong Baedyagun and Luang Suvejj Subhakich (eds), *Transactions of the eighth congress of the Far Eastern Association of Tropical Medicine*, Bangkok Times Press, 1931, pp. 53–64.

113. L. S. Huizenga, 'Autogenous serum treatment for opium addicts', *Chinese Medical Journal*, 48, no. 8 (Aug. 1934), pp. 741–4; see also Christian Reformed World Missions' Archives, Calvin College, collection 122, 'Lee S. Huizenga', 'Het gebruik van serum van den patient', 1935, box 14 f. 4.

114. L. S. Huizenga, 'Autogenous serum treatment for opium addicts', *Chinese Medical Journal*, 49, no. 7 (July 1935), pp. 719–21.

115. R. H. Mumford, 'Auto-haemotherapy in opium addiction', *Chinese Medical Journal*, 49, no. 9 (Sept. 1935), p. 1061.

116. Shanghai shili hubei jieyan yiyuan (ed.), *Shanghai shili hubei jieyan yiyuan nianbao* (Yearly report of the Zhabei anti-opium hospital), Shanghai: Shanghai shili hubei jieyan yiyuan, 1935.

117. Morinaka, 'Chronic morphine intoxication', pp. 792–3.

118. Zhang Shitao, 'Jieyan zhi fa' (Detoxification methods), *Yiyao daobao*, 2, no. 5 (March 1936), pp. *zhuan* 11–14.

119. Gu Xueqiu, *Yapian* (Opium), Shanghai: Shangwu yinshuguan, 1936, p. 101.

120. William L. White, *Slaying the dragon: The history of addiction treatment and recovery in America*, Bloomington, IL: Chestnut Health Systems, 1998, p. 126; however, W. D. Reddish was already using Modinos's serum method in Lexington, Kansas, in the early 1930s; since the Department of Justice designated a set of barracks at Fort Leavenworth, Kansas, as an annex to the main Leavenworth Penitentiary for the segregation and treatment of all convicted drug addicts while a new institution was being built near Lexington in 1929, it is likely that the serum method was used in Kansas before it emerged in Colorado; see RA, Bureau of Social Hygiene, III–I, box 4, f. 134, W. D. Reddish, 'The treatment of morphine addiction by blister fluid injections', pp. 1–9, n.d., and RA, Bureau of Social Hygiene, III–I, box 4, f. 146, 'Proposed experimental studies in the treatment of chronic opium poisoning', c. 1930.

121. The abstraction of the individual from his social milieu, implied by the search for a magical bullet, was already criticised in 1937 in Bingham Dai, *Opium addiction in Chicago*, Montclair, NJ: Patterson Smith, 1970 (orig. 1937), p. 9.

122. Ma Wen-chao, 'The effect of the lecithin on opium addicts', *China Medical Journal*, 46, no. 5 (May 1932), pp. 806–19; Ma Wen-chao et al., 'A comfortable and spontaneous cure of the opium habit by means of a lecithin diet' in Wu Lien-teh (ed.), *Transactions of the ninth congress of the Far Eastern Association of Tropical Medicine*, Nanjing, 1935, vol. 2, pp. 381–7.

123. Gu, *Yapian*, pp. 101–8.

124. Zhang Chongxi, *Jieyan diaoyan ji zhiliao* (A diagnosis for opium addiction and its cure), Hangzhou: Songjinglou shudian, 1936, p. 11.

125. Nanjing shi, *Nanjing shi jieyan yiyuan ershiwu nian gongzuo nianbao*, pp. 15–24.

126. 'Nanning yishi Luo Lebin dui yangfen keduan yapian yanyin fabiao tanhua' (A speech by Luo Lebin concerning the use of goat droppings to cure opium

addiction), *Judu yuekan*, no. 92 (Oct. 1935), pp. 18–20; see also Wu Liande, 'The ancient Chinese on poisoning', *China Medical Journal*, 30, no. 3 (May 1916), pp. 175–8.

127. Xia Shenchu, *Jieyan zhinan* (Guide to detoxification), Shanghai: Zhenliaoyi baoshe, 1936, pp. 58–60.

128. 'Biekai shengmian de xinli jieyanfa' (Unique spiritual cure against opium addiction), *Judu yuekan*, no. 101 (July 1936), p. 45.

129. BJ, J181/19/9807, 'Jiaoyangju guanyu Han Zeng jieyan yinbing siwang zhi an' (Report from the reform centre regarding the death of Han Zeng from illness whilst undergoing drug rehabilitation), 1915.

130. BJ, J181/19/9806, 'Jiaoyangju guanyu Song Jitang jieyan yinbing siwang zhi yi'an' (Report from the reform centre regarding the death of Song Jitang from illness whilst undergoing drug rehabilitation), 1915.

131. JS, 1002/2/3473, 'Yanmin siwang ji qiangjue yanfan juan' (Files concerning cases of death and execution among drug criminals), 1946.

132. NJ, 11/11/147, 'Yunnan sheng 1937 nian 6 yue zhi 1938 nian 1 yue jindu gongzuo baogao' (Report on anti-narcotic work in Yunnan from June 1937 to Jan. 1938), 1938.

133. Shanghai shili, *Shanghai shili hubei jieyan yiyuan nianbao fuce*, pp. 2–12; morphine remained the best treatment to alleviate tuberculosis in republican China; see Sun Youxin, 'Zhiliao feijiehe zhi xiao jingyan' (An experiment in the treatment of tuberculosis), *Shehui yibao*, no. 208 (Feb. 1934), pp. 4706–12.

134. 'Man executed for drug habit: Heroin addict pays extreme penalty', *North China Herald*, 28 Nov. 1934, p. 330.

135. 'Death sentence on opium addicts', *North China Herald*, 24 April 1935, p. 136.

136. '3,500 drug addicts register: Enforcement of compulsory measure next month', *North China Herald*, 25 Sept. 1935, p. 512.

137. 'Nanhui mafei chongfan, Shi Fenglou panchu sixing' (Repeat morphine offender Shi Fenglou sentenced to death), *Judu yuekan*, no. 94 (Dec. 1935), pp. 17–18.

138. 'Hospital gives opium addicts new start', *North China Herald*, 5 Aug. 1936, p. 251; NJ, 12/1077, 'Geshengshi 1935 1936 zhixing yandufan sixing renshubiao' (Statistics on executions of drug-related criminals carried out in 1935 and 1936), 1937–8.

139. 'Jinyan weiyuanhui zonghui tezai tonggao' (Public announcement by the National Opium Suppression Commission), *Judu yuekan*, no. 99 (May 1936), p. 22.

140. 'Rigid anti-opium measure: Three years imprisonment or capital punishment', *North China Herald*, 11 March 1936, p. 439.

141. 'Sian's anti-opium campaign: Nine narcotics vendors executed in public', *North China Herald*, 13 May 1936, p. 273.

142. 'Planters of opium will be shot', *North China Herald*, 20 May 1936, p. 320.

143. 'Drug dealer shot in Peiping: First witnesses bonfire of narcotics', *North China Herald*, 3 June 1936, p. 403.

144. 'Capital punishment for addicts: new anti-opium laws come into force', *North China Herald*, 10 June 1936, p. 447.

145. 'Excessive sentences', *The Shanghai Times*, 6 March 1937.

146. The licensing system is described in Alan Baumler, 'Opium control versus opium suppression: The origins of the 1935 six-year plan to eliminate opium and drugs' in Timothy Brook and Bob T. Wakabayashi (eds), *Opium regimes: China, Britain, and Japan, 1839–1952*, Berkeley: University of California Press, 2000, pp. 270–91.

147. Lai Shuqing (ed.), *Guomin zhengfu liunian jinyan jihua ji qi chengxiao, 1935–40* (The nationalist government's Six-Year Opium Suppression Plan and its results), Taipei: Guoshiguan, 1986, pp. 83–4.

148. Zhou Yongming, *Anti-drug crusades in twentieth-century China: Nationalism, history, and state-building*, Lanham, MD: Rowman and Littlefield, 1999, pp. 83–4.

149. 'Szechuen political conditions', *North China Herald*, 10 June 1937, p. 453.

150. Qin Heping, *Yunnan yapian wenti yu jinyan yundong* (The anti-opium movement and the problem of opium in Yunnan), Chengdu: Sichuan minzu chubanshe, 1998, p. 315.

151. NJ, 12/920, 'Fujian jinyan tepaiyuan Qiu Hongjun chengbao tuixing jinyan yin zhuyi gexiang qingxing an' (Qiu Hongjun, the opium prohibition inspector to Fujian, reports on various matters to be considered during the prohibition movement), 1938.

152. NJ, 12/775, 'Jiangsu diyijian gonghan gei Nanjing jingbei silingbu junzhengbu' (Official letter from the Jiangsu Number One Prison to the headquarters of the Nanjing Military Police Department), 1937, pp. 21–2.

153. *Sichuan sishi niandai jinzheng gaikuang* (An overall view of the anti-opium policy in Sichuan in the 1940s), Chengdu: Sichuan sheng zhengfu jinyan shanhou dulichu, 1942, p. 26.

154. NJ, 12/2/358, 'Shaanxi sheng 1936 nian 9 yue 1937 nian 12 yue jinyan jindu gongzuo baogao' (Report on the anti-opium work in Shaanxi from Sept. 1936 to Dec. 1937), 1937.

Chapter 8   Pills and Powders: The Spread of Semi-Synthetic Opiates (*c.* 1900–1940)

1. Arnould de Liedekerke, *La Belle Époque de l'opium*, Paris: Éditions de la Différence, 2001, pp. 99–100.

2. Virginia Berridge, *Opium and the people: Opiate use and drug control policy in nineteenth and early twentieth century England*, London: Free Association Books, 1999, pp. 138–41.

3. Royal Commission on Opium, *Royal Commission on Opium*, London: Eyre and Spottiswoode, 1894–5, vol. 2, p. 114.

4. Ibid., p. 16.

5. G. S. Muir, 'The traffic in morphia: Origin and growth of the trade', *North China Herald*, 24 Dec. 1915, p. 915.

6. See the report on opium and opium smoking by H. McCallum, Hong Kong, 6 March 1881, which possibly documents the first instance of clinical morphine being used for leisure purposes in Hong Kong; RCO, vol. 5, pp. 195–6.

7. 'The spread of morphia', *North China Herald*, 25 April 1900, pp. 725–6.

8. Ibid., p. 726.

9. Isabella L. Bird, *The Yangtse Valley and beyond: An account of journeys in China, chiefly in the province of Sze Chuan and among the Man-Tze of the Somo territory*, London: John Murray, 1899, pp. 508–10.

10. W. H. Park (ed.), *Opinions of over 100 physicians on the use of opium in China*, Shanghai: American Presbyterian Mission Press, 1899, pp. 43–9.

11. Xu Xuejun, *Shanghai jindai shehui jingji gaikuang (haiguan shinian baogao yibian)* (A survey of Shanghai's modern society and economy including a translation of ten years of customs reports), Shanghai: Shanghai shehui kexue chubanshe, 1985, pp. 183–7.

12. Wu Liande, 'Jinggao mafei zhi weixian' (Warning against the dangers of morphine), *Zhonghua yixue zazhi*, 3, no. 2 (June 1917), p. 3; see also 'Japan and the opium trade in China', *China Medical Journal*, 33, no. 5 (Sept. 1919), p. 515.

13. Wu Lien-teh, 'The latest phase of the narcotic problem', *Zhonghua yixue zazhi*, 6, no. 2 (June 1920), pp. 69–70.

14. Wu Lien-teh, *Plague fighter: The autobiography of a modern Chinese physician*, Cambridge: Heffer, 1959, pp. 484–5.

15. Ibid., p. 489.

16. Wu, 'The latest phase', p. 66.

17. YDL, International Missionary Council Archive, RG 46/6, 'The Manchuria issue: A new Opium War', 16 Dec. 1931, p. 4.

18. 'Morphia evil in Shantung', *North China Herald*, 24 Jan. 1925, p. 137.

19. LN, JC23/4281, 'Pi Lingyuan xian zhishi' (Formal instruction to the governor of Lingyuan county), 1915.

20. LN, JC23/6959, 'Cha mafei yi'an ling gexian jiu difang qingxing tuoni zhangcheng yifa guiban' (Investigation over the morphine case and order to the local counties to carry out legislation according to circumstances), 1918.

21. 'Morphia pill habit in China', *North China Herald*, 31 Jan. 1925, p. 181.

22. LN, JC23/12661, 'Lundun fu you dabang mafei huiguo' (A huge quantity of morphine imported from London), 5 April 1920.

23. LoN, OC294 (a), Advisory Committee on Traffic in Opium, *List of seizures reported to the League of Nations since August 1925*, 22 April 1926, pp. 27 and 35.

24. 'Morphia pill habit in China', p. 181.

25. *Shenbao*, 17 April 1874.

26. Su Zhiliang, *Zhongguo dupin shi* (History of narcotics in China), Shanghai: Shanghai renmin chubanshe, 1995, p. 247.

27. Shanghai shehui kexueyuan (ed.), *Shanghai jindai xiyao hangye shi* (A history of modern pharmaceutical commerce in Shanghai), Shanghai: Shanghai shehui kexueyuan chubanshe, 1988, p. 33; Su, *Zhongguo dupin shi*, pp. 246–7.

28. Cao Bingzhang, *Yapianyin jiechufa* (Opium detoxification methods), Shanghai: Zhongyi shuju, 1931, pp. 20–35.

29. SH, U1/16/922, 'Joint petition to Mayor from the Bureaux of Public Safety and Public Health', 1933.

30. BJ, J5/1/1879, 'Beiping shi zhengfu weishengchu xunling' (Instruction from the Beiping Municipal Health Bureau), 1933, pp. 9–12.

31. NJ, 12/1185, 'Junwei Sichuan sheng jinyanhui tepaiyuan Xiao Zhiping qing quti shishang yiqie jieyan yaowan' (Plea by Xiao Zhiping, opium prohibition inspector for Sichuan province, to ban all anti-opium medicines on the market), 1936; on morphine in opium treatment pills in Nanjing, see D. T. Yü (*sic*), 'Nanjing shinei jieyanwan zhi huayan chengji biao' (Results of a chemical analysis of opium treatment pills in Nanjing), *Shehui yibao*, no. 192 (June 1933), pp. 4021–2.

32. Frank Dikötter, *Crime, punishment and the prison in modern China*, London: Hurst; New York: Columbia University Press, 2002, p. 21.

33. Sun Jiazhen, *Xu Haishang fanhuameng* (Sequel to the vanity fair of Shanghai), Shanghai: Jinbu shuju, 1916, vol. 3. pp. 5–11, 20–3.

34. Li Bingxin, Xu Junyuan and Shi Yuxin (eds), *Jindai Zhongguo yandu xiezhen* (The real story of narcotics in modern China), Shijiazhuang: Hebei renmin chubanshe, 1997, vol. 1, p. 23, 68–9.

35. 'Illicit traffic in opium', *China Medical Journal*, 33, no. 1 (Jan. 1919), pp. 51–2.

36. *China Medical Journal*, 33, no. 1 (Jan. 1919), p. 202.

37. 'The pharmaceutical situation in China', *Chinese Medical Journal*, 47, no. 4 (April 1933), p. 405.

38. Lin Yutang, *History of the press and public opinion in China*, Oxford University Press, 1937, p. 143.

39. The *National Medical Journal*, quoted in Herbert D. Lamson, *Social pathology in China: A source book for the study of problems of livelihood, health, and the family*, Shanghai: Commercial Press, 1935, p. 291; for a similar observation, see also Lin, *History of the press*, p. 143; for an analysis of medical advertisements in the press, see Huang Kewu, 'Cong *Shenbao* yiyao guangbao kan minchu de yiliao wenhua yu shehui shenghuo, 1912–1926' (Medical culture and social life in the early republican era as seen through the medical advertisements of the *Shenbao*, 1912–1926), Zhongyang yanjiuyuan jindaishi yanjiusuo jikan, 17, no. 2 (Dec. 1988), 141–94.

40. See for instance Roy Porter, *Health for sale: Quackery in England, 1660–1850*, Manchester University Press, 1989, and J. H. Young, *The medical messiahs: A social history of health quackery in twentieth century America*, Princeton University Press, 1967.

41. For sample analyses of deep brown, dirty-looking 'opium mania' cures in the United States, see Stanford Emerson Chaille, 'The opium habit and "opium mania cures"', *The New Orleans Medical and Surgical Journal*, May 1876, pp. 773–5.

42. The appeal by the association's president for a 'pure drugs supply' was published in the *China Medical Journal*, 23, no. 2 (March 1909), p. 107, and the first responses compiled in *China Medical Journal*, 23, no. 3 (May 1909), pp. 215–18, 23, no. 5 (Sept. 1909), pp. 267–73, 365–8, and 23, no. 6 (Nov. 1909), p. 421. Seasickness pills, such as *Zoto's*, were nothing else than pink (i.e. 'red') pills; see *China Medical Journal*, 23, no. 4 (July 1909), pp. 256–7.

43. 'The very useful formulae', *China Medical Journal*, 23, no. 6 (Nov. 1909), p. 406.

44. NJ, 1036/3, 'Chouyi chuangshe weijin yaopin guanliju banfa ji niju yusuan youguan wenjian' (A proposal for the creation of a bureau of illicit drugs and estimated costs), 1920.

45. Wu Lien-teh, 'Financing public health in China', *National Medical Journal of China*, 15, 1 (Feb. 1929), p. 51.

46. 'Proposed regulations governing patent and proprietary medicines', *China Critic*, 3, no. 21 (May 1930), p. 500; 3, no. 22 (May 1930), p. 522.

47. *Shanghai jindai xiyao hangye shi*, p. 309.

48. According to D. Barat, officer of the Association of Licensed Pharmacists in Shanghai; D. Barat, 'The pharmaceutical situation in China', *Chinese Medical Journal*, 47, no. 4 (April 1933), p. 405.

49. 'Patent medicine law', *Chinese Medical Journal*, 51, no. 1 (Jan. 1937), pp. 99–101.

50. Yip Ka-che, *Health and national reconstruction in nationalist China: The development of modern health services, 1928–1937*, Ann Arbor: Association for Asian Studies, 1995.

51. See H. Dale Beckett, 'Heroin: The gentle drug', *New Society*, 26 July 1979.

52. Berridge, *Opium and the people*, p. 162.

53. On the early history of heroin in the United States, see David F. Musto, *The American disease: Origins of narcotic control*, Oxford University Press, 1999, pp. 101–2 and 198–200.

54. LoN, C124/M113/1940/XI, Advisory Committee on Traffic in Opium and other Dangerous Drugs, *Annual reports of governments on the traffic in opium and other dangerous drugs for the year 1938*, 27 Aug. 1940, p. 17; On Egypt, see LoN, C329/M200/1932/XI, Advisory Committee on Traffic in Opium and other Dangerous Drugs, *Summary of annual reports of governments on the traffic in opium and other dangerous drugs for the years 1929 and 1930*, 22 March 1932, pp. 23–25, and United Nations Office for Drug Control and Crime Prevention, 'History of heroin', *Bulletin on Narcotics*, no. 2 (1953), pp. 3–16.

55. 'Heroin', *China Medical Missionary Journal*, 15, no. 1 (Jan. 1901), p. 31.

56. 'Hongwan baiwan jindan' (Red pills, white pills and golden elixir), *Judu yuekan*, no. 22 (June 1928), p. 28.

57. C. P. Fairchild, 'The rise and fall of the pink pill', manuscript, Centre for Criminology, University of Hong Kong, p. 2, dates the origins of the red pill to 1921, but the red pill was already outlawed in Zhejiang province in 1912; see 'Zhejiang suqing dupin zanxing tiaoli' (Temporary regulations for the suppression of narcotics), reprinted in Ma Mozhen (ed.), *Zhongguo jindu shi ziliao* (Archival materials on the history of drug prohibition in China), Tianjin: Tianjin renmin chubanshe, 1998, pp. 594–5.

58. Ren Jiyu (ed.), *Zhongguo daojiao shi* (A history of Daoism in China), Shanghai: Shanghai renmin chubanshe, 1990, p. 596.

59. 'Heihua zhi Shanxi', *Judu yuekan*, no. 75 (April 1934), pp. 6–7.

60. LoN, C258/M130/1935/XI, Advisory Committee on Traffic in Opium and other Dangerous Drugs, *Summary of annual reports of governments on the traffic in opium and other dangerous drugs for the year 1933*, 5 June 1935, p. 51.

61. UN Drug Control and Crime Prevention, 'The mysterious heroin pills for smoking', *Bulletin on Narcotics*, no. 2 (1953), p. 50.

62. 'Guonei zhi hongwan dupin' (The red pill in China), *Judu yuekan*, no. 82 (Dec. 1934), p. 22.

63. SH, U1/4/2690, 'Report by the Shanghai Municipal Council for the calendar year 1935 on the traffic in opium and other dangerous drugs', 1935, pp. 198 and 351. Narcotic pills with added caffeine could be compared to caffeinated beverages such as coca-cola or the use of clove and other spices in Indonesian kretek cigarettes. See Mark Pendergrast, *For God, country and Coca-Cola: The definitive history of the world's most popular soft drink*, London: Orion, 2000 and Mark Hanusz, *Kretek: The culture and heritage of Indonesia's clove cigarettes*, Singapore: Equinox, 2000.

64. LoN, C258/M130/1935/XI, Advisory Committee on Traffic in Opium and other Dangerous Drugs, *Summary of annual reports of governments on the traffic in opium and other dangerous drugs for the year 1933*, 5 June 1935, p. 67.

65. SH, U1/4/2690, 'Report by the Shanghai Municipal Council for the calendar year 1935 on the traffic in opium and other dangerous drugs', 1935, p. 198.

66. 'Guonei zhi hongwan dupin', p. 20.

67. SH, U1/4/2691, 'Report', 1936, pp. 168–9.

68. 'Guonei zhi hongwan dupin', p. 20.

69. Ibid., p. 21; SH, U1/4/2690, 'Report', 1935, p. 198.

70. Luo Yunyan, *Dupin wenti* (The problem of narcotics), Shanghai: Shangwu yinshuguan, 1931, pp. 9–10.

71. SH, U1/4/2690, 'Report', p. 206.

72. 'The mysterious heroin pills for smoking', p. 49.

73. 'Dope haunts in "beggar land"', *North China Herald*, 21 April 1937, p. 126.

74. 'Heroin traffic flourishing', *North China Herald*, 14 April 1937, p. 81.

75. 'Guonei zhi hongwan dupin', p. 21.

76. *Report of the Government of Hong Kong for the calendar year 1930 on the traffic in opium and other dangerous drugs*, Hong Kong: Noronha, 1931, p. 4.

77. 'The mysterious heroin pills for smoking', p. 50; see also C. P. Fairchild, 'The rise and fall of the pink pill', manuscript, Hong Kong: Centre for Criminology, n.d.

78. *Report of the Government of Hong Kong for the calendar year 1930*, p. 2.

79. LoN, C218/M146/1939/XI, Advisory Committee on Traffic in Opium and other Dangerous Drugs, *Annual reports of governments on the traffic in opium and other dangerous drugs for the year 1937*, 22 July 1939, p. 39.

80. Harold Traver, 'Opium to heroin: Restrictive legislation and the rise of heroin consumption in Hong Kong', *Journal of Policy History*, 4, no. 3 (1992), p. 315.

81. Cf. description contained in *Report of the Government of Hong Kong for the calendar year 1928 on the traffic in opium and other dangerous drugs*, Hong Kong: Noronha, 1929, p. 2.

82. Bing Miao, 'Yanxia zhuiyu' (Embellished words for smoking clouds), *Jinyan zhuankan* (Special publication on opium prohibition), Shanghai: Shanghai jinyan weiyuanhui, 1935, p. 29.

83. Wang Bingshi, 'Tonghai zhi hongwan du' (The harm of red pills in Nantong and Haimen), *Judu yuekan*, no. 60 (Sept. 1932), pp. 70–1.

84. *Report of the Government of Hong Kong for the calendar year 1934 on the traffic in opium and other dangerous drugs*, Hong Kong: Noronha, 1935, p. 2; saving time was already cited in 1910 as a reason by consumers in Beijing, where 'it was

very difficult to purchase opium... illicitly'; 'Opium suppression: Progress in China', *North China Herald*, 14 Jan. 1910, pp. 270–1.

85. *Report of the Government of Hong Kong for the calendar year 1937 on the traffic in opium and other dangerous drugs*, Hong Kong: Noronha, 1938, pp. 2–4.

86. On pill smuggling into the United States, see LoN, C256/M105/1934/XI, Advisory Committee on Traffic in Opium and other Dangerous Drugs, *Report to the Council on the work of the eighteenth session, held at Geneva from May 18th to June 2nd, 1934*, June 1934, p. 15, and LoN, C237/M136/1938/XI, Advisory Committee on Traffic in Opium and other Dangerous Drugs, *Report to the Council on the work of the twenty-third session, held at Geneva from June 7th to 24th, 1938*, 24 June 1938, pp. 31–2.

87. D. Eskes and J. K. Brown, 'Heroin-caffeine-strychnine mixtures: Where and why?', *Bulletin on Narcotics*, no. 1 (1975), pp. 67–9.

88. Yu Ende, *Zhongguo jinyan faling bianqian shi* (The changing history of opium prohibition in China), Beijing: Zhonghua shuju, 1934, pp. 324–5.

89. 'Morphia evil in Shantung', *North China Herald*, 24 Jan. 1925, p. 137.

90. 'Jinan zhi baiwan wei yapian zhi jindi' (White pills from south of Henan compete with opium), *Judu yuekan*, no. 44 (Oct. 1931), pp. 21–6.

91. 'Hongwan baiwan jindan', p. 28; 'Heihua zhi Shanxi' (Narcotics in Shanxi), *Judu yuekan*, no. 75 (April 1934), pp. 6–15.

92. NJ, 1048/138–141, 'Shanxi sheng fanmai yapianzui' (Traffic in opium in Shanxi), NJ, 1048/1918–1981, 'Shanxi sheng fanmai yapianzui' (Traffic in opium in Shanxi), NJ, 1048/3558–3580, 'Shanxi sheng fanmai yapianzui' (Traffic in opium in Shanxi), NJ, 1048/4696–4734, 'Shanxi sheng fanmai yapianzui' (Traffic in opium in Shanxi), and NJ, 1048/6012–6077, 'Shanxi sheng fanmai yapianzui' (Traffic in opium in Shanxi), all on 'immortality pills', 1919.

93. 'Shanxi' (Report on narcotics suppression), *Judu yuekan*, no. 23 (July 1928), p. 22; 'Gesheng jianli sifa gexian zhengfu chahuo mazui dupin shuliang tongji' (Statistics on narcotics confiscated by local authorities in Shanxi), *Zhongguo yanhuo nianjian*, no. 3 (1927–8), p. 21.

94. 'Great Britain and the opium traffic in China', *China Medical Journal*, 34, no. 1 (Jan. 1920), pp. 68–70.

95. 'Hebei', *Zhongguo yanhuo nianjian*, no. 3 (1927–8), p. 63.

96. 'Baimian zhiguo de Shanxi' (Shanxi, country of white powder), *Judu yuekan*, no. 44 (Jan. 1931), p. 26.

97. 'Hebei', *Zhongguo yanhuo nianjian*, no. 3 (1927–8), p. 63.

98. *Jindan* was thus used for 'traditional' herbal drugs and for 'modern' synthetic ones, including opiates such as heroin. Yu Jiaxi, 'Hanshisan kao' (A study on cold-eating powder) in *Yu Jiaxi lunxue zazhu* (Essays by Yu Jiaxi), Beijing: Zhonghua shuju, 1963, pp. 181–226, and Kristofer Schipper, *The Daoist body*, Berkeley: University of California Press, 1993, p. 180.

99. 'Drug traffic in the interior exposed', *North China Herald*, 21 Nov. 1934, p. 316.

100. On the practice of doping cigarettes, see Martin Booth, *Opium: A history*, London: Pocket Books, 1997, p. 165, as well as 'Floods spoil crops in North', *North China Herald*, 30 September 1930, p. 504.

101. *Narcotic drugs in Hong Kong*, Hong Kong: Rotary Club, 1969, p. 16.

102. Tao Yunde, *Yapian zhi jinxi* (A history of opium), Shanghai: Yuzhoufeng chubanshe, 1937, p. 6; 'Hebei', *Zhongguo yanhuo nianjian*, no. 3 (1927–8), p. 63.

103. Tao, *Yapian zhi jinxi*, pp. 24–5; SH, U1/4/2690, 'Report', 1935, p. 205; SH, U1/4/2691, 'Report', 1938, p. 169.

104. United Nations Office for Drug Control and Crime Prevention, 'The smoking of heroin in Hong Kong', *Bulletin on Narcotics*, no. 3 (1958), pp. 6–7.

105. *Tianjin dagongbao*, 14 Oct. 1930; 'Heihua zhi Shanxi', pp. 6–7.

106. *Report of the Government of Hong Kong for the calendar year 1937 on the traffic in opium and other dangerous drugs*, Hong Kong: Noronha, 1938, pp. 2–4.

107. 'Smokers of white drug', *North China Daily News*, 23 May 1936, p. 9.

108. Peter Valaer, 'The red pill, or the opium substitute', *American Journal of Pharmacy*, no. 107 (1935), pp. 199–207.

109. 'Jiaoji yanxian dupin liuxing' (The spread of narcotics in counties along the Jiaodong peninsula), *Judu yuekan*, no. 73 (Feb. 1934), p. 25.

110. 'Heihua zhi Shanxi', pp. 6–7.

111. 'Qianjiang shangyou zhi hongwan' (The red pill in the upper reaches of the Qiantang River), *Judu yuekan*, no. 57 (June 1932), p. 49.

112. SH, U1/4/2690, 'Report', 1935, pp. 205–6.

113. 'The mysterious heroin pills for smoking', p. 52; see also 'Hairen tingwen zhi Wuxi hongwan jiguan' (Terrifying facts about the red pill business in Wuxi), *Judu yuekan*, no. 53 (Feb. 1932), p. 38 and SH, U1/4/2690, 'Report', 1935, pp. 205–6.

114. 'Guonei zhi hongwan dupin', p. 20 and Bing, 'Yanxia zhuiyu', p. 29.

115. Taisheng, 'Mafei yu hongwan' (Morphine and the red pill), *Judu yuekan*, no. 83 (Jan. 1935), pp. 6–7.

116. 'The opium question', *Shanghai Times*, 9 July 1937.

117. Tao, *Yapian zhi jinxi*, p. 24; U1/4/2690, 'Report', 1935, p. 205.

118. National Anti-Opium Association of China, 'The narcotic situation in China', *Zhonghua yixue zazhi*, 15, no. 2 (April 1929), p. 270.

119. Ibid., p. 271.

120. K. Morinaka, 'Chronic morphine intoxication', *Zhonghua yixue zazhi*, 15, no. 6 (Dec. 1929), pp. 766 and 771.

121. SH, U1/4/2691, 'Report', 1938, p. 169.

122. T'ang Leang-li, *Reconstruction in China*, Shanghai: China United Press, 1935, pp. 120–1.

123. LoN, C88/M44/XI, League of Nations, *Second Opium Conference: 22 July 1924, Geneva*, 1924, p. 5 for the development of the Japanese narcotics trade between 1920 and 1924.

124. LoN, C76/M31/1938/XI, *Annual reports by governments for 1936, China*, Feb. 1938, p. 3.

125. The definitions can be found in League of Nations, *International Opium Convention, signed at The Hague, January 23rd, 1912*, Geneva: D'Ambilly, 3 April 1923, article 8.

126. 100 kilos of base morphine were required to produce 135 kilos of heroin; 'Drug barons and China', *North China Herald*, 7 June 1933, pp. 395–6.

127. William B. McAllister, *Drug diplomacy in the twentieth century: An international history*, London: Routledge, 2000, pp. 91–2.

128. 'A record seizure of drugs', *North China Herald*, 2 Dec. 1930, p. 301.

129. Zhu Qingbao, Jiang Qiuming and Zhang Shijie, *Yapian yu jindai Zhongguo* (Opium and modern China), Nanjing: Jiangsu jiaoyu chubanshe, 1995, p. 35.

130. 'Police make huge narcotics haul', *North China Herald*, 29 May 1935, p. 338.

131. Material on the 1928 law appears in Shanghai shi dang'anguan (ed.), *Qingmo minchu de jinyan yundong he wanguo jinyanhui* (The anti-opium movement and the anti-opium conferences of the League of Nations during the late Qing and early Republic), Shanghai: Shanghai kexue jishu wenxian chubanshe, 1996, pp. 496–506.

132. SH, U1/4/2690, 'Report', 1935, p. 198.

133. 'Drug traffic in the interior exposed', *North China Herald*, 21 Nov. 1934, p. 316.

134. 'Jiangsu' (Jiangsu), *Zhongguo yanhuo nianjian*, no. 3 (1927–8), p. 78.

135. Lang Xiaocang, *Duhuo jian* (Historical facts on the opium evil), Beijing: Guonan zhuanbaoshe, 1934, p. 25.

136. 'Drug traffic menace: Enormous profits in Far East', *North China Herald*, 26 April 1933, p. 156.

137. YDL, International Missionary Council Archive, RG 46/6, 'Recent opium situation in China', Geneva, microfilm collection, part 6: Asia, 1933, pp. 1–2.

138. SH, U1/4/2690, 'Report', 1935, pp. 49–52, 116–17, 187–9; see also NJ, 12/938, 'Shanghai gonggong zujie bufang puohuo sizhi dupin baogao zhaiyao' (Shanghai Municipal Police seized various clandestine factories in the international settlement), 1934.

139. 'Raid on new heroin factory', *North China Herald*, 29 Aug., 1934, p. 313.

140. 'Police make huge narcotic haul', *North China Herald*, 29 May 1935.

141. 'Heroin in form of floor polish', *North China Herald*, 14 Sept. 1929, p. 402.

142. SH, U1/4/2690, 'Report', p. 83.

143. Ibid., p. 87.

144. SC, 58/449, 'Chuan Kang Dian Qian qu yandu jianchatuan Jiang zuzhang Tianxi jiancha Chengdu shi jindu qingxing zhaiyao biao' (A brief report by Jiang Tianxi, head of the Sichuan-Xikang-Yunnan-Guizhou opium prohibition commission on the situation in Chengdu), 1941; Wu Shaobo, 'Jiu Chengdu de "yanhuo"' (The 'opium plague' in old Chengdu) in Feng Zhicheng (ed.), *Lao Chengdu* (Old Chengdu), Chengdu: Sichuan wenyi chubanshe, 1999, pp. 131–2.

145. Su, *Zhongguo dupin shi*, pp. 436–8; Zeng Junchen, 'Jingying "teye" wunian jilüe' (Brief account of five years of managing the 'special business') in Li, Xu and Shi, *Jindai Zhongguo yandu xiezhen*, vol. 2, p. 54; Yu Yanfu, 'Jiu Xikang yanhuo jianwen ji' (A report on the opium evil in old Xikang) in Li, Xu and Shi, *Jindai Zhongguo yandu xiezhen*, vol. 2, pp. 74–5; Ning Wenguang, 'Ningshu jinzheng jianwen' (Prohibition policy in Ningshu) in Li, Xu and Shi, *Jindai Zhongguo yandu xiezhen*, vol. 2, pp. 210–11.

146. NJ, 12/1265, 'Chahuo Ribenren xiedai dupin yantu' (Japanese discovered carrying opium and narcotics), 1937; NJ, 12/1269, 'Chahuo Chaoxianren siyun dupin' (Koreans discovered smuggling narcotics), 1937.

147. The role of Japan as a global hub in semi-synthetic drugs during the early 1920s is evidenced in LoN, OC294, Advisory Committee on Traffic on Opium, *List of seizures reported to the League of Nations since 1921*, 22 Aug. 1925, pp. 62–3, 74–5 and 82–3 and LoN, C52/M/20/1923/XI, Traffic in Opium, *Movement in opium and other dangerous drugs in European possessions and countries in the Far East*, 5 Jan. 1923, pp. 1–2.

148. YDL, International Missionary Council Archive, RG 46/6, Report dated 1 March 1932, pp. 4–7.

149. Ibid., p. 6.

150. NJ, 41(2)/38, 'Neizhengbu Hebei Henan diqu jinyan gongzuo baogao' (The report of the Ministry of Internal Affairs on opium prohibition in Hebei and Henan), 1946–8; Wang Long, 'Rijun baobixia Tianjin zhidu neimu' (The clandestine narcotics industry in Tianjin under Japanese occupation) in Li, Xu and Shi, *Jindai Zhongguo yandui xiezhen*, vol. 1, pp. 160–4.

151. See Frederic Wakeman, *Policing Shanghai 1927–1937*, Berkeley: University of California Press, 1995, pp. 264–5.

152. For further reading on Du Yuesheng, see Brian G. Martin, *The Shanghai Green Gang: Politics and organized crime, 1919–1937*, Berkeley: University of California Press, 1996; see also Zhu, Jiang and Zhang, *Yapian yu jindai Zhongguo*, p. 34.

153. Yiwen, 'Yapian dafanzi Ye Qinghe' (Opium boss Ye Qinghe) in Li, Xu and Shi, *Jindai Zhongguo yandui xiezhen*, vol. 1, pp. 131–4.

154. Zhu, Jiang and Zhang, *Yapian yu jindai Zhongguo*, pp. 35–8.

155. The report compiled for the League of Nations contains figures, facts and maps concerning opium cultivation and consumption in China; see, for instance, LoN, C635/M254/1930/XI, Commission of Enquiry into the Control of Opium-Smoking in the Far East, *Report to the Council*, Nov. 1930.

156. LoN, C202/M131/1939/XI, Advisory Committee on Traffic in Opium and other Dangerous Drugs, *Report to the Council on the work of the twenty-fourth session, Held at Geneva from May 15th to June 12th, 1939*, 30 June 1939, p. 9.

157. 'Guangzhou yanshi shumiao' (A sketch of the opium market in Canton), *Judu yuekan*, no. 90 (Aug. 1935), p. 2.

158. 'Fujian', *Zhongguo yanhuo nianjian*, no. 3 (1927–8), pp. 80–2; 'Tanhuashi' (Opium parlours).

159. 'Anhui' and 'Jiangxi', *Zhongguo yanhuo nianjian*, no. 3 (1927–8), pp. 73–6.

160. Wu Yu, Liang Licheng and Wang Daozhi, 'Jiu Zhongguo yandu gaishu' (A brief history of narcotics in China before 1949) in Li, Xu and Shi, *Jindai Zhongguo yandu xiezhen*, vol. 1, p. 48.

161. 'Wairen zongdu qingxing zhi yiban' (Facts about drug peddling by foreigners), *Zhongguo yanhuo nianjian*, no. 3 (1927–8), p. 47 ff.

162. Qiu Xia, 'Malipeng yanshi jishi' (The opium market in Malipeng), *Judu yuekan*, 93 (Nov. 1935), pp. 2–11.

163. Xie Zaosheng, 'Yi Sichuan yanhuo' (Memories of the opium problem in Sichuan), *Sichuan wenshi ziliao jicui* (Compendium of historical sources on Sichuan), Chengdu: Sichuan renmin chubanshe, 1996, vol. 6, pp. 498–502.

164. Liao Jiwei and Bai Jingchun, 'Yapianyan zai Chengdu' (Opium in Chengdu) in Li, Xu and Shi, *Jindai Zhongguo yandu xiezhen*, vol. 2, p. 111.

165. Xie, 'Yi Sichuan yanhuo', pp. 499–500; see also Shang Ke, 'Jiu Chengdu de lüguanye' (Hotel business in old Chengdu), *Longmenzhen*, no. 6 (1983), pp. 23–4.

Chapter 9   Needle Lore: The Syringe in China (*c.* 1890–1950)

1. Frank Dikötter, *Sex, culture and modernity in China: Medical science and the construction of sexual identities in the early republican period*, London: Hurst; Honolulu: Hawai'i University Press, 1995; Frank Dikötter, *Imperfect conceptions: Medical knowledge, birth defects and eugenics in China*, London: Hurst; New York: Columbia University Press, 1998.

2. For a comparable study on Africa, see Ernest Drucker, 'The injection century: Massive unsterile injections and the emergence of human pathogens', unpublished paper, London School of Hygiene and Tropical Medicine, University of London, 20 March 2002.

3. A. Duchaussoy, *Des injections par les veines dans le traitement du choléra épidémique*, Paris: Hamel, 1855, pp. 9, 19–23, 114–15. Such injectables seem to have replaced earlier attempts to orally infuse curative substances; see Jean Joseph Chassanis, *Dissertation sur la maladie épidémique qui a regné à Lodève et autres villes du royaume en 1751*, Avignon: Garrignan, 1753, pp. 164–7.

4. Patricia Ann Rosales, 'A history of the hypodermic syringe, 1850s–1920s', doctoral dissertation, Harvard University, 1997, pp. 35–6.

5. Ibid., pp. 39, 105.

6. Lu Gwei-djen and Joseph Needham, *Celestial lancets: A history and rationale of acupuncture and moxa*, London: Routledge Curzon, 2002.

7. Chimin K. Wong and Wu Lien-teh, *History of Chinese medicine*, Tianjin: The Tientsin Press, 1932, p. 29.

8. For an update on the most recent scholarship on the history of acupuncture, see Vivienne Lo's introduction to Lu Gwei-djen and Needham, *Celestial lancets*, pp. xxv–li.

9. Deng Tietao, *Zhongyi jindai shi* (A history of Chinese medicine in modern China), Canton: Guangdong gaodeng jiaoyu chubanshe, 1999, p. 432. For further readings on the history of acupuncture, see Yamada Keiji, *The origins of acupuncture, moxibustion and decoction*, Kyoto: International Research Center for Japanese Studies, 1998; Jacqueline Filshie and Adrian White (eds), *Medical acupuncture*, Edinburgh and London: Churchill Livingstone, 1998.

10. Chen Boxi, *Shanghai yishi daguan* (Old Shanghai), 1st edn 1924, Shanghai: Shanghai shudian, 1999, p. 359; see also Zou Yueru, 'Chi tiaosha zhi hai' (On the harm of *tiaosha*), *Shehui yibao*, no. 122 (July 1930), p. 1078; similar methods are known as *meihua zhen* or plum-blossom cluster, and the *qixing zhen* or seven stars cluster. They are also called 'multiple-needle acupuncture.' Five or seven needles are fixed into a light hammerhead and tapped with varying degrees of strength or delicacy; Lu and Needham, *Celestial lancets*, p. 164.

11. Royal Commission on Opium, *Royal Commission on Opium*, London: Eyre and Spottiswoode, 1894–5, vol. 5, pp. 209–11.

12. Martin Booth, *Opium: A history*, London: Pocket Books, 1997, pp. 150–1.

13. Harold Traver, 'Opium to heroin: Restrictive legislation and the rise of heroin consumption in Hong Kong', *Journal of Policy History*, 4, no. 3 (1992), p. 316.

14. W. H. Park (ed.), *Opinions of over 100 physicians on the use of opium in China*, Shanghai: American Presbyterian Mission Press, 1899, p. 47.

15. Wu Lien-teh, *Plague fighter: The autobiography of a modern Chinese physician*, Cambridge: Heffer, 1959, pp. 484–5.

16. Virginia Berridge, *Opium and the people: Opiate use and drug control policy in nineteenth and early twentieth century England*, London: Free Association Books, 1999, pp. 141–2.

17. *Shenbao*, 5 Dec. 1906.

18. Ke Quanshou and Chen Jinfang, 'Badaweiya jieyan xinfa' (Clinical reports on new opium cure methods), *Judu yuekan*, no. 41 (July 1930), pp. 53–7.

19. BJ, J181/18/8942, 'Putong baogao' (Ordinary reports), 1917.

20. Yu Ende, *Zhongguo jinyan faling bianqian shi* (The changing history of opium prohibition in China), Beijing: Zhonghua shuju, 1934, pp. 136–8.

21. Zhu Peizhang, 'Xing shenjing shuairuo zhi zhiliao' (The treatment of sexual neurasthenia), *Shehui yiyaobao*, 2, no. 5 (June 1934), pp. 39–41.

22. Bayer Co., *Bai'er liangyao* (Good medicine from Bayer), Shanghai: Bai'er dayaochang, 1924, p. 79.

23. These pharmaceutical products were widely advertised in medical journals, for instance the *Shehui yiyaobao*, the *Zhonghua yixue zazhi* and the *Xin yiyao kan*.

24. *Shanghai yiyao zhi* (History of medicine in Shanghai), Shanghai: Shanghai shehui kexueyuan chubanshe, 1988, p. 65.

25. Zhang Jian, *Zuixin zhushe liaofa* (Newest treatment by injection), Shanghai: Zhonghua shuju, 1925, pp. 3, 42.

26. Wang Yufeng, *Gebing zhushe liaofa daquan* (Encyclopaedia on the hypodermical treatment of various diseases), Shanghai: Xinyi zhensuo, 1926; Zhu Shenjiang, *Zhushe qianshuo* (Introduction to injections), Shanghai: Shangwu yinshuguan, 1933; Zhang Chongxi, *Gezhong zhushe liaofa* (Various treatments by injection), Hangzhou: Songjinglou shudian, 1936; and Jiang Ziyu (ed.), *Zhushefa ji zhusheyao* (Injection methods and injected medications), Xinhua: Xinan yixue shudian, 1941.

27. Haipu, *Zhushe zhiliao baofa* (Treasure raft of injected treatments), Shanghai: Haipu zhiyaochang, 1930.

28. Xingpai, *Xingpai tezhi yaopinlei shuoming*, pp. 211–16.

29. Rosales, 'A history of the hypodermic syringe', p. 123.

30. Peter Keating, 'Vaccine therapy and the problem of opsonins,' *Journal of the History of Medicine and Allied Sciences*, 43 (1988), pp. 275–96, quoted in Rosales, 'A history of the hypodermic syringe', p. 121.

31. SH, U1/16/921, 'Importation and sale of hypodermic syringes,' 1938.

32. Allan M. Brandt, *No magic bullet: A social history of venereal disease in the United States since 1880*, Oxford University Press, 1985, p. 41.

33. Frank Dikötter, 'A history of sexually transmitted diseases in China' in Scott Bamber, Milton Lewis and Michael Waugh (eds), *Sex, disease, and society: A*

comparative history of sexually transmitted diseases and HIV/AIDS in Asia and the Pacific, Westport, CT: Greenwood Press, 1997, pp. 67–84.

34. Wu Liande [Wu Lien-teh], 'Problem of venereal diseases in China', *China Medical Journal*, 41, no. 1 (Jan. 1927), p. 34.

35. BJ, J5/3/646, 'Wei fengzhun fenfa jieyanyao dingyaoye chongzuo geyuansuo zhentongyao yong' (On the distribution of anti-opium cures as painkillers to various hospitals), 1948.

36. BJ, J5/3/536, 'Hou Qinglin deng zhidu' (Hou Qinglin and others manufacture narcotics), 1945.

37. Luise White, "'They could make their victims dull": Genders and genres, fantasies and cures in colonial southern Uganda', *The American Historical Review*, 100, no. 5 (Dec. 1995), pp. 1389–96; Terence Ranger, 'Godly medicine: The ambiguities of medical mission in southeast Tanzania, 1900–1945', *Social Science and Medicine*, 15, no. 3 (1981), p. 265.

38. Gerda Theuns de Boer, 'Bubonic plague in Bombay, 1896–1914', *International Institute of Asian Studies Newsletter*, 25 (July 2001), p. 20.

39. Francis L. K. Hsü, *Religion, science and human crises: A study of China in transition and its implications for the West*, London: Routledge, 1952, p. 79.

40. Ibid., pp. 78–82.

41. H. D. Lamson, *Social pathology in China*, Shanghai: Commercial Press, 1935, pp. 287–90.

42. Chen Wenda, 'Fei jiehebing zhiliao zhi jingguo' (Self-medication in the case of pulmonary tuberculosis), *Zhonghua yixue zazhi*, 14, no. 3 (June 1928), pp. 147–8.

43. NJ, 1036/65, 'Baihou dusu hunheye zhaoshi diaocha baogao' (Report on an accident involving an antitoxin against whooping cough), 1927.

44. BJ, J5/3/453, 'Xinminhui Beijingshi zonghui guoyi fenhui cheng' (Letter from the traditional medicine department of the Xinminhui headquarters in Beijing), Oct. 1942, pp. 4–5.

45. Wu, *Plague fighter*, pp. 484–5.

46. 'Beisheng jinyan zhuangkuang' (The situation on opium prohibition in provinces in the north), *Shenbao*, 19 Jan. 1919, p. 3; 'Beifang zhi liyuan yu mafei' (The poppy and morphine in the north), *Shenbao*, 17 Jan. 1919, p. 4; see also the editorial by the China Medical Association on 'The indiscriminate selling of drugs in China', *China Medical Journal*, 28, no. 4 (July 1914), p. 287.

47. BJ, J181/19/37807, 'Liu Wentong jijin zhizao mafeizhen yi'an' (The case of Liu Wentong who repaired morphine needles), 1923.

48. 'Heroin injection horrors,' *North China Herald*, 8 July 1936, p. 82.

49. L. S. Huizenga, 'Autogenous serum treatment for opium addicts', *Chinese Medical Journal*, 49, no. 7 (July 1935), pp. 719–21.

50. Zhonghua quanguo jidujiao xiehui judu weiyuanhui, *Duji wenda* (Questions and answers regarding narcotics), Shanghai: Zhonghua guomin juduhui, 1925, p. 11.

51. 'Heroin injection horrors,' *North China Herald*, 8 July 1936, p. 82.

52. Tao Yunde, *Yapian zhi jinxi* (A history of opium), Shanghai: Yuzhoufeng chubanshe, 1937, pp. 24–5.

53. *Jinyan tekan* (Special issue on opium prohibition), Chongqing: Neizhengbu jinyan weiyuanhui, 1939, p. 14.

54. Wu Liande, 'Two unusual cases of morphinism', *Zhonghua yixue zazhi*, 6, no. 2 (June 1920), pp. 62–3.

55. Yu, *Zhongguo jinyan faling bianqian shi*, pp. 136–8.

56. *Zhongguo yanhuo nianjian*, no. 3 (1927–8), pp. 33–44.

57. *Zhongguo yanhuo nianjian*, no. 3 (1927–8), pp. 63, 91; 'Liaoning sanjiao didai dupin zhi shikuang' (The situation of narcotic consumption in the triangle region of Liaoning), *Judu yuekan*, 86 (March 1935), p. 21.

58. 'Harbin zhi duyao shijie' (Harbin's drug world), *Judu yuekan*, 37 (March 1930), p. 47.

59. SH, U1/4/2690, 'Report,' 1935, p. 85.

60. Wu, 'Public health', p. 423.

61. Wu Liande, 'Jinggao mafei zhi weixian' (Warning against the dangers of morphine), *Zhonghua yixue zazhi*, 3, no. 2 (June 1917), p. 3.

62. Frank Dikötter, *Crime, punishment and the prison in modern China*, London: Hurst; New York: Columbia University Press, p. 97.

63. K. Morinaka, 'Chronic morphine intoxication,' *Zhonghua yixue zazhi*, 15, no. 6 (Dec. 1929), pp. 764–5.

64. YDL, International Missionary Council Archive, RG 46/6, microfilm collection, part 6: country file, Asia, 'The Manchuria issue: A new Opium War', 16 Dec. 1931, p. 4.

65. Dai Bingheng, 'Dongbei yanhuo shikuang' (The evils of opium in Manchuria), *Judu yuekan*, no. 42 (Aug. 1930), pp. 40–1.

66. 'Xisheng' (Sacrifice), *Judu yuekan*, no. 86 (March 1935), pp. 16–17.

67. 'Opium question,' *Shanghai Times*, 9 July 1937.

68. 'Shanghai zhi da mafei zhenzhe' (Shanghai's morphine injections), *Judu yuekan*, no. 40 (June 1930), p. 38.

69. 'Drug traffic experience in Shanghai,' *North China Daily News*, 23 May 1936, p. 2.

70. Rosales, 'A history of the hypodermic syringe,' p. 111.

71. Bingham Dai, *Opium addiction in Chicago*, Montclair, NJ: Patterson Smith, 1970 (orig. 1937), p. 118.

72. Michael Gossop, *Living with drugs*, London: Ashgate, 2000, p. 49.

73. 'Yapian liudu shengfen' (Opium and narcotics in various provinces), *Judu yuekan*, 22 (June 1928), p. 28; 'Jiangsu' (Jiangsu), *Zhongguo yanhuo nianjian*, no. 3 (1927–8), p. 78.

74. 'Shandong', 'Jiangsu' and 'Zhejiang', *Zhongguo yanhuo nianjian*, no. 3 (1927–8), pp. 64–5, 79–80.

75. 'Hubei', *Zhongguo yanhuo nianjian*, no. 3 (1927–8), p. 73.

76. Ruxin, 'Renli chefu yu mafeiguan' (Rickshaw pullers and morphine dens), quoted in Tao, *Yapian zhi jinxi*, p. 61.

77. Ibid. For medical references see P. B. Besson and W. McDermott (eds), *Cecil-Loeb textbook of medicine*, 11th edn, Philadelphia: W. B. Saunders, 1963, p. 1746.

78. T'ang Leang-li, *Reconstruction in China*, Shanghai: China United Press, 1935, pp. 120–1.

79. J. M. Jennings, 'The forgotten plague: Opium and narcotics in Korea under Japanese rule, 1910–1945', *Modern Asian Studies*, 29, no. 4 (Oct. 1995), pp. 795–815.

80. Joseph Westermeyer, 'The pro-heroin effects of the anti-opium laws in Asia', *Archives of General Psychiatry*, no. 33 (1976), pp. 1135–9.

81. Traver, 'Opium to heroin', pp. 316 and 319.

Chapter 10 China's Other Drugs (*c*. 1900–1950)

1. NJ, 12/1193, 'Tai'ouning ji mi'erkayin' (Dionine and novocaine), 1936.

2. LoN, C88/M44/XI, *Second Opium Conference*, 22 July 1924, part 2, p. 51, 'Estimated annual requirements of opium and its derivatives reduced to their morphine contents, together with estimated requirements of cocaine and other narcotics'.

3. RA, Bureau of Social Hygiene, series III–I, box 5, f. 151, 'Report from Opium Advisory Committee, League of Nation', 1926–33, pp. 12–13.

4. 'Control of new morphine derivatives', *Zhonghua yixue zazhi*, 14, no. 5 (Oct. 1928), pp. 336–7 and SH, U1/16/735, 'Hospitals for treatment of addicts to opium within the international settlement', 9 April 1925. A detailed list compiled by the opium suppression authorities is contained in LoN, C299/M182/1936, Advisory Committee on Traffic in Opium and other Dangerous Drugs, *Summary of annual reports of governments on the traffic in opium and other dangerous drugs for the year 1934*, 14 July 1936, p. 92.

5. 'Control of new morphine derivatives', *Zhonghua yixue zazhi*, 14, no. 5 (Oct. 1928), pp. 336–7.

6. Xia Shenchu, *Jieyan zhinan* (Guide to detoxification), Shanghai: Zhenliaoyi baoshe, 1936, pp. 40–3.

7. Piero Camporesi, *Bread of dreams*, London: Polity, 1989, pp. 124–5.

8. Hou Guangdi, 'Jieyan jingyan tan' (Discussion of an experiment in detoxification), *Zhonghua yixue zazhi*, 14, no. 3 (June 1928) pp. 21–3.

9. Yu Fengbin, 'Yapian yu mafei zhi liudu' (The pernicious influence of opium and morphine), *Zhonghua yixue zazhi*, 7, no. 2 (June 1921), pp. 77–80.

10. Li Wenlan, *Jieyan xinfa* (New methods on treating opium addiction), Guilin: Tongweichu, 1942; Zheng Qingshan, 'Yapian chengyin zhi yuanli jiqi jiechufa' (The cause of opium craving and its treatment), *Jinyan zhuankan*, 1935, pp. 15–17.

11. 'Jizhong hanyou duzhi de yaopin' (Various medicines containing narcotics), *Judu yuekan*, 50 (Dec. 1931), pp. 48–50.

12. SH, U1/4/2693, 'Joint petition to the mayor from the Bureaux of Public Safety and Public Health', 1933, p. 26.

13. A brief summary of the opium treatment activities in Japanese and GMD-held areas during the war appears in LoN, C237/M136/1938, Advisory Committee on Traffic in Opium and other Dangerous Drugs, *Report to the Council on the work of the twenty-third session, held at Geneva from June 7th to 24th, 1938*, 24 June

1938, pp. 13–15, 18–20 and LoN, C51/M51/1946, Traffic in Opium and other Dangerous Drugs, *Annual reports of governments for the year 1941*, 1 June 1946, pp. 14 and 20.

14. Su Zhiliang, *Zhongguo dupin shi* (History of narcotics in China), Shanghai: Shanghai renmin chubanshe, 1995, pp. 418.

15. Ibid., p. 430.

16. Thomas J. Payte, 'A brief history of methadone in the treatment of opioid dependence: A personal perspective', *Journal of Psychoactive Drugs*, 23 (1991), pp. 103–7.

17. BJ, J5/3/965, 'Ling yishi gonghui xinyaoye gonghui' (Order to physicians and pharmacists), 1947; SC, 58/282, 'Wei fengling qudi dimeilu ji anerdong yi'an' (Order to proscribe demerol and amidone), 1947.

18. Steven B. Karch, 'Japan and the cocaine industry of Southeast Asia, 1864–1944' in Gootenberg, *Cocaine*, pp. 146–7.

19. William Shrubshall, 'Cocaine as an anaesthetic', *China Medical Missionary Journal*, 4 (Dec. 1890), pp. 259–60.

20. Patricia G. Erickson, *The steel drug*, Toronto: Lexington Book, 1987, p. 8.

21. Arnould de Liedekerke, *La Belle Époque de l'opium*, Paris: Éditions de la Différence, 2001, pp. 208–9.

22. Ernst Jöel and F. Fränkel, *Der Cocainismus. Ein Beitrag zur Geschichte und Psychopathologie der Rauschgifte*, Berlin: Justus Springer, 1924, pp. 15–17. The organ of the German medical association, the *Deutsche Medizinische Zeitschrift*, advocated cocaine as a cure for breaking the nicotine habit; ibid., pp. 15–17.

23. Jöel and Fränkel, *Cocainismus*, p. 14.

24. RA, Bureau of Social Hygiene, III–I, box 6, f. 159, E. Poulsson, 'The properties, use and abuse of cocaine', *The World's Health*, p. 474, and Jöel and Fränkel, *Cocainismus*, p. 20.

25. David T. Courtwright, 'The rise and fall of cocaine in the United States' in Jordan Goodman, Paul E. Lovejoy and Andrew Sheratt (eds), *Consuming habits: Drugs in history and anthropology*, London: Routledge, 1995, pp. 206–28.

26. Karch, 'Japan and the cocaine industry', p. 148 and Joseph F. Spillane, 'Making a modern drug: The manufacture, sale and control of cocaine in the United States, 1880–1920' in Gootenberg, *Cocaine*, p. 24.

27. Karch, 'Japan and the cocaine industry', pp. 148–50.

28. On the consequences of wartime on the German cocaine economy, see Friman, 'Germany and the transformation of cocaine', pp. 95–97.

29. Karch, 'Japan and the cocaine industry', pp. 152–3.

30. RA, Bureau of Social Hygiene, III–I, box 1, f. 95, 'Kenneth Caldnell Papers', 1928–1930.

31. Tim Madge, *White mischief: A cultural history of cocaine*, Edinburgh: Mainstream Publishing, 2001, p. 123. For examples of cocaine smuggled in the engine rooms of ships to India, see LoN, OC294, Advisory Committee on Traffic in Opium, *List of seizures reported to the League of Nations since 1921*, 22 Aug. 1925, p. 83.

32. David T. Courtwright, *Forces of habit: Drugs and the making of the modern world*, Cambridge, MA: Harvard University Press, 2001, p. 50.

33. League of Nations, Advisory Committee on Traffic in Opium and other Dangerous Drugs, *Minutes of the 13th session*, Geneva: League of Nations, 20 Jan.–14 Feb. 1930, pp. 18 and 113.

34. LoN, C253/M125/1935/XI, Advisory Committee on Traffic in Opium and other Dangerous Drugs, *Report to the Council on the work of the twentieth session, held at Geneva from May 20th to June 5th, 1935*, 18 June 1935, p. 18 and LoN, C278/M168/1936, Advisory Committee on Traffic in Opium and other Dangerous Drugs, *Report to the Council on the work of the twenty-first session, held at Geneva from May 18th to June 5th, 1936*, 1 July 1936, p. 23.

35. LoN, C88/M44/XI, *Second Opium Conference*, 22 July 1924, p. 5 and NJ, 41/20, 'Weishengbu zhiding Taiwan sheng zhongzhi gukashu guanli banfa fu gukaye nianchanliang biao' (The ministry of health's regulation regarding the plantation of coca trees in Taiwan, with annual figures for coca leaf production in the region); see also the attachment to the file, entitled 'Taiwan kekaye buchong ziliao' (Supplementary materials concerning coca leaves in Taiwan), 1948.

36. League of Nations, Advisory Committee on Traffic in Opium and other Dangerous Drugs, *Minutes of the 13th session*, Geneva: League of Nations, 20 Jan.–14 Feb. 1930, p. 231. 95 kilos of Taiwanese coca were necessary to produce just one of cocaine, only half the amount needed by South American coca farmers. See Karch, 'Japan and the cocaine industry', p. 155.

37. Su, *Zhongguo dupin shi*, p. 245.

38. 'Drug seizure at Shanghai', *China Medical Journal*, 36, no. 6 (Nov. 1922), pp. 549–50.

39. LoN, C121/M39/1930/XI, *Minutes of the thirteenth session held at Geneva*, 20 Jan.–14 Feb. 1930, p. 222 and 331–4; see also LoN, C656/M234/1924/XI, *Second Opium Conference*, part 1, 'Summary of the information received from the governments with regard to the production and manufacture of raw opium and coca leaves, opium derivatives and cocaine, with statistical tables (years 1920, 1921, 1922 and 1923)', 1924, p. 46.

40. LoN, C121/M39/1930/XI, *Minutes of the thirteenth session held at Geneva*, 20 Jan.–14 Feb. 1930, p. 235.

41. 'Haiguan chahuo wairen siyun mazuipin laihua tongji' (Statistics on foreign nationals smuggling narcotics into China), *Zhongguo yanhuo nianjian*, 3 (1927–8), pp. 32–44.

42. J. Nelson Teeter, 'A case of cocaine poisoning', *China Medical Missionary Journal*, 9, no. 4 (Dec. 1895), p. 245.

43. A detailed description can be found in Dugald Christie, 'Cocaine as a local anaesthetic', *China Medical Missionary Journal*, 2, no. 2 (June 1888), pp. 67–68.

44. 'Hongwan baiwan jindan' (Red pills, white pills and golden elixir), *Judu yuekan*, no. 22 (1928), p. 28.

45. 'Drug traffic experience in Shanghai', *North China Daily News*, 23 May 1936.

46. 'Cocaine and cafés chantants', *North China Herald*, 14 June 1924, p. 418.

47. See the statement by Malcom DeLevingne, RA, Bureau of Social Hygiene, III–I, box 4, f. 136.

48. NJ, 12/1193, 'Tai'ouning ji mi'erkayin' (Dionine and novocaine), 1936.

49. YDL, Yale China Record Project Miscellaneous Personal Paper Collection, RG 8, box 204, Joseph Oscar Thomson, 'Cycle of Cathay', pp. 173, 195–7 and 331. The author was a medical missionary who worked at a Canton hospital in 1910–41.

50. RA, Bureau of Social Hygiene, III–I, box 2, f. 115, Chen to Richards, Department of Pharmacology, School of Medicine, Johns Hopkins University, Baltimore, 2 July 1928, and letter by Carl F. Schmidt to Dr Terry, Laboratory of Pharmacology, School of Medicine, University of Pennsylvania, Philadelphia, 16 July 1928.

51. RA, Bureau of Social Hygiene, III–I, box 2, f. 115, translation of letter to Dr I. Wasserberg, Health Section, League of Nations, 15 May 1928.

52. RA, Bureau of Social Hygiene, III–I, box 2, f. 115, 'League learns of new drug like cocaine', *New York Herald Tribune*, 24 June 1928 [unpaginated].

53. For further readings on cannabis see Patrick Matthew, *Cannabis culture*, London: Bloomsbury, 2000, as well as Vera Rubin (ed.), *Cannabis and culture*, The Hague: Mouton, 1975. The full range of the names used for cannabis in northern China is listed in *Beizhi Mengjiang malei zhi diaocha* (Survey of hemp types used in northern China and along the Mongolian border), Diaocha ziliao di 20 hao, Huabei chanye kexue yanjiusuo (Agricultural Sciences Research Centre for Northern China), 1941, pp. 1–3. Traffic in cannabis was first internationally regulated by chapter IV of the International Opium Convention of 1925; see *Convention internationale de l'opium et protocole, signés à Genève le 19 février 1925*, Cairo: Imprimerie Nationale, 1929, p. 9.

54. Zhao Zhongming, *Wushi, wushu, mijing* (Magic healers, magic art and mysterious worlds), Yunnan: Yunnan daxue chubanshe, 1993, p. 35; see also He Yumin and Zhang Ye, *Zouchu wushu conglin de zhongyi* (Magic and Chinese medicine), Shanghai: Wenhui chubanshe, 1994, p. 360.

55. More examples appear in Tian Daihua, *Zhiwuming shitukao changbian* (An illustrated encyclopaedia of plants), Beijing: Renmin weisheng chubanshe, 2002, vol. 1, pp. 3–18.

56. Cited in Frédéric Obringer, *L'aconit et l'orpiment. Drogues et poisons en Chine ancienne et médiévale*, Paris: Fayard, 1997, pp. 181–2, note 161; see also Hui-Lin Li, 'The origin and use of cannabis in East Asia: Their linguistic-cultural implications' in Rubin, *Cannabis and culture*, pp. 51–62.

57. For instance Chen Jiamo, *Bencao mengquan* (A collection of materia medica), orig. 1565 or 1573, Beijing: Renmin weisheng chubanshe, 1988, pp. 281–2, and Liu Wentai, *Bencao pinhui jingyao* (A choice collection of materia medica), completed in 1505, but only published in 1700, Shanghai: Shangwu yinshuguan, 1936, pp. 813–14.

58. NJ, 41/113, 'Xinjiang sheng jinzhong mayan shixiang juan' (Prohibition of the cultivation of hemp for smoking in Xinjiang), Oct. 1947.

59. SH, U1/4/2690, 'Report', 1935, p. 77.

60. NJ, 41/113, 'Xinjiang sheng jinzhong mayan shixiang juan' (Prohibition of the cultivation of hemp for smoking in Xinjiang), Oct. 1947.

61. *Beizhi Mengjiang malei zhi diaocha*, pp. 4 and 7.

62. Courtwright, *Forces of habit*, pp. 39–42.

63. William Brooke O'Shaughnessy, *On the preparations of the Indian hemp, or gunjah, (cannabis indica) their effects on the animal system in health, and their utility in the treatment of tetanus and other convulsive disorders*, Calcutta: Bishop's College Press, 1839, p. 7.

64. James H. Mills, *Madness, cannabis and colonialism*, London: St Martin's Press, 2000.

65. Ahmad M. Khalifa, 'Traditional patterns of hashish use in Egypt' in Rubin, *Cannabis and culture*, p. 199.

66. Luo Yunyan, *Dupin wenti* (The problem of narcotics), Shanghai: Shangwu yinshuguan, 1931, p. 9.

67. A.-F. Legendre, *Au Yunnan et dans le massif du Kin-Ho (Mission A.-F. Legendre)*, Paris: Plon 1913, pp. 79–80.

68. Courtwright, *Forces of habit*, p. 114.

69. Shanghai shizhengfu shehuiju, *Shanghai shi gongren shenghuo chengdu* (The living standards of workers in Shanghai), Shanghai: Shanghai shizhengfu shehuiju, 1934, p. 157.

70. E. J. Dingle, *Across China on foot: Life in the interior and the reform movement*, Bristol: Arrowsmith, 1911, pp. 100–1.

71. W. Y. Fullerton and C. E. Wilson, *New China: A story of modern travel*, London: Morgan and Scott, 1910, p. 84; on BAT advertisements in Shanghai, see Sherman Cochran, 'Transnational origins of advertising in early twentieth-century China' in Sherman Cochran (ed.), *Inventing Nanjing Road: Commercial culture in Shanghai, 1900–1945*, Ithaca, NY: Cornell University East Asia Programme, 1999, pp. 37–58.

72. A. S. Roe, *Chance and change in China*, London: Heinemann, 1920, p. 81.

73. Sherman Cochran, *Big business in China: Sino-foreign rivalry in the cigarette industry, 1890–1930*, Cambridge, MA: Harvard University Press, 1980, p. 27.

74. C. I. Tinling, *Bits of China: Travel-sketches in the Orient*, New York: Fleming Revell, 1925, p. 14.

75. RA, China Medical Board Collection, RG IV–I, box 8, folder 90, 'Letter to Mr Greene at CMB', 1915, pp. 2–3.

76. Cochran, *Big business in China*, p. 246.

77. John Logan, *China old and new*, Hong Kong: South China Morning Post, 1982, p. 55.

78. Wingate M. Johnson, 'Tobacco smoking', *China Medical Journal*, 43, no. 11 (Nov. 1929), p. 1184.

79. Tinling, *Bits of China*, pp. 41–2; see also the critical Gu Baoluo, 'Xi xiangyan de haichu' (The harm of cigarette smoking), *Shehui yiyaobao*, 2, no. 9 (June 1935), pp. 50–1.

80. H. D. Lamson, *Social pathology in China*, Shanghai: The Commercial Press, 1935, p. 285.

81. Xu Borong, 'Xiangyan yu waishang' (Cigarettes and foreign merchants), *Longmenzhen*, no. 4, 1996, pp. 96–7.

82. See for instance the *Lüxing zazhi*, 3, nos 3–4, 1929.

83. LoN, C635/M254/XI, Commission of enquiry into the control of opium-smoking in the Far East, *Report to the Council*, Nov. 1930, vol. 1, p. 27.

84. 'Zhongguo juanyan gongye de guoqu yu xianshi' (The past and present of the cigarette industry in China), *Jingji zhoubao*, 21 Aug. 1947, reprinted in Chen Zhen (ed.), *Zhongguo jindai gongye shi ziliao* (Primary sources on the history of modern industry in China), Beijing: Sanlian shudian, 1961, vol. 4, p. 436.

85. Chiang Monlin, *Tides from the West: A Chinese autobiography*, New Haven: Yale University Press, 1947, pp. 34–5.

86. Quanguo jingji weiyuanhui, *Huochai gongye baogaoshu* (Report on the match industry), Nanjing: Quanguo jingji weiyuanhui, 1935, pp. 1–6.

87. Sidney D. Gamble, *How Chinese families live in Peiping*, New York: Funk and Wagnalls, 1933, pp. 159–60.

88. Xu, 'Xiangyan yu waishang', p. 96.

89. Zhu Xiang, 'Yanjuan' (Cigarettes) in Lao Pin, *Mingjia bixia de yanjiuchadian* (Famous people talking about tobacco, alcohol, tea and dim sum), Beijing: Zhongguo guoji guangbo chubanshe, 1994, pp. 298–300.

Chapter 11 Conclusion

1. Jordan Goodman, Paul E. Lovejoy and Andrew Sherratt (eds), *Consuming habits: drugs in history and anthropology*, London: Routledge, 1995, p. 16.

2. On the role of the United States in pushing a policy of strict prohibition at all cost, see David R. Bewley-Taylor, *The United States and international drug control, 1909–1997*, London: Pinter, 1999.

3. Harold Traver, 'Opium to heroin: Restrictive legislation and the rise of heroin consumption in Hong Kong', *Journal of Policy History*, 4, no. 3 (1992), pp. 320–1.

4. Ch'en Yung-fa, 'The blooming poppy under the red sun: The Yan'an way and the opium trade' in Tony Saich and Hans van de Ven (eds), *New perspectives on the Chinese communist revolution*, New York: Sharpe, 1995, pp. 263–98; his findings are confirmed in NJ, 41/78, 'Neizhengbu Hebei ji Ping Jin shi 1946–1948 niandu yandu dujin gongzuo jihua baogao' (Annual reports on opium suppression in 1946–8 from the Beijing and Tianjin divisions of the Ministry of Internal Affairs), 1946–8, pp. 26–42 and attached report.

5. See various contributions in Ma Weigang (ed.), *Jinchang jindu* (Eliminate prostitution and eradicate opium), Beijing: Jingguan jiaoyu chubanshe, 1993; see also Zhou Yongming, *Anti-drug crusades in twentieth-century China: Nationalism, history, and state-building*, Lanham, MD: Rowman and Littlefield, 1999.

6. James R. Rush, 'Opium in Java: A sinister friend', *Journal of Asian Studies*, 44, no. 3 (May 1985), p. 557.

7. Anthony Reid, 'From betel-chewing to tobacco smoking in Indonesia', *Journal of Asian Studies*, 44, no. 3 (May 1985), p. 538.

8. Emily Hahn, 'The big smoke', *Times and places*, New York: Thomas Cromwell, 1970, p. 5.

9. 'The opium question', *The Shanghai Times*, 9 July 1937.

10. Jean Cocteau, *Opium: Diary of a cure*, London: Icon, 1957, p. 18.

11. John Logan, *China old and new*, Hong Kong: South China Morning Post, 1982, p. 55.

12. Sherman Cochran, *Big business in China: Sino-foreign rivalry in the cigarette industry, 1890–1930*, Cambridge, MA: Harvard University Press, 1980.

13. Iris Cheng, Virginia L. Ernster and He Guanqing, 'Tobacco smoking among 847 residents of east Beijing, People's Republic of China', *Asia-Pacific Journal of Public Health*, 4, nos 2–3, 1990, pp. 156–63.

14. Zhou, *Anti-drug crusades in twentieth-century China*, pp. 113–30.

15. See for instance Pierre-Arnaud Chouvy and Joël Meissonnier, *Yaa Baa. Production, trafic et consommation de méthamphétamine en Asie du Sud-Est continentale*, Paris: L'Harmattan, 2002.

16. Karen Joe Laidler, Jeffrey Day and David Hodson, 'A study of the psychoactive substance abuse problem in Hong Kong', Hong Kong: Centre for Criminology, 2002, p. 123.

17. Embassy of the People's Republic of China in the United States of America, 'Narcotics control in China', June 2000.

18. Embassy of the People's Republic of China in the United States of America, 'Official: Drugs situation grim in China', June 2002.

BIBLIOGRAPHY

ARCHIVAL SOURCES

(1) Di'er Lishi Dang'anguan (No. 2 National Archives), Nanjing (abbreviation: NJ)

1001	various files on opium pro-hibition	Neizhengbu, 1912–28
1002	various files on opium pro-hibition	Beiyang Zhengfu Guowuyuan, 1912–28
1010	various files on opium pro-hibition	Beiyang Zhengfu Hujun Guanlichu, 1915–24
1036	files 3–30	Beiyang Zhengfu Fangyichu, 1919–28
1039	various files on opium pro-hibition	Beiyang Zhengfu Waijiaobu, 1912–28
1048	various files on narcotic in Shanxi	Beiyang Zhengfu Zongjian chating, 1912–28
2	files 1376–1512	Xingzhengyuan, 1928–49
7	various files on opium pro-hibition	Sifa Xingzhengbu, 1928–1947
12	files 340–360, 550–1275	Neizhengbu, 1928–37
41	files 1–829	Neizhengbu Jinyan Weiyuanhui, 1938–49

(2) Jiangsu Sheng Dang'anguan (Jiangsu Provincial Archives), Nanjing (abbreviation: JS)

1002/2	files 3385, 3403–3480, 3544–6	Jiangsu Sheng Minzhengting, 1927–49
1047/17 and 25	various files	Jiangsu Gaodeng Fayuan, 1927–48
1054	various files on opium in prisons	Sifa, 1912–49

(3) Liaoning Sheng Dang'anguan (Liaoning Provincial Archives), Shenyang (abbreviation: LN)

JC 23	various files on opium prohibition	Rehe Sheng Zhanggongshu, 1914–33

(4) Heilongjiang Sheng Dang'anguan (Heilongjiang Provincial Archives), Changchun (abbreviation: HLJ)

51	various files on opium prohibition	Heilongjiangcheng Yamen, 1899–1908
62/3	files 462–941	Heilongjiang Zhengfu Neizheng, 1912–32
62/8	files 61–1725	Heilongjiang Zhengfu Neizheng, 1912–32
132	various files on opium prohibition	Longjiang Daoyin Gongshu, 1914–29

(5) Sichuan Sheng Dang'anguan (Sichuan Provincial Archives), Chengdu (abbreviation: SC)

58	files 1–2500	Sichuan Sheng Jinyan Shanhou Dulichu, 1936–48
132	file 8123	Xichuan Youzheng Guanliju, 1930–49

(6) Yunnan Sheng Dang'anguan (Yunnan Provincial Archives), Kunming (abbreviation: YN)

11/11	files 147–50, 404–551, 1455–1522, 1762–1778	Yunnan Minzhengting, 1900–50
29/2	various files on opium prohibition	Yunnan Sheng Gong'anting, 1940

(7) Beijing Shi Dang'anguan (Beijing Municipal Archives), Beijing (abbreviation: BJ)

J5	files on opium	Beijing Shi Weishengju, 1937–49
J181	files on opium	Beiping Shi Jingchaju, 1911–37

(8) Shanghai Shi Dang'anguan (Shanghai Municipal Archives), Shanghai (abbreviation: SH)

U1/4	files 2690–5	Shanghai Gongbuju Zongbanchu, 1871–1945
U1/16	files 914–1055, 2564–2881	Shanghai Gongbuju Weishengchu, 1871–1945
Q1/10	various files	Guomin Zhengfu Shanghai Zhengfu, 1943
Q400	various files	Shanghai Shi Weishengju, 1945–9
Q177	various files	Shanghai Jianyu, 1939–49

(9) League of Nations Archives, London, New York, Geneva (abbreviation: LoN)

OC	files on China	Advisory Committee on Traffic in Opium, 1921–46
XI	annual reports	Opium and Other Dangerous Drugs, 1921–46

(10) Public Record Office, London (abbreviation: PRO)

FO 228	files 631–755	Consulates and Legations, China, 1834–1930
FO 233	files on opium	Consulates and Legations, China, 1727–1951

(11) Rockefeller Foundation Archives, New York (abbreviation: RA)

RG 1	series 601, box 44	Projects-China, 1912–49
RG 4/2/B9	box 120	China Medical Board, 1913–29
BSH	series III–I, box 1–6, folders 94–161	Bureau of Social Hygiene, 1927–35
BSH	series IV–I, box 1–2, folders 550–568	Bureau of Social Hygiene, 1921–28

(12) Yale Divinity Library (Special Collections), New Haven (abbreviation: YDL)

ms 85 series III, 260023	International Missionary Council Archives, 1910–61
RG 46	World Student Christian Federation, 1895–1945
RG 5	Smith Family Papers, Foochow, 1901–51

RG 10   Miner Searle Bates Papers, Nanking, 1920–50
RG 23   Franklin and Bertha Ohlinger Papers, 1880–1910
ms 116   China through Western Eyes, 1792–1942

(13) Christian Reformed World Missions' Archives, Calvin College

collection 122   various files   Lee S. Huizenga, 1901–49

(14) Archives des Missions Étrangères de Paris (abbreviation: AME)

449–450   Chine, Lettres, 1805–57
527–530   Se-tchoan, 1843–65
541   Yun-nan, 1844–97
549S   Kouy-tcheou, Question de l'opium
549T   Kouy-tcheou, Correspondence

SPECIALISED JOURNALS

Judu yuekan (Anti-Narcotics Monthly), Shanghai, nos 1–113 (incomplete), 1926–36.

China Medical Missionary Journal, Shanghai, vols 1–21, 1887–1907; continued as *China Medical Journal*, vols 22–45, 1908–31; continued as *Chinese Medical Journal*, vols 46–59, 1932–45.

Mercy and Truth, London, vols 3–43 (incomplete), 1897–1939.

North China Herald, Shanghai, 1880–1938.

Sichuan jinyan yuekan (Sichuan Prohibition Journal), Chengdu, 1938–47.

Sichuan jinyan huibao (Sichuan Prohibition News), Chengdu, 1942–46.

Sichuan yuebao (Sichuan Prohibition Monthly), Chengdu, vols 9–12, 1936–39.

Yiyao pinglun (Periodicus Medico-Pharmaceutical), Shanghai, nos 1–151, 1929–37.

Yiyao daobao (Medico-Pharmaceutical Guide), Shanghai, Chongqing, vols 1–5, 1933–44.

Zhongguo yanhuo nianjian (China Yearbook on the Opium Plague), Shanghai, nos 1–4, 1926–31.

Zhonghua yixue zazhi (Chinese Medical Journal), Shanghai, vols 1–29, 1915–48.

PRINTED PRIMARY SOURCES

'3,500 drug addicts register: Enforcement of compulsory measure next month', *North China Herald*, 25 Sept. 1935, p. 512.

Anon., *China as it was, and as it is: With a glance at the tea and opium trades*, London: Cradock, 1842.

'A record seizure of drugs', *North China Herald*, 2 Dec. 1930, p. 301.

A Ying (ed.), *Yapian zhanzheng wenxue ji* (Collection of literary writings on the Opium War), Beijing: Guji chubanshe, 1957.

Abel, Clarke, *Narrative of a journey in the interior of China, and of a voyage to and from that country in the years 1816 and 1817*, London: Longman, 1818.

'The abolition of opium smoking', *North China Herald*, 23 Nov. 1906, p. 451.

Aiton, William, *Dissertations on malaria, contagion and cholera*, London: Longmans, 1832.

Albespy, Daniel, *Du traitement du cancer par l'autosérothérapie*, Sens: Société Générale d'Imprimerie, 1921.

Alexander, Robert, *The rise and progress of British opium smuggling and its effects upon India, China, and the commerce of Great Britain: Four letters addressed to the Right Honourable Earl of Shaftesbury*, London: Seeley, Jackson and Halliday, 1856.

Allan, David, *Notes on the treatment of spasmodic cholera: As successfully employed in many instances that occurred in India and China*, Edinburgh: Stillies Brothers, 1832.

Anselmino, O., 'ABC of drugs' in *Opium and other dangerous drugs*, Geneva: League of Nations Publication, 9, 1931, pp. 20–21.

Aspland, Graham W. H., 'Abuse of the drugs caffeine and strychnine', *China Medical Journal*, 41, no. 2 (Feb. 1927), p. 180.

'Baimian zhiguo de Shanxi' (Shanxi, country of white powder), *Judu yuekan*, no. 44 (Jan. 1931), p. 26.

Bao Tianxiao, *Chuanyinglou huiyilu* (Memoirs from Chuanying mansion), Hong Kong: Xianggang daohua chubanshe, 1971.

Barat, D., 'The pharmaceutical situation in China', *Chinese Medical Journal*, 47, no. 4 (April 1933), p. 405.

Barrow, John, *Travels in China, containing descriptions, observations, and comparisons*, London: Cadell and Davies, 1804.

Bayer Co., *Bai'er liangyao* (Good medicine from Bayer), Shanghai: Bai'er dayaochang, 1924.

'Beifang zhi liyuan yu mafei' (The poppy and morphine in the north), *Shenbao*, 17 Jan. 1919, p. 4.

'Beisheng jinyan zhuangkuang' (The situation on opium prohibition in provinces in the north), *Shenbao*, 19 Jan. 1919, p. 3.

Beizhi Mengjiang malei zhi diaocha (Survey of hemp types used in northern China and along the Mongolian border), Diaocha ziliao di 20 hao, Huabei chanye kexue yanjiusuo (Agricultural Sciences Research Centre for Northern China), 1941.

'Biekai shengmian de xinli jieyanfa' (Unique spiritual cure against opium addiction), *Judu yuekan*, no. 101 (July 1936), p. 45.

Bierbaum, J., *Das Malaria-Siechthum vorzugsweise in sanitäts-polizeilicher Beziehung*, Wesel: Bagel, 1853.

Bing Miao, 'Yanxia zhuiyu' (Embellished words for smoking clouds), *Jinyan zhuankan* (Special publication on opium prohibition), Shanghai: Shanghai jinyan weiyuanhui, 1935.

Bird, Isabella L., *The Yangtse Valley and beyond: An account of journeys in China, chiefly in the province of Sze Chuan and among the Man-Tze of the Somo territory*, London: John Murray, 1899.

Blofeld, John E. C., *City of lingering splendour: A frank account of old Peking's exotic pleasures*, London: Hutchinson, 1961.

Bonnet, Georges, *Sur l'autosérothérapie intramuqueuse dans l'asthme et ses équivalents*, Paris: Masson, 1934.

Cai Jinjun, 'Shanghai shi jinyan wenti' (Problems with the suppression of opium in Shanghai), *Yiyao pinglun*, 7, no. 9 (1935), pp. 17–20.

Cao Bingzhang, *Yapianyin jiechufa* (Opium detoxification methods), Shanghai: Zhongyi shuju, 1931.

'Capital punishment for addicts: New anti-opium laws come into force', *North China Herald*, 10 June 1936, p. 447.

Chaille, Stanford Emerson, 'The opium habit and "opium mania cures"', *The New Orleans Medical and Surgical Journal*, May 1876, pp. 773–5.

Chassanis, Jean Joseph, *Dissertation sur la maladie épidémique qui a regné à Lodève et autres villes du royaume en 1751*, Avignon: Garrignan, 1753.

Chen Boxi, *Shanghai yishi daguan* (Old Shanghai), 1st edn 1924, Shanghai: Shanghai shudian, 1999.

Chen Jiamo, *Bencao mengquan* (A collection of materia medica), orig. 1565 or 1573, Beijing: Renmin weisheng chubanshe, 1988.

Chen Xingzhen, *Huoluan zizhifa* (Self-medication against cholera), Shanghai: Wenming shuju, 1926.

Chen Wenda, 'Fei jiehebing zhiliao zhi jingguo' (Self-medication in the case of pulmonary tuberculosis), *Zhonghua yixue zazhi*, 14, no. 3 (June 1928), pp. 147–8.

Chiang Monlin, *Tides from the West: A Chinese autobiography*, New Haven: Yale University Press, 1947.

'China battle opium on long front', *North China Herald*, 19 Aug. 1936, p. 338.

Choksy, N. H., 'The opium habit among lepers', *China Medical Missionary Journal*, 8, no. 1 (March 1894), pp. 18–20.

Christie, Dugald, 'Cocaine as a local anaesthetic', *China Medical Missionary Journal*, 2, no. 2 (June 1888), pp. 67–68.

'Cocaine and cafés chantants', *North China Herald*, 14 June 1924, p. 418.

Cocteau, Jean, *Opium: Diary of a cure*, London: Icon, 1957.

'Coffee and strychnine', *China Medical Journal*, 40, no. 12 (Dec. 1926), pp. 1245–6.

Collis, Maurice, *Foreign mud*, London: Faber, 1946.

Coltman, Robert, *The Chinese: Their present and future*, Philadelphia and London: F. A. Davis, 1891.

'Control of new morphine derivatives', *Zhonghua yixue zazhi*, 14, no. 5 (Oct. 1928), pp. 336–7.

Cooke, George W., *China: Being 'The Times' special correspondence from China in the years 1857–58*, orig. 1858, Wilmington, Delaware: Scholarly Resources, 1972.

Cordier, G., *La province du Yunnan*, Hanoi: Imprimerie Mac-Dinh-Tu/Le-Van-Tan, 1928.

Correspondence respecting the opium question in China, London: His Majesty's Stationary Office, 1908.

Courtellemont, Gervais, *Voyage au Yunnan*, Paris: Plon, 1904.

Cousland, P. B., 'Some observations on the opium habit', *China Medical Missionary Journal*, 10, no. 1 (Jan. 1896), p. 20.

Cranmer-Byng, J. L., *An embassy to China: Being the journal kept by Lord Macartney during his embassy to the emperor Ch'ien-lung 1793–1794*, London: Longmans, 1962.

Dai Bingheng, 'Dongbei yanhuo shikuang' (The evils of opium in Manchuria), *Judu yuekan*, no. 42 (Aug. 1930), pp. 23–44.

Dai, Bingham, *Opium addiction in Chicago*, orig. 1937, Montclair, NJ: Patterson Smith, 1970.

Daly, H. D., *Report on the political administration of the territories within the Central India Agency for the year 1873–74* [Selections from the Records of the Government of India, CXIV], Calcutta: Foreign Department Press, 1874.

Dane, R. M., 'Historical memorandum', in Royal Commission on Opium, *Volume VII: Final report of the Royal Commission on Opium; Part II: Historical appendices; together with an index of witnesses and subjects, and a glossary of Indian terms used in the evidence and appendices. Presented to both houses of Parliament by command of Her Majesty*, London: Eyre and Spottiswoode, 1895, appendix B, pp. 28–63.

Davidson, G. F., *Trade and travel in the Far East; or recollections of twenty-one years passed in Java, Singapore, Australia and China*, London: Madden and Malcolm, 1846.

De Mei, 'Shanghai xiacheng shehui jianying yiye' (A reflection on the life of the lower classes in Shanghai), *Judu yuekan*, no. 101 (May 1936), pp. 36–8.

de Mol, A. van Otterloo and A. Bonebakker, 'Over de doeltreffenheid van de ontwenningskuur volgens Modinos voor opiumschuivers', *Geneeskundig Tijdschrift voor Nederlandsch-Indië*, vol. 79 (1931), pp. 862–72.

De Quincey, Thomas, *The confessions of an English opium eater*, orig. 1822, London: Bodley Head, 1930.

'Death sentence on opium addicts', *North China Herald*, 24 April 1935, p. 136.

Dechambre, Amédée, *Dictionaire encyclopédique des sciences médicales*, Paris: Lahure, 1854–89.

Ding Shaoyi, *Dongying shilüe* (A brief account of the eastern seas), orig. 1873, Taipei: Zhonghua shuju, 1957.

Dingle, E. J., *Across China on foot: Life in the interior and the reform movement*, Bristol: Arrowsmith, 1911.

Discorso sopra la mal'aria, e le malattie che cagiona principalmente in varie spiaggie d'Italia e in tempo di estate, Rome: Luigi Perego Salvioni, 1793.

Doolittle, Justus, *Social life of the Chinese*, New York: Harper, 1865.

Downs, Norton, 'Opium-poisoning treated with potassium permanganate', *China Medical Missionary Journal*, 9, no. 4 (Dec. 1895), pp. 245–7.

'Dr. Ayres on opium smokers in the Hongkong Gaol', *China Medical Missionary Journal*, vol. 3, no. 4 (Dec. 1889), p. 134.

'Dope haunts in "beggar land"', *North China Herald*, 21 April 1937, p. 126.

'Drug barons and China', *North China Herald*, 7 June 1933, pp. 395–6.

'Drug dealer shot in Peiping: First witnesses bonfire of narcotics', *North China Herald*, 3 June 1936, p. 403.

'Drug seizure at Shanghai', *China Medical Journal*, 36, no. 6 (Nov. 1922), pp. 549–50.

'Drug traffic experience in Shanghai', *North China Daily News*, 23 May 1936.

'Drug traffic in the interior exposed', *North China Herald*, 21 Nov. 1934, p. 316.

'Drug traffic menace: Enormous profits in Far East', *North China Herald*, 26 April 1933, p. 156.

Duburquois, Alexandre, *Notes sur les maladies des Européens en Chine et au Japon*, Paris: Faculté de Médecine, 1872.

Duchaussoy, A., *Des injections par les veines dans le traitement du choléra épidémique*, Paris: Hamel, 1855.

Eames, James Bromley, *The English in China: Being an account of the intercourse and relations between England and China from the year 1600 to the year 1843 and a summary of later developments*, London: Isaac Pitman, 1909.

Edkins, Joseph, 'Historical note on opium and the poppy in China', in Royal Commission on Opium, *First Report of the Royal Commission on Opium with minutes of evidence and appendices*, London: Eyre and Spottiswoode, 1894, vol. 1, pp. 146–58.

Eskes D. and J. K. Brown, 'Heroin-caffeine-strychnine mixtures: Where and why?', *Bulletin on Narcotics*, no. 1 (1975), pp. 67–9.

Fairchild, C. P., 'The rise and fall of the pink pill', manuscript, Centre for Criminology, University of Hong Kong, n.d.

Fang Shao, *Bozhai bian* (Collected work from years of wandering), orig. *c.* 1125, Beijing: Zhonghua shuju, 1983.

Fang Yizhi, *Wuli xiaoshi* (Knowledge regarding nature), Taiwan: Shangwu yinshuguan, 1974.

Farrère, Claude, *Fumée d'opium*, Paris: Mille et Une Nuits, 2002.

Fleming, George, *Travels on horseback in Mantchu Tartary: Being a summer's ride beyond the Great Wall of China*, London: Hurst and Blackett, 1863.

'Floods spoil crops in North', *North China Herald*, 30 Sept. 1930, p. 504.

Fortune, Robert, *Three years' wandering in the northern provinces of China, including a visit to the tea, silk, and cotton countries: With an account of the agriculture and horticulture of the Chinese, new plants, etc.*, London: John Murray, 1847.

Foster, A., 'The Report of the Opium Commission', *China Medical Missionary Journal*, 10, no. 1 (March 1896), pp. 1–16.

Fu Chongju, *Chengdu tonglan* (A survey of Chengdu), orig. 1909, Chengdu: Bashu shushe, 1987.

'Fujian', *Zhongguo yanhuo nianjian*, no. 3 (1927–8), pp. 80–2.

Fullerton, W. Y. and C. E. Wilson, *New China: A story of modern travel*, London: Morgan and Scott, 1910.

Galle, P. E., *Shanghai au point de vue médical: Contributions à la climatologie médicale*, Paris: André Delahaye, 1875.

Gamble, Sidney D., *How Chinese families live in Peiping*, New York: Funk and Wagnalls, 1933.

'Gedi jinyan jindu baogao' (Report on narcotics suppression), *Judu yuekan*, no. 23 (July 1928), p. 22.

'Gesheng jianli sifa gexian zhengfu chahuo mazui dupin shuliang tongji' (Statistics on narcotics confiscated by local authorities in Shanxi), *Zhongguo yanhuo nianjian*, no. 3 (1927–8), p. 21.

Giles, Herbert, *Some truths about opium*, Cambridge: Heffer, 1923.

'Great Britain and the opium traffic in China', *China Medical Journal*, 34, no. 1 (Jan. 1920), pp. 68–70.

Greig, James A., 'Notes on a few instructive cases', *Chinese Medical Missionary Journal*, 8, no. 4 (Dec. 1894), pp. 173–6.

Gu Xueqiu, *Yapian* (Opium), Shanghai: Shangwu yinshuguan, 1936.

'Guangzhou yanshi shumiao' (A sketch of the opium market in Canton), *Judu yuekan*, no. 90 (Aug. 1935), p. 2.

Guomindang zhongyang zhixing weiyuanhui (ed.), *Jinyan xuanchuan zhuankan* (Special publication on opium prohibition), Nanjing: Zhongguo Guomindang zhongyang zhixing weiyuanhui, 1929.

'Guonei zhi hongwan dupin' (The red pill in China), *Judu yuekan*, no. 82 (Dec. 1934), pp. 19–25.

Guo Songtao, *Guo Songtao riji* (The diaries of Guo Songtao), Changsha: Hunan renmin chubanshe, 1982.

Haipu, *Zhushe zhiliao baofa* (Treasure raft of injected treatments), Shanghai: Haipu zhiyaochang, 1930.

Hahn, Emily, *Times and places*, New York: Thomas Cromwell, 1970.

'Haiguan chahuo wairen siyun mazuipin laihua tongji' (Statistics on foreign nationals smuggling narcotics into China), *Zhongguo yanhuo nianjian*, no. 3 (1927–8), pp. 32–44.

'Hairen tingwen zhi Wuxi hongwan jiguan' (Terrifying facts about the red pill business in Wuxi), *Judu yuekan*, no. 53 (Feb. 1932), p. 38.

'Hangzhou tongxun: Qingmo Hangzhou' (Correspondence from Hangzhou: Hangzhou during the late Qing), *Judu yuekan*, no. 98 (April 1936), pp. 6–9.

'Harbin zhi duyao shijie' (Harbin's drug world), *Judu yuekan*, 37 (March 1930), p. 47.

Hart, Robert, *China Imperial Maritime Customs: II. Special Series: No. 4 Opium*, Shanghai: State Department of the Inspectorate General, 1881.

Haslewood, W. and W. Mordey, *History and medical treatment of cholera, as it appeared in Sunderland in 1831*, London: Longmans, 1832.

'Hebei', *Zhongguo yanhuo nianjian*, 3 (1927–8), p. 63.

'Hebei jianyu' (Hebei prisons), *Judu yuekan*, no. 91 (Sept. 1935), p. 12.

'Heihua zhi Shanxi' (Narcotics in Shanxi), *Judu yuekan*, no. 75 (April 1934), pp. 6–7.

'Heroin', *China Medical Missionary Journal*, 15, no. 1 (Jan. 1901), p. 31.

'Heroin in form of floor polish', *North China Herald*, 14 Sept. 1929, p. 402.

'Heroin in sordid demi-monde', *North China Herald*, 24 June 1936.

'Heroin injection horrors', *North China Herald*, 8 July 1936, p. 82.

'Heroin traffic flourishing', *North China Herald*, 14 April 1937, p. 81.

'Hongwan baiwan jindan' (Red pills, white pills and golden elixir), *Judu yuekan*, no. 22 (1928), p. 28.

Hosie, Alexander, *Three years in western China: A narrative of three journeys in Ssuch'uan, Kuei-chow, and Yün-nan*, London: George Philip, 1890.

'Hospital gives opium addicts new start', *North China Herald*, 5 Aug. 1936, p. 251.

'Hospital reports', *China Medical Missionary Journal*, 19, no. 3 (May 1905), pp. 122–3.

Hou Guangdi, 'Jieyan jingyan tan' (Discussion of an experiment in detoxification), *Zhonghua yixue zazhi*, 14, no. 3 (June 1928), pp. 21–3.

'Hubei', *Zhongguo yanhuo nianjian*, no. 3 (1927–8), p. 73.

Huang Guanxiu, *Bencao qiuzhen* (Authentic materia medica), orig. 1769, Shanghai: Shanghai kexue jishu chubanshe, 1959.

Huang Shujing, *Taihai shichai lu* (Journal of a mission to Taiwan), orig. 1736, Shanghai: Shangwu yinshuguan, 1935.

Hughes, Richard, *Foreign devil: Thirty years of reporting from the Far East*, London: Deutsch, 1972.

Huizenga, Lee S., 'Autogenous serum treatment for opium addicts', *Chinese Medical Journal*, 48, no. 8 (Aug. 1934), pp. 741–4.

———, 'Autogenous serum treatment for opium addicts', *Chinese Medical Journal*, 49, no. 7 (July 1935), pp. 719–21.

'Illicit traffic in opium', *China Medical Journal*, 33, no. 1 (Jan. 1919), pp. 51–2.

'Imports of caffeine into China', *China Medical Journal*, 41, no. 1 (Jan. 1927), p. 99.

'The indiscriminate selling of drugs in China', *China Medical Journal*, 28, no. 4 (July 1914), p. 287.

International Anti-Opium Association, *The war against opium*, Tianjin: Tientsin Press, 1922.

'The International Opium Convention', *China Medical Journal*, 26, no. 3 (May 1912), pp. 178–80.

'Japan and the opium trade in China', *China Medical Journal*, 33, no. 5 (Sept. 1919), p. 515.

'Jinan zhi baiwan wei yapian zhi jindi' (White pills from south of Henan compete with opium), *Judu yuekan*, no. 44 (Oct. 1931), pp. 21–6.

'Jizhong hanyou duzhi de yaopin' (Various medicines containing narcotics), *Judu yuekan*, 50 (Dec. 1931), pp. 48–50.

Jiang Jieshi, *China's destiny*, London: Dobson, 1947.

'Jiangsu' (Jiangsu), *Zhongguo yanhuo nianjian*, 3 (1927–8), p. 78.

Jiangsu sheng minzhengting (ed.), *Jiangsu sheng jinyan gaikuang* (Survey of drug repression in Jiangsu province), Nanjing: Jiangsu sheng minzhengting, 1936.

Jiang Ziyu (ed.), *Zhushefa ji zhusheyao* (Injection methods and injected medications), Xinhua: Xinan yixue shudian, 1941.

'Jiaodong yuanxian dupin liuxing' (The spread of narcotics in counties along the Jiaodong peninsula), *Judu yuekan*, no. 73 (Feb. 1934), p. 25.

'Jieyan zhuanhao' (Special edition on addiction treatment), *Judu yuekan*, no. 84 (Feb. 1935).

'Jinshi jieyansuo yipie' (A glance at the detoxification centre in Tianjin), *Judu yuekan*, no. 87 (May 1935), p. 16.

Jinyan tekan (Special issue on opium prohibition), Chongqing: Neizhengbu jinyan weiyuanhui, 1939.

Jinyan weiyuanhui tongjishi (ed.), *Quanguo ge shengshixian jieyan yiyuan yilan* (Overview of detoxification centres in the various provinces, cities and counties), Nanjing: Jinyan weiyuanhui tongjishi, 1935.

'Jinyan weiyuan zonghui de tonggao' (Public announcement by the National Opium Suppression Commission), *Judu yuekan*, no. 99 (May 1936), p. 22.

Jöel, Ernst and Fränkel, F., *Der Cocainismus. Ein Beitrag zur Geschichte und Psychopathologie der Rauschgifte*, Berlin: Justus Springer, 1924.

Johnson, Wingate M., 'Tobacco smoking', *China Medical Journal*, 43, no. 11 (Nov. 1929), p. 1184.

'Jukao suppresses opium', *North China Herald*, 5 Dec. 1934, p. 370.

'Judu de di sandao fangxian' (The third problem concerning opium prohibition), *Judu yuekan*, no. 57 (June 1932), pp. 34–5.

Engelbert D. Kaempfer, *Amoenitatum exoticarum: politico-physico-medicarum—quibus continentur variae relationes, observationes, et descriptiones. Rerum persicarum et ulterioris asiae multa attentione in peregrationibus per universum orientem, collectae ab auctore Engelberto Kaempfero*, Lemgo (Lippe): Heinrich Wilhelm Meyer, 1712.

Kequan, 'Gailiang fengsu lun' (On reforming popular customs), *Dongfang zazhi*, 1, no. 8 (Aug. 1904), pp. 153–8.

Ke Quanshou and Chen Jinfang, 'Badaweiya jieyan xinfa' (Clinical reports on new opium cure methods), *Judu yuekan*, no. 41 (July 1930), pp. 53–7.

Kwa Tjoan Sioe and Tan Kim Hong, 'The mass treatment of drug addiction by the Modinos' phlycten method' in Phya Damrong Baedyagun and Luang Suvejj Subhakich (eds), *Transactions of the eighth congress of the Far Eastern Association of Tropical Medicine*, Bangkok Times Press, 1931, pp. 53–64.

————, 'Opiumontwenningskuren met blaarserum', *Geneeskundig Tijdschrift voor Nederlandsch-Indië*, vol. 79 (1931), pp. 138–51.

Lamson, Herbert D., *Social pathology in China: A source book for the study of problems of livelihood, health, and the family*, Shanghai: The Commercial Press, 1935.

Lan Dingyuan, *Luzhou chuji* (First impressions of Taiwan), orig. 1722, in *Siku quanshu* (Complete library of the four treasuries), Shanghai: Shanghai guji chubanshe, 1987.

Lang Xiaocang, *Duhuo jian* (Historical facts on the opium evil), Beijing: Guonan zhuanbaoshe, 1934.

Lauze, Jean, *Contribution à l'étude de l'autosérothérapie de l'ascite*, Montpellier: Imprimerie Générale du Midi, 1911.

'League learns of new drug like cocaine', *New York Herald Tribune*, 24 June 1928.

League of Nations, *International Opium Convention, signed at The Hague, January 23rd, 1912*, Geneva: D'Ambilly, 1923.

Lecomte, Louis, *Nouveaux mémoires sur l'état présent de la Chine*, Paris: Jean Anisson, 1696.

Lee, James S., *The Underworld of the East*, London: Green Magic, 2000.

Legendre, A.-F., *Au Yunnan et dans le massif du Kin-Ho (Mission A.-F. Legendre)*, Paris: Plon 1913.

Legge, James, *Li Chi: Book of rites*, New York: New York University Books, 1967.

Lester Chinese Hospital, *Annual report of the Lester Chinese Hospital*, Shanghai: Lester Chinese Hospital, 1930.

Li Jianhua, *Jianyuxue* (Penology), Shanghai: Zhonghua shuju, 1936.

Li, K. H., 'Public health in Soochow', *Zhonghua yixue zazhi*, 9, no. 2 (June 1923), p. 122–31.

Li Shizhen, *Bencao gangmu* (Materia medica), orig. 1578, Beijing: Renmin weisheng chubanshe, 1957.

Li Ting, *Yixue rumen* (Introduction to medicine), orig. 1575, Tianjin: Tianjin kexue chubanshe, 1999.

Li Wenlan, *Jieyan xinfa* (New methods on treating opium addiction), Guilin: Tongweichu, 1942.

Li Zhiyong (ed.), *Zhang Jingyue yixue quanshu* (The medical treatises of Zhang Jingyue), Beijing: Zhongguo zhongyiyao chubanshe, 1997.

'Liaoning sanjiao didai dupin zhi shikuang' (The situation of narcotic consumption in the triangle region of Liaoning), *Judu yuekan*, 86 (March 1935), p. 21.

Libermann, Henri, *Les fumeurs d'opium en Chine. Étude médicale*, Paris: Victor Rozier, 1862.

Lin Ji, 'Jianyan yanfan yijian' (Opinions on the examination of opium addicts), *Zhonghua yixue zazhi*, 19, no. 3 (June 1933), pp. 362–6.

Lin Yutang, *History of the press and public opinion in China*, Oxford University Press, 1937.

Little, Archibald John, *Through the Yang-tse gorges, or Trade and travel in western China*, London: Sampson Low, 1898.

Little, Mrs Archibald, *Intimate China: The Chinese as I have seen them*, London: Hutchinson, 1899.

Liu Wentai, *Bencao pinhui jingyao* (A choice collection of materia medica), completed in 1505, but only published in 1700, Shanghai: Shangwu yinshuguan, 1936.

Lockhart, William, *The medical missionary in China: A narrative of twenty years' experience*, London: Hurst and Blackett, 1861.

Logan, John, *China old and new*, Hong Kong: South China Morning Post, 1982.

Lu Yu (Francis Ross Carpenter, tr.), *Chajing* (The tea canon), Boston: Little, Brown, 1974.

Luoluo jushi (Zhong Zufen), 'Zhao yinju' (The charm of living in seclusion) in A Ying (ed.), *Yapian zhanzheng wenxue ji* (Collection of literary writings on the Opium War), Beijing: Guji chubanshe, 1957, vol. 2, pp. 645–55.

Luo Yunyan, *Dupin wenti* (The problem of narcotics), Shanghai: Shangwu yinshuguan, 1931.

Lyall, James B., 'Note on the history of opium in India and of the trade in it with China' in Royal Commission on Opium, *Volume VII: Final report of the Royal Commission on Opium; Part II: Historical appendices; together with an index of witnesses and subjects, and a glossary of Indian terms used in the evidence and appendices. Presented to both houses of Parliament by command of Her Majesty*, London: Eyre and Spottiswoode, 1895.

Ma Boying, *Zhongguo yixue wenhua shi* (A history of medical culture in China), Shanghai: Shanghai renmin chubanshe, 1994.

Ma Wen-chao, 'The effect of the lecithin on opium addicts', *China Medical Journal*, 46, no. 5 (May 1932), pp. 806–19.

———, *et al.*, 'A comfortable and spontaneous cure of the opium habit by means of a lecithin diet' in Wu Lien-teh (ed.), *Transactions of the ninth congress of the Far Eastern Association of Tropical Medicine*, Nanjing, 1935, vol. 2, pp. 381–7.

McAll, P. L., 'The opium habit', *China Medical Missionary Journal*, 17, 1 (Jan. 1903), pp. 1–10.

Macculloch, John, *Malaria: an essay on the production and propagation of this poison and on the nature and localities of the places by which it is produced: with an enumeration of the diseases caused by it, and of the means of preventing or diminishing them, both at home and in the naval and military service*, London: Longmans, 1827.

Maitland, Charles T., 'Phosphorus poisoning in match factories in China', *China Journal of Science and Art*, 3, nos 2–3 (Feb. and March 1925), pp. 103–113, 169–78.

'Man executed for drug habit: Heroin addict pays extreme penalty', *North China Herald*, 28 Nov. 1934, p. 330.

Martin, Ludwig, *Aerztliche Erfahrungen über die Malaria der Tropen-Länder*, Berlin: Springer, 1889.

Martin, R. M., *China: Political, commercial, and social*, London: James Madden, 1847.

———, *Opium in China, extracted from 'China: Political, commercial, and social'*, London: James Madden, 1846.

Marx, Karl and Friedrich Engels, *On colonialism*, Moscow: Progress Publishers, 1959.

Maugham, William Somerset, *On a Chinese screen*, London: William Heinemann, 1922.

Medhurst, Walter Henry (junior), *The foreigner in far Cathay*, London: Edward Stanford, 1872.

Mei Gongren, *Wangguo miezhong de yapian yanhuo* (The opium plague leads to racial extinction), Beijing: Minyou shuju, 1935.

Merwin, Samuel, *Drugging a nation: The story of China and the opium curse*, New York: Fleming Revell, 1908.

Modinos, Polys, 'La guérison des toxicomanes par le sérum du vésicatoire', *Revue Pratique des Maladies des Pays Chauds*, vol. 10 (Feb. 1930), pp. 68–77.

————, *Le traitement des toxicomanes par la phlycténothérapie*, Paris, Baillière: 1932.

Morinaka, K., 'Chronic morphine intoxication', *Zhonghua yixue zazhi*, 15, no. 6 (Dec. 1929), pp. 764–94.

Morley, Arthur, 'The opium cure: A plea for gradual withdrawal', *China Medical Missionary Journal*, 4, no. 3 (Sept. 1890), pp. 250–2.

'Morphia evil in Shantung', *North China Herald*, 24 Jan. 1925, p. 137.

'Morphia pill habit in China', *North China Herald*, 31 Jan. 1925, p. 181.

Morrison, G. E., *An Australian in China*, London: Cox, 1895.

Muir, G. S., 'The traffic in morphia: Origin and growth of the trade', *North China Herald*, 24 Dec. 1915, p. 915.

Mumford, R. H., 'Auto-haemotherapy in opium addiction', *Chinese Medical Journal*, 49, no. 9 (Sept. 1935), p. 1061.

'Nanhui mafei chongfan, Shi Fenglou panchu sixing' (Repeat morphine offender Shi Fenglou sentenced to death), *Judu yuekan*, no. 94 (Dec. 1935), pp. 17–18.

Nanjing shi jieyan yiyuan (ed.), *Nanjing shi jieyan yiyuan gongzuo nianbao* (Yearly report of the detoxification hospital in Nanjing), Nanjing: Nanjing shi jieyan yiyuan, 1936.

'Nanking's campaign against opium', *North China Herald*, 19 Dec. 1934, p. 448.

'Nanning yishi Luo Lebin dui yangfen ke duan yapian yanyin fabiao tanhua' (A speech by Luo Lebin concerning the use of goat droppings to cure opium addiction), *Judu yuekan*, no. 92 (Oct. 1935), pp. 18–20.

Narcotic drugs in Hong Kong, Hong Kong: Rotary Club, 1969.

National Anti-Opium Association of China, 'The narcotic situation in China', *Zhonghua yixue zazhi*, 15, no. 2 (April 1929), pp. 270–1.

Neizhengbu, 'Gesheng shi xian chouban qiangmin gongchang banfa' (Regulation concerning the establishment of Citizen-Strengthening Factories in all provinces, cities and counties), *Jinyan tekan*, Chongqing: Neizhengbu, 1939.

Nian Xiyao, *Jiyan liangfang* (A collection of good remedies), [n.p.], 1724.

'Opium addicts help to build roads', *North China Herald*, 26 May 1937, p. 318.

'The opium habit in children', *China Medical Missionary Journal*, 14, no. 1 (Jan. 1900), p. 16.

'Opium in Formosa', *North China Herald*, 28 Feb. 1896, p. 308.

'The opium question', *Shanghai Times*, 9 July 1937.

'Opium restrictions in Shansi: Honest attempt to check evil, but morphia position well-nigh hopeless', *North China Herald*, 21 Feb. 1925, p. 301.

'Opium suicide', *North China Herald*, 16 Oct. 1896.

'Opium suppression: Progress in China', *North China Herald*, 14 Jan. 1910, pp. 270–1.

O'Shaughnessy, William Brooke, *On the preparation of the Indian hemp, or gunjah, (Cannabis Indica), their effects on the animal system in health, and their utility in the treatment of tetanus and other convulsive disorders*, Calcutta: Bishop's College Press, 1839.

Osgood, Elliott J., 'Some experiences with patients breaking opium', *China Medical Missionary Journal*, 17, no. 2 (March 1903).

Otte, J. A., 'Treatment of the opium habit', *China Medical Journal*, 24, no. 4 (July 1910), pp. 237–8.

Park, W. H. (ed.), *Opinions of over 100 physicians on the use of opium in China*, Shanghai: American Presbyterian Mission Press, 1899.

———, 'Opium smoking in China', *China Medical Missionary Journal* 19, no. 3 (May 1905), p. 80.

'Patent medicine law', *Chinese Medical Journal*, 51, no. 1 (Jan. 1937), pp. 99–101.

Peck, A. P., 'The antidotal treatment of the opium habit', *China Medical Missionary Journal*, 3, no. 4 (Dec. 1889), pp. 49–51.

Peiqing, 'Lun Zhongguo shehui zhi xianxiang jiqi zhenxing zhi yaozhi' (The current situation of Chinese society and the key to its restoration), *Dongfang zazhi*, vol. 1, no. 12 (Dec. 1904), pp. 279–80.

'Peking prisoners and freedom', *North China Herald*, 2 Sept. 1930, p. 348.

'Permanganate of potassium in opium-poisoning', *China Medical Missionary Journal*, 10, no. 3 (Sept. 1896), pp. 150–1.

'The pharmaceutical situation in China', *Chinese Medical Journal*, 47, no. 4 (April 1933), p. 405.

Pichon, Louis, *Un voyage au Yunnan*, Paris: Plon, 1893.

'Planters of opium will be shot', *North China Herald*, 20 May 1936, p. 320.

'Police make huge narcotics haul', *North China Herald*, 29 May 1935, p. 338.

'Potassium permanganate as an antidote for morphine', *China Medical Missionary Journal*, 9, no. 2 (June 1895), p. 108.

'Proposed regulations governing patent and proprietary medicines', *China Critic*, 3, no. 21 (May 1930), p. 500; 3, no. 22 (May 1930), p. 522.

Qi Sihe, *Huang Juezi Xu Naiji zouyi hekan* (A combined edition of Huang Juezi and Xu Naiji's memorials), Beijing: Zhonghua shuju, 1959.

'Qianjiang shangyou zhi hongwan' (The red pill in the upper reaches of the Qiantang River), *Judu yuekan*, no. 57 (June 1932), pp. 48–9.

Qiu Xia, 'Malipeng yanshi jishi' (The opium market in Malipeng), *Judu yuekan*, 93 (Nov. 1935), pp. 2–11.

Quanguo jingji weiyuanhui, *Huochai gongye baogaoshu* (Report on the match industry), Nanjing: Quanguo jingji weiyuanhui, 1935.

'Raid on new heroin factory', *North China Herald*, 29 Aug., 1934, p. 313.

Report of the Government of Hong Kong for the calendar year 1928 on the traffic in opium and other dangerous drugs, Hong Kong: Noronha, 1929.

Report of the Government of Hong Kong for the calendar year 1930 on the traffic in opium and other dangerous drugs, Hong Kong: Noronha, 1931.

Report of the Government of Hong Kong for the calendar year 1934 on the traffic in opium and other dangerous drugs, Hong Kong: Noronha, 1935.

Report of the Government of Hong Kong for the calendar year 1937 on the traffic in opium and other dangerous drugs, Hong Kong: Noronha, 1938.

von Richthofen, Ferdinand, *Tagebücher aus China*, Berlin: Reimer, 1907.

'Rigid anti-opium measure: Three years imprisonment or capital punishment', *North China Herald*, 11 March 1936, p. 439.

Roberts, William, 'Anarcotine: A neglected alkaloid of opium', *Chinese Medical Missionary Journal*, 9, no. 4 (Dec. 1895), p. 287–90.

Rocher, Émile, *La province chinoise du Yün-nan*, Paris: Ernest Leroux, 1880.

Rockhill, W. W., *Diary of a journey through Mongolia and Tibet in 1891 and 1892*, Washington: Smithsonian Institution, 1894.

Roe, A. S., *Chance and change in China*, London: Heinemann, 1920.

Rohmer, Joseph, *De l'autosérothérapie en ophthalmologie*, Angers: Grassin, 1913.

Rousset, Léon, *À travers la Chine*, Paris: Hachette, 1886.

Royal Commission on Opium, [Report of the] *Royal Commission on Opium*, London: Eyre and Spottiswoode, 1894–5.

St Luke's Hospital for Chinese, *Annual reports*, Shanghai: St Luke's Hospital for Chinese, 1887–1900.

Schwalbe, C., *Beiträge zur Kenntnis der Malaria-Krankheiten*, Zürich: Meyer and Zeller, 1869.

'Shandong', *Zhongguo yanhuo nianjian*, no. 3 (1927–8), pp. 64–5.

Shanghai General Hospital, *Report of the Shanghai General Hospital*, Shanghai General Hospital, 1934.

'Shanghai gonggong zujie zhuhuo yanfan zhi yanjiu' (A study on the drug criminals in the Shanghai International Settlement), *Judu yuekan*, no. 54 (April 1932), pp. 10–14.

'Shanghai shili ge jieyan yiyuan zhuyuan guize' (Regulations for inmates of all Shanghai detoxification hospitals), *Jinyan zhuankan*, Shanghai, 1935.

Shanghai shili hubei jieyan yiyuan (ed.), *Shanghai shili hubei jieyan yiyuan nianbao* (Yearly report of the Zhabei anti-opium hospital), Shanghai: Shanghai shili hubei jieyan yiyuan, 1935.

Shanghai shizhengfu shehuiju, *Shanghai shi gongren shenghuo chengdu* (The living standards of workers in Shanghai), Shanghai: Shanghai shizhengfu shehuiju, 1934.

'Shanghai zhi da mafei zhenzhe' (Shanghai's morphine injections), *Judu yuekan*, no. 40 (June 1930), p. 38.

'Shijie mazui wenti toushi' (A study on the narcotic problem worldwide), *Judu yuekan*, no. 91 (Sept. 1935), pp. 41–2.

Shrubshall, William W., 'Cocaine as an anaesthetic', *China Medical Missionary Journal*, 4 (Dec. 1890), pp. 259–60.

Shushan, 'Yapian yu zuojia' (Opium and writers), *Lunyu banyuekan*, no. 30 (Dec. 1933), pp. 277–9.

'Sian's anti-opium campaign: Nine narcotics vendors executed in public', *North China Herald*, 13 May 1936, p. 273.

'Sichuan sheng jinyan xize' (Opium suppression regulations of Sichuan in detail), *Zhengfu gongbao*, 8 Feb. 1915, no. 989.

Sichuan sishi niandai jinzheng gaikuang (An overall view of the anti-opium policy in Sichuan in the 1940s), Chengdu: Sichuan sheng zhengfu jinyan shanhou dulichu, 1942.

Sifa xingzhengbu (ed.), *Sifa tongji (1929 niandu)* (Judicial statistics: 1929), Nanjing: Sifa xingzhengbu, 1931.

Sifa xingzhengbu (ed.), *Sifa tongji (1931 niandu)* (Judicial statistics: 1931), Nanjing: Sifa xingzhengbu, 1934.

'Smokers of white drug', *North China Daily News*, 23 May 1936, p. 9.

Soubigou, Xavier, *Contribution à l'étude du traitement de la tuberculose par une méthode d'autosérothérapie*, Bordeaux: Imprimerie de l'Académie et des Facultés, 1930. 'The spread of morphia', *North China Herald*, 25 April 1900, pp. 725–6.

Stanley, Arthur, *Health department annual report*, Shanghai Municipal Council, 1902.

Staunton, George, *An historical account of the embassy to the emperor of China undertaken by order of the king of Great Britain*, London: Stockdale, 1797.

Steifensand, C. A., *Das Malaria-Siechthum in den niederrheinischen Landen. Ein Versuch in der medizinischen Geographie*, Crefeld: Funcke and Müller, 1848.

———, *Die asiatische Cholera auf der Grundlage des Malaria-Siechthums*, Crefeld: Funcke and Müller, 1848.

Stuart, G. A., *Chinese materia medica*, Taipei: Southern Materials Center, 1987.

Su Song, *Bencao tujing* (Illustrated materia medica), orig. 1062, Hefei: Anhui kexue jishu chubanshe, 1994.

Su Zhe, *Su Zhe ji* (A collection of Su Zhe's work), orig. twelfth century, Beijing: Zhonghua shuju, 1990.

Sun Jiazhen, *Xiaoxiang haishang fanhuameng* (The vanity fair of Shanghai with portraits), Shanghai: Shangwu yinshuguan, 1915.

———, *Xu Haishang fanhuameng* (Sequel to the vanity fair of Shanghai), Shanghai: Jinbu shuju, 1916.

———, *Tuixinglu biji* (Journal of a hermit), orig. 1925, Shanghai: Shanghai shudian, 1996.

Sun Shu'an, *Yonghua shipin* (A annotated collection of poetry on flowers), Nanchang: Jiangxi renmin chubanshe, 1996.

Sun Youxin, 'Zhiliao feijiehe zhi xiao jingyan' (An experiment in the treatment of tuberculosis), *Shehui yibao*, no. 208 (Feb. 1934), pp. 4706–12.

Sun Zhongshan, *Sun Zhongshan quanji* (The complete works of Sun Yatsen), Beijing: Zhonghua shuju, 1982.

Suvoong, V. P., 'Observations on opium', *China Medical Missionary Journal*, 7, no. 3 (Sept. 1893), pp. 172–9.

Swan, J. M., 'Opium poisoning treated with atropia-sulphate', *China Medical Missionary Journal*, 3, no. 4 (Dec. 1889), pp. 46–48.

'Szechuen political conditions', *North China Herald*, 10 June 1937, p. 453.

Taisheng, 'Mafei yu hongwan' (Morphine and the red pill), *Judu yuekan*, no. 83 (Jan. 1935), pp. 6–7.

T'ang Leang-li, *Reconstruction in China*, Shanghai: China United Press, 1935.

Tao Yunde, *Yapian zhi jinxi* (A history of opium), Shanghai: Yuzhoufeng chubanshe, 1937.

Teeter, J. Nelson, 'A case of cocaine poisoning', *China Medical Missionary Journal*, 9, no. 4 (Dec. 1895), p. 245.

Terry, Charles E. and Mildred Pellens, *The opium problem*, New York: Committee on Drug Addiction, 1928.

Tinling, C.I., *Bits of China: Travel-sketches in the Orient*, New York: Fleming Revell, 1925.

Toussaint, François, *Description du choléra-morbus, suivi de considérations topographiques*, St Nicolas: Trenel, 1835.

'Treatment of cholera', *Zhonghua yixue zazhi*, 13, no. 5 (Oct. 1927) p. 419.

Turner, F. S., *British opium policy and its results to India and China*, London: Low and Marston, 1876.

Turner, John A., *Kwang Tung, or five years in south China*, Hong Kong: Oxford University Press, 1988 (1st edn 1894).

United Nations Office for Drug Control and Crime Prevention, 'The mysterious heroin pills for smoking', *Bulletin on Narcotics*, no. 2 (1953), pp. 49–54.

———, 'History of heroin', *Bulletin on Narcotics*, no. 2 (1953), pp. 3–16.

———, 'The smoking of heroin in Hong Kong', *Bulletin on Narcotics*, no. 3 (1958), pp. 6–7.

Ure, Andrew, *The general malaria of London and the peculiar malaria of Pimlico; investigated, and the means of their economical removal ascertained*, London: William Orr, 1850.

'The use of coffee in the treatment of Asiatic cholera', *China Medical Missionary Journal*, 9, no. 2 (June 1895), p. 155.

Valaer, Peter, 'The red pill, or the opium substitute', *American Journal of Pharmacy*, no. 107 (1935), pp. 199–207.

'The very useful formulae', *China Medical Journal*, 23, no. 6 (Nov. 1909), p. 406.

'Wairen zongdu qingxing zhi yiban' (Facts about drug peddling by foreigners), *Zhongguo yanhuo nianjian*, 3 (1927–8), pp. 47–50.

Wall, Martin, *Clinical observations on the use of opium in low fevers and in the synochus*, Oxford: Clarendon Press, 1786.

Wang Ang, *Bencao beiyao* (Essential materia medica), orig. 1694, Taipei: Shangwu yinshuguan, 1955.

Wang Bingshi, 'Tonghai zhi hongwan du' (The harm of red pills in Nantong and Haimen), *Judu yuekan*, no. 60 (Sept. 1932), pp. 70–1.

Wang Gui, *Taiding yangsheng zhulun* (A treatise on nurturing life), orig. 1338, Jinan: Yuelu shushe, 1996.

Wang Jingming, 'Dupin manyan yu nongcun shehui' (The spread of narcotics and agricultural society), *Judu yuekan*, no. 43 (Sept. 1930), pp. 22–5.

Wang Penggao, 'Yapian texie' (Special feature on opium), *Judu yuekan*, no. 97 (March 1936), pp. 2–17.

Wang Shizhen, *Xiangzu biji* (Travel notes) in *Siku quanshu* (Complete library of the four treasuries), Shanghai: Shanghai guji chubanshe, 1987.

Wang Yanchang, *Wangshi yicun* (Writings of Wang Yanchang), orig. 1871, Hangzhou: Jiangsu kexue jishu chubanshe, 1983.

Wang Yufeng, *Gebing zhushe liaofa daquan* (Encyclopaedia on the hypodermical treatment of various diseases), Shanghai: Xinyi zhensuo, 1926.

Watson, Ernest, *The principal articles of Chinese commerce*, Shanghai: Chinese Maritime Customs, 1930.

'Weidu yanshi pianxia' (A sketch of the opium market in Changchun), *Judu yuekan*, no. 96 (Feb. 1936), pp. 2–4.

Whitney, H. T., 'The medical missionary and the opium habitué', *China Medical Missionary Journal*, 5, no. 2 (June 1891), pp. 86–7.

Wilkinson, G., 'Among the small-tooth comb makers', *Mercy and Truth*, 15, no. 170 (Feb. 1911), pp. 52–4.

Wilson, Thomas, *An enquiry into the origin and intimate nature of malaria*, London: Henry Renshaw, 1858.

Wolf, Eugen, *Meine Wanderungen (I). Im Innern Chinas*, Stuttgart: Deutsche Verlags-Anstalt, 1901.

Wu Liande (Wu Lien-teh) (ed.), *Plague fighter: The autobiography of a modern Chinese physician*, Cambridge: Heffer, 1959.

————, *Transactions of the ninth congress of the Far Eastern Association of Tropical Medicine*, Nanjing, 1935.

————, 'Financing public health in China', *National Medical Journal of China*, 15, 1 (Feb. 1929), p. 51.

————, 'Problem of venereal diseases in China', *China Medical Journal*, 41, no. 1 (Jan. 1927), p. 34.

————, 'Note by Dr. Wu Lien Teh', *China Medical Journal*, 40, no. 12 (Dec. 1926), p. 1248.

————, 'Public health aspects of the narcotic problem', *Zhonghua yixue zazhi*, 11, no. 6 (Dec. 1925), pp. 413–25.

————, 'The latest phase of the narcotic problem', *Zhonghua yixue zazhi*, 6, no. 2 (June 1920), pp. 65–70.

————, 'Two unusual cases of morphinism', *Zhonghua yixue zazhi*, 6, no. 2 (June 1920), pp. 62–3.

————, 'Jinggao mafei zhi weixian' (Warning against the dangers of morphine), *Zhonghua yixue zazhi*, 3, no. 2 (June 1917), pp. 1–6.

————, 'The ancient Chinese on poisoning', *China Medical Journal*, 30, no. 3 (May 1916), pp. 175–178.

Wu Yiluo, *Zhenzhu bencao congxin* (New materia medica), orig. 1757, Shanghai: Shanghai guangyi shuju, 1953.

'Xi'an tongxun' (Correspondance from Xi'an), *Judu yuekan*, no. 90 (Aug. 1935), pp. 17–21.

'Xidufan jiechuhou de shanhou weiti' (Relevant issues following the treatment of addicts), *Jinyan jinian tekan*, Nanjing: Neizhengbu jinyan weiyuanhui, 1935.

'Xisheng' (Sacrifice), *Judu yuekan*, no. 86 (March 1935), p. 17.

Xia Shenchu, *Jieyan zhinan* (Guide to detoxification), Shanghai: Zhenliaoyi baoshe, 1936.

Xiaoliu, 'Xianzi shou', *Judu yuekan*, no. 85 (1935), p. 24.

Xingpai, *Xingpai tezhi yaopinlei shuoming* (Handbook on special pharmaceutical products from Star Brand), Shanghai: Xingpai, 1929.

'Xisheng' (Sacrifice), *Judu yuekan*, no. 86 (March 1935), p. 17.

'Xiuzheng guanli zhusheqi zhushezhen zanxing guize' (Revised regulations on the supervision of hypodermic syringes), *Zhonghua yixue zazhi*, 21, no. 4 (April 1935), pp. 431–2.

Xu Boling, *Yinjingjuan* (The works of Xu Boling) in *Siku quanshu* (Complete library of the four treasuries), Shanghai: Shanghai guji chubanshe, 1987.

Xu Borong, 'Xiangyan yu waishang' (Cigarettes and foreign merchants), *Longmenzhen*, no. 4, 1996, pp. 96–7.

Xu Guozhen, *Yuyao yuanfang* (Prescriptions issued by the Imperial Medicine Bureau), orig. 1267, Beijing: Renmin weisheng chubanshe, 1991.

Xu Hongzu, *Xu Xiake youji* (The travels of Xu Xiake), orig. 1638, Shanghai: Shanghai guji chubanshe, 1980.

Xu Ke, *Qingbai leichao* (Fictitious history of the Qing), Shanghai: Shangwu yinshuguan, 1984.

'Yapian liudu shengfen' (Opium and narcotics in various provinces), *Judu yuekan*, 22 (June 1928), p. 28.

'Yapian zhi hai' (The evil of opium), *Judu yuekan*, no. 80 (Oct. 1934), pp. 23–4.

Yan Fu, *Yan Fu ji* (Collected writings of Yan Fu), Beijing: Zhonghua shujiu, 1986.

'Yanmin bingyuan nianling tongji' (Statistics about various illness as the cause for using opium and users' age), *Judu yuekan*, no. 38 (April 1930), p. 41.

Yü, D. T., 'Nanjing shinei jieyanwan zhi huayan chengji biao' (Results of a chemical analysis of opium treatment pills in Nanjing), *Shehui yibao*, no. 192 (June 1933), pp. 4021–2.

Yu Fengbin, *Huoluan congtan* (Notes on cholera), Shanghai: Yu Fengbin, 1922.

———, 'Yapian yu mafei zhi liudu' (The pernicious influence of opium and morphine), *Zhonghua yixue zazhi*, 7, no. 2 (June 1921), pp. 75–82.

Yu Jiao, *Mengchang zaji* (Notes from a dreamy cabin), Beijing: Wenhua yishu chubanshe, 1988.

Ye Mengzhu, *Yueshi bian* (Collected notes), Shanghai: Shanghai guji chubanshe, 1981.

Yu Yunxiu, 'Liuxingxing huoluan yu Zhongguo jiu yixue' (Cholera epidemics and Chinese traditional medicine), *Zhonghua yixue zazhi*, 29, no. 6 (Dec. 1948), pp. 273–88.

Yu Zhengxie, *Guisi leigao* (Collection of notes), orig. 1884, Shanghai: Shangwu yinshuguan, 1957.

Zhang Changjia, 'Yanhua' (On opium) in A Ying (ed.), *Yapian zhanzheng wenxue ji* (Collection of literary writings on the Opium War), Beijing: Guji chubanshe, 1957, vol. 2, pp. 755–78.

Zhang Chongxi, *Gezhong zhushe liaofa* (Various treatments by injection), Hangzhou: Songjinglou shudian, 1936.

———, *Jieyan diaoyan ji zhiliao* (A diagnosis for opium addiction and its cure), Hangzhou: Songjinglou shudian, 1936.

Zhang Jian, *Zuixin zhushe liaofa* (Newest treatment by injection), Shanghai: Zhonghua shuju, 1925.

Zhang Shitao, 'Jieyan zhi fa' (Detoxification methods), *Yiyao daobao*, 2, no. 5 (March 1936), pp. *zhuan* 11–14.

Zhao Chen, *Jianyuxue* (Penology), Shanghai: Shanghai faxue bianyishe, (1st edn 1931) 1948.

Zhao Xuemin, *Bencao gangmu shiyi* (A supplemented edition to the Materia Medica), orig. 1765, Shanghai: Shangwu yinshuguan, 1954.

'Zhejiang', *Zhongguo yanhuo nianjian*, no. 3 (1927–8), p. 80.

Zhejiang sheng minzhengting (ed.), *Jinyan xiaoce* (A small handbook on opium prohibition), Hangzhou: Zhejiang sheng minzhengting, 1933.

Zheng Qingshan, 'Yapian chengyin zhi yuanli jiqi jiechufa' (The cause of opium craving and its treatment), *Jinyan zhuankan*, 1935, pp. 15–17.

Zhongguo shixue xuehui (ed.), *Yapian zhanzheng* (Historical documents on the Opium War), Shanghai: Shenzhou guoguangshe, 1954.

Zhonghua quanguo jidujiao xiejinhui judu weiyuanhui, *Duji wenda* (Questions and answers on narcotics), Shanghai: Zhonghu guiming judu hui, 1925.

Zhu Di, *Pujifang* (Collection of popular remedies), Harbin: Heilongjiang kexue jishu chubanshe, 1996.

Zhu Mengmei, *Huoluan yufang fa* (Preventive measures against cholera), Shanghai: Shangwu yinshuguan, 1926.

Zhu Peizhang, 'Xing shenjing shuairuo zhi zhiliao' (The treatment of sexual neurasthenia), *Shehui yiyaobao*, 2, no. 5 (June 1934), pp. 39–41.

Zhu Shenjiang, *Zhushe qianshuo* (Introduction to injections), Shanghai: Shangwu yinshuguan, 1933.

Zhu Shijie, *Xiao liuqiu manzhi* (A travel account of Taiwan), orig. 1765, Taipei: Datong shuju, 1960.

Zou Yueru, 'Chi tiaosha zhi hai' (On the harm of *tiaosha*), *Shehui yibao*, no. 122 (July 1930), p. 1078.

SECONDARY SOURCES

Aixinjueluo Yingsheng and Yu Runqi, *Jingcheng jiusu* (Old customs of Beijing), Beijing: Yanshan chubanshe, 1998.

Alatas, S. H., *The myth of the lazy native: A study of the image of the Malays, Filipinos and Javanese from the 16th to the 20th century and its function in the ideology of colonial capitalism*, London: Frank Cass, 1977.

Aoki Yoshio, '"Drinking" tobacco: the customs and aesthetics of smoking in early modern Japan', paper presented at *Beverages in early modern Japan and their international context, 1660s–1920s: A conference organised by the Sainsbury Institute for the Study of Japanese arts and cultures*, London: School of Oriental and African Studies, 9–11 March 2001.

Baum, Dan, *Smoke and mirrors: The war on drugs and the politics of failure*, Boston: Little, Brown, 1997.

Baumler, Alan, *Modern China and opium: A reader*, Michigan: University of Michigan Press, 2001.

————, 'Opium control versus opium suppression: The origins of the 1935 six-year plan to eliminate opium and drugs' in Timothy Brook and Bob T. Wakabayashi (eds), *Opium regimes: China, Britain, and Japan, 1839–1952*, Berkeley: University of California Press, 2000, pp. 270–91.

————, 'Playing with fire: The Nationalist government and opium in China, 1927–1941', doctoral dissertation, University of Illinois, 1997.

Beeching, Jack, *The Chinese Opium Wars*, New York: Harcourt, 1975.

Bello, David, 'Opium in Xinjiang and beyond' in Timothy Brook and Bob T. Wakabayashi (eds), *Opium regimes: China, Britain, and Japan, 1839–1952*, Berkeley: University of California Press, 2000, pp. 127–51.

Benedict, Carol, *Bubonic plague in nineteenth-century China*, Stanford University Press, 1996.

Benn, James, 'Temperance, tracts and teetotallers during the T'ang: Buddhism, alcohol and tea in medieval China', MA dissertation, School of Oriental and African Studies, University of London, 1994.

Virginia Berridge, *Opium and the people: Opiate use and drug control policy in nineteenth and early twentieth century England*, London: Free Association Books, 1999.

Bewley-Taylor, David R., *The United States and international drug control, 1909–1997*, London: Pinter, 1999.

Bianco, Lucien, 'The responses of opium growers to eradication campaigns and the poppy tax, 1907–1949' in Timothy Brook and Bob T. Wakabayashi (eds), *Opium regimes: China, Britain, and Japan, 1839–1952*, Berkeley: University of California Press, 2000, pp. 292–319.

Blunden, Caroline and Mark Elvin (eds), *Cultural atlas of China*, Oxford: Phaidon Press, 1983.

Booth, Martin, *Opium: A history*, London: Pocket Books, 1997.

Brandt, Allan M., *No magic bullet: A social history of venereal disease in the United States since 1880*, Oxford University Press, 1985.

Braudel, Fernand, *The structures of everyday life: Civilisation and capitalism, 15th to 18th century*, New York: Harper and Row, 1979.

Brook, Timothy and Bob T. Wakabayashi (eds), *Opium regimes: China, Britain, and Japan, 1839–1952*, Berkeley: University of California Press, 2000.

Boyes, Jon and S. Piraban, *Opium fields*, Bangkok: Silkworm Books, 1991.

Braun, Stephen, *Buzz: The science and lore of alcohol and caffeine*, New York: Oxford University Press, 1996.

Brown, J. B., 'Politics of the poppy: The Society for the Suppression of the Opium Trade, 1874–1916', *Journal of Contemporary History*, 8, no. 3 (July 1973), pp. 97–111.

Burnett, John, *Liquid pleasures: A social history of drinks in modern Britain*, London: Routledge, 1999.

Paul Butel, *Histoire du thé*, Paris: Éditions Desjonquères, 1989.

———, *L'opium, histoire d'une fascination*, Paris: Perrin, 1995.

Butler, Anthony R., 'A treatment for cardiovascular dysfunction in a Dunhuang medical manuscript', unpublished paper.

Camporesi, Piero, *Bread of dreams: Food and fantasy in early modern Europe*, Oxford: Polity Press, 1989.

Chang T'ien-tse, *Sino-Portuguese trade from 1514 to 1644: A synthesis of Portuguese and Chinese sources*, Leiden: E. J. Brill, 1934.

Chaudhuri, K. N., *The trading world of Asia and the English East India Company, 1660–1760*, Cambridge University Press, 1978.

Chen Songfeng, *Yanshi wenjian lu* (Stories on tobacco), Beijing: Zhongguo shangye chubanshe, 1989.

Chen Zhen (ed.), *Zhongguo jindai gongye shi ziliao* (Primary sources on the history of modern industry in China), Beijing: Sanlian shudian, 1961.

Ch'en Yung-fa, 'The blooming poppy under the red sun: The Yan'an way and the opium trade' in Tony Saich and Hans van de Ven (eds), *New perspectives on the Chinese communist revolution*, New York: Sharpe, 1995, pp. 263–98.

Cheng, Iris, Virginia L. Ernster and He Guanqing, 'Tobacco smoking among 847 residents of east Beijing, People's Republic of China', *Asia-Pacific Journal of Public Health*, 4 nos 2–3, 1990, pp. 156–163.

Cheong, Weng Eang, *The Hong merchants of Canton: Chinese merchants in Sino-Western trade*, Richmond: Curzon Press, 1997.

Chouvy, Pierre-Arnaud and Joël Meissonnier, *Yaa Baa. Production, trafic et consommation de méthamphétamine en Asie du Sud-Est continentale*, Paris: L'Harmattan, 2002.

Ch'ü T'ung-tsu, *Local government in China under the Ch'ing*, Stanford University Press, 1969.

Clarence-Smith, William Gervase, *Cocoa and chocolate, 1765–1914*, London: Routledge, 2000.

Clunas, Craig, *Superfluous things: Material culture and social status in early modern China*, Cambridge: Polity Press, 1991.

Cochran, Sherman, 'Marketing medicine and advertising dreams' in Yeh Wen-hsin (ed.), *Becoming Chinese: Passages to modernity and beyond*, Berkeley: University of California Press, 2000.

———, 'Transnational origins of advertising in early twentieth-century China' in Sherman Cochran (ed.), *Inventing Nanjing Road: Commercial culture in Shanghai, 1900–1945*, Ithaca, NY: Cornell University East Asia Programme, 1999, pp. 37–58.

————, *Big business in China: Sino-foreign rivalry in the cigarette industry, 1890–1930*, Cambridge, MA: Harvard University Press, 1980.

Connors, Richard, 'Opium and imperial expansion: The East India Company in eighteenth century Asia' in Stephen Taylor, Richard Connors and Clyve Jones (eds), *Hanoverian Britain and empire: Essays in memory of Philip Lawson*, Suffolk: Boydell Press, 1998, pp. 248–66.

Courtwright, David. T., *Forces of habit: Drugs and the making of the modern world*, Cambridge, MA: Harvard University Press, 2001.

————, 'The rise and fall of cocaine in the United States' in Jordan Goodman, Paul E. Lovejoy and Andrew Sheratt (eds), *Consuming habits: Drugs in history and anthropology*, London: Routledge, 1995, pp. 206–28.

Christie, Nils and Bruun, Kettil, *Den goda fienden. Narkotikapolitik i Norden* (The good enemy: Narcotics policy in Scandinavia), Kristianstad: Rabén and Sjögren, 1985.

Cotterell, Yong Yap, *The Chinese kitchen: A traditional approach to eating*, London: Weidenfeld and Nicolson, 1986.

Davenport-Hines, Richard, *The pursuit of oblivion: A social history of drugs*, London: Phoenix Press, 2002.

Davies, John B., *The myth of addiction*, Amsterdam: Harwood, 1992.

de Boer, Gerda Theuns, 'Bubonic plague in Bombay, 1896–1914', *International Institute of Asian Studies Newsletter*, 25 (July 2001), p. 20.

de Liedekerke, Arnould, *La Belle Époque de l'opium*, Paris: Éditions de la Différence, 2001.

Deng Tietao, *Zhongyi jindai shi* (A history of Chinese medicine in modern China), Canton: Guangdong gaodeng jiaoyu chubanshe, 1999.

Dermigny, Louis, *La Chine et l'Occident. Le commerce à Canton au XVIIIe siècle, 1719–1833*, Paris: S.E.V.P.E.N., 1964.

Dikötter, Frank, *Crime, punishment and the prison in modern China*, London: Hurst; New York: Columbia University Press, 2002.

————, *Imperfect conceptions: Medical knowledge, birth defects and eugenics in China*, London: Hurst, New York: Columbia University Press, 1998.

————, 'A history of sexually transmitted diseases in China' in Scott Bamber, Milton Lewis and Michael Waugh (eds), *Sex, disease, and society: A comparative history of sexually transmitted diseases and HIV/AIDS in Asia and the Pacific*, Westport, CT: Greenwood Press, 1997, pp. 67–84.

————, *Sex, culture and modernity in China: Medical science and the construction of sexual identities in the early republican period*, London: Hurst; Honolulu: University of Hawai'i Press, 1995.

————, *The discourse of race in modern China*, London: Hurst; Stanford University Press, 1992.

Dillon, Patrick, *The much-lamented death of Madam Geneva: The eighteenth-century gin craze*, London: Review, 2002.

Dong Yiming, 'Étude sur le problème de l'opium dans la région du sud-ouest de la Chine (pendant les années 1920 et 1930)', doctoral dissertation, Paris: École des Hautes Études en Sciences Sociales, 1997.

Drucker, Ernest, 'The injection century: Massive unsterile injections and the emergence of human pathogens', unpublished paper, London School of Hygiene and Tropical Medicine, University of London, 20 March 2002.

Elvin, Mark, *The retreat of the elephants: An environmental history of China*, New Haven: Yale University Press, 2004.

Erickson, Patricia G., *The steel drug*, Toronto: Lexington Book, 1987.

Escohotado, Antonio, *Historia de las drogas*, Madrid: Alianza Editorial, 1989.

Evans, J. C., *Tea in China: The history of China's national drink*, New York: Greenwood Press, 1992.

Fairbank, John K., 'The creation of the treaty system' in Denis Twitchett and John K. Fairbank (eds), *The Cambridge history of China*, Cambridge University Press, 1978, vol. 10, part 1, pp. 213–63.

Fay, Peter Ward, *The Opium War, 1840–1842: Barbarians in the Celestial Empire in the early part of the nineteenth century and the war by which they forced her gates ajar*, New York: Norton, 1976.

Feng Erkang and Chang Jianhua, *Qingren shehui shenghuo* (Everyday life in the Qing dynasty), Shenyang: Shenyang chubanshe, 2002.

Feng Erkang, Xu Shengheng and Yan Aimin, *Yongzheng huangdi quanzhuan* (Complete biography of the Yongzheng emperor), Beijing: Xueyuan chubanshe, 1994.

Feng Zhicheng, *Lao Chengdu* (Old Chengdu), Chengdu: Sichuan wenyi chubanshe, 1999.

Filshie, Jacqueline and Adrian White (eds), *Medical acupuncture*, Edinburgh and London: Churchill Livingstone, 1998.

Fletcher, Joseph, 'The heyday of the Ch'ing order in Mongolia, Sinkiang and Tibet' in D. Twitchett and J. K. Fairbank (eds), *The Cambridge history of China*, Cambridge University Press, 1978, vol. 10, part 1, pp. 375–85.

Friman, H. Richard, 'Germany and the transformations of cocaine, 1880–1920' in Paul Gootenberg (ed.), *Cocaine: Global histories*, London: Routledge, 1999, pp. 83–104.

Gardella, Robert, *Harvesting mountains: Fujian and the China tea trade, 1757–1937*, Berkeley: University of California Press, 1994.

von Glahn, Richard, *Fountain of fortune: Money and monetary policy in China, 1000–1700*, Berkeley: University of California Press, 1996.

Golas, Peter J., 'The Sung wine monopoly', doctoral dissertation, Harvard University, 1972.

Goldberg, Ted, *Demystifying drugs: A psychosocial perspective*, Basingstoke: Macmillan, 1999.

Golvers, Noël, *François de Rougemont, S. J., missionary in Ch'ang-shu (Chiang-nan): A study of the Account Book (1674–1676) and the Elogium*, Leuven: Leuven University Press, 1999.

Gong Yingyan, *Yapian de chuanbo yu duihua yapian maoyi* (The spread of opium and the opium trade with China), Beijing: Dongfang chubanshe, 1999.

Goodman, Jordan, Paul E. Lovejoy and Andrew Sherratt (eds), *Consuming habits: Drugs in history and anthropology*, London: Routledge, 1995.

Goodman, Jordan, *Tobacco in history: The cultures of dependence*, London: Routledge, 1993.

Goodrich, L. Carrington, 'Early prohibitions of tobacco in China and Man-churia', *Journal of the American Oriental Society*, no. 58 (1938), pp. 638–57.

Gootenberg, Paul (ed.), *Cocaine: Global histories*, London: Routledge, 1999.

Gossop, Michael, *Living with drugs*, London: Ashgate, 2000.

Gray, Jack, *Rebellions and revolutions: China from the 1800s to the 1980s*, Oxford University Press, 1990.

Greenberg, Michael, *British trade and the opening of China 1800–42*, Cambridge University Press, 1951.

Groeneveldt, W. P., 'De eerste bemoeiingen om den handel in China en de vestiging in de Pescadores (1601–1624)', *De Nederlanders in China*, The Hague: Martinus Nijhoff, 1898.

Hanes, W. T. and Frank Sanello, *The Opium Wars: The addiction of one empire and the corruption of another*, Naperville, IL: Sourcebooks, 2002.

Hanusz, Mark, *Kretek: The culture and heritage of Indonesia's clove cigarettes*, Singapore: Equinox, 2000.

He Lingxiu, *Qingshi luncong* (Essays on Qing history), Beijing: Hebei jiaoyu chubanshe, 1999.

He Yumin and Zhang Ye, *Zouchu wushu conglin de Zhongyi* (Magic and Chinese medicine), Shanghai: Wenhui chubanshe, 1994.

Henriot, Christian, *Prostitution and sexuality in Shanghai: A social history, 1849–1949*, Cambridge University Press, 2001.

Ho, Virgil K. Y., 'The city of contrasts: Perceptions and realities in Canton in the 1920s and 1930s', doctoral dissertation, Oxford University, 1995.

Howard, P. W., 'Opium suppression in Qing China: Responses to a social problem, 1729–1906', doctoral dissertation, University of Pennsylvania, 1998.

Hsü, Francis L. K., *Religion, science and human crises: A study of China in transition and its implications for the West*, London: Routledge, 1952.

Huang Kewu, 'Cong *Shenbao* yiyao guangbao kan minchu de yiliao wenhua yu shehui shenghuo, 1912–1926' (Medical culture and social life in the early republican era as seen through the medical advertisements of the

Shenbao, 1912–1926), *Zhongyang yanjiuyuan jindaishi yanjiusuo jikan*, 17, no. 2 (Dec. 1988), 141–94.

———, 'Yan Fu de yixing qingyuan yu sixiang jingjie' (Yan Fu's emotional and intellectual life) in Huang Kewu (ed.), *Sixiang, zhengquan yu shehui liliang* (Knowledge, politics and social power), Taipei: Zhongyang yanjiuyuan jindaishi yanjiusuo, 2002, pp. 97–136.

Hubert, Annie and Philippe Le Faillier (eds), *Opiums: Les plantes du plaisir et de la convivialité en Asie*, Paris: L'Harmattan, 2000.

Inglis, Brian, *The Opium War*, London: Hodder and Stoughton, 1976.

Jay, Mike, *Artificial paradises: A drugs reader*, London: Penguin, 1999.

———, *Emperors of dreams: Drugs in the nineteenth century*, Sawtry: Daedalus, 2002.

Jennings, J. M., 'The forgotten plague: Opium and narcotics in Korea under Japanese rule, 1910–1945', *Modern Asian Studies*, 29, no. 4 (Oct. 1995), pp. 795–815.

Jiao Yang, 'Yaodong "chutu" yapiangao' (Opium paste unearthed from cave), *Chengdu shangbao*, 12 Dec. 2001, special supplement, p. B9.

Jonnes, Jill, *Hep-cats, narcs, and pipe dreams*, Baltimore: The Johns Hopkins University Press, 1996.

Julien, Robert M., *A primer of drug action*, New York: Freeman, 1996.

Karch, Steven B., 'Japan and the cocaine industry of Southeast Asia, 1864–1944' in Paul Gootenberg (ed.), *Cocaine: Global histories*, London: Routledge, 1999, pp. 146–61.

Katz, Paul R., *Demon hordes and burning boats: The cult of Marshal Wen in late imperial Chekiang*, New York: State University of New York Press, 1995.

Kiernan, Victor G., *Tobacco: A history*, London: Hutchinson Radius, 1991.

Kohn, Marek, *Narcomania: On heroin*, London: Faber and Faber, 1987.

Kuhn, Cynthia, Scott Swatzwelder and Wilkie Wilson, *Buzzed: The straight facts about the most used and abused drugs from alcohol to ecstacy*, New York: Norton, 1998.

Lai Shuqing (ed.), *Guomin zhengfu liunian jinyan jihua ji qi chengxiao, 1935–40* (The nationalist government's Six-Year Opium Suppression Plan and its results), Taipei: Guoshiguan, 1986.

Laidler, Karen Joe, Jeffrey Day and David Hodson, 'A study of the psychoactive substance abuse problem in Hong Kong', Hong Kong: Centre for Criminology, 2002.

Lao Pin, *Mingjia bixia de yanjiuchadian* (Famous people talking about tobacco, alcohol, tea and dim sum), Beijing: Zhongguo guoji guangbo chubanshe, 1994.

Lee, Peter, *The big smoke: The Chinese art and craft of opium*, Bangkok: Lamplight Books, 1999.

Lenson, David, *On drugs*, Minneapolis: University of Minnesota Press, 1995.

Li Bingxin, Xu Junyuan and Shi Yuxin (eds), *Jindai Zhongguo yandu xiezhen* (The real story of narcotics in modern China), Shijiazhuang: Hebei renmin chubanshe, 1997.

Li, Hui-Lin, 'The origin and use of cannabis in Eastern Asia: Their linguistic-cultural implications' in Vera Rubin (ed.), *Cannabis and culture*, The Hague: Mouton, 1975, pp. 51–62.

Li Ling, *Zhongguo fangshu xukao* (Supplementary studies on the esoteric arts in China), Beijing: Dongfang chubanshe, 2000.

Liao Jiwei and Bai Jingchun, 'Yapian zai Chengdu' (Opium in Chengdu) in Li Bingxin, Xu Junyuan and Shi Yuxin (eds), *Jindai Zhongguo yandu xiezhen* (The real story of narcotics in modern China), Shijiazhuang: Hebei renmin chubanshe, 1997, vol. 2, p. 111.

Lin Manhong, *Zhangnao yu wan Qing Taiwan* (Tea, sugar, sandalwood and late Qing Taiwan), Taipei: Taiwan yinhang jingji yanjiu shi, 1996.

————, 'Qingmo shehui liuxing xishi yapian yanjiu: Gongjimian zhi fenxi (1773–1906)' (A study of opium consumption in late Qing society: A supply-side analysis, 1773–1906), doctoral dissertation, Taipei: National Normal University, 1985.

Lodwick, Kathleen S., *Crusaders against opium: Protestant missionaries in China, 1874–1917*, Lexington: The University Press of Kentucky, 1996.

Lu Dong, Xi Ma and Thann, François, *Les maux épidémiques dans l'empire chinois*, Paris: L'Harmattan, 1995.

Lu Geting, 'Chunxilu shang de "xiaojinku"' (Money spending holes on Chunxi Street) in Feng Zhicheng, *Lao Chengdu* (Old Chengdu), Chengdu: Sichuan wenyi chubanshe, 1999, pp. 133–5.

Lu Gwei-djen and Joseph Needham, *Celestial lancets: A history and rationale of acupuncture and moxa*, London: Routledge Curzon, 2002.

Ma Mozhen (ed.), *Zhongguo jindu shi ziliao* (Archival materials on the history of drug prohibition in China), Tianjin: Tianjin renmin chubanshe, 1998.

Ma Weigang (ed.), *Jinchang jindu* (Eliminate prostitution and eradicate opium), Beijing: Jingguan jiaoyu chubanshe, 1993.

McAllister, William B., *Drug diplomacy in the twentieth century: An international history*, London: Routledge, 2000.

McNeill, W. H., *Plagues and peoples*, London: Penguin, 1979.

Madancy, Joyce, 'Revolution, religion and the poppy: Opium and the rebellion of the "Sixteenth Emperor" in early republican Fujian', *Republican China*, 21, no. 1 (Nov. 1995), pp. 1–41.

Madge, Tim, *White mischief: A cultural history of cocaine*, Edinburgh: Mainstream Publishing, 2001.

Marshall, Jonathan, 'Opium and the politics of gangsterism in nationalist China, 1927–1945', *Bulletin of Concerned Scholars*, 8, no. 3 (July 1976), pp. 19–48.

Martin, Brian G., *The Shanghai Green Gang: Politics and organized crime, 1919–1937*, Berkeley: University of California Press, 1996.

Maveety, Patrick J., *Opium pipes, prints and paraphernalia*, Stanford University Museum of Art, 1979.

Meeker, Oden, *The little world of Laos*, New York: Scribner's, 1959.

Miller, Richard L., *The case for legalizing drugs*, New York: Praeger, 1991.

Milligan, Barry, *Pleasures and pains: Opium and the Orient in nineteenth-century British culture*, Charlottesville: University Press of Virginia, 1995.

Mills, James H., *Madness, cannabis and colonialism*, St Martin's Press, 2000.

Mintz, Sidney, *Caribbean transformations*, New York: Columbia University Press, 1974.

———, *Sweetness and power: The place of sugar in modern history*, Harmondsworth: Penguin Books, 1985.

Moore, Robert I., *The formation of a persecuting society: Power and deviance in Western Europe, 950–1250*, Oxford: Blackwell, 1987.

Morse, Hosea Ballou, *The chronicles of the East India Company: Trading to China 1635–1834*, Oxford: Clarendon Press, 1926.

———, *International relations of the Chinese empire*, London: Longmans, 1910.

———, *The trade and administration of the Chinese empire*, London: Longmans, 1908.

Murdock, C. G., *Domesticating drink: Women, men, and alcohol in America, 1870–1940*, Baltimore: Johns Hopkins University Press, 1998.

Murray, Dian H., *Pirates of the South China Coast, 1790–1810*, Stanford University Press, 1987.

Musto, David F., *The American disease: Origins of narcotic control*, Oxford University Press, 1999.

Narcotic drugs in Hong Kong, Hong Kong: Rotary Club, 1969.

Neale, Joanna, *Drug users in society*, Basingstoke: Palgrave Macmillan, 2001.

Newman, Richard K., 'Opium smoking in late imperial China: A reconsideration', *Modern Asian Studies*, 29 (Oct. 1995), pp. 765–94.

———, 'Opium as a medicine in nineteenth-century India' in Sanjoy Bhattacharya and Biswamoy Pati (eds), *Imperialism, medicine and South Asia (1800–1950)*, Hyderabad: Orient Longman, 2004.

Ning Wenguang, 'Ningshu jinzheng jianwen' (Prohibition policy in Ningshu) in Li Bingxin, Xu Junyuan and Shi Yuxin (eds), *Jindai Zhongguo yandu xiezhen* (The real story of narcotics in modern China), Shijiazhuang: Hebei renmin chubanshe, 1997.

Nguyen Te Duc, *Le livre de l'opium*, Paris: Éditions de la Maisnie, 1979.

Obringer, Frédéric, *L'aconit et l'orpiment. Drogues et poisons en Chine ancienne et médiévale*, Paris: Fayard, 1997.

Ogawa Kooraku, 'Sencha and Japanese literati', paper presented at the *Beverages in early modern Japan and their international context, 1660s–1920s: A conference organised by the Sainsbury Institute for the Study of Japanese arts and cultures*, School of Oriental and African Studies, 9–11 March 2001.

Owen, D. E., *British opium policy in China and India*, New Haven: Yale University Press, 1934.

Parssinen, Terry, *Secret passion, secret remedies: Narcotic drugs in British society, 1820–1930*, Philadelphia: Institute for the Study of Human Issues, 1983.

Payte, Thomas J., 'A brief history of methadone in the treatment of opioid dependence: A personal perspective', *Journal of Psychoactive Drugs*, 23 (1991), pp. 103–107.

Peele, Stanton, *Diseasing of America*, New York: Lexington Books, 1995.

———, *The meaning of addiction: An unconventional view*, New York: Lexington Books, 1985.

Pendergrast, Mark, *For God, country and Coca-Cola: The definitive history of the world's most popular soft drink*, London: Orion, 2000.

Philips, John Edward, 'African smoking and pipes', *Journal of African History*, no. 24 (1983), pp. 303–19.

Picard, Liza, *Dr Johnson's London: Life in London, 1740–1770*, London: Phoenix Press, 2000.

Polachek, James M., *The inner Opium War*, Cambridge, MA: Harvard University, Council on East Asian Studies, 1992.

Poo Mu-Chou, 'The use and abuse of wine in ancient China', *Journal of the Economic and Social History of the Orient*, 42, part 2 (May 1999), pp. 123–51.

Porter, Roy, *Health for sale: Quackery in England, 1660–1850*, Manchester University Press, 1989.

Porter, Roy and Mikulas Teich, *Drugs and narcotics in history*, Cambridge University Press, 1995.

Price, Jacob M., 'Tobacco use and tobacco taxation: A battle of interests in early modern Europe', in Jordan Goodman, Paul E. Lovejoy and Andrew Sherratt (eds), *Consuming habits: Drugs in history and anthropology*, London: Routledge, 1995, pp. 165–181.

Ptak, Roderich (ed.), *China and the Asian seas: Trade, travel, and visions of the other (1400–1750)*, Aldershot: Ashgate Publishing, 1998.

Qin Heping, *Yunnan yapian wenti yu jinyan yundong: 1840–1940*, (The problem of opium in Yunnan and the anti-opium movement), Chengdu: Sichuan minzu chubanshe, 1998.

Ranger, Terence, 'Godly medicine: The ambiguities of medical mission in southeast Tanzania, 1900–1945', *Social Science and Medicine*, 15, no. 3 (1981), pp. 261–77.

Reid, Anthony, 'From betel-chewing to tobacco-smoking in Indonesia', *Journal of Asian Studies*, 44, no. 3 (May 1985), pp. 529–48.

Reins, Thomas D., 'Reform, nationalism and internationalism: The opium suppression movement in China and the Anglo-American influence, 1900–1908', *Modern Asian Studies*, 25, no. 1 (Feb. 1991), pp. 101–42.

Ren Jiyu (ed.), *Zhongguo daojiao shi* (A history of Daoism in China), Shanghai: Shanghai renmin chubanshe, 1990.

Richards, John F., 'Opium and the British Indian empire: The Royal Commission of 1895', *Modern Asian Studies*, 36, part 2 (May 2002), pp. 375–420.

———, 'Indian empire and peasant production of opium in the nineteenth century', *Modern Asian Studies*, 15 (1981), pp. 59–82.

———, 'Opium and the British empire', Kingsley Martin Lecture, Cambridge University, 23 May 2001, pp. 1–22.

Rosales, Patricia Ann, 'A history of the hypodermic syringe, 1850's–1920's', doctoral dissertation, Harvard University, 1997.

Rubin, Vera (ed.), *Cannabis and culture*, The Hague: Mouton, 1975.

Rush, James R., *Opium to Java: Revenue and Chinese enterprise in colonial Indonesia, 1860–1910*, Ithaca: Cornell University Press, 1990.

———, 'Opium in Java: A sinister friend', *Journal of Asian Studies*, 44, no. 3 (May 1985), pp. 549–62.

Schipper, Kristofer, *The Daoist body*, Berkeley: University of California Press, 1993.

Schivelbusch Wolfgang, *Tastes of paradise: A social history of spices, stimulants, and intoxicants*, New York: Pantheon Books, 1992.

Scott, J. M., *The white poppy: A history of opium*, London: Heinemann, 1969.

Shang Ke, 'Jiu Chengdu de lüguanye' (Hotel business in old Chengdu), *Longmenzhen*, no. 6 (1983), pp. 17–24.

Shanghai shehui kexueyuan (ed.), *Shanghai jindai xiyao hangye shi* (A history of modern pharmaceutical commerce in Shanghai), Shanghai: Shanghai shehui kexueyuan chubanshe, 1988.

Shanghai shi dang'anguan (ed.), *Qingmo minchu de jinyan yundong he wanguo jinyanhui* (The opium prohibition movement during the late Qing and early Republic and the anti-opium meetings of the League of Nations), Shanghai: Shanghai kexue jishu wenxian chubanshe, 1996.

Shanghai yiyao zhi (History of medicine in Shanghai), Shanghai: Shanghai shehui kexueyuan chubanshe, 1988.

Shaw, Thurstan, 'Early smoking pipes: Africa, Europe, and America', *Journal of the Royal Anthropological Institute of Great Britain and Ireland*, 90 (1960), pp. 272–305.

Slack, Edward R., *Opium, state, and society: China's narco-economy and the Guomindang, 1924–1937*, Honolulu: University of Hawai'i Press, 2000.

———, 'The National Anti-Opium Association and the Guomindang state, 1924–1937' in Timothy Brook and Bob T. Wakabayashi (eds), *Opium regimes: China, Britain, and Japan, 1839–1952*, Berkeley: University of California Press, 2000, pp. 248–69.

Sommer, Matthew H., *Sex, law, and society in late imperial China*, Stanford University Press, 2000.

Song Xian, *Huihui yaofang kaoshi* (A critical translation of the Muslim materia medica), Beijing: Zhonghua shuju, 2000.

Spence, Jonathan D., 'Opium smoking in Ch'ing China' in Frederic Wakeman and Carolyn Grand (eds), *Conflict and control in late imperial China*, Berkeley: University of California Press, 1975, pp. 143–73.

Spillane, Joseph F., 'Making a modern drug: The manufacture, sale and control of cocaine in the United States, 1880–1920' in Paul Gootenberg (ed.), *Cocaine: Global histories*, London: Routledge, 1999, pp. 21–45.

Su Zhiliang, *Zhongguo dupin shi* (History of narcotics in China), Shanghai: Shanghai renmin chubanshe, 1995.

Suzuki, Barney T., *The first English pipe smoker in Japan. Le premier fumeur de pipe anglais au Japon: William Adams, the pilot and the English trade house in Hirato (1600–1621)*, Paris: Académie Internationale de la Pipe, 1997.

Sweet, Matthew, *Inventing the Victorians*, London: Faber and Faber, 2001.

Szasz, Thomas Stephen, *Ceremonial chemistry: The ritual persecution of drugs, addicts and pushers*, London: Routledge and Kegan Paul, 1974.

Tan Chung, *China and the brave new world: A study of the origins of the Opium War (1840–1842)*, Durham, NC: Carolina Academic Press, 1978.

Traver, Harold, 'Opium to heroin: Restrictive legislation and the rise of heroin consumption in Hong Kong', *Journal of Policy History*, 4, no. 3 (1992), pp. 307–24.

Trocki, Carl A., 'Drugs, taxes and Chinese capitalism' in Timothy Brook and Bob Tadashi Wakabayashi (eds), *Opium regimes: China, Britain, and Japan, 1839–1952*, Berkeley: University of California Press, 2000, pp. 79–104.

———, *Opium, empire and the global political economy: A study of the Asian opium trade 1750–1950*, London: Routledge, 1999.

Tian Daihua, *Zhiwuming shitukao changbian* (An illustrated encyclopaedia of plants), Beijing: Renmin weisheng chubanshe, 2002.

Vanvugt, Ewald, *Wetting opium: 350 jaar Nederlandse opiumhandel in de Indische archipel*, Haarlem: In de Knipscheer, 1985.

von Gernet, Alexander, 'Nicotian dreams: The prehistory and early history of tobacco in eastern North America' in Jordan Goodman, Paul E. Lovejoy and Andrew Sherratt (eds), *Consuming habits: Drugs in history and anthropology*, London: Routledge, 1995, pp. 67–87.

Wagner, Rudolph, 'Lebensstil und Drogen im chinesischen Mittelalter', *T'oung Pao*, 59 (1973), pp. 79–178.

Wakeman, Frederic E., *Strangers at the gate: Social disorder in south China, 1839–1861*, Berkeley: University of California Press, 1997.

————, *Policing Shanghai 1927–1937*, Berkeley: University of California Press, 1995.

Waley, Arthur, *The Opium War through Chinese eyes*, London: Allen and Unwin, 1958.

Wang Gungwu, 'The Nanhai trade: A study of the early history of Chinese trade in the South China Sea', *Journal of the Malayan Branch of the Royal Asiatic Society*, 31, part 2 (June 1958), pp. 74–112.

Wang Hongbin, *Jindu shijian* (Historical evidence about the prohibition movement), Changsha: Yuelu shushe, 1997.

Wang Lihua, *Zhonggu Huabei yinshi wenhua de bianqian* (The changes in eating and drinking culture in the north of China during the ancient and mediaeval periods), Beijing: Zhongguo kexue chubanshe, 2000.

Wang Long, 'Rijun baobixia Tianjin zhidu neimu' (The clandestine narcotics industry in Tianjin under Japanese occupation) in Li Bingxin, Xu Junyuan and Shi Yuxin (eds), *Jindai Zhongguo yandu xiezhen* (The real story of narcotics in modern China), Shijiazhuang: Hebei renmin chubanshe, 1997, vol. 1, pp. 160–4.

Weinberg, B. A. and B. K. Bealer, *The world of caffeine: The science and culture of the world's most popular drug*, London: Routledge, 2001.

Welsh, Frank, *A borrowed place: The history of Hong Kong*, New York: Kodansha International, 1993.

Welter, Albert, 'A Buddhist response to the Confucian revival: Tsan-ning and the debate over *wen* in the early Sung' in Peter N. Gregory and Daniel A. Getz (eds), *Buddhism in the Sung*, Honolulu: University of Hawaii Press, 1999.

Westermeyer, Joseph, *Poppies, pipes and people: Opium and its use in Laos*, Berkeley: University of California, 1982.

————, 'The pro-heroin effects of the anti-opium laws in Asia', *Archives of General Psychiatry*, no. 33 (1976), pp. 1135–9.

White, Luise, '"They could make their victims dull": Genders and genres, fantasies and cures in colonial southern Uganda', *The American Historical Review*, 100, no. 5 (Dec. 1995), pp. 1389–96.

White, William L., *Slaying the dragon: The history of addiction treatment and recovery in America*, Bloomington, IL: Chestnut Health Systems, 1998.

Wolf, Eric R., *Peasants*, Englewood Cliffs, NJ: Prentice Hall, 1966.

Wills, John E., *Pepper, guns and parleys: The Dutch East India Company and China, 1622–1681*, Cambridge, MA: Harvard University Press, 1974.

Winther, Paul, *Anglo-European science and the rhetoric of empire: Malaria, opium, and British rule in India, 1756–1895*, Lanham, MD: Lexington Books, 2003.

Wong, Chimin K. and Wu Lien-teh, *History of Chinese medicine*, Tianjin: The Tientsin Press, 1932.

Wong, J. Y., *Deadly dreams: Opium, imperialism and the Arrow War (1856–1860)*, Cambridge University Press, 1998.

Wu Zhihe, *Ming Qing shidai yincha shenghuo* (Tea culture during the Ming and Qing), Taipei: Boyuan chuban youxian gongsi, 1990.

———, 'Mingdai sengren, wenren dui cha tuiguang zhi gongxian' (The contribution of monks and scholars to the spread of tea during the Ming), *Mingshi yanjiu zhuankan*, no. 3 (Sept. 1980), pp. 1–74.

Wylie, Jerry and Richard E. Fike, 'Chinese opium smoking techniques and paraphernalia' in Priscilla Wegars (ed.), *Hidden heritage: Historical archaeology of the overseas Chinese*, Amityville, NY: Baywood, 1993, pp. 255–303.

Wyman, Judith, 'Opium and the state in late-Qing Sichuan' in Timothy Brook and Bob Tadashi Wakabayashi (eds), *Opium regimes: China, Britain, and Japan, 1839–1952*, Berkeley: University of California Press, 2000, pp. 212–27.

Xiao Yishan, *Qingdai tongshi* (A general history of the Qing), Taipei: Shangwu yinshuguan, 1962.

Xie Zaosheng, 'Yi Sichuan yanhuo' (Memories of the opium problem in Sichuan), *Sichuan wenshi ziliao jicui* (Compendium of historical sources on Sichuan), Chengdu: Sichuan renmin chubanshe, 1996.

Xu Hairong (ed.), *Zhongguo yinshi shi* (History of food and drink in China), Beijing: Huaxia chubanshe, 1999.

Xu Xuejun, *Shanghai jindai shehui jingji gaikuang (haiguan shinian baogao yibian)* (A survey of Shanghai's modern society and economy including a translation of ten years of customs reports), Shanghai: Shanghai shehui kexue chubanshe, 1985.

Yamada Keiji, *The origins of acupuncture, moxibustion and decoction*, Kyoto: International Research Center for Japanese Studies, 1998.

Yiwen, 'Yapian dafanzi Ye Qinghe' (Opium boss Ye Qinghe) in Li Bingxin, Xu Junyuan and Shi Yuxin (eds), *Jindai Zhongguo yandu xiezhen* (The real story of narcotics in modern China), Shijiazhuang: Hebei renmin chubanshe, 1997, vol. 1, pp. 131–4.

Yip Ka-che, *Health and national reconstruction in nationalist China: The development of modern health services, 1928–1937*, Ann Arbor: Association for Asian Studies, 1995.

Young, J. H., *The medical messiahs: A social history of health quackery in twentieth century America*, Princeton: Princeton University Press, 1967.

Yu Ende, *Zhongguo jinyan faling bianqian shi* (The changing history of opium prohibition in China), Beijing: Zhonghua shuju, 1934.

Yu Jiaxi, *Yu Jiaxi lunxue zazhu* (Essays by Yu Jiaxi), Beijing: Zhonghua shuju, 1963.

Yu Zhao, *Beijing jiushi* (Old Beijing), Beijing: Xueyuan chubanshe, 2000.

Yuan Tingdong, *Zhongguo xiyan shihua* (A history of smoking in China), Beijing: Shangwu yinshuguan, 1995.

Zhang Deyi, *Hanghai shuqi* (Travels abroad), Changsha: Yuelu shushe, 1985.

Zhao Zhongming, *Wushi, wushu, mijing* (Magic healers, magic art and mysterious worlds), Yunnan: Yunnan daxue chubanshe, 1993.

Zheng Chaoxiong, 'Cong Guangxi Hepu Mingdai yaozhi nei faxian ci yandou tanji yancao chuanru woguo de shijian wenti' (The question of the timing of the spread of tobacco in China discussed on the basis of the discovery of clay pipes in Hepu, Guangxi province), *Nongye kaogu*, (1986), pp. 383–91.

Zheng Tianyi and Xu Bin, *Yan wenhua* (Smoking culture), Beijing: Zhongguo shehui kexue chubanshe, 1992.

Zhongguo shixue xuehui (ed.), *Yapian zhanzheng* (Historical documents on the Opium War), Shanghai: Shenzhou guoguangshe, 1954.

Zhou Yongming, *Anti-drug crusades in twentieth-century China: Nationalism, history, and state-building*, Lanham, MD: Rowman and Littlefield, 1999.

Zhu Qingbao, Jiang Qiuming and Zhang Shijie, *Yapian yu jindai Zhongguo* (Opium and modern China), Nanjing: Jiangsu jiaoyu chubanshe, 1995.

CHARACTER LIST

afurong 阿芙蓉
anbu 安瓿
Anhui 安徽
anmian san 安眠散
anquan huocha 安全火柴
anshen 安神
anti yaopian 安體藥片
apian 阿片

baijingfen 白精粉
baimian 白麵
baimianguan 白麵館
baipitu 白皮土
baiwan 白丸
baiyangyao 白洋藥
baiyao xian 白藥仙
baiyaofen 白藥粉
bantu 班土
Bao Tianxiao 包天笑
baojia 保甲
baoyang 保癢
baozi 包子
Bencao tujing 本草圖經
biyan 鼻煙
bositu 波斯土
bufeizhen 補肺針
bushen 補腎
buxue 補血
buzhengwan 補正丸

caizhi feilei ping'an yaoshui
　蔡製飛雷平安藥水
canren 殘忍
Cao Bingzhang 曹炳章
caomayou 草蔴油

caoyan 草煙
chaguan 茶館
chang 長
chang 常
Channing 禪寧
chapu 茶舖
chasi 茶肆
chatan 茶攤
chawu 茶屋
Chen Boxi 陳伯熙
Chen Xingzhen 陳醒篋
Chen Yuan 陳遠
Chongqing 重慶
chou 臭
choupao jieyanfa
　抽泡戒煙法
chuantu 川土
chunfangyao 春房藥
cishi 磁石
cuimian 催眠
culiao 粗料

Dai Xinsan 戴新三
Dalian 大連
dan 丹
danhuangsu jieyanfa
　蛋黃素戒煙法
danliao 丹料
dansha 丹砂
danyao 丹藥
danrouguo 淡肉果
danbagu 淡巴菰
danbagu fu 淡巴菰賦
dao yuezhong 到月中
Daoguang 導光

daoyinju 導淫具
datu 大土
Deng Xiaoping 鄧小平
diandeng 点燈
diaohua 刁滑
Ding Yongzhu 丁永鑄
Dongfang zazhi 東方雜誌
Dongya bingfu 東亞病夫
doumen san 鬥門散
du 毒
Du Yuesheng 杜月笙
duanyinsan 斷癮散
duwanchu 毒丸處

Er Ya 爾雅

Fang Yizhi 方以智
fangyao 房藥
fangzhong yao 房中藥
fanwei 反胃
feifa kaoda 非法拷打
Fengtian 奉天
fengwo 蜂窩
fu 福
Fujian 福建

ganhua 感化
Gansu 甘肅
gejian weiliang 革姦為良
gezi 個子
gongsibai 公司白
Guangdong 廣東
Guangxi 廣西
Guangxu 光緒
guaqing 寡情
guijiu 鬼臼
Guizhou 貴州
guji 固疾

gujing 固精
Guo Songtao 郭嵩燾
Guomindang 國民黨
guyangyao 沽洋藥

hai 害
hailuoyin 海洛因
Hainan 海南
Han Tan 韓菼
Han Zeng 韓增
hang 行
Hangzhou 杭州
hanshisan 寒石散
He Yongqing 何永清
hefurong 合甫融
He Qiwei 何其偉
heihaixing 黑海星
hongqian qiyao 紅鉛奇藥
hongwan 紅丸
hongyi 紅夷
Hou Guangdi 侯光迪
huajing 滑精
huanchang wan 換腸丸
huang 黃
Huang Chujiu 黃楚九
Huangfu Mi 黃甫謐
Huang Guanxiu 黃官綉
Huang Juezi 黃爵滋
Huangdi neijing 黃帝內經
huangjiu 黃酒
huayanjian 花煙間
Hubei 湖北
Hunan 湖南
huoluan 霍亂
huzai 虎仔

jian 漸
Jiang Jieshi 蔣介石

Jiangnan 江南
Jiangsu 江蘇
jianshang 奸商
jiaoyang gongchang
　教養工廠
jiemen 解悶
jieyan jianshen wan
　戒煙健身丸
jieyanyao 戒煙藥
jieyan zhuanjia 戒煙專家
Jin Ping Mei 金瓶梅
jindan 金丹
jingluo 經絡
jingmai zhushe 靜脈注射
jingshen jieyan fa
　精神戒煙法
jingzuo 靜坐
jinhuatu 金花土
jinqian 金錢
jinsixun 金絲醺
jinsiyan 金絲煙
jiqibang 機器棒
jiqipao 機器炮
jisuanwan 忌酸丸
Jiyan liangfang
　集驗良方
Jiyun 集韻
Judu weiyuanhui
　拒毒委員會
juzhong 聚眾

Kangxi 康熙
Kong Molin 孔墨霖
Kong Zhaogan 孔昭乾
kuaishangkuai 快上快
kuaizi 塊子
kudeng 苦簦

laohai 老海
lazhuangtu 喇庄土
Lei Jin 雷瑨
Li Hongzhang 李鴻章
Li Shizhen 李時珍
Li Ting 李挺
liang 兩
Liang Qichao 梁啟超
Liaoning 遼寧
Lin Ji 林几
Lin Yutang 林語堂
Lin Zexu 林則徐
linse 吝墙
Liu Guangsan 劉光三
Liu Qitong 劉啟彤
Liu Ruiheng 劉瑞恆
Liu Yuanliang 劉員亮
Liu Yushan 劉玉山
liuhualin huochai
　硫化磷火柴
Longhua 龍華
longtou shui 龍頭水
longtou zha 龍頭渣
Lu Quanbao 陸全保
luanlinzhi jieyanfa
　卵膦肢戒煙法
Luo Bangshi 羅幫實
Luo Lebin 羅樂斌
Luo Yunyan 羅運炎

Ma Wenzhao 馬文昭
Mabo 麻勃
mafei 嗎啡
mafeiguan 嗎啡館
mafeizhen 嗎啡鍼
mafen 馬糞
mafen 麻蕡
mahuang 麻黃

Mao Zedong 毛澤東
Mei Gongren 梅公任
mengyi 夢遺
mie ren zhi zhong
　滅人之種
miezhong 滅種
miezu 滅族
mijiu 米酒
mingde 明德
Mingyi bielu 名醫別錄
mofan jieyansuo
　模范戒煙所
molihua 茉莉花
mukang 木炕

Nandao 南島
Nanjing 南京
Nanjing jingbei silingbu
　南京警備司令部
Ningbo 寧波
ningfei san 寧肺散
nuanshen buyaoqi
　暖身補腰膝

pangguang 膀胱
pi 癖
pilaozhen 辟癆針
pixia zhushe 皮下注射
Pu'er 普洱

Qi 氣
Qianlong 乾隆
qingshui 清水
Quan Zuwang 全祖望

santao 三桃
se 澀

shahuan 痧瘓
Shanxi 山西
Shaanxi 陝西
Shandong 山東
shangdaren 上大人
Shanghai 上海
Shanghai shi xinyao shangye
tongye gonghui
　上海市新藥商業同業工會
shanghan 傷寒
shangyin chengpi 上癮成癖
shaojiu 燒酒
Shen Zhongyan 沈鐘彥
Shenbao 申報
shengzhiling 生殖靈
Shennong bencaojing
　神農本草經
shenzhen 神針
Shi Fenglou 石鳳樓
si shenxian 似神仙
shidan 石膽
shidansuan 石膽酸
shiwai taoyuan zhi xinjing
　世外桃園之心境
shou 熟
shou 壽
Shuowen jiezi 説文解字
Shunzhi 順治
Shushan 曙山
shuyi 鼠疫
Sichuan 四川
Siku quanshu 四庫全書
song 鬆
Song Jitang 宋吉堂
Song Liang 宋亮
suan 酸
Suzhou 蘇州

taijiquan 太極拳
Taiwan 臺灣
Tang Jiyao 唐繼堯
Tang Liangli 湯良禮
tanhuashi 談話室
tanzhi 痰滯
tianhuo 天禍
Tianjin 天津
tianran jieyanwan
　天然戒煙丸
tianwan 甜丸
tiaosha 挑痧
tishen 提神
tisi jiaoxia 涕泗交下

Wang Ang 汪昂
Wang Gui 王珪
wang ren zhi guo
　亡人之國
Wang Shizhen 王士禎
Wang Tao 王韜
Wang Xi 王璽
Wang Yanchang 王燕昌
wangguo 亡國
Wanli 萬曆
Wei Moshen 魏默深
weidun 委頓
wenyi 瘟疫
Wu Liande 伍連德
Wu Yiluo 吳儀洛
Wuchi 無恥
wulai guntu 無賴棍徒
Wuxi 無錫
wuxiang 烏香
wuyan 烏煙

xi 吸
xi 喜

Xi Liang 錫良
Xia Shenchu 夏慎初
Xiamen 廈門
xianfeng daogu 仙風道骨
xianzi shou 攕子手
Xiao Yishan 蕭一山
Xiao Zhiping 蕭治平
xiaojinku 銷金窟
xiaoqian 消遣
xiaotu 小土
xie 邪
Xie Chunfeng 謝純酆
xiejiao 邪教
xiere 邪熱
xiliao 細料
Xinjiang 新疆
xinjiao 心焦
xionghuang 雄黃
xiongshi 雄石
xiyisuo 習藝所
Xu Boling 徐伯齡

Yan Fu 嚴復
Yan Xishan 閻錫山
yancao 煙草
yancha 煙茶
yangqi 陽氣
yangyao 洋藥
yanhuajian 煙花間
yanhui 煙灰
yanyin 煙癮
yanzhen 煙鍼
yangui 煙鬼
yao 藥
Yao Lü 姚旅
Yao Chunpu 姚春圃
yaocai 藥材
yaotouwan 搖頭丸

yapian 雅片
yapianyan 雅片煙
yarong 亞榮
ye ju xiao san 夜聚曉散
Ye Mengzhu 葉夢珠
yeman 野蠻
Yilin jiyao 醫林集要
yin 淫
yin 癮，引，陰
yingchou 應酬
yingsu 罌粟
yingsuhua 罌粟花
yingsuke 罌粟殼
yingsuzhang 罌粟瘴
yong'e loulie 庸惡陋劣
Yongzheng 雍正
Youxi 遊戲
Yu Fengbin 俞鳳賓
Yu Jiao 俞蛟
Yu Zhengxie 俞正燮
Yuan Shikai 袁士凱
Yunnan 雲南
yuntu 雲土
yuqing 娛情
Yuyao yuanfang 禦藥院方

zaoxie 早泄
Zeng Guofan 曾國蕃

Zhabei 閘北
zhaguan 拃管
Zhang Jian 張堅
Zhang Jiebin 張介賓
Zhang Tianhui 張天匯
Zhang Zhidong 張之洞
zhangqi 瘴氣
Zhao Xuemin 趙學敏
zhapi 拃皮
Zhejiang 浙江
Zheng Guanying 鄭觀應
zhengliushui 蒸餾水
zhongcai 重財
zhongliao 中料
zhou yishen 周一身
Zhu Jingying 朱景英
Zhu Mengmei 朱夢梅
Zhu Shijie 朱仕介
zhu yangshi 助陽事
zhuangjing 壯精
zhuangyan 裝煙
zhuilong 追龍
zhupi liao 豬皮料
zijia xueqing jieyanfa
    自家血清戒煙法
ziyin 滋陰
zougou 走狗

INDEX

Abel, Clarke, 40
acupuncture, 81, 175–6
addiction, see dependence
addiction treatment, 120–2, 131–42, 178
agency houses, 41
alcohol, 13–6, 196
alcoholism, 99, 101
America, 24–5, 42, 45, 66–7, 95, 159–60, 167, 174, 196, 203, 207
amphetamines, 194, 210–1
Andong, 149, 170
Anhui, 142, 165, 171, 189
anodyne, 76, 84, 87; see also pain relief and effects of opium
anti-opium hospitals, 123–4, 132
anti-opium movement, 94–5, 109–10, 114
antispasmodic, 85, 91, 135, 205
anxiety, 30, 32, 35, 65, 69, 193
aphrodisiac, see opium, as sex aid
areca, 25, 40
Armenian traders, 41
arsenic, 30, 63, 71, 72, 78, 81–3, 124–5, 182
aspirin, 3, 74–75, 79, 88, 139, 180, 194
atropine, 72, 118, 124–5, 138, 194

Baotou, 194
Bayer, 166, 191–2
beer, 8, 11–4, 15–6, 18, 66
Beijing, 63, 66, 87, 129, 132, 134, 141, 143, 148, 164, 168, 169, 170, 182, 184, 185, 187, 204–5
belladonna, 81, 120, 194
Bencao tujing, 76
betel, 25, 27–28, 73, 84, 197, 208

blister method, 138–9
Bontekoe, Cornelis, 11
boredom, 28, 32, 69, 102
brick opium, 63
Burroughs, William, 193

caffeine, 4, 10, 120–1, 146, 156–9, 180; see also coffee
cannabis, 3, 19, 24, 197, 199–201, 266 (n. 53)
Canton, 40–2, 56, 69, 80, 86–7, 123, 149, 158, 168, 170, 177, 198
Cao Bingzhang, 114, 152
capital punishment, see execution of drug users
ceremonies, 21, 24, 28, 54–5, 62
Changchun, 67, 150, 170, 187–8
Channing, 28
'chasing the dragon', 162; see also consumption modes
Chen Xingzhen, 80
Chengdu, 152, 168, 172
children, 13, 16, 18, 40, 47, 52–53, 113, 171, 183, 202
Chinese emigrant communities, 70, 94, 151, 177
chocolate, 11–3
cholera, 18, 70, 74, 80, 85, 174, 176, 181, 183, 206, 232 (n. 32)
Chongqing, 48, 135, 144, 145, 152, 169, 172
cigarettes, 162–3, 165, 201–5, 209–10; see also tobacco
cinchona, see quinine
cinnabar, see immortality drugs
coca, 69, 116, 195–7

313